THE POLITE AMERICANS

BOOKS BY GERALD CARSON

The Old Country Store
Cornflake Crusade
The Roguish World of Doctor Brinkley
One for a Man, Two for a Horse
The Social History of Bourbon
The Polite Americans
A Wide-Angle View of our More or Less Good Manners

The
POLITE
AMERICANS

A WIDE-ANGLE VIEW OF OUR
MORE OR LESS GOOD MANNERS
OVER 300 YEARS

★ ★ ★

Gerald Carson

"If ours the faults, the virtues too are ours. . . ."

ROYALL TYLER in the
Prologue to *The Contrast* (1787)

New York

WILLIAM MORROW & Company

1 9 6 6

Some of the chapters of this book appeared in slightly different form as articles in *American Heritage, The New England Galaxy,* and *The Georgia Review.*

The author and publishers wish to thank the following for permission to reproduce material, as follows: The Bobbs-Merrill Company, Inc., for permission to quote from *The Good New Days,* by Merriman Smith, copyright © 1962 by Merriman Smith; *Harper's Magazine* for permission to quote a passage from "The Country Newspaper" by William Allen White, May, 1916; and Win Stracke for permission to quote from the lyrics of his song, *The Forty-Third Ward.*

Published simultaneously in Canada
by George J. McLeod Limited, Toronto.
Printed in the United States of America.
by H. Wolff, New York
Library of Congress Catalog Card Number 66–12087

FOR
MY FAVORITE POLITE AMERICANS
Sara Gay Forden
Daniel Warner Forden

ACKNOWLEDGMENTS

I have already expressed in general terms the great sense of gratitude I feel toward the reference librarians of the United States in a speech, "Some of My Best Friends Are Librarians," delivered before the dinner meeting of the American Library Trustees Association, in Detroit, July 3, 1965. To be specific, I have received courtesies and substantial help from C. K. Shipton and M. A. McCorison, Director and Librarian of the American Antiquarian Society; B. Joseph O'Neil, Coordinator of General Reference Services, Boston Public Library; Paul A. Angle, recently retired Director, Margaret Scriven, Librarian, and Grant Talbot Dean, of the Chicago Historical Society; Roscoe Eads, Librarian of *The Cincinnati Enquirer;* and John Mullane, Librarian, History and Literature Department, The Public Library of Cincinnati and Hamilton County.

Extraordinary help came from Jean K. Taylor, Head, Business and Technology Department, Cleveland Public Library. I also thank Miss Jane Carson, Research Associate, Colonial Williamsburg; B. M. Redington of the *Daily News* (New York); Mrs. Alys Freeze, Head, Western History Department, Denver Public Library; Mrs. C. F. Manwaring,

Assistant, Washingtoniana Division, District of Columbia Central Library; and at the Enoch Pratt Free Library, Mrs. Margaret Harris, Miss Jacqueline Sanders and Mrs. Elizabeth C. Litsinger. I am under obligation to Mrs. Dorothy Thomas Cullen, Curator and Librarian, The Filson Club; and at The Free Library of Philadelphia, Miss Julia L. Crawford and H. F. Berolzheimer; also W. H. Harrison, Director, Fruitlands Museum at Harvard, Mass.; and at the Harvard College Library, Kimball C. Elkins and Janet Tracy.

Also helpful were Watt P. Marchman, Director, The Rutherford B. Hayes Library; R. N. Williams, II, Director, the Historical Society of Pennsylvania; Mrs. C. E. Berry and Mrs. Frank Mercer, of The Edsel Ford Memorial Library at Hotchkiss School; Miss Margaret A. Flint, of the Illinois State Historical Library; and at the Kansas State Historical Society my ever-cooperative friend, Nyle H. Miller, Secretary, and his associates Joe Snell and Bob Richmond. I thank, too, Miss Virginia Daiker and Milton Kaplan of the Prints and Photographs Division, Library of Congress, and Irving Lowens, Assistant Head, Reference Section; and at the Little Rock Public Library, Mrs. Margaret Burkhead, Director, and Mrs. Margaret Moser, Reference Librarian; also Mrs. Elizabeth Schlegel, Principal Librarian, Science & Technology, Los Angeles Public Library.

I owe a special salute to Leon Karpel, Director, Mid-Hudson Libraries; Mary E. Schutz, Reference Coordinator, and her staff and her predecessor, Mrs. Polly Anderson; and all the institutions who cooperated with Mid-Hudson in granting me inter-library loans—among them, Cornell University Library, Swarthmore College, the university libraries of Iowa, Minnesota and Wisconsin. Mrs. Malcolm Hunter, Librarian, Milterton Free Library, provided many reference materials. Michael Brook, Reference Librarian, Minnesota Historical Society, helpfully answered a vague question. My particular thanks go out to Miss Geraldine Beard, former Chief, Reading Room. The New-York Historical Society; Gerald D. McDonald of The New York Public Library; Miss Ida M. Cohen, Assistant Librarian of the General Reference Section and Mary V. Jennings, Assistant Librarian, Reference Department, at The New York State Library; and Miss Catherine Fennelly, Director of Research and Publications, Old Sturbridge Village.

I acknowledge gratefully a lift on my way from William Ramirez, Principal Librarian, Department of Rare Books and Special Collections, San Francisco Public Library; Ken Donelson, Coordinator for Special Services, State University of Iowa; Elizabeth Tindall, of the St. Louis Public Library Reference Department; also Mabel Smith, Texas State Library; John Preston, Librarian, and Frederick A. McKechnie and Jim Archer of the University Club (New York); Lawrence

S. Thompson, Director, University of Kentucky Libraries; Prof. P. L. Myhre, School of Journalism, University of Missouri; William S. Powell, Librarian, North Carolina Collections, University of North Carolina Library; at the University of Texas Library, Miss Llerena Friend and R. A. Seeliger.

D. R. Haynes, Reference Assistant, Alderman Library, University of Virginia, answered a question for me. Dorothy A. Plum at Vassar College handled several, as did Mrs. Alene Lowe White, Librarian, The Western Reserve Historical Society; and the same is true of J. A. Servies, Librarian, College of William and Mary; Mrs. Barbara Miller Solomon, Director, The Women's Archives, Radcliffe College; and at Yale University Library, Dorothy W. Bridgwater and Judith A. Schiff.

Friends and even strangers who have generously given me help as individuals or representatives of organizations not connected professionally with the retrieval of information, include: John Bakeless, V. E. Barrett, Mrs. W. J. Bates, John Caples, W. J. C. Carlin, Kenneth Fiester, Professor J. T. Flanagan, Lewis Gannett, Mrs. Nancy Gross, L. E. Grove, Richard Gump, John Hager, Tom Haines, Mr. and Mrs. Philo H. Higley, G. K. Hutchens, H. A. Ingraham, Mrs. Joan Kerr, Professor Leslie A. Koempel, Herman Kogan, Germaine Krettek, and Mrs. Berenice Lowe, who has devotedly fed me material over a span of years that was invariably pertinent to my needs.

I am also indebted to Mrs. Mildred Milligan, Milton Moskowitz, Mrs. M. M. Murphy, Robert Nuese, Stewart D. Owen, E. L. Raymond, J. W. Ripley, Francis Robinson, Dr. Harry L. Shapiro, Hal Stebbins, Paul Stevenson, E. G. Strable, Win Stracke, C. V. Truax, R. G. W. Vail, Carl Vitz and Professor J. H. Young. I warmly acknowledge years of help and guidance by Willis Kingsley Wing and am under obligation to all at William Morrow and Company who have lavished their talents upon this book. I should like to borrow words uttered over three hundred years ago by George Wither to say of my editor at Morrow, Lawrence Hughes, that he is ". . . An honeſt Stationer [or Publisher] . . . no meere Bookeſeller. . . . The reputation of Schollars is as deare unto him as his owne. . . . In a word, he is such a man that the State ought to cheriſh him; Schollers to louve him; good Cuſtomers to frequent his shopp; and the whole Company of Stationers to pray for him."

Lastly, I thank my wife, Lettie Gay Carson, by now an expert in all the pathologies of the writer's life, who has shared the bumps and hard places and freely extended to the book and the author the immeasurable gifts of confidence and good counsel, not to mention her typing skills.

G.C.

Contents

Illustrations

Foreword

This book offers a bird's-eye view of the folkways, conventions and inherited ideas governing civilized behavior which have been followed—or flouted—among the English-speaking inhabitants of the United States. The topics discussed, and various odd matters that creep in tangentially, are illustrative rather than exhaustive. They represent only a quick sampling of a richly varied social legacy, since the time-span runs from the planting of the first American settlements by men of the seventeenth century to the age of the telephone, the cigarette, the cocktail and the automobile.

Many aspects of our more or less polite conduct, such as ceremonious ways of shaking hands, the vagaries of costume, make no sense. They are, in the literal meaning of the word, irrational. Others have their own rigorous logic which is inescapable once one understands it. Eating with a knife came to be frowned upon. Why? Because a better implement became available—the four-pronged fork. The open fireplace produced its own patterns of politeness, involving such injunctions as don't spit in the fire or grab the cosiest corner. Why did gentlemen start removing their hats in the house? Because wigs were in vogue and a full-bottomed wig and a hat were too much of a good thing.

The author is pushing no thesis, slays no dragons, rights no wrongs, but does hope to demonstrate that Americans have always been socially mobile, responding to such modifiers as political change, the trek to the cities, the expanding factory system and striking alterations in the position of women. The physical environment is deeply involved, too. This is reflected in the remark of a Kansas editor who once wrote: "Whether or not it is polite to drink out of the same bucket after your pony depends entirely on the distance the water has to be drawn."

Contrasts between doctrine and practice being what they are, these pages have their lighter moments. But the author has tried to avoid that kind of condescension toward the past which is both poor history and bad manners, remembering the warning sounded long ago by the English scholar, Elias Ashmole: "And Posterity will pay us in our own Coyne, should we deride the behaviour and dress of our Ancestors."

American manners in our time may not have taken any quantum jump. Gains and losses occur and have to be balanced off against each other, and there is no absolute scale of measurement. What appears to traditionalists to be an appalling falling away may often be a necessary adaptation to new conditions. We peer anxiously, then see through the dawn's early light that the flag is still there. Beneath the frivolities, snobberies and pudency of the past and present it is possible to find encouraging outcroppings which suggest that we have preserved in American life something of those ideals of civil manners which are a part of universal history. Herodotus and Tacitus and Chinese scholars of the Han dynasty considered, in Professor Clyde Kluckhohn's apt phrase, that "types and manners of men [were] worth talking about. . . ." The life style of a modern, mobile people who have reached for the graces, sometimes on the run, is presented here as an interesting and important subject to write and read about.

Obligations to individuals and institutions who have rendered material assistance are gratefully acknowledged elsewhere. Chapter notes contain bibliographical information. Picture credits appear as a legend with each illustration.

G.C.

Carson Road
Millerton, New York
October, 1965

I

The colonial inheritance

★ ★ ★

1

DUKES DON'T EMIGRATE

For more than three centuries, English-speaking Americans have been adapting older ideas of what is proper social behavior as the universal problems of people living together have appeared in the American environment. Changes in life styles have modified traditional forms to fit new circumstances. The introduction of the fork in the seventeenth century, for instance, or the wig in the eighteenth, the hoop skirt of the Civil War period and, in our own fast-changing century, new customs associated with the car pool, mixed drinking and the mores of the independent bachelor girl, may be cited as instances which have required the editing of old conceptions and the development of new responses.

New people have always been moving up in our mobile society, acquiring, as a consequence, the discipline of social learning. Descendants of the buckskinned frontiersmen glorified the Victorian parlor and were bemused, for a time, with an effete gentility. Sons and daughters of later immigrants have been armed against vulgar errors by the warnings printed in their newspapers. This upward thrust of emerging social groups may be observed, as strong today as ever, in the publications of union labor which concern themselves with the ceremonial aspects of the church wedding and with the propriety of cutting up a lettuce salad with one's knife. Even before the Great Society is fairly launched, *The Electrical Workers' Journal* prints gourmet recipes for crepes suzette and beef stroganoff. So the human heart continues to long for elegance. Social aspiration will doubtless continue to be one of the facts of life as long as the citizens of the United States are free to become, as the late Professor Arthur M. Schlesinger has phrased it, as unequal as they can.

It would be difficult to imagine a group of less social brilliance than the congregation of simple Nottinghamshire separatists who arrived at Plymouth on Massachusetts Bay in December, 1620. Some may have been saints, but none were gentlemen, a term reserved in English life for those who, regardless of personal character or whether they exhibited gentlemanly traits, could live without working. A somewhat more diversified population settled around the Boston and Salem area following the chartering of the Massachusetts Bay Company in 1629. When John Winthrop, the Governor of the Bay Colony, arrived in the *Lady Arbella,* the passenger list included a mixed company—Puritans and plowmen, indentured servants, horses, cows and dogs, the daughter of an earl and a very small sprinkling of other persons of gentle breeding.

The inhabitants of both Plymouth and the Bay Colony accepted the premise of a rigidly stratified society, the only kind they were acquainted with. "It is very meete and necessary," ran a quaint tract of the time, entitled *A Health to the Gentlemanly Profession of Serving Men; or the Servingman's Comfort . . . by I. M.* (London: 1598), "that there shoulde be men of all manners, conditions, and callinges: as the Princes or Potentats, Dukes, Earles, Barons, Knights, Esquires, Gentlemen, Yeomen, Husbandmen: Taylor, Tanner and Tinker: Cowper, Carter, and Cobbler, with men of all other estates, degrees and professions . . . without every of these professions there can be no well governed Common wealth. . . ." According to Richard Allestree, the putative author of a long-influential guide to the conduct of life, *The Gentleman's Calling,* the English social system was arranged by God who, the author wrote, "in his wisdom, discerning that Equality of Conditions would breed Confusion in the World, has ordered several States, designed some to Poverty, others to Riches, only annexing to the Rich the Care of the Poor. . . ."

A man could rise in the ranks of English life. It wasn't done easily, but it did occur, as John Winthrop's paternal grandfather had demonstrated. A bright country lad with no taste for the plow, Adam Winthrop went up to London, and learned the mysteries of the wool trade. By the time he was forty-six he had made a fortune and could devote his attention to improving his social position. The grandsir purchased the estate of Groton Hall in Suffolk, the living of Groton Church, and took his place on the bench as a judge at the quarter sessions and the grand assizes. The next Adam, son of the self-made man, bought a coat of arms, further solidifying the family position among the country gentry.

The adventurers who sailed three thousand miles west of England to establish a new Israel did not leave behind them the normal stirrings of social ambition. Coopers, tailors, weavers, tenant farmers, men who could not have taken the essential upward step in England—the acquisition of land—became freeholders (voters) in the new Canaan, with a pew in the meetinghouse and a reasonable hope that their sons might attend Harvard College and sign their names with the suffix, "Gent."

This is not to denigrate the religious motives and moral earnestness of many who left England for Massachusetts, men who risked all to purify the church, escape bishops, sinecures and church courts and to secure freedom of worship for themselves, however reluctant they may have been to extend it to others. There was no double-talk among the "visible Saints" about this. In fact, the Reverend Samuel Willard pointed out that the Puritans never intended to establish toleration in New England, and suggested to the Baptists that they go and hew out their own lands from the wilderness instead of troubling the colonies established by others.

The Puritan merchants, farmers, shipbuilders and fishermen, looking with complacency upon their social arrangements, a "Right Worshipful" at the top, lubberly serving maids and rustic laborers at the bottom, did not doubt but what the same system was followed—a place for everyone and everyone in his place—in Heaven. Economic advantage, social aims and spiritual values, then, all weighed heavily on the same side of the balance with men who, despite their independent views on the Anglican Church, were after all conventional Englishmen in their general outlook.

In the Massachusetts scheme of things, the gentry consisted of the higher functionaries of government, the ministers and the man who, as Professor Thomas J. Wertenbaker has said, "brought his rank with him." But the principle of an hereditary aristocracy did not cross the water; not because the immigrants were convinced democrats—Governor Winthrop had warned of democracy ". . . there is no such government in Israel"—but because the Puritans held to the peculiarly Protestant concept of *calling*. Men were called to a life-task set by God. It might be preaching or ruling or trading in furs or exterminating the Indians, in harmony with the text in Proverbs: "Seest thou a man diligent in his business? He shall stand before kings." The doctrine was often useful in practical situations. When certain English Puritans of exalted rank offered to emigrate to New England if the Bay Colony would create a House of Lords in which they and their descendants would sit forever, the word was passed back with many flowery compliments that it was possible their remote offspring might not be called to govern; that is, they might be fools. It would be improper, then, "if we should call them forth, when God hath not, to public authority."

As environmental factors worked upon English traditions, modifying older ideas and codes of manners, the Puritan slowly dissolved and the Yankee appeared. Intelligence, good character, thrift and property became the test of social position. But the greatest of these was property. In 1667 this was made very explicit in Swansea. There the town divided the people into three grades who, if taken up by the constables for some infraction of the statutes, paid differing fines. This system of differentiation, observed William B. Weeden, nineteenth century social historian of New England, was "the cheapest order of nobility ever known."

Owing to the vast empty land, the absence of any preceding civilization, the scarcity of capital, the need for labor, men of position could under certain circumstances perform homely work without loss of face. When Governor Winthrop was not occupied with public affairs, he labored beside his servants. A man could be a gentleman and also tread clams on the tidal flats, if the pot supplies were critically low, without dishonor. He could be the proprietor of a grist mill, as was Brian Pendleton of Saco. John Davy, town clerk, constable and New London farmer, was barefoot in his fields when he learned he had succeeded to his grandfather's baronetcy in England. But the price on any deviation from orthodox congregationalism was high. It worked this way. A man couldn't vote unless he was a member of the church. He couldn't be a member of the church unless he was a supporter of Calvinism and the status quo. The voters were, in Cotton Mather's phrase, "visible subjects of our Lord Jesus Christ" and subject to His representatives, the local theocrats who carried out the Lord's desires so far as Massachusetts was concerned.

Captain John Underhill, doughty Indian fighter, who adopted somewhat casually the outward forms of Puritanism, found out to his cost how the system operated. Underhill was fond of gaudy attire, tobacco, rum and a neighbor's wife who was young, beautiful and jovial in disposition. When asked by the authorities of the First Church of Boston why he was frequently found at her home with the door locked, the Captain said they were in private prayer together. This answer was received as being both false and frivolous. But worse was yet to come. Underhill imprudently compared the orthodox churchmen of Boston to the scribes and Pharisees censured by Christ. Although Captain Underhill enjoyed great prestige and had scattered the Pequots at Mystic, he was thrown out of the church and ordered to leave the colony. Only by humbling himself, in the style of self-incrimination made familiar in our own time by Communism, was Underhill finally forgiven for his offenses against church and state and rehabilitated à la Russe.

Below the gentlefolk and the clergy came the upper middle class, merchants, shopkeepers, independent freeholders tilling their own land. These men, like those who built and commanded the schooners in the fishing fleet, could aspire to participate in public life on a modest scale, as selectman, officer of the 'tillery company, church elder, surveyor of the fences, hog reeve or petit juror. The lower end of the middle group consisted of temporarily bonded servants working out the cost of their passage, apprentices and orphans. Their way of life was grimly circumscribed by law and custom. They could not trade, sing ribald songs, take a toddy of rum or play shuffleboard. Marriage or any kind of sexual outlet was denied them, with such dark results as John Winthrop recorded: "One Hackett, a servant in Salem . . . was found in buggery with a cow, upon the Lord's day." Man and cow were executed.

The lowest social level was occupied by indentured servants, unskilled laborers, slaves, Negroes and Indians. They lived not by bread alone for, according to court records, they could choose water porridge if they wished. Social differentiation was functional, based upon what a man worked at. If the son of a magistrate regularly followed a mean occupation, he slipped from the position he formerly occupied. By the end of the century social prerogatives were clearly associated with goods rather than godliness. A Massachusetts merchant, for example, if sufficiently successful in the fur trade, could marry into one of the best families and sit at the council table despite the fact that he might hold heterodox views on infant damnation, justification, sanctification, adoption, regeneration, repentance, free grace, reprobation, original sin or other nice points of Calvinist divinity. This falling away from the test of strict orthodoxy was even more marked in New Hampshire, with its more secular spirit and among the urbane Narragansett planters, the Virginians of the North.

The holder of a university degree was considered to be a gentleman. Ministers were accorded the title because they were men of learning and did not perform manual labor. Governors were gentlemen *ex officio,* and members of the upper house of the bicameral assemblies; also sons of genuine English baronets if they behaved themselves. The elite were endogamous. The idea was to keep the land and the power in safe hands.

Shrewd alliances kept the Dudleys, Leveretts, Appletons and Winthrops on top in Massachusetts, lent luster to the Wyllyses in Connecticut, reinsured the position of the Hazards, Throckmortons and Coggeshalls of Rhode Island. The father controlled the family. But the clergy controlled the father. A certain amount of inbreeding was the natural result. As John Winthrop the Younger, Governor of Connecticut, remarked as he looked about for a suitable son-in-law, the choice was not as wide as one could wish.

The ranks closed when there was a scandal. Mistress Elizabeth Perkins, the wife of a gentleman, according to the testimony of witnesses sported in a secluded orchard with one James Creeke, a man of little property. The community conscience was shocked by her "adulterous carriage," but even more by her irresponsibility in entering into dalliance with "such an one as he. . . ."

The gentry enjoyed immunity from degrading punishments. When Josiah Plaistowe stole some corn from the Indians, according to the *Massachusetts Colonial Records,* his servants were severely flogged. Plaistowe was let off with a fine but was stripped of his social rank; that is, it was directed he should pay five pounds and thereafter be "Josias" and not a "Mister."

Social gradations were reinforced by the distribution of complimentary titles. High officials were addressed orally or in writing as Worshipful Sir, The Right Worshipful, Your Excellency, or Honorable. Candidates for the master of arts degree at Harvard College were entitled to be called Sir. Ministers enjoyed the honorific "Reverend Mister." Lay church officials received the title of elder or deacon. Run-of-mine members were brother or sister. Esquire or "squire" was used erratically in association with the lower judiciary.

The oral form for gentleman was Master, abbreviated in writing to Mr. Those at the upper limits of the middle class were Misters—the teachers, all who held the master of arts degree and the substantial landowners. Wives of gentlemen received the salutation of respect, Madam. This was continued into the eighteenth century when Mary Lynde, for instance, wife of Benjamin Lynde, the Chief Justice of Massachusetts, was known as Madam Lynde.

The term of civility for the respectable middle class man of modest property was Goodman. His wife was Goodwife or "Goody." Professor Norman H. Dawes and others have shown that usage was often loose and modified by local circumstances. Military titles were applied with more precision than others. The importance of defense gave them real validity. As Dawes has remarked, when only about twelve per cent of the population received a prefix of respect, a man did not lightly scorn the name of corporal. And men cherished the privileges which went with position. At Windsor, Connecticut, as an example, the magistrates and clergy established an order of precedence for boarding the ferry: they went first. And sometimes the civil and spiritual authorities squabbled among themselves over matters of protocol. Judge Samuel Sewall recorded in his diary the great difficulty he had on one occasion in persuading the Reverend Samuel Willard to dine with him. The prominent divine was in a pet because the civil authorities had marched ahead of the ministers in the procession celebrating the ascension of Queen Anne to the throne of England.

While William Bradford, Governor at Plymouth, hoped devoutly to see in his time "ye churches of God reverte to their ancient puritie," what he actually saw was something much more human and worldly, an interesting procedure called "seating the meeting." In the meetinghouse all, theoretically, were equal. But the poorer Saints sat in the back. Each member was allotted his place, those closest to the teacher being the most exalted. The assignment of pews was public evidence of the community consensus about family position. No one wanted to be seated near the roof beams with the blacks, but to get as near as possible to God; or at least, in Ipswich, if not nearer to God, then to the Winthrops, Saltonstalls, Dudleys and Bradstreets; at New Haven to the Eatons, Goodyears, Malbons, Davenports and Hooks. The leaders were flatfooted about it: "Goody Gates to sit at the end of the Deacon's seat. Goody Wines to sit in the Gallery."

One can sense the social dynamics involved when Judge Sewall complacently set it down how he sat "in the Fore-seat at the Sacrament" with Thomas Hinckley, Governor of Plymouth Colony, and Major Thomas Pynchon, proprietor of immense landed property in the Connecticut Valley. The outraged feelings of Goody Elizabeth Randall reverberated down through three centuries as she pushed her way into the seat she felt was rightfully hers, climbing to get there over the tops of benches "four or five feet high." Whittier describes how the meeting was seated in his "Mary Garvin":

> *To the goodly house of worship, where in order due and fit,*
> *As by public vote directed, classed and ranked the people sit;*
> *Mistress first and goodwife after, clerkly squire before the clown,*
> *From the brave coat, lace-embroidered to the gray frock shading down.*

There are numerous entries in the old town records of unmannerly shoving, of the discharge of firearms in the church, of a man riding into the congregation mounted on a horse, of scurrilous remarks comparing the parson with barking dogs and bawling bears. It was a risky business to utter hard words about a minister. When John Veering, of Boston, called the Reverend James Allen "a black hypocritical Rogue" he was fined ten pounds, had to post a bond for future good behavior or sit publicly on a stool with a placard on his chest proclaiming him A PROPHANE AND WICKED SLANDERER AND IMPIOUS REVILER OF A MINISTER OF THE GOSPEL. At Salem, Lydia, wife of Eliakim Wardwell, a woman of good reputation, came into the meetinghouse naked as a protest against the wickedness of the "priests and rulers." For this breach of decorum and her subversive opinions, Mrs. Wardwell was tied to the fence post of the tavern at Ipswich and lashed with between twenty and thirty stripes.

When names appeared on official lists they were usually arranged in the order of dignities and titles. This custom probably gave rise to the modern belief that family position determined the ranking of students in the class lists at Harvard. This practice was not followed in this century but did prevail for a part of the eighteenth century at both Harvard and Yale. Benjamin Franklin expressed the bitter thoughts of an unpropertied youth in Boston when he wrote, under the anonymn Silence Dogood, of how Mrs. Dogood had had an allegorical dream about Harvard College. There, Franklin wrote, two sturdy porters named *Riches* and *Poverty* kept the gate and only those recommended by *Riches* were admitted. Learning sat neglected on a high throne while the students flocked to attend upon Madam Idleness and "her Maid Ignorance." As a result, many of the graduates, unless they could fall back upon family wealth, lived as poor as church mice, "being unable to dig and ashamed to beg, and to live by their Wits it was impossible . . ." for at Harvard they learned "little more than how to carry themselves handsomely and enter a room genteelly (which might as well be acquir'd at a Dancing-School . . .)."

The Puritan, believing in total virtue, total evil, had a rigid standard of conduct for himself and his neighbor. Introspective, conscious always of the eternal world, the Calvinists took their recreations with caution. Laws existed against drinking healths, playing at bowls and dancing, with an inquisitorial system to back them up. If a man smoked a pipe, walked out to the woodlands to gather chestnuts or played a game of shuffleboard, there was always the lurking fear that Old Scratch would in some way snare him through his innocent play. Permitted diversions were town elections, the militia trainings in spring and autumn, the Commencement exercises at Cambridge and the minister's Thursday lecture —the "great and Thursday"—which was followed by the announcement of interesting public notices such as a dissection or the burning of an heretical book by the public executioner. The Great and Thursday was a sermon unaccompanied by prayer or other devotions. Attendance was voluntary as distinct from the two services on the Lord's Day which were compulsory.

There was about as much drinking and fighting and somewhat more litigation in Massachusetts Bay as would be found among men in the same stage of civilization elsewhere. "As to truth and godliness," wrote Jasper Danckaerts, an entertaining Dutch observer of New England manners, "you must not expect more of them than of others." Danckaerts was, in a small way, an early victim of American nativism. He was received in New England coolly, for he seemed to have no business in Boston, could speak several languages and was therefore suspected of being a Jesuit. The feelings of apprehension which Danckaerts committed to his journal were not without foundation. Only a year before a Frenchman, Peter Lorphelin, accused of being a stranger and the cause of the great fire of August 8-9, 1679, had both his ears cut off, though no evidence was ever produced connecting him with the fire.

John Josselyn, the naturalist and travel writer, who wrote *An Account of Two Voyages to New-England,* also looked for truth and godliness but found in Boston many women whom he termed strange women "in Solomon's sense, more the pitty." It is possible he was present when the notorious madam, Alice Thomas, was whipped through the streets for "giving secret and unreasonable Entertainm[en]t in her house to Lewd Lascivious and notorious persons of both sexes giving them opportunity to commit carnal wickedness."

The asceticism of Puritan regulations worked no hardship on the teachers themselves. They had as their portion the thrill of manipulating the levers of power, knew the pleasures of study, meditation and conniving and looked forward confidently to sitting on the dais in the kingdom of Heaven. The social mechanism which divided those who ruled from those who were born to be ruled, even operated in such areas as dress and hair styles. Long before, in the fifteenth century, the English poet, Thomas Occleve, had expressed regret that one could no longer rely upon costume to place a stranger in his proper social niche.

> *Some (time) ago, men might lordes know*
> *By their array from other folk . . .*

In New England, when the General Court was not occupied with the extermination of the Indians or the encouragement of the fisheries, it turned its attention to regulating fashion. "One end of apparel," wrote Urian Oakes, poet, clergyman and President of Harvard, "is to distinguish and put a difference between persons according to their places and Condition." In the spirit of Oakes's statement the Massachusetts General Court declared its "utter detestation and dislike, that men or women of mean condition, should take upon them the garb of Gentlemen, by wearing Gold or Silver lace, or Buttons, or Points at their knees, or to walk in great Boots; or Women of the same rank to wear Silk or Tiffiny hoods, or Scarfes. . . ." This they declared to be "intollerable" and ordered that "gaudy apparrell" could be worn only by those who had a capital of over £200. Exceptions were made for military officers who were gentlemen, judges and the university man who had been moneyed but was "now decayed."

Farmers and artisans wore coarse linen smocks in summer, wool in winter, made of a material called "frocking." The garment went on overhead, and was tied with a string. Copley's portrait of Paul Revere as silversmith shows him wearing such a mechanic's frock. Common laborers wore leather aprons or deerskin jerkins. Men of social position were clad in doublets and silk stockings, slashed their sleeves, wore "falling bands," ancestor of the necktie, a beaver hat with a steeple crown, elaborately embroidered gloves. When a gentleman went out upon the town he carried a silver-headed cane or wore a rapier. Until about 1685 hats were worn inside the houses at all times including meal times.

Gentlemen began to remove their hats in homes, churches or public buildings, as a matter of comfort, after heavy wigs became the mode. The removal of the hat was gradually incorporated into the code of good behavior as a gesture of politeness. Meals, incidentally, were taken in the "hall"—kitchen in modern usage—the most cheerful, picturesque room in the house, with huge open fireplace and a dresser displaying a few pieces of shining pewter. Seats were stools or benches. Trenchers (plates) were made of wood. Forks were unknown, but fingers, supplemented by plenty of napery, met the demands of table manners. In the up-country districts the trenchers were spoken of as having "the dinner side and the pie side." Two persons often ate from the same dish. If a hard-handed beau and his sunburned belle shared a trencher it was considered that they were betrothed.

Matrons whose husbands possessed the requisite estate of £200 wore bonnets, caps, forehead cloths, cloaks and ruffs, gowns of silk and satin, and enjoyed the possession of muffs, lace and fans, finger rings, tortoise shell combs, shoes with French heels and silver buckles. Little Puritan children must sometimes have reflected upon the difference between what they heard and what they saw as they learned from the Reverend Isaac Watts, author of *Divine Songs for Children,* to sing:

> *Why should our garments, made to hide*
> *Our parents' shame, provoke our pride?*
> *The art of dress did ne'er begin*
> *Till Eve, our mother, learned to sin.*

Connecticut agreed with Massachusetts that it was a function of dress to advertise the social position of the wearer and that it was a proper function of government to see to it that the indications of status were not abused. Rhode Island did not establish sumptuary regulations because of its more liberal outlook upon the nature of man. Plymouth was spared the problem because all were poor.

In Tudor England the man of fashion wore his hair banged in front and bobbed to cover the ears, topped with a black velvet hat with a beret crown. Full beards flourished in conformity with the charge in Leviticus "Ye shall not . . . mar the corners of thy beards." Lawyers, soldiers, courtiers, merchants wore beards and devoted a sinful amount of time and money, as the Nonconformists saw the matter, in perfuming, trimming, dusting them with orris powder and crisping with curling irons. Elizabeth I sent an ambassador to the Russian court whose mission, incidentally, was greatly facilitated by a splendid beard two feet long, accepted by the Russians as a mark of manhood, wisdom and philosophy.

The more fanatic of the English religious sectaries regarded long hair as an ensign of pride. There was much scruple in New England about this subject. Governor Endecott was especially stiff and persuaded the magistrates to issue a manifesto opposing shoulder-length locks. The Reverend Charles Chauncey preached against long hair. The college rules at Harvard in 1655 decreed ". . . neither shall it bee lawfull for any to weare Long haire, Locks or foretops, nor to use Curling, Crisping, parting or powdering their haire." At the restoration of the English monarchy, men cut off their hair, but only in order to don an enormous periwig (corruption of the French, *perruque*). The wig, worn generally in England, gained favor rapidly in New England following the Glorious Revolution in England which settled the question of the Protestant succession and brought William and Mary to the throne. Judge Sewall, who hated wigs for their frivolity and the lack of warrant in Scriptures even more intensely than he detested the feast of Christmas, was gratified to observe in 1686 that "Wm. Clendon, Barber and Perriwig-maker, dies miserably."

It is not known that Increase Mather ever wore wigs which he once called "Horrid Bushes of Vanity." Portraits which exist show him wearing long, naturally colored hair, probably his own. But Cotton Mather, his eldest son, is shown with a wig on his head in Pelham's portrait which now hangs on the south wall of the main reading room of the American Antiquarian Society in Worcester, Massachusetts, just above the card catalogue. The younger Mather once preached a sermon in which he suggested that it was straining at a gnat and swallowing a camel "to be zealous against an innocent fashion (while) being guilty of great Immoralities." Sewall wrote sadly, "I expected not to hear a vindication of Perriwigs in Boston Pulpit by Mr. Mather." The story of the subsequent rise and fall of artificial hair pieces and of facial hair will be resumed in a later chapter (Chapter 10).

The New England settlements in the seventeenth century were a microcosmos. Life was monotonous, dreary and not without the threat of daily peril from the magistrates. They boldly attempted to punish "sin" judicially even when it did not represent any offense under English law. There were, of course, no bishops' courts. Yet a document dating from 1643 and still in existence, lists Biblical authority, not statutory law, for punishing fifteen offenses by death, with precedents cited from Deuteronomy, Exodus, Leviticus, Numbers and Samuel. Scolds were gagged and set in their doors for a prescribed period of hours. Kissing a woman in the street, "though in the way of civil salute," Josselyn explained, or a "single fornication," were punished equally by a whipping or a fine. For swearing or cursing the judges either whipped, fined, or ordered that the unfortunate sinner have his tongue bored through with a hot iron. Considerable ingenuity and diligence was expended in devising penalties. Robert Shorthouse, "for swearing by the blood of God," had to stand for half an hour with a cleft stick pinching his tongue. The supervision of private life was extraordinarily minute, with the constables required to report on "tobacco-takers, and all other persons who could give no good account how they spent their time."

Emotional release came in theological controversies, reading the Geneva Bible or shuddering over Michael Wigglesworth's frightening poem, *The Day of Doom*. Life gained drama if not dignity in fierce disputes over small personal affairs.

Despite the Puritan faith that life on this earth was but a short trial heat which would be followed by eternal bliss or torment, the manners of the colonists were often tinctured with coarseness. A man was fined for beating his daughter with a flail. Women struck their husbands and vice versa. A girl pounded the peace officer with her Bible. John Combe of Plymouth was a problem drinker. Michael Mitton seduced Mary Martin up Casco way, while George Palmer was set in the stocks "having committed folly with Margary Ruggs through her allurement. . . ." Since Margary enticed him, she was "severely whipped." Joshua Parker forged a deed, became in consequence the first Harvard man to have his ears cut off. To be precise, it was only one ear. Parker, incidentally, was described in the writs as a gentleman because his father held town offices and a brother was a minister.

The instances of "light carriage" and the application of the law of Moses are not the whole story. There were, of course, gentle customs and affable social relations which reflected the good sense and native good heart of the New Englanders. "There are many sincere and religious people amongst them," Josselyn, usually a critic of the Calvinists, acknowledged. There was a leavening of men educated at Oxford and Cambridge who owned, read and pondered ancient "courtesy books" which kept alive the ideal, as Chaucer expressed it, "That he is gentil that doeth gentil dedis."

2

GENTLE IS AS GENTLE DOES

It was on Italian soil, in the fifteenth and sixteenth centuries, that there grew an ideal of beauty, not of person but of style. The Greek conception of the perfect man was the philosopher-king. The Romans favored the orator and citizen; the age of chivalry the knight. Each vocation was obviously open only to a very few individuals. With the appearance of the idea of the gentleman in sixteenth century England, the base was broadened to admit the scholar, the lawyer, the merchant (wholesale, not retail), the politician and civil servant.

New writings, known as "courtesy books," placed before Europeans a standard of simplicity of demeanor, of generosity and personal honor, of consideration for others and in ordinary intercourse a freedom from affectation. Among such books which reached England in translation were *Il Galateo* of Giovanni della Casa, *La Civile Conversazione* of Stefano Guazzo, and Count Baldesar Castiglione's dialogue, *Il Cortegiano,* or *The Book of the Courtier,* most influential of the courtesy books in England, written by

Castiglione early in the sixteenth century and Englished in 1561 by Sir Thomas Hoby.

The conduct books became so widely diffused that they were, in effect, English books. As such, they passed over into the New England cultural inheritance, along with trace elements accumulated from the classics, the church fathers and the Bible. So when the Reverend Cotton Mather expressed the hope that the young men of New England would "do genteel deeds" he attached himself to a social ideal more gracious and far older than the teachings of John Calvin. The accident of noble birth might entitle a man to wear the crest of one of England's great families, but, Richard Brathwaite emphasized in an analysis of the nature of the gentleman, "his own actions expresse himself."

The gentleman was a child of the Renaissance. But he was supposed to be a good Christian, too. Shakespeare made use of this mingling of sometimes contradictory pagan and Christian elements when he had Portia say, flippantly: "How oddly he is suited! I think he bought his doublet in Italy, his round hose in France, his bonnet in Germany and his behaviour everywhere."

Whether he was secure in his station because of his own accomplishments or those of illustrious ancestors, the gentleman in seventeenth century doctrine was distinguished for mental rather than manual or mechanical abilities, an early appearance of the white-collar, blue-collar polarities. The gentleman was indifferent to material gain and under an obligation to make his talents available to the state through some form of public service. The longbow in the hands of stout English yeomen and the common soldier with arquebus and caliver had ended the career of the knight on horseback as a fighting man. The esquire, then, if his wits were good, turned to the law, the art of governing, to the church or medicine.

In his contacts with the world around him, a gentleman was expected to be courteous to all, but with a nice sense of what was due to each, his inferior, his equal or superior in the social scheme. His sense of personal honor was quite touchy, the result, one may conjecture, of a traumatic experience, the loss of his effectiveness as a fighter. Out of this hypersensitivity came the theory and practice of dueling, which later became deeply rooted in America and flourished remarkably in the southern and western regions of the United States (see Chapter 9). A gentleman was also expected to be a scholar, an association of ideas that is still familiar. "Alas," exclaimed George Pettie, who turned Stefano Guazzo's *La Civile Conversazione* into vigorous Elizabethan English, "you wyll be but ungentle Gentlemen, yf you be no Schollers."

The qualities which an age possesses are not always those it professes to admire. Many Englishmen of noble lineage left edifying counsels for their descendants on how to manage their lives, written while the author was awaiting execution for the conduct of his own. La Rochefoucauld touched upon the point in a maxim well-known in England: "Old men delight in giving good advice as a consolation for the fact that they can no longer set bad examples."

The writings on courtesy, whether informal or systematic, were concerned with dress, table manners, drinking, gambling, dancing, pride, the choice of suitable companions, the art of agreeable conversation. Don't repeat your dreams, warned della Casa, or boast of your money. Avoid double meanings, and if they occur in the speech of others, make them understand you accept the innocent sense only. When your interlocutor obviously thinks he has "a Joly grace in telling a tale," do not disabuse him of his illusion, or reply "that you doe know it well." And say nothing against God or the saints, even though you have thought of something very witty. The books on courtesy are markedly different from the modern book of etiquette. Their concern is with the universal rules of good taste, the behavior of the well-bred man of all countries and periods, rather than the prevailing mode of a particular clique.

Judge Sewall spent many pleasant hours reading Calvin on the psalms and it has become commonplace to suppose that the men of his generation had available to them only books of sermons and devotional works such as Richard Baxter's *Saint's Everlasting Rest* or John Foxe's *Book of Martyrs*. John Dunton, a Boston bookseller, who was familiar with New England society just below the upper ranks, recorded the preference of one woman customer for plays, romances and "Books of Gallantry." Modern analysis has shown that the people of the Bay Colony read their share of trashy literature. There was, too, a sub-literature of anal humor whose aim was—anything for a laugh. Readers bought joke books and narratives of low life as well as romantic accounts of the marvelous exploits of wandering knights who rescued virgins kidnapped by giants, and lubricious tales about nuns' escapades, which offered a pleasing blend of erotic titillation with congenial anti-papist passages. On a higher level, books offering a ground-plan of polite behavior were imported in significant quantities, often turning up later in inventories of estates under some haphazard notation as "one book of manners." Seventeen copies of the anonymous but popular *Academy of Complements* reached one bookseller within a six-month period, providing Bostonians with standard models to imitate when they had to write a letter. Specimen conversational gambits were set out for those who might find themselves in select company with nothing to say. There were definitions of especially difficult words and even "Songs and catches à la mode."

Elder William Brewster of Plymouth owned Guazzo's *Civile Conversazione* in Pettie's translation. Guazzo had been an ambassador, counsellor and courtier, setting down late in life his reflections upon the world and men. He wrote for the middle group rather than the aristocratic audience; a reason, along with his eminently good sense and realistic dialogue, for his enduring popularity. The book is encyclopedic in scope, regarded by modern investigators as a probable source of some of Shakespeare's material on dress, customs and the nature of social man. One editor of Guazzo has argued persuasively that the book Hamlet is reading in Act Two, Scene ii is the *Civile Conversazione*.

The Massachusetts authorities, when they issued regulations governing women's costumes, may well have been in debt to Guazzo for saying:

"If a man offer abuse to an honest matron, being attyred like a harlot . . . let women therefore bee carefull to apparell themselves so modestly, that they may thereby, rather please their husbands . . . for they ought to consider, that menne suppose, that there is always a light mind, lodged in a gorgeous body."

William Brewster also owned the versified *Description of a Good Wife* by Richard Brathwaite, author of the widely known *The English Gentleman*. The book was also in the Harvard College library early in the eighteenth century. Brathwaite was a country gentleman himself, not a Puritan but touched by Puritan ethics and seriousness. Castiglione's *The . . . Courtier* was among Governor John Winthrop, Jr.'s books in a Latin version. Castiglione wrote of a group of noble friends who gathered around Elizabeth, Duchess of Urbino, to discuss the character, duties and accomplishments of the ideal courtier. Here the Renaissance man is presented in his most attractive guise. The definition which emerged from the dialogue remains, with some shifts of emphasis, that of the timeless man of breeding. The word courtier is used in a high sense

with no implication of the placeman or trimmer. The courtier
lived with grace, understood the use of arms, of kindness, of nonchalance, of jesting and of silence.

In one amusing passage, as pertinent today as it was when the
patrician author was writing at Urbino and at Rome, the Count
warns of the dangers of trying to be the life of the party. If one is
successful in getting off an engaging anecdote, Count Castiglione
urges, stop while still ahead. No wonder, in view of the enduring
validity of such advice, that *The . . . Courtier* has passed through
more than one hundred and forty editions and been plundered
countless times by later writers of less finesse.

Other manuals dealing with similar subject matter which
reached colonial America included Henry Peacham's *The Compleat Gentleman* and *The Whole Duty of Man* which was, its title
page continued lengthily, *Laid Down in a plain and familiar Way,
for the Use of all, but especially the meanest Reader, Divided into
XVII Chapters. One whereof being read every Lord's Day, the
whole may be read over thrice in the Year. Necessary for all Families. With Private Devotions for several Occasions.* The authorship
of this tome, which enjoined its readers "to behave themselves so in
this World that they may be happy for ever in the next," is generally but not unanimously attributed to Richard Allestree, royalist
divine. The book, with its comfortable Established Church ideas
and political slant, its homilies on deceit, fair dealing and respect
due all men, exerted a strong influence in shaping the aristocratic
code of the American South.

New York has the distinction of bringing out the first book
printed in America on manners. It appears to have been a reprint
of a London publication, Richard Lyngard's *Letters of Advice to a
Young Gentleman leaving the University concerning his behaviour and conversation in the World.* The book appeared in 1696.
In it the youth is urged to get out of the academic atmosphere and
supplement what he has learned from books by observing men. Be
sincere, open-hearted, informal, the author counsels. English
bluntness and French cunning both represent extremes. Grant favors. Keep promises and return borrowed books. Don't confuse the
acquaintance and the true friend. It is wise, the author says, to
choose one friend from each profession. Do we catch here, one
wonders, the seminal idea of Rotary International, which admits
only one member to a Club from each occupation?

The first book of American authorship dealing with correct deportment was the *School of Good Manners. Composed for the Help of Parents in teaching their Children how to behave during their Minority* (New London: 1715). It was quickly followed by *A Sermon for the Reformation of Manners* (Boston: 1716), written by Benjamin Colman, pastor of Brattle Street Church in Boston. The *School of Good Manners* was probably compiled by Eleazar Moody, who conducted a writing school in Boston near Prison Lane, now Court Street. Although Moody's little work had a French precursor, the New England adapter managed to give his book an authentic Bostonian and Congregational flavor. In the section dealing with behavior at the meetinghouse, for instance, one encounters such counsel as:

"Decently walk to thy seat or pew; run not or go wantonly.

"Fix thine eye on the minister; let it not wildly wander to gaze on any person or thing.

"Be not hasty to run out of the meeting-house when the worship is ended, as if thou wert weary of being there."

When one recalls the Sabbath pushing and shoving at the church door mentioned by an historian of Windsor, Connecticut, and Goody Randall climbing over the backs of pews in defense of her social position, it is easy to believe that the deportment proscribed in the *School of Good Manners* was an observable feature of life in the New England Zion.

After walking home in a sober manner, thinking over what he has heard from the pulpit, making a formal bow when he entered his home with head uncovered, the good American boy of Puritan times addressed his parents with some title of respect, as Sir or Madam, bore with meekness any reproof they thought the occasion required. Arriving at the table washed and combed and without getting into a scrap with his brothers or sisters, the little paragon, if he followed Mr. Moody's training, sat silently while the older generation did the talking. He did not blow upon his meat to cool it, or pick it up for closer inspection. When "moderately satisfied" he rose, made a low leg again and retired. As the family reassembled later, the boy did not interrupt. If spoken to he stood up, "not wriggling with thy body hither and thither," said Sir to male elders and again spoke briefly.

If a "superior" got mixed up in trying to tell his favorite story, the model youth was to "snigger not." Guazzo would have appreciated that. On school days the young scholar was told to go directly to school and return straight home and "stand not talking with boys."

Decorum manuals of American provenience remained the exception until the nineteenth century when the presses poured out etiquette books of native authorship. Americans were in the main content to take their instruction in politeness from English authorities. This was especially true among the southern planters. In any plantation library there was apt to be a well-thumbed copy of Peacham, Brathwaite or the *Whole Duty of Man*. The last was owned by George Washington and Thomas Jefferson among others; and Dr. Franklin recommended it to his daughter, Sally.

A surprisingly large number of American colonials visited London in the seventeenth century where they occupied a social position similar to that of the Australians today. This was a singular migration in the history of a people who have, historically, faced west. Between 1640 and 1660, during the Interregnum, about half of the alumni of Harvard College went to England for further study, to preach, teach, practice medicine, claim inheritances or comb the Herald's Office for armigerous ancestors. By the beginning of the eighteenth century the growth of trade and rising prosperity drew men to make the voyage for other reasons—to look after business affairs, act as commercial agents, perform the functions of a consular service or seek political advancement. Jeremiah Dummer, for example, received the degree of Doctor of Philosophy from Leyden University, attached himself to Lord Bolingbroke, became a mirror of fashion, a religious skeptic and was gossiped about for keeping a seraglio of beauteous young females at his estate in Plaistow.

Dummer stayed in England because that was where his opportunity lay. The Reverend John Barnard went over for pleasure, wore a wig and put on a sword so successfully that he was often taken by country squires for a member of the court circle. When he returned to Boston, the prestige and polish he had acquired through his travels were so great that he was able to deliver his old sermons over again without a murmur from his flock.

Americans were conscientious tourists three hundred years ago, as they are now. They visited the Guildhall, saw the crown jewels at the Tower, enjoyed the pageantry of the Horse Guards, tip-toed reverently in the twilight of the Abbey, and took in a spectacle no longer available—the public executions at Tyburn. Then as now men drew together when upon foreign soil. Philadelphians located each other at the Pennsylvania Coffee House, compared notes upon the high cost of travel, the wickedness of London sparks who led country girls astray. The clannish Bostonians saw St. James's Park and thought nostalgically of another one, the Boston Common, shared the Lucullan pleasures of a dinner of salt fish and, when they could obtain so toothsome a rarity, an Indian meal pudding.

Such goings and comings across the ocean introduced to the New World the newest minuet, cocked hat or the smartest nonce phrase which a hostess would value as coming directly from the fashionable drawing rooms of London; as, "Split me, Madam" or "Damn me." There were casualties, of course. Some colonists lost their characters abroad, some committed apostasy and returned to bishops and the liturgy. Others hoped to acquire *ton* while carrying on necessary commercial activities abroad. That was how it was with Henry Laurens, gentleman-merchant of South Carolina, who referred whimsically to the subject when he wrote to a friend back home:

"I promised this voyage should polish me and make me quite polite; but really I believe my time will be so taken up with business that I shall return just the fellow that left you in September last. . . ."

Some men chose America because of the dictates of conscience. Some came to save their necks; some to engage in riotous living; some to catch fish. The view of the Congregationalist teachers seems to have been that the people came to hear threatening sermons.

"It is my design by God's assistance," declared Mr. Israel Loring, minister at Sudbury, "to entertain you at this time with a solemn and awakening Discourse of Hell."

Every Sabbath the well-brought-up child stepped forth into the mid-aisle, faced the pulpit, "made his manners"—the girls curtseying, the boys jerking their heads in what passed for a bow—and answered by rote and through fear of punishment both immediate and eternal, the questions the pastor launched at them from the loathed Westminster Assembly's Shorter Catechism:

Q. What shall be your condition in hell?
A. I shall be dreadfully tormented . . .

Q. If you should go to hell how long must you continue there?
A. For ever and ever.

Because of the severity of the theocrats and their bleak doctrines, human nature could not long continue to spend a lifetime trying to atone for the error of having been born. The colonial wars of the eighteenth century—Queen Anne's, the Indian forays of 1722-24, the Old French War, the movements of troops and increases in population and wealth—modified the crabbed pattern of life in the American provinces. The royal governors, their ladies and official retinues, helped to spread a more amiable social atmosphere throughout the settlements. When a royal prince was married or the queen had an accouchement or the king a birthday, the church bells of loyal Boston rang out, the governor inspected the troops and in the evening there was a ball.

Meanwhile, in the seaports a new sophistication appeared. Merchants grown rich in the West India trade were having their portraits painted by Smibert and Blackburn and going to hear Dr. Colman and Dr. Cooper, if not out of piety then to set an example in decorum to the lower classes. And there was fun to be found in Boston—a fire, a frolic, a riot, an execution, a funeral procession winding its way up Copp's Hill or, on Guy Fawkes Day, the town's children begging and breaking windows. Peter Faneuil ordered a chariot and coachman from London, the latest cookbooks and a dozen silver forks with three tines and his coat of arms incised upon them. After the necessities are served, as Franklin noted, men on the make think of the embellishments. As the Puritan image faded, a new American type appeared, later known as the Self-Made Man, quick to grasp the doctrine subsequently to be made an article of faith by the telephone companies and air lines, that politeness pays.

THE ART OF WORLDLY SUCCESS

With the close of the Puritan century, new men who were wholly
the product of the American environment were in the positions of
leadership in New England. Time had made it possible for a man
to have a family tree which included a member of the provincial
Council, a governor or two and numerous doctors of divinity.
Wealth, either honestly acquired or old enough so that its shady
past had been forgiven, was producing a new plutocracy, the land-
hungry Livingstons of the Hudson Valley, a flourishing haut bour-
geoisie of traders and shippers, Amorys of Boston, Browns of Providence, Crugers and Lows of New York, Willings and Whartons of
Philadelphia. These brisk enterprisers had already set foot on the
path that led to the opulent, plush age of the railroad magnates,
the nineteenth century fortunes in timber, coal and iron, the
profits from manufacturing patented harvesting machinery. Entre-
preneurs and daring speculators were pleased to learn, as Lord
Burghley had said so long before, that "Gentilitie is nothing but
ancient Riches."

The founders of new economic dynasties who were pushing energetically to the front found counsellors available whose emphasis fell congenially upon manipulating men rather than upon the traditional teachings of Christian ethics. Such a personage was Baron Adolph Franz Friedrich Ludwig von Knigge, who had been gentleman-in-waiting at the German courts of Hesse-Cassel and Weimar. Knigge's social treatise was published here as *Practical Philosophy of Social Life . . . Adapted to American Use . . .* Don't try to shine, the Baron wrote. Let others appear to advantage and you gain ascendancy over them. Be still and you create an impression of wisdom. Submit patiently to fashionable chatter and you will be called a wit.

A similarly self-seeking motivation was frankly set forth in Francis Osborne's *Advice to a Son. . . .* The author recommended travel because it advances one's reputation, a form of upmanship. Gratuities distributed at the end of a stay are wasted. Pay first, the Baron urged, enjoy later. "A small drop of silver will carry you more safe than a Sword." Conscience should be kept under control, subordinate to "our own honest, safe and wholsom conveniences." Be temperate in public, Osborne wrote, for anything may be done in private. The only inducement to marriage which he could imagine was the acquisition of a wife's great estate. Why, otherwise, give up freedom for thralldom, fornication for adultery? In times of political unrest, keep out of harm's way: "A Living Dogg is better than a Dead Lyon."

Schoolmasters in the eighteenth century taught manners and morals as a part of the curriculum, and encouraged young scholars to keep a commonplace book in which they copied extracts from the best authors they had read. Such a compilation has come down to us from the 1740's which reveals much about the climate of the times and about the copier who was young George Washington. Later contemporaries thought they saw evidence that Washington modeled his conduct in adult life upon his boyish *Rules of Civility and Decent Behaviour in Company and Conversation.* One maxim set forth the importance of showing the world a pleasant, grave countenance. This early became a habit with Washington. When he was twenty-eight years old his friend and companion in arms, Captain George Mercer, said of him, "In conversation he looks you full in the face, is deliberate, deferential and engaging."

Much good sense is encapsulated in such pithy aphorisms as:

"Mock not nor Jest at anything of Importance break no Jest that are Sharp Biting and if you Deliver anything witty and Pleasant abstain from Laughing thereat yourself."

"Give not Advice without being Ask'd & when desired do it briefly."

"Speak not in an unknown Tongue in Company but in your own language and that as those of Quality do and not as ye Vulgar. . . ."

Social conditions may be inferred from:

"Kill no Vermin as Fleas, lice ticks &c in the Sight of Others. . . ."

Also in:

"Spit not in the Fire, nor Stoop low before it neither Put your Hands into the Flames to warm them, nor Set your Feet upon the Fire especially if there be meat before it."

Could better advice be given today to one about to call upon a friend in the hospital than this?

"In visiting the Sick, do not Presently play the physician if you be not Knowing therein."

The name of the compiler who put together what are called Washington's *Rules* is not known. There are interesting parallels with an Elizabethan work, *The Babees Boke,* "a lytyl reporte of how young people should behave," translated from the Latin in the fifteenth century. Compare, for example, "Kutte withe your knyfe youre brede, and breke yt nouhte," with Washington's ". . . Feed not with Greediness; cut your Bread with a Knife, lean not on the table."

Someone, at any rate, possibly his father, placed before young Washington a collection of gnomic sayings about decorum and "carriage." We need not be detained here with the complicated and conjectural sources. There may be a debt to Moody's *School of Good Manners.* There is evidence that the *Rules* derive from an English version of an earlier French work. The point is that in many societies there has been substantial agreement that certain acts are graceless. It is not surprising, then, that different writers used similar words to speak of the same gaucheries: the undainty eater, the conversation-killer, the interrupter, the clumsy fellow who claws his clothing, investigates publicly his body's orifices, does not hesitate when in company to fire his stern guns.

When the states of the new American Confederation had

achieved their political separation from the English homeland, some voices were raised in favor of a social declaration of independence as well. Enos Hitchcock, Congregational clergyman and ardent patriot, urged that the European style of life was unsuited to American circumstances. "We have already suffered much," he wrote, "by too great an avidity for British customs and manners; it is now time to become independent in our maxims, principles of education, dress, and manners, as we are in our laws and government." And a contributor to Mathew Carey's *American Museum,* the first successful American magazine, declared in the days of the Confederation, "I sincerely wish that we may abolish many disgustful, embarrassing, destructive English customs. . . ." One usage which the writer denounced especially was the complimentary gesture of health-drinking in which every guest at a dinner was expected to toast every other guest individually, "calling out across the table to know the name of mr. and mrs. such-a-one, that you may have the pleasure of drinking their healths." The consequence: noise, confusion, the gentlemen soon "disguised with liquor." And, since all drank out of one vessel, grease, tobacco and other foreign objects could be floating in the liquor and there was "the risk of contracting a venereal taint."

But the protests of iconoclasts against the ascendancy of the English social world were atypical. The first impression which London made upon the American painter, Copley, led him to say "in comparison with the people of this country, we Americans are not half removed from a state of nature." Young Edward Shippen, although he hailed from Philadelphia, then the second city in the British Empire, wrote defensively while reading law in the Middle Temple, of "How much we are excelled by those in Europe." New Yorkers imitated the manners of fashionable English life, the ladies following London in the "silly Trick of taking Snuff with such a Cocquet Air," the returned traveler boasting of his familiarity with the newest minuets and of having seen Garrick act. A Boston satirist observed ironically of the women there that they were "neglecting the affairs of their families with as good a grace as the finest ladies in London."

When the letters of fatherly counsel written by Philip Dormer Stanhope, fourth Earl of Chesterfield, to his illegitimate son, Philip, were published they quickly made their way to the colonies. Graceful in style, the distillation of the life experience of one of the foremost English statesmen of the age, these letters on the art of pleasing and being pleased were written in polished English, Latin and French and so filled with sage observations so happily phrased that many of the Earl's felicities have become as familiar in quotation as Shakespeare. It was agreed that the Earl spoke with unusual authority. Yet certain portions of his book gave offense and stirred up a storm of adverse comment. The bone in the throat was that Lord Chesterfield appeared to separate good breeding from good morals and to recommend polite behavior solely upon the grounds of expediency.

For example, His Lordship said of dancing that it was "one of those established follies," but that people of sense should be able to dance well. "Dress," Chesterfield told his son, "is a very foolish thing; and yet it is a very foolish thing for a man not to be well dressed. . . ." Diogenes, the Cynic, the Earl continued, was a wise man for despising the customs of society but a fool for showing it. When young Stanhope was touring Europe his father wrote that the way to gain the friendship of people was to find out their strengths and weaknesses, then ". . . do justice to the one, and something more than justice to the other." Self-interest was the key to success, dissimulation the lock. Women are important because what they say can affect a man's position in the world; but they can be managed through flattery; "scarce any . . . is too gross for them to swallow."

It has often been overlooked that Chesterfield did urge honor and morality in the *Letters* because sexual morality was not included. When the son reached Paris on his tour, he being then eighteen years old, the Earl warned that he would not pay for actresses, dancers, whores and surgeons—they all went together—and all were quite unnecessary, since in Paris "gallantry is both the profession and the practise of every woman of fashion." Philip was urged by his father to make an assault upon the virtue of a Madame de Blot who was still pretty and faithful to her husband though married a whole year; also the more experienced Madame du Pin, who would provide *tournure,* direction and style. The father thought an arrangement could be made since she was no longer in "the glare and éclat of youth."

Despite the "glossy duplicity" recommended in the *Letters* and the anxiety lavished by the busy Secretary of State upon making his son a roué—these observations appear in Boswell's *Life of Johnson*

—young Stanhope seems to have been from the point of view of his father something of a dud. He contracted a secret marriage with an English woman of humble origin and died young, leaving the widow, Eugenia, and two sons. Lord Chesterfield took his disappointment philosophically, behaved admirably toward Mrs. Stanhope and her children. It is only fair to say of the *Letters* that they were never intended to be published.

In America Chesterfield's advice was widely read because he was recognized as an arbiter of elegance, because of the charm of his intellect and because he was an English lord. The *Letters* were read in their original form during the Revolutionary struggle, circulated later in expurgated versions such as *The American Chesterfield by "A Member of the Philadelphia Bar."* Every nation, writes the anonymous Philadelphia lawyer, has its peculiarities which call for reproof. He incorporates into the book the special offenses committed against decorum by "the young gentlemen of the United States." They include chewing tobacco, spitting on the floor and lolling back on the two rear legs of a chair, with feet elevated in an indecent posture. This social crudity led to another unpleasantness, a grease spot on the wallpaper.

Chesterfield's *Letters* were perhaps our first taste of what was later called success literature, a genre which has always possessed an irresistible attraction and descends without interruption through the Reverend William M. Thayer, who collected anecdotes about successful men under such titles as *Men Who Win* and *Pluck and Purpose* and the prolific sermonizing of Orison Swett Marden. Chesterfield's influence in shaping the American attitude toward success is probably second only to that of Benjamin Franklin. The Earl's book was in Washington's personal library. John Adams read him but thought the work unsuitable reading for his wife. Abigail read the book anyway, scorned the author as "a Hypocritical polished Libertine, a mere Lovelace," referring to the attractive but unscrupulous man of fashion in Samuel Richardson's novel, *Clarissa Harlowe.* A Reverend John Bennet, himself the author of a book of unquestioned rectitude, *Letters to a Young Lady,* said forthrightly that Chesterfield's treatise ought to be burned.

Chesterfield's influence is apparent in the ideas of Samuel Pickering Gardner, prosperous merchant and Boston gentleman. Gardner told his two sons that he owned "a little book filled with excellent remarks . . . extracted from Earl Chesterfield's *Letters to*

His Son." In the spirit of these "remarks" Gardner warned his boys against getting involved in "trifling pursuits" among which he enumerated "public employments which occupy much time and confer little or no distinction."

The deep respect for money among the Americans was noticed in the eighteenth century even before the Almighty Dollar existed. At a dancing party given for a select company in Philadelphia by the Chevalier de La Luzerne in 1780, the Marquis de Chastellux, soldier, *philosophe* and strong friend of the American cause, remarked slyly that Mrs. Robert Morris was given precedence, "an honor rather generally bestowed on her, as she is the richest woman in the city, and all ranks here being equal, men follow their natural bent by giving preference to wealth."

Similar claims were advanced, not too successfully as it turned out, by John Hancock, the richest man in New England to choose the patriot side in the American Revolution. When President Washington made his tour of New England in the autumn of 1789 to see for himself how the people were disposed toward the national government, the pompous Hancock, then the Governor of Massachusetts, kept the President waiting at the town line of Boston while a committee struggled with a problem of etiquette. Should the nation's chief magistrate be greeted by the state's governor or the town's selectmen? With Washington and his suite shivering in a biting wind, it was finally determined that he should be received by the municipal authorities. It was a rude affront. So, with a ringing of church bells, royal salutes from the French frigates off the Long Wharf and joyous Federal greetings from the local artillery companies, the Father of his Country rode to the State House. There he got to see the Lieutenant Governor but not the Governor.

Then came the question of who would pay the first visit to whom. Hancock sat tight, claiming that he was the chief of an independent state whereas Washington was merely the head of a confederation of sovereign states. The Governor also announced that he didn't feel very well. But the pressures built up. Hancock was persuaded at last to yield and "enveloped in red baise," went in his great coach the next evening to call upon the President of the United States to the great glee of the citizens of Boston.

A clash between widely different social theories occurred when the attempt was made to place the *jeunesse dorée* of New England automatically at the top of the class lists at Harvard and Yale colleges. The application of social criteria reflected many pressures. But the determination of who was who had practical importance. It involved the marching order of splendid academic processions, who sat at the head of the table at commons and the question of seniority at prayers. Rank was also useful in maintaining discipline. It was invoked, to cite one instance, to discipline James Ward, member of the Harvard Class of 1645. Ward was dropped to the next-to-last place. The reason: burglary.

When first introduced, the ranking appears to have been based upon an educated guess as to a student's probable academic performance. But later, at the insistence of ambitious parents, the faculty succumbed to the deceptively simple plan of permitting Family to fix the class order. This appeared reasonable to men accustomed to the grand principle of subordination as found in the Scriptures. But the method soon introduced new contradictions. The father of Samuel Phillips raised such a dust-up over the fact that his son was ranked below a boy whose father had not been a Justice of the Peace as long as the elder Phillips, that the Overseers retreated. An alphabetical arrangement was adopted.

"There is no evidence," remarks the modern historian of Harvard, Professor Samuel Eliot Morison, "that democratic feeling had anything to do with the change. . . ." It was merely that "the task of placating provincial pomposity [became] more difficult."

At Yale, from the earliest days of the College, the names of the students had stood, in Latin, in the *Triennial Catalogue* in the order of family standing, but the rule was rescinded in favor of the alphabetical order in 1768, the year before Harvard made the same decision. David Avery, Yale '69, wrote happily of the change to Dr. Eleazar Wheelock, the Congregational pastor at Lebanon, Connecticut, who was soon to found Dartmouth College.

"It is not he that has got the finest coat or largest ruffles that is esteemed here at present. And as the class henceforthward are to be placed alphabetically, the students may expect marks of distinction put upon the best scholars and speakers."

The question of "placing" students upon any other basis than performance did not arise at the College of William and Mary, second oldest college in the United States because, Miss Jane Carson, Research Assistant at Colonial Williamsburg, has concluded, "Where status is clearly understood, there is no need for formal labels."

Amusements during the eighteenth century in the seaport towns centered around parties, plays, dancing assemblies and al fresco fetes. Newport enjoyed tripe suppers and "turtle frolicks." This involved sailing over to Goat Island in a sloop, dinner at two o'clock prepared by a skillful Guinea-boy, and a generous supply of limes, arrack and Barbados rum for running up a glorious punch, with dancing later under the stars. New Yorkers rode out the Bowery Road in sleighs for skating and shooting, carried on an old Dutch custom of deep drinking and visits of ceremony to mark the arrival of the New Year. Of the sleighing parties, Alexander Macraby, a young British army officer, wrote shortly before the Revolution, "You can have no idea of the state of the pulse seated with pretty women mid-deep in straw, your body armed with furs and flannels, clear air, bright sunshine . . . every feeling turned to joy and jollity." The plain people, apprentices, servants and mechanics of the city developed such a taste for gambling in the public houses that an enactment was passed restricting the privilege to the merchants and gentlemen of the town who presumably had the moral stamina to keep the habit under control and the money to afford it. In New England, Calvinism relaxed its grip slowly. While New Yorkers were gambling, following the hounds on Long Island and holding race meetings, Robert Hale of Beverly, Massachusetts, chose as his recreation reading the Bible one hundred and thirty-four times.

The socially elect young women of Maryland and Virginia rode to the dancing assemblies in scarlet riding habits worn over their ball gowns, performed the figures of the stately minuet with high-bred courtesy. In Cincinnati the ladies dressed too thinly, laced too tightly and stayed up too late, according to Dr. Daniel Drake. The Doctor also observed among the male Cincinnatians that there were numbers of citizens "who daily but quietly became intoxicated." Philadelphia took its amusements seriously. Colonel John Mitchell exercised the office of manager of a subscription ball with such strictness that when a young woman forgot her turn in a figure, the Colonel roared at her:

"Come, come . . . do you think you are here for pleasure?"

The French, who led the Old World in the polite accomplishments, often encountered traumatic experiences in endeavoring to put some polish on the people of the New. When Samuel Moody, son of the gifted but eccentric parson, "Handkerchief" Moody, became the first headmaster of Dummer Academy, he hired a Frenchman to knock the rust off his pupils. Tradition has it that when the dancing teacher arrived in Byfield, the two of them stood bowing and scraping at the door until the Reverend became disgusted, picked up the polite little dancing master and threw him into the room.

Hardly less trying was an incident which occurred in Louisville when that thriving town was taking shape at the Falls of the Ohio. M. Jean Nickle opened a dancing school, introduced the dances known in Paris, the vivacious *branle,* the graceful minuet, the ceremonious *pavane.* But Nickle was "too scientific" for the Ohio valley. The boys played leap frog when they were supposed to be doing the *branle.* During the minuet, the girls held their linsey-woolsey dresses out like sails, skipped across the floor with heads down, like so many geese dodging stones; and in the *pavane* all strutted and cried like pea fowls until the distracted Nickle wished "he were in hell" and yielded the scene to an old Negro named Cato Watts. Cato gave the dancers what they wanted, Virginia reels and Irish jigs. Cato had another distinction, his last. He was the first man ever hung in Louisville, an event which caused much sorrow among the young people.

The annals of those whom John Adams called "the simple men" are always scanty. Something of the conditions of life may be inferred from a reminiscence of Oliver E. Ellsworth, one of the first U.S. senators from Connecticut and later Chief Justice of the Supreme Court, whose ancestors had lived for generations in Windsor. Ellsworth told his son that he did not think that in the eighteenth century there was "such a thing as a privy or necessary-house in the town. . . ." Under the prod of biological necessity the inhabitants of Windsor could take to the bushes. Or another common arrangement is suggested in the token of affection which a Harvard class of the mid-century presented to a famous college "character," the well-beloved tutor, Henry Flynt. In solemn procession on Commencement morning the class carried to Tutor Flynt a handsome solid silver chamber pot. It was inscribed with a scatological jest which is repeated here but will not be translated:

Mingere cum bombis
Res est saluberrima lumbis.

In the South the "simple men" took their pleasure in fighting. In New England they were always lawing. "Fite they wood," said Timothy Dexter, the merchant and eccentric, "they went to Jinrel

Cort to be sot of." Nor could plain, republican simplicity always be counted upon to supply the courtesy which nurture had failed to cultivate. Chastellux, who admired all things American when he honestly could, paid for a good dinner with wine for two American travelers, strangers to him, at an inn in Trenton, New Jersey. After eating and drinking, the men rose without a word and departed. The Marquis remarked with unusual asperity: "There are more ceremonies than compliments in America. All their politeness is mere form . . . none of it arises from feeling; in a word, politeness here is like religion in Italy. . . ."

An extraordinary instance of what established usage can do to legitimize rough customs was a rite known as bundling. This was a usage in which a suitor paid night visits to a respectable girl and courted her, fully clothed, in a feather bed. Bundling developed out of the environment in New York, New Jersey, Pennsylvania and New England, involving a cold climate, poor housing, lack of privacy and the absence of daytime leisure among those who toiled from sunup to sundown. Bundling was also common in the southern states from the Revolutionary times to the early years of the nineteenth century as a convenience to travelers when public accommodations were lacking and beds were scarce.

Numerous instances have been recorded in which strangers shared a bed with the daughter of the household. In 1777 Lieutenant Thomas Anbury, an officer in Burgoyne's captive army, was billeted at Williamstown, Massachusetts, in a house where the old matriarch indicated the two beds available—"Jonathan and I will sleep in this and our Jemima and you shall sleep in that." Jemima, black-eyed and very pretty, archly remarked that it "will be with the first Britainer." Even straight-laced John Adams, when he considered the serious objections he had to the arranged marriage, concluded, "I cannot wholly disapprove of Bundling." But out of local bundling incidents and the *contes drolatiques* told along the counters of ancient country stores come almost certainly the body of *sub rosa* folk tales and bawdry which may be referred to collectively as The Traveling Salesman and the Farmer's Daughter.

Fought by the churches, ridiculed by the almanac writers, bundling passed its peak around 1800. Cape Codders are said to have held out the longest for featherbed wooing. As with the early Christian fathers who lived with young virgins to test their strength in the struggle between the flesh and the spirit, the battle was sometimes lost and a pregnancy resulted in the girl's father entering suit for damages. But the courts held that a father who consented to such broad-minded hospitality could not collect; *volenti non fit injuria*. A student of bundling who wrote a book about this curious subject a hundred years later remarked that probably our ancestors were neither better nor worse than ourselves and, speaking as the father of daughters, he decided that bundling was perhaps less dangerous than the Victorian sofa.

By the end of the eighteenth century the old cities of the North had taken on the individualities which were to remain with them as a part of their personality and ethos. New York acquired sophistication when it became for a short but important period the seat of the Federal Government. This eminence brought the latest fashions, novelties and luxuries, the formality of European court etiquette and, at the same time, the uncombed job hunters in relentless pursuit of political plunder. Looking over the Congressional scene, Adams declared that he had not encountered one well-bred man since he came to town.

Philadelphia already possessed maturity and aplomb, polite tastes and the nearest thing to an hereditary in-group which the United States was ever to see. The Old Philadelphian did not, then or later, have to get ahead. He was born ahead. There was little to worry about or vex him except whether it was good form to be too distinguished. Progress, too, was noticed in Boston. Henry Wansey, the English clothier who saw a fair slice of this country in 1794, wrote of the Hub: "They no longer hang old women for witchcraft . . . maintain a decent sobriety of manners. . . ." The standard female type later known as the Boston Amazon, who wore funny hats, sensible shoes and muslin drawers, apparently had not appeared in the mid-eighteenth century. When Dr. Alexander Hamilton, the urbane and observant Maryland physician, visited Boston in 1744, he commented in his diary upon the fine "ring of ladys" there and added: "I must take notice that this place abounds with pritty women."

Long before the Wednesday evening genealogical page in the Boston *Transcript* came to exercise jurisdiction in matters social and armorial, Bostonians with a sense of Family looked for social clarification, in those unusual instances when it was necessary, in the Harvard catalogue. Josiah Quincy, sixth in descent from forebears who came to the Colony with John Cotton, kept the Bible on his desk and the *Harvard Triennial Catalogue*. When an unfamiliar name came to his attention he would consult the catalogue.

"If a man was in it," he once explained, "that's who he was; if he wasn't in it, who was he?"

By the time the 1800's arrived, the posture of the "fine gentleman" who wore his manners for display and kept his morals in the deep freeze was challenged by the rise of a sober, industrious, trading class, the spread of Methodism, the popularity of novels of sensibility which countered the cold calculation of Chesterfield's *Letters* with a revival of emotion and moral earnestness. In apposition to the "fine gentleman" was the "true gentleman" who combined Christian ethics with the classical doctrine of moderation in all things, subject to limitation in certain areas, since it would plainly be a vice to practice moderation in honesty, in kindness or in chastity.

A major influence in the reappraisal of what constituted the well-bred man was Samuel Richardson, the English author of *Pamela, or Virtue Rewarded, Clarissa Harlowe* and *The History of Sir Charles Grandison*. . . . The last purports to be the portrait of a perfect gentleman—always calm, self-possessed, virtuous and, to the taste of later generations, a very tedious character. Richardson had a genius for expressing himself through the form of letters. When still a youth, he had been employed as penman for girls of his acquaintance in the conduct of their love affairs. He was fifty years old when two printers asked him to prepare for them "a little volume of letters, in a common style, on such subjects as might be of use to those country readers who were unable to indite for themselves."

The result was *Letters Written to and for Particular Friends* . . . issued without indication of authorship. The book appeared in 1741, the year after Richardson's phenomenally successful *Pamela*. The author gave not only patterns for style but for thinking and acting "Justly and Prudently . . ." with especial attention to the perils surrounding young, good-looking girls who went out into the world as domestics. It may be objected that in Richardson virtue is protected by a mechanical following of the rules of propriety rather than by inner sanction. He was, nevertheless, received with joy in America. For he expressed what American conservatives wanted after the political upheaval of the American Revolution—the continuity of the social tradition.

Six editions of what came to be called the *Familiar Letters* were issued during Richardson's life, a seventh soon after. Eighty-two American compilers of similar works helped themselves to the durable little classic, changing English geographical references, such as Vauxhall and Caper's Gardens, to Central Park. Sometimes they didn't bother to edit out the Briticisms. One American work, *The Letter Writers Own Book,* which appeared in 1848, borrowed one of Richardson's model letters about the honorable offer of marriage a young woman had received from a "linen-draper," an occupation or at least a term that is not known in the United States. She takes the proposal up with her father. This is the way she puts the matter:

> *Honoured Father,*
> *My duty teaches me to acquaint you, that a gentleman of this town, whose name is Smith, and by business a linen-draper, has made some overtures to my cousin, Arnold, in the way of courtship to me. My cousin has brought him once or twice into my company, as he has a high opinion of him and his circumstances. He has been set up three years, possesses a very good business, and lives in credit and fashion. He is about twenty-seven years old, and is likely in his person. He seems not to want sense nor manners, and is come of a good family. He has broken his mind to me, and boasts how well he can maintain me; but I assure you, sir, I have given him no encouragement, yet he resolves to persevere, and pretends extraordinary affection and esteem. I would not, sir, by any means, omit to acquaint you with the beginning of an affair, that would show a disobedience unworthy of your kind indulgence and affection. Pray give my humble duty to my honoured mother, love to my brother and sister, and respects to all friends.*
> *I remain your ever dutiful daughter.*

The father did not approve. So of course that was the end of the matter.

With American enthusiasm for the principles of the French Revolution there came a new appreciation, based upon philosophic grounds, of the natural man whose native worth, uncorrupted by reading Chesterfield, showed through an often shaggy exterior. The smart mode in dress was the disheveled look. Long trousers replaced the knee-length breeches and long stockings. Formalities were dropped in social intercourse. The dramatic portrait of a new kind of American appeared for the first time in an American play, Royal Tyler's *The Contrast*. The play's bluff old Colonel Manly, lately come down to New York from Massachusetts wearing his old regimental coat, had a large amount of Richardson in him. The Colonel, a home-grown specimen of nobility, and no fool either, exposes the villainy of one Billy Dimple, who had traveled in Europe and read Chesterfield. The odious Dimple gets his comeuppance, of course, exits with a speech aimed directly at the audience:

"I take my leave, and you will please to observe in the case of my deportment, the contrast between a gentleman who has read Chesterfield and received the polish of Europe, and an unpolished, untraveled American."

The triumph of Colonel Manly, a kind of backwoods Sir Charles Grandison, comes as a warning that the Christian gentleman rather than the cynical fop is to dominate the polite code in the century to come. As it turned out, a felicitous way was found to bring into harmony the morality of the Protestant churches and the self-serving precepts for getting ahead in material affairs. The practice of the Puritan virtues, it was found, assured advancement in this world as well as the next. If a boy was brave, honest, manly and polite, it made no difference that his father was not able to provide him with a pony. If he had the requisite character, stamina and style he would get the pony himself. It is significant that much of the inspirational literature preaching the art of worldly success came from the busy pens of clergymen, like Horatio Alger or Russell Herman Conwell, popular lecturer and pastor of the largest Protestant church in the United States, who thundered from pulpit and platform, "You should be a righteous man, and if you were you would be rich." Conwell's doctrine filled the correspondence and night schools, the Y.M.C.A. training classes. "Find out the world's need," he said, and thousands went into taxidermy, started a popcorn stand or got up a patented collar button in response to the Reverend's parable of success which held out the vision of *all this, and Heaven too.*

SOCIETY AT THE SOUTH

While the Puritans liked to compare themselves with the Judeans in exile at Babylonia, the men of the South sought the more comfortable title of English gentlemen. Of all the men who thought of England as "home," the southerners cultivated most assiduously the attitudes of a feudal aristocracy, accepted and enjoyed the responsibilities and perquisites of leadership and supported religion as a necessary underpinning of a stable society. In one important respect the environment was against them; land was too abundant for the establishment of a permanent upper class. But the habits of thought, customs, even the gossip of London were all within their grasp.

The emigrants who sailed westward on the *Goodspeed,* the *Susan Constant* and the *Discovery* found no gold. But with tobacco and peanuts, Carolina rice and indigo, they flourished well enough, although they possessed "a Country over-run with Woods and Briers, and for many years infested with the Incursions of the barbarous Indians . . ." as was pointed out in the preface to the

Statutes of the College of William and Mary in Virginia. But their descendants developed the plantation mind, the plantation tradition and the plantation economy, by virtue of the blessings called in those forthright days, "land and niggers." Prevailing winds made intercourse with England easier than with the colonies to the North. Hospitality was easy and gracious in a sense denied to a Yankee situated as was Dr. Abner Hersey of Barnstable, Massachusetts, and a professor of medicine at Harvard. Dr. Hersey once wrote, when his sister-in-law proposed to pay him a visit: "Madam, I can't have you here; I am sick, and my wife is sick; I have no hay or corn for your horses: I have no servants; and I had rather be chained to a galley-oar than wait on you myself."

The inclination of the southern planters toward lavish entertainment was stimulated by the absence of large towns, the great distances involved in the maintenance of social relations, the abundance of home-processed food and unlimited service. Even funerals were social as well as solemn occasions. Prolonged feasting was a feature of mourning involving the barbecuing of a steer and several sheep. A barrel of strong beer would be broken out and brandy by the gallon, while Pompey or Cato handed around a sweet wine for the ladies.

Europeans had affirmed more or less seriously for a thousand years the existence of an Earthly Paradise located somewhere to the west. If Virginia was not the fabled garden, it "may be justly esteemed" wrote the historian and loyal Hanovarian, Hugh Jones, "the happy retreat of true Britons and true churchmen." So a landed gentry able to live out the idylls of the plantation kings sent their sons to be made barristers at the Inns of Court, to acquire an outlook on life in the country houses of England to which they had admittance. Thomas Pinckney wrote that in addition to reading law he had learned to dance the cotillion and to fence, following a conscious plan "of blending the Gentleman into the Scholar." Among Maryland families which sent two or more sons abroad for schooling were the Galloways and Dulanys. Charles Carroll of Carrollton was absent from Maryland for as long as sixteen years. Henry Laurens of South Carolina sent two sons to Geneva. Medical students gathered at Edinburgh. South Carolina Draytons and Izards were educated in England, as were the Randolphs, Lees, Blands, Meades and Carters of Virginia, all representing families of political and social importance. Some young colonials bought a

horse and journeyed in style to see Salisbury Cathedral and Stone-
henge. Some lost themselves in the flesh pots of London. Others
went north to inspect the manufacture of buttons.

Colonial Virginia offers a spectacular instance of the opportunity which American life has presented for men of energy to make
their way up in the world. A few emigrants, a small proportion of
the total population, were of aristocratic lineage, for the most part
younger sons with no expectations from their fathers. Many were
merchants or sons of the merchant class. The first Virginia Byrd
was the son of a goldsmith. He came to Virginia as a young man,
traded pots, pans, guns and rum for Indian furs, married the
daughter of a Cavalier gentleman, pushed ahead in the business of
dealing in tobacco and bond servants, did some blackbirding as
owner of the slaver, the *William and Jane.* In the mix of emigrants
were mercers, maltsters, members of craft guilds, soldiers captured
in the Parliamentary, Scotch and Irish wars. For some the choice
was Virginia instead of Newgate. Sufficient numbers had been
burnt in the hand for Dr. Johnson to say of the Virginians, un-
fairly yet not as a complete invention, "Sir, they are a race of con-
victs." Enough persons of good family did come out to leave an
impression of courtly manners and a certain infuriating hauteur. If
they were not all lords they could at least act like lords, indulge a
passion for fast horses, silver plate and handsome sideboards
equipped with cut decanters. They created an attitude and a style
without which our national folklore would have been the poorer.
The significant point, after all, is not what they were, but what
they became.

The gentleman of Virginia had pressing administrative duties
competing for his attention—at the stock barn, the wharf and ware-
houses, the sawmill, the dovecote and the buttery. He consulted
with the overseer about the field hands and directed the carving in
mahogany of a capital for the new great hall in the family mansion.
The Virginia grandee helped choose the new rector for the college
at Williamsburg, dozed in church if he felt like it, walked in his
garden in the cool of the evening and had the Negro, Tom,
whipped, as William Byrd II noted in his diary, "for not telling me
that he was sick." The Virginia Englishman followed the hounds
and hit the bottle as regularly as did his progenitors, moldering
under the chancels of rural parish churches in Devon or Surrey.

Following the English custom, the planters gave names to their estates, many with a romantic flavor, such as the broad acres of the Harrisons, known as "Berkeley Hundred," "Exeter Lodge" or "Drayton," which honored the ancient seat of the Purifoys in Leicestershire. Under the social system of the upper classes, the father and master was a kind of Old Testament character, august, martial, arrogant, his estates a little kingdom. This is not a modern, romanticized idea we have thrust upon the past. The analogy occurred to Colonel Byrd at the time he was living out the dream. He wrote from his "Westover" to his English friend, the Earl of Orrery:

"I have my flocks and my herds, my bondmen and bondwomen, and every sort of trade amongst my own servants, so that I live in a kind of independence of everyone but Providence." But he points out that he has to work, too. "I must take care to keep all my people to their duty, to set all the springs in motion, and to make everyone draw his equal share to carry the machine forward." "We sit securely," he concludes, "under our vines and our fig trees without any danger to our property. We have neither public robbers nor private, which your lordship will think very strange. . . ."

William Byrd II, one of the most accomplished of the gentlemen to emerge from Virginia, was educated in England, entered the Middle Temple and was admitted to the bar in 1695. Byrd was the mirror of the urbane aristocrat, equally at home with the Council of State, with scouts and surveyors in the wilds of the Appalachian frontier, or in the coffee houses of London. Byrd had a reputation in London as a social climber. But he was successful at it. He won access to the best society, moved in the court circles and had the honor of watching George I throw dice. Elected a Fellow of the Royal Society, Byrd sent his colleagues an American opossum, a live rattlesnake, boxed, and told his fellow-members how to distill peach brandy. Kneller painted him, and the Restoration wits, Congreve, Nicholas Rowe and Wycherley, admitted him to their company. Crossing the ocean five times, the Colonel, in later years a wealthy widower, pursued heiresses for their assets and women of the town for the moment's necessities. Byrd was a virtuoso, complex, gifted, ambitious and conniving, with an eye always out for a pretty woman or a place of power. His candid diaries present a fascinating and minute view of his studies and religious devotions, what he ate, how he fondled a tavern maid, when he washed his feet and whether he said, or forgot to say, his prayers. The diary entries often end with this conventional note, "I had good health, good thoughts, and good humor, thanks be to God Almighty," to which on one occasion he added, "only I feared I was going to have the piles."

The prefix "Mister" marked the social position of a gentleman as in New England. But the term "Esquire" was used even more sparingly. Members of the Council of State were esquires, a title practically equivalent to a patent of nobility. "Honorable" was used in connection with a great office with only one incumbent, such as the Governor, Secretary or Treasurer. As in the North, wives of high officials were addressed as "Madam," women of lower rank as "Goody." "Goody" Layton, for example, told Madam Thoroughgood to her face that her late husband, Captain Adam Thoroughgood, was well known to be *slow pay*. The cocked hat was a prerogative of the upper classes. An anecdote is preserved of William Randolph who ran a taut ship when sitting as judge on the Henrico County bench. He fined a presumptuous Thomas Holmes twelve hundred pounds of tobacco because Holmes did "put on his hat, cock it up, sit down, and begin to sing . . . to ye great abuse and dishonour of all authority."

The Virginian of the plantation class breakfasted in colonial times between eight and nine o'clock on bread, butter, venison, ham, beef, with tea or coffee as beverages. He dined in the middle of the day, between two and three, took a light supper at eight or nine o'clock in the evening. The plain people ate cold turkey and fried hominy with cider at the morning meal, dined on corn pone, greens and cabbage with some form of pork, took no supper. Women of social position presided over richly appointed mahogany dinner tables. Yet the food must often have been tepid and limp, since it was prepared in an outdoor kitchen, served by slack waiters whose rustic maneuvers contrasted strangely with the elegance of the linen, the glowing silver and fine English bone china.

Cookbooks popular in the seventeenth and early eighteenth centuries provided engraved "schemes" for the proper arrangement of dishes on the table and explained the etiquette of serving. All meats, vegetables and side dishes which made up the first course were put on the table at once. The mistress of the house carved and served. Guests helped themselves from the nearest dishes, and passed their plates for the rest. The food was rich, highly seasoned, often complicated. Ragouts and meat pies were popular, served with rich stuffings and elaborate sauces. A gravy for veal cutlets, for instance, called for such ingredients as white wine, butter, oysters and sweetbreads. Cakes and puddings, which made up the second course, required lavish use of butter, heavy cream, eggs and spices. After the dessert course the cloth was removed. Apples and nuts appeared and the wine bottle was set out.

When Josiah Quincy, Jr., Boston lawyer and Revolutionary patriot, visited Charleston in 1773, he dined with four other gentlemen at the home of David Deis, described the table as "decent and not inelegant." A young Deis daughter gave a toast "very creditably" and the ladies withdrew. On another occasion, at Roger Smith's, a lady, called on for a toast, gave: "When passions rise may reason be the guide"; a course which South Carolina unfortunately did not follow at a later date when Fort Sumter offered a tempting target for the Charleston batteries. Healths having been drunk, the Smith ladies withdrew, leaving the male guests free to indulge in further drinking and in conversation too free for the ears of gentlewomen.

The majority of the people of the South were always plain folks, yeoman farmers, small planters settled on tracts of modest size, who had a corn patch, made pot ashes, dressed out beaver skins and cut cedar logs. They read their Bible and the almanac, sang Scotch-Irish ballads, attended fish fries and gloried in the flowery rhetoric of the lawyers on court day. Although generous and friendly and not lacking in a native, inner courtesy, their manners were rude, for the world had not been too much with them. Many were not agriculturists at all, but traversed the piney-woods regions as herdsmen and hunters. The rifle-gun hung over the fireplace. A few rows of tobacco grew in the "deadening" among the blackened stumps of pitch pine. The people on the settlement line were not universally admired. George Washington, who came among them as a young surveyor, called the frontiersmen "a parcel of barbarians," who all lay down together at night before the fireplace upon a little straw or fodder, "and happy's he that gets the Birth nearest the fire."

Women were scarce in "the Back Parts." The need for their labor and company gave them an importance and a partnership in family life beyond what had been known in older societies, even though they wore plain blue shifts, weeded the corn, hoed collards in their bare feet. Many of them arrived from England for the wife market by the shipload, described as young, handsome maids, "of honest life and carriage," a bargain at $80 in leaf tobacco; or as white bond servants who rose later to good social position after their term of servitude had run out. In remarking upon these arrangements for relieving the shortage of marriageable girls, Colonel Byrd wondered, possibly with tongue in cheek, why the Indian women had been overlooked: "I may safely venture to say, the Indian women would have made altogether as Honest Wives for the first Planters, as the Damsels they us'd to purchase from aboard the Ships. It is Strange, therefore, that any good Christian Shou'd have refused a wholesome, Straight Bed-fellow, when he might have had so fair a Portion with her, as the Merit of saving her Soul."

A modern scholar, Professor Frank L. Owsley, has theorized that out of the large but relatively unnoticed middle class in the Old South came the famous Southern accent, the slow drawl being in a white man a form of politeness, in a slave a sign of deference. Men spoke softly. "To be unfriendly was dangerous, for it was regarded as a challenge to a personal encounter by people whose fighting spirit and mores did not permit the refusal of such a challenge."

Among the common people the rural church was the nerve center of community life. Here slave and master gathered to hear the gospel expounded. The young bucks stayed outside, were often presented to the grand jury for swearing and scrapping near holy ground. After church the older men and women moved in small groups to the graveyard where they visited the family dead, observed with Christian resignation where they themselves would in the fullness of time be laid. It was a sacred place, yet they were not overwhelmed with death since they were sustained by a faith which promised resurrection and taught that unrestrained grief questioned God's wisdom and love. After the visit to the graves there was chat of gardens, chickens, weddings and quiltings. Nor did the nearness of God's Acre prevent the relating of tall tales and spicy anecdotes. While lovers strolled to the spring, the members of the parish went home with friends to eat a late Sunday dinner if they were "expected": and it was not against the principles of the devout to uncork the brown jug of corn squeezings which put a razor edge on appetite.

The small farmers and herders of the back country found their recreation in cooperative work like candle-dipping and corn-shucking. The men gathered for cock fights, barbecues, and oratory on county court day. This day, always on Monday, as James Lane Allen has written with affection, "the Kentuckian regularly did his fighting. Another noticeable recreation of the day was the drinking. Indeed, the two pleasures went marvelously well together. The drinking led up to the fighting, and the fighting led up to the drinking; and this amiable co-operation might be prolonged at will. . . ."

In the older regions the little market towns offered more decorous amusements. In Annapolis, the sound of the fiddle and French horn were frequently heard and welcomed in an atmosphere of "Universal Mirth and Glee . . . amongst all Ranks of People. . . ." There were balls in the provincial capitals "in publick times" and a great coming and going of governors, councillors, milliners and dressmakers, French hair dressers and barbers' boys rushing freshly groomed wigs to their owners. The notices of dancing teachers appeared frequently in the *Virginia Gazette*. The widow Stagg, as a drawing card for her classes, promised to raffle off a "likely young negro fellow" while a rival, Madame Degraffereidt, went her one better by advertising that at her next ball she would put up "a likely young Virginia negro woman fit for house business and her child."

Gentlemen chatted about prices—of land, tobacco and Negroes. There was much profanity and uninhibited, rural frankness of language among men and women of all ranks. The Reverend Jonathan Boucher, Anglican clergyman and stout upholder of the established order, resented being subjected to hearing "obscene Conceits and broad Expressions." He singled out for especial praise sixteen-year-old Priscilla Carter because she "never swears, which is here a distinguished virtue." The planters put down countless bowls of arrack, won or lost at loo, followed hounds with lilting names like Sweetlips, Chanter, Truelove and Musick. As a youth, George Washington ranged pleasantly through the social whirl of this snug and pleasant world. His cash accounts show him paying his share of club repasts at Yorktown, Williamsburg and Port Royal, attending the theater or laying out four shillings at Fredericksburg fair "By Treating the Ladies" to see "a Lyoness" and a "Tyger"; so we are justified in believing that the future Father of Our Country was a circus buff.

In the South, even more than in New England, the celebration of royal birthdays and the accessions of a new ruler provided occasion for the expression of joyful allegiance to king and country, a release from daily discipline and restraint. Then the great guns boomed from the ramparts and were handsomely answered by the ships in the river. There was an illumination of fireworks, a dance at the Governor's Palace with "a splendid Appearance of Ladies" in rustling brocades and high headdresses; and the common sort got a free glass of rum. Just before the end of these Arcadian days, in May, 1774, when the Virginia House of Burgesses met, the public life in Williamsburg had become so stylized that a court herald published a code of etiquette to guide those who governed in the proper management of their pleasures and official duties. The birthday of Queen Charlotte in January, 1775, was the last royal occasion marked by the amenities of an elaborate dancing party at Williamsburg. Within a matter of months Lord Dunmore, the Governor, and his family, including a tiny daughter who had been christened Virginia in compliment to the colony, had slipped away to England, universally execrated.

A prohibitionist in colonial America would have been considered a lunatic. The planter drank peach brandy of local provenience or a julep built upon a rum base to "clear his pipes" when he got up in the morning. What did they use for ice? Ice. Coasting schooners were ballasted with ice cut on Fresh Pond and Spy Pond near Boston. It is quite possible that many of the prosperous southrons regularly enjoyed the luxury of ice to a degree unknown in New England where the ice came from. In the practice of hospitality the toddy was indispensable. Southerners were also well-provided with imported wines—champagne, burgundy, claret, Fayal, Madeira, and hock.

The "island wines" from the Azores and Canary Islands enjoyed a particular esteem. In the Carolinas, according to Quincy, the favorite "liquors," as he called them, were claret and port. It was in bumpers of Madeira, most popular wine for a century and a half, that men of quality toasted the healths of the King, the Queen, the Prince and Princess of Orange, all the Royal Highnesses and the more respectable dukes.

The books which were owned and presumably read by planters, churchmen, doctors, lawyers and public officials have been ferreted out of old wills and inventories of estates, itemized and subjected to minute analysis by modern cultural historians. That the books were indeed read is strongly suggested by such information as is supplied by hasty notations included in the appraisals of estates, such as occurs in connection with one decedent, Thomas Casson, "a pcell of old books all in pecis." Poetry and polite letters are scantily represented. Men owned books which served practical purposes—dictionaries, medical handbooks, works on midwifery. Such volumes recall the circumstances of life on isolated plantations where diagnosis and treatment were carried out by master or mistress. Other subjects reflect a pattern of life—books on agriculture, distilling and surveying and polemical writings sounding a tocsin against that "snake in the grass," Quakerism.

Social aspirations are indicated in the frequent appearance of such titles as *The English Gentleman* and Castiglione's *Courtier.* *The Accomplished Courtier* was a guide to a career in politics popular with Cavalier readers. Peacham's *The Compleat Gentleman* . . . turns up frequently. Robert (King) Carter owned *The Gentleman's Calling* and that most popular of all conduct books, *The Whole Duty of Man.* . . . Almost every man of position in Virginia from the seventeenth century Ralph Wormeley down to Washington and Jefferson owned a copy of *The Whole Duty of Man.* It was one of the first books published in Virginia when William Parks established his press in Williamsburg. Indeed, a list of all the owners of this book in the first two hundred years of this country's history would be very nearly a genealogical register of the first families of the Old South. The pious moralizing of *Duty of Man* was presumably a lamp to the feet of those concerned with developing their private character and public reputation.

The degree to which daily conduct conformed to the standard remains an elusive question. Behind outward dignity in public there was often a coarseness in private life and a freedom of behavior especially when the young bucks were "worsted by the frolick of yesterday." Ebenezer Cook introduced into his poem, "The Sot-Weed Factor," the uncouth son of the Maryland planter

> *Who ne'er by Fathers Pains and Earning*
> *Had got at Mother Cambridge Learning.*

Two girls, Nancy and Milly, out for a stroll, complained of being seized by "two Horred Mortals," Corbin Washington and a Mr. Pinkard, and thrown into disarray by being forcibly kissed a dozen times. On another occasion the osculatory Washington chased the girls all around the garden and was quite impertinent. Among Pinkard's other "pleasantries" mentioned by the girls was a taste for dressing up in women's clothes. Colonel Byrd could say his prayers while Jenny was being whipped. His handsome father-in-law, Colonel Daniel Parke, admonished a daughter, Frances, to behave like a gentlewoman. But according to a contemporary, a hostile witness to be sure, Colonel Parke stole the wife of a gentleman of London and brought her to Virginia as his "cousin Brown." In a fit of rage when a sermon was preached against adultery at Bruton Church in Williamsburg, Parke dragged the wife of James Blair, deputy in Virginia of the Bishop of London, out of her pew. Parke died in an insurrection in the Leeward Islands leaving two illegitimate children there. But he was, for all his escapades, a member of The Establishment.

When an esquire heard the Church of England prayer, "For Our Country," which included the words "Bless our land with honorable industry, sound learning, and pure manners," he expected the rector to follow the model provided by the English sporting parson. The ecclesiastic was to behave like a southern gentleman, appreciate an anecdote if it wasn't too raw and demonstrate in his life and works that good Christians didn't have to be Stoics. The priest got by handily if he preached short sermons and could read the service. But the quality of the preaching is suggested in a lively vignette by Molly Tilghman, daughter of the noted Tilghman family of Talbot County, Maryland. Referring to her religious experience on a Sunday at Chestertown, Maryland, shortly after the Revolution, Molly wrote:

". . . I broil'd 6 Miles by Water, to the Bay Side Church in such a sun, it was enough to coddle common flesh. I was then so stupefied with old Gordon's slow croaking, that I began to dream a dozen times before the Sermon was over. . . ."

American history is crowded with instances of local loyalties and geographical snobberies. The Yankees looked down their noses at the Dutch. The east side of the Hudson River patronized the west side and the people of the Highlands returned the sentiment. The coastal regions looked askance at the buckskins streaming over the Allegheny ridges. Southerners disapproved of the manners of Philadelphians. The people of Philadelphia scorned the Germans while the latter ridiculed *die dummer Irisher* who passed through Lancaster County lugging their bright copper whiskey stills. When a young graduate of Princeton College was considering going to Virginia to tutor the children of Robert Carter III at Nomini Hall, his friends tried to dissuade him by assuring him that Virginia was a benighted land where there were no books on Calvinism. Colonel Byrd, in turn, spoke harshly of the North Carolinians whom he declared to be lazy, ignorant, dirty, unchurched and given over to an absurd status symbol: they lived in miserable hovels but splurged on enormous privies. Later a distinguished North Carolinian, Edwin Anderson Alderman, President of the University of Virginia, made the riposte, "I come from North Carolina, that lowly valley between twin peaks of conceit."

Most provincialism based upon ethnocentric allegiances was harmless enough. But southern sectional snobbery directed toward the North—"I hate their government—I hate their religion—I hate their *levelling*"—as Carter Braxton said of New Englanders, undoubtedly contributed to the charged atmosphere leading up to the Civil War. "We are the gentlemen of this country," declared Robert Toombs, a U. S. Senator from Georgia; and the Muscogee, Georgia, *Herald* lumped all northern society together as a "conglomeration" of mechanics, mill hands, radical theorists and tight-fisted farmers "hardly fit for association with a southern gentleman's body servant." It was a conception that led the South deep into fantasy. The fact is that the people of English origin in both North and South came from the same social strata, mostly the middle level. The differences between them arose from the influences of climate, soil, geography, religion and the land system—the human ecology of the regions.

As a humorous instance of the exquisite self-discipline of the southern gentleman, Joseph Clark Baldwin wrote in *The Flush Times of Alabama and Mississippi* (1853) that the Virginia aristocrat "never throws up to a Yankee the fact of his birthplace," and drew the analogy of a man of delicate feelings who would not speak of ropes in the presence of one whose brother had been hanged. "So far do they carry this refinement," Baldwin declared, "that I have known one of my countrymen, on occasion of a Bostonian owning where he was born, generously protest that he had never heard of it before."

The War destroyed the old social order. But out of military defeat came a legend made up of selected elements taken from the past, none entirely false in itself. But the effect was to create a mythical Golden Age when life was lived, so to speak, to an obligato of violins and hautboys. Even as the veterans of the late Confederacy hitched up the mule to do the spring plowing, they became scions all of Stuart cavaliers, Jeffersonian in their intellectual achievements, brave as Robert E. Lee, though somewhat susceptible to drink.

A professor of English at the University of Tennessee, our contemporary, C. P. Lee, remembers that when he was a college freshman, sitting there among the sons of men who operated an automobile agency, a coal yard or hardware store, all gathered from the real world of modern southern life, the old values were still strong.

"Of course," Lee has written, "we did not say 'Good morning, southern gentlemen.' The adjective was considered tautological."

The popular conception of life in the Old South still needs overhauling and the removal of accretions resulting from nineteenth century sentimentalism and shameless exploitation by mass communication media. Much history had to be ignored to create the panoramic set piece—the high born social group playing cricket on parklike lawns; in the background a tidal river; on one side a sleek, saddle horse held by a Negro hostler in bright livery; and, to balance the composition, the inevitable white columns of the great house. The detail would include a noble little heir in charge of his faithful Mammy, while the master lifts his fog-cutter from the butler's silver tray.

The Harrisons, the Burwells and the Carters who lived before the War, it seems safe to say, would have looked upon the charming scene with incredulity and amusement.

WOMEN: THEIRS NOT TO REASON WHY

The social role of women in colonial America was marked out not only by established convention but by Christian doctrine. The conservative theorists assigned women a definitely inferior position. The clergy took their stand upon the teachings of St. Paul which exhorted the wife to be a crown to her husband, to wear modest raiment, obey her husband's superior judgment in all things, to find self-expression in bearing children: "I will not suffer a woman to teach," said the Apostle, "nor to usurp authority over the man." It was uncommonly gracious, then, of Captain John Underhill, when he was wounded by the Pequots, that he took his wife's advice not to remove the Indian arrow that struck him. And he recovered. "God," he reflected, "useth weak means to keep his purpose unviolated."

Above all, silence was enjoined upon women, but not always achieved, at least in New England, as witness this biography-in-brief incised in native granite:

Here lies as silent clay
Miss Arabella Young
Who on the 21st of May
1771
Began to hold her tongue

The writer of these chapters records with humility the existence of a trouble-making ancestress, Deborah Hewes, who in 1686 acknowledged to Concord Meeting of Friends in what was then Chester County but later Delaware County, Pennsylvania, that she had circulated a slander, and confessed that she had "reported things of Jacob Chanler & Sarah Usher which are fals. . . ." One can surmise the nature of her remarks and why she took upon herself "ye shame . . . for publishing such a thing." Similarly, Joane Barnes of Plymouth, Massachusetts, was put in the stocks wearing a large sign announcing that she was a slanderer. Women of Maine whose tongues wagged maliciously were gagged. In East Hampton, New York, cleft sticks were slipped over too-busy tongues, while a Dutch Mrs. Van Corlear of Manhattan was haled into court for declaring that Mrs. Everardus Bogardus, wife of the dominie, held her petticoats high enough to display her ankles of which she was inordinately proud.

When an American goodwife died who was deemed to have lived an exemplary life, she became the subject of a funerary eulogy in which her meekness under her husband's rule, her skill and industry with spindle and distaff and her piety were favorably compared with the character of the virtuous woman in the Book of Proverbs. In tombstone inscriptions, which often reveal social attitudes, the wife was praised as being affectionate, kind to the servants, a tender mother and obedient to her husband. One such tribute to "Lettice" said of her: "From a Child she knew the Scriptures. . . . She was Beautiful But not Vain: Witty But not Talkativ."

For women of spirit and capacity the way toward self-fulfillment was rocky in a male-oriented world, with the power of the church arrayed against them. And, subjectively, they lived with the guilty knowledge that it was Eve who brought about mankind's expulsion from the Garden of Eden. So women assented to their subordination. It was only just. It was a part of their view of themselves. Even the brilliant Martha Laurens Ramsay, wife of Dr. David

Ramsay, who could read the New Testament in French and Greek and was acquainted with Mary Wollstonecraft's *Vindication of the Rights of Women,* accepted the limitations which contemporary culture placed upon her sex. As her husband wrote admiringly, she felt them as "a part of the curse denounced on Eve."

Education was not thought to be necessary for "females in common life" beyond what they could acquire in dame school. The majority of the women of the plantation class in the seventeenth century could not sign their full names to a paper; they had to make their mark. Old deeds show that even a century later less than forty per cent could do any better. This situation was not peculiar to the South. In 1788, Northampton, Massachusetts, later famous as a seat of learning for women, voted to incur no expense at all for schooling girls whose mission in life, after all, was to tend bees, cut up chickens, fetch wood, suckle children, make butter and cheese and keep the loom clacking from dawn to dusk.

The ability to read was somewhat more widely diffused among women since contact with the sacred writings would strengthen young women in their religious life. Fortunately, not all husbands were authoritarian in their domestic outlook. There is abundant evidence of tenderness, respect and felicity. When the lovely Arbella, daughter of the third Earl of Lincoln, died in Salem, Massachusetts, soon after the colony was planted, her husband, Isaac Johnson, survived her by only one month. It had been a love match. A contemporary said of Johnson, who would probably have succeeded John Winthrop as Governor: "He for a little tried to live without her, liked it not, and died."

Many early wills set forth minute and tender provisions for the maintenance and comfort of widows, such as the use of the "great lower" room, of bed and bedding and a "good gentle riding horse." Governor Benedict Arnold of Rhode Island, ancestor of the Revolutionary patriot and traitor, left his widow the services of three Negresses and a gray horse to be kept in a particular pasture. But sons usually fared better than daughters when the will was read, a partial following of English custom.

In the upper levels of southern society men and women associated with a degree of formality. Quincy made the inevitable comparison between the women of the South and of New England. Attending a concert of the St. Cecilia Society in Charleston, he concluded that the Charleston ladies surpassed those of Boston in richness of dress, but made an equal amount of noise. Few wives called their husbands by their first names. A love letter from a lady to her absent husband began customarily "My dear Mr. Blaine," or whatever. A gentleman treated women of his own class with deference, although this did not prevent Colonel Byrd from entertaining a woman correspondent with a ribald tale of a lady afflicted with a "Horizontal chest" who equipped herself with an ingenious pneumatic device which rendered her bosom so tight she could crack a louse on it. The firm hillocks suddenly collapsed at a ball, Byrd said, with "a sound that was a little unseemly. . . ."

Women occupied the superior position in these areas: the education of children, management of the household, genealogical reckonings, support of church and charities and the ceremonial side of social life. Divorce was rare, infidelity seldom sufficiently notorious to be recorded and in America, wrote Tocqueville, "no one thinks of relating affairs of gallantry." Where women of another class or race were concerned, a southern chevalier could transgress the Seventh Commandment without jeopardizing his position. Sins of the flesh could be overlooked or forgiven, but not meanness, cowardice, cheating at cards, lying or a failure in natural courtesy.

Another French observer may be cited in support of Tocqueville's judgment of American morals. The martial Marquis de Chastellux, who recited Ossian's poetry with Jefferson at Monticello, drank Madeira with General Washington and rode gaily along the highways and trails of eastern America with a blue jay's feather in his cap, remarked on the liberty which existed between the unmarried, yet found that abuses were rare, even among the common people. "Licentious manners," he wrote, ". . . are so foreign in America that conversation with a young woman leads no further . . . " and remarked that American freedom "bears a character of modesty unknown to our . . . false reserve." When the Marquis came, as he sometimes did, upon a case of bastardy, he thought it was not quixotic to say that it merely proved "how pure and respectable are the manners of the Americans. . ." for he regarded a slip resulting from passion as no different from an accidental illness. The error was venial, seldom repeated and mitigated by the arrival of a lusty new citizen urgently needed to fill up an empty country.

The southern coquette who had danced the gavotte at the fashionable assemblies and reveled in being the object of an elaborate courtship found that she had her work cut out for her once she became mistress of a household and head of the plantation's department of health, education and welfare. The chatelaine rose early, visited the various storehouses and the smokehouse where the hams and jowls hung from dark, fragrant beams. Her badge of office was the little key basket on her wrist, filled with tiny keys which unlocked her sewing table, escritoire or the linen press; big ones which opened the ponderous locks to the wine cellar. Such a matron, in her close cap with lace border, crimped frill about the neck, never touched a broom or made the beds. But she "gave out" for the day's cooking, measured quantities of flour, butter, sugar, molasses, lard, bacon middling for the servants' dinner, wine and brandy for the sauces. Gentlewomen personally washed the breakfast china, glassware and silver, arranged the cruets, mustard, salt-cellars, pickle vases and all the apparatus of the dinner table; but a lady of high standing, like Eliza Pinckney, had Ebba to fetch wood, Daphne to knead the bread, Moses as houseman and Peg to wash and milk. The mistress nursed the sick and when there was a lull in the day's affairs, she sat with her embroidery while her little name-daughter perched on a cricket beside her and tackled *Pamela,* or put aside her book to hear of family memories of long ago—of tea-drinking and tambour work, of spangles, hair powder and snuff boxes and how great-grandmama had stood straight and regal in her satin paduasoy and hose with silver clocks to receive General Braddock and his staff when he visited Alexandria.

The southern matron of colonial times found herself in the straw about as often as human biology permitted. A woman living in the Greenville District of South Carolina had thirty-four children. Grandmothers of thirty were not unusual. "Mrs. Harrison is well recovered from her lying in," Rebecca Dinwiddie, wife of the Governor of Virginia, wrote to her friend, the wife of the President of William and Mary College, "though by the time you gett this she may be in the way again." Death notices of a kind frequently published in the South testify to the consequences of constant childbearing: "Of a Miscarriage of Twins, on the 10th Instant, died here, in the 24th Year of her age, one of the most pious and accomplished young Women in these Parts . . ." and so on.

Little girls played with dolls and found even more striking ways of anticipating their future. Frances Ann Tasker Carter, wife of Robert Carter II, was pregnant most of the time, which suggested to two of her little daughters a caper in which their tutor caught them. "I discovered . . ." he wrote, *"Fanny* & *Harriot* by stuffing rags & other Lumber under their Gowns just below their Apron-Strings, were prodigiously charmed at their resemblance to Pregnant Women! They blushed, however, pretty deeply on discovering that I saw them. . . ."

By the time a capable southern girl was able to hem her own chemises and take her own laxatives she had been thoroughly trained in a culture which stressed charm, vivacity, small talk and grace under pressure.

Colonel Byrd gives a memorable illustration of this last point. On one occasion he called at the residence of former Governor Alexander Spotswood to find only Mrs. Spotswood at home. She received him graciously in her drawing room which was elegantly set off with magnificent pier-glasses. The room was also occupied at the moment by two unusual pets, a brace of tame deer. One took fright at seeing his own image in the mirror and sprang to the attack over the tea table. The mirror was shattered. The deer fell back into the tea things, making, wrote the Colonel, "a terrible Fracas among the China." Mrs. Spotswood was "perfectly frighten'd" but Byrd commended her warmly for her social poise. "I was worth all the Damage," he said, "to shew the Moderation and good humour with which she bore this disaster."

The woman living out on the fringe of civilization occupied no pedestal, but stood beside her husband in the egalitarianism of the new West. She understood not only the household handicrafts, but could handle firearms, help with the distilling, tie up a hog and knock down a beef animal with an ax. But the wife and daughters of a man who had any regard for his own standing never worked in the fields. Even so, some observers thought the wives did more than their full share. Byrd scornfully called the men of the back country "Sloathfull in everything but getting Children."

The ideal of the frontier woman, from a male point of view, was set forth in Mordecai Manuel Noah's drama, *She Would Be a Soldier* (1819), which held the stage for many years. In the play, a country girl with a good education has refused an ignorant farmer as a husband. The rejected suitor remarked magnanimously that he did not "mind how larned she was" but asked "Can she milk—knit garters—make apple butter and maple sugar—dance a reel after midnight, and ride behind her husband on a pony, to see the trainings of our sogers—that's the wife for my money."

The real-life story of how Hugh Henry Brackenridge, jurist and author, chose his second wife is one of the classic frontier tales of western Pennsylvania. Princeton classmate of Philip Freneau and James Madison, painted by Gilbert Stuart and described by his son as "a gentleman of the old school," Brackenridge was one of a group of lawyers riding in Washington County, when they saw a barefooted nymph named Sabina Wolfe leap a rail fence without touching it to head off the cows she was driving.

"If she does that again, I'll marry her," exclaimed Brackenridge.

She did. Later the lawyer asked the astonished father for the hand of his Sabina. Perhaps a pause is indicated here to explain this extraordinary action. A contemporary poet wrote of Sabina's charms:

> *Nut brown were her Locks, her Shape was full strait,*
> *Her Eyes were as black as a Sloe;*
> *Milk white were her teeth, full smart was her Gait,*
> *And sleek was her skin as a Doe.*

But to get back to Wolfe: he objected that he needed the services of his daughter in shrubbing his meadow as it would otherwise put him to the expense of about ten dollars. Brackenridge promptly laid down the ten-spot, obtained the young woman's consent and married her, sending her to Philadelphia for a year's polishing under the eye of "a reputable female Character," whose business it was, according to one old account, to "wipe off the Rusticities which Mrs. *Brackenridge* had acquired whilst a *Wolfe*. An epithalamial poem published in the *Pittsburgh Gazette* predicted that no heroine of romance or lady "of polish'd France" could equal the newly molded Sabina, "In Manners soft, and true Gentility."

If a woman of the eighteenth century was uncertain about what she was supposed to be, there was a copious literature at hand to tell her. While the gentlemen were occupied with Robert Anderson's *The Genuine Use and Effects of the Gun* . . . madam was closeted with *The Ladies Calling* or the *Academy of Complements*. Guides of this sort were mainly discourses on the vanities of this world with an insistence, macabre to modern taste, upon the nearness of worm and shroud. Mostly of English origin, they defined woman's place, borrowing without hesitation or acknowledgment from the ancients or each other. Other works of homiletic character include *The Practise of Piety, Meditations on Eternity,* William Sherlock's *Practical Discourse concerning Death,* and Lord Halifax's *The Ladies- New-Years-Gift; or, Advice to a Daughter, as to religion, husband, house, family, and children* (1688). Halifax was the grandfather of the even more famous composer of maxims, Lord Chesterfield. One of the more piquant ideas expressed by Lord Halifax was that women were not managed by their husbands. It was quite the other way, the governing being done by *looks* and *tears.* With a duplicity worthy of his grandson, His Lordship advised his feminine readers to let it appear to *him* and to the world that he was in charge.

Some of the moralists lived picturesquely riotous lives in sharp contrast to their sententious teachings, a reminder of what Mark Twain once said on the subject: "To be good is noble, but to teach others to be good is nobler—and far less trouble." One pious work entitled *The Whole Duty of a Woman . . . by a Lady. Written at the desire of a Noble Lord* (London: 1753), which ran through nine American editions before the end of the century, was a hack job turned out by a notorious rogue and tosspot named William Kendrick, who lectured in the taverns of London on perpetual motion, which he thought he had discovered. With the help of Kendrick and her prayer book, the godly woman was expected to know enough about God's ordinances to save her soul, especially, said Mason Locke (Parson) Weems, the greatest American book peddler of all time, if her reading matter came "cloth^d in splendid binding." Fénelon said that young virgins should have religious instruction, but without raising theological issues which they could not possibly understand; and the Abbé D'Ancourt declared in his *The Lady's Preceptor* (1743) that all that was required of a young lady in church was simply to pay attention, "with gravity."

Wily men, to turn to a more interesting subject than sermons, schemed to gain victories over what the worldly Abbé called "the most rigid virtue." A young woman should maintain an attitude of polite skepticism when fine and flattering things are said to her. Evasive action was recommended, with "a gentle Smile . . . to shew that you are neither a Prude or a Coquette." The Abbé D'Ancourt was referring of course to Frenchmen and their well-known ways. But the Virginia girls, those delicious young fillies who visited Williamsburg for the balls and made Chastellux think of the nymphs of Diana, found the advice of the Abbé pertinent to their circumstances. Chastellux noted: "Though they did not lead the chase [they] inspired a taste for it . . . knew how to defend themselves from the hunters, but did not crush with their arrows those who dared to look at them." When honorable proposals were made, a young woman replied, if she followed the rules, that she was not the person to be consulted but referred all reasonable offers to her father. After marriage, according to Lord Halifax, the discreet wife should "affect ignorance" if her spouse turned out to be a philanderer. If he was ill-natured, an alcoholic or a witless fool, she could console herself with the thought that she cut "a better Figure, for her Husband's making no great one."

Parson Weems's sprightly letters to his publisher, Mathew Carey —"Let the Moral & Religious," he wrote, "be as highly dulcified as possible"—indicate a brisk demand for *A Father's Legacy to his Daughters,* by Dr. John Gregory, professor of moral philosophy at Aberdeen University, *The Lady's Pocket Library* and similar works. The anxiety-ridden guardians of the prevailing moralities and conventions exercised a powerful influence in fixing the conception of the nature of woman. She was the weaker vessel, encouraged to think of herself with an exaggerated sex consciousness. The seducer lurked behind every bush and many a cautionary tale was told to demonstrate that the girl who put her trust in the generosity of young men got just what she hadn't asked for—a baby without a last name.

The girl of the middle or lower class with little experience in life was the object of a volume which appeared in Boston in 1810 under the title *Advice from Farmer Trueman to his Daughter Mary*. It was a new version of an earlier book with an interminable title of which I shall give only enough to identify it, *Virtue in Humble Life* . . . (London: 1777). The book was the production of an odd stick named Jonas Hanway, a traveler, moralist and philanthropist and said to have been the first man to carry an umbrella in London. Hanway adopted the favorite literary device of the eighteenth century, the dialogue. Through the mouths of a father and daughter he told the edifying story of a young girl who was "ruined" by a gentleman identified as "Francis" who beat down her defenses and "gratified his sinful desires." She died of shame, hoping to the last to be restored to respectable society by the wedding ring she never got. Francis got a delayed reaction. He, too, expired, overcome by remorse for having robbed the cookie jar. The daughter in the dialogue, who speaks for Hanway, wrapped up the point: "This . . . should be a lesson to young men."

Any touch of cleverness was highly suspect in a woman. Women should rather cultivate, according to Dr. Gregory, a "soft delicacy," an "exquisite sensibility." Delicacy of spirit suggested the companion thought, delicacy of the body, the Camille touch. These were not completely new ideas. Long before, Castiglione had advised women not to engage in the same exercises and recreations as men, instructed them in how to dance and sing as *women,* what musical instruments a gentle-woman could play. "Imagine," he wrote with a shudder, "how unlovely it would be to see a woman play drums."

The conduct writers took a conservative view of dress. Castiglione thought it was proper for a woman to choose styles which were becoming to her in an unobtrusive way. But he would not have approved of gimmicks like the sari, the Chadou (a four-cornered headdress with sleeves) or the fishnet effects. A fifteenth century mother of humble position in life, about to depart on a pilgrimage to a holy place, left instructions for her daughter: "hang not thy girdle too low," spoke clearly about showing drawers or "hosen," each a sufficient cause for men to say, "of thy body thou carest but little." What, one speculates, would Castiglione and Casa and the Tudor mother-pilgrim have thought of the Canadian mother of three who recently entered a Toronto discount store wearing a topless bathing suit and two zinnias?

Women never seem to be like their grandmothers. Governor William Livingston of New Jersey spoke for the quidnuncs of all time when he mourned that the young women of early Federal days preferred to spend their time with French dancing masters rather than at the spinning wheel. Similarly, President Timothy Dwight of Yale College, an imperious man who dominated The Establishment in Connecticut in his time, feared for the souls of women, believing that they used even their accomplishments for low ends, such as doing embroidery to show off or developing their musical gifts to win applause. Brissot de Warville asked God to grant that the women of Boston be saved from piano-playing, an art "never attained but at the expense of the domestic virtues."

Women were always doing something upsetting such as going about without their mob caps, wearing too few petticoats or showing their bare elbows, once the height of indecency. And after hoop skirts became the fashion, it was used as a handle against them that they artfully elevated their skirts upon the pretext of avoiding dirt, dust or mud. What modern reader of either sex cannot fully comprehend the plight of Anna Green Winslow, sent from Nova Scotia to Boston to be "finished" during Revolutionary times. Anna was appalled at the prospect of appearing in Sudbury Street wearing her unsuitable "red Dominie [cloak] & black Hatt." She wrote home with anguish, "Dear Mama, you don't know the fation here—I beg to look like other folk."

Beauty, after all, as was so frequently and tiresomely pointed out, is a fading thing. Fortunately the ladies of the South, whom the amiable English divine, Andrew Burnaby, found "rather handsome," were not inclined to accept such a gloomy view of a pretty face. They knew better. Molly Tilghman gave her appraisal when she said to her cousin, Polly Pearce, "Wisdom says it [beauty] is a fading flower, but fading as it is, it attracts more admiration than wit, goodness or anything else in the world."

Gentlemen did not require that a pretty woman also be a Brain. John Ewing, tutor at the College of New Jersey at Princeton, after an hour's strenuous talk with the President's wife, Esther Edwards Burr, wished that women would keep to topics they understood and avoid trying to put on more sail than they could carry. Mrs. Burr, for her part, sensed his views and thought they were "sordid." Freiherr von Knigge recommended the company of women for smoothing off the rough edges, but confessed, "I am always seized with a kind of shivering, when I am placed near a woman who pretends to learning." A suggestion tending in the same direction came from *The Lady's Library:* "Women seldom have Materials to furnish a long discourse." To become, as one observer put it, "Fine Lady Mrs. Talkative" might lead on to other unfeminine forms of aggression. A *frisson* passed through Philadelphia social circles when it became known that the usually discreet Chastellux had written of Mrs. Samuel Powel that she not only talked too much but "contrary to American custom, she plays the leading role in the family—*la prima figura,* as the Italians say. . . ." The Marquis later consented to soften this passage, at the suggestion of Thomas Jefferson, in deference to Philadelphian sensibilities.

It was perhaps, then, such warnings as these and Dr. Gregory's suggestion to his readers to conceal "your *good sense*" and "if you happen to have learning, keep it a profound secret," which brought forth the apparently bird-brained southern flirt. But a low estimate of the capacity of women was also apparent in the North. John Winthrop, meditating upon the evils of educating women too much, noted the sad case of Ann, wife of Edward Hopkins, Governor of Connecticut, and aunt of Elihu Yale. She meddled "in

Inſtances of Ill Manners, to be carefully avoided, by Youth, of both Sexes.

OMITTING to pay proper reſpect to Company, on entering or leaving a Room; or paying it only to one perſon when more are preſent.

Paſſing between the Fire, and perſons ſitting at it.

Whiſpering, or Pointing, in company, and ſtanding between the light, and any perſon wanting it.

Sitting ſtill, on the entrance of Superiors.

Swinging the Arms, and all other aukward geſtures, eſpecially in the ſtreet, and in Company.

Drumming with Feet or Hands in Company; and omitting the proper attention, when waited on by Superiors.

Laughing loudly, when in Company.

Dirtying or Defacing Apartments, or Furniture, and every thing which may be called *Sluttiſh* or *Slovenly.*

All actions that have the moſt remote tendency to Indelicacy.

Putting fingers in the Noſe or Ears.

Leaning on the Shoulder or Chair of another Perſon, and overlooking Perſons who are writing or reading.

Throwing things, inſtead of handing them, and crowding others in a paſſage, or running againſt their elbows.

Contempt in looks, words, or actions, for a partner in Dancing, or other perſon.

All inſtances of that ill-judged Familiarity, which breeds contempt.

Lolling on a Chair, when ſpeaking or ſpoken to: And looking perſons earneſtly in the face, without any apparent cauſe.

Surlineſs of all kinds, eſpecially on receiving a compliment.

Diſtortion of countenance, and Mimickry.

Ridicule, of every kind, Vice or Folly excepted.

A conſtant Smile or ſettled frown on the countenance.

Interrupting others, who are any way engaged.

Scandal and Slander, in the ſmalleſt degree.

Unreaſonable refuſals to oblige others.   Vulgariſm in expreſſion.

Omitting to reply, on being aſked a queſtion.

Paſſing by any thing on the floor, which ſhould be taken up.

Making reply to a queſtion put to another.

Every ſhadow of indelicacy, written or ſpoken.

Too much attention to the faults of others and too little to our own.

Omitting to notice excellencies, when you point out defects.

Being offended at friendly reproofs.

Omitting to pay every attention to a Stranger, which good manners demand.

By Your humble Servant,

JOHN GRIFFITH.

How many of the precepts appearing above may be disputed as being possibly suited to other times, but not ours? One finds in reading them that they are, simply, the ageless rules of universal courtesy.

Freestyle eating as practiced in the refreshment area during President Ulysses S. Grant's first Inaugural Ball, March 4, 1869. It was sketched by the famous cartoonist, Thomas Nast, who had a special talent for the picture which made a social comment.

Joseph Palmer, Massachusetts farmer, enemy of slavery, liquor and the razor, went to jail for defending his right not to shave. Palmer's face, beard and martyrdom are memorialized (*right*) at Leominster, Massachusetts.

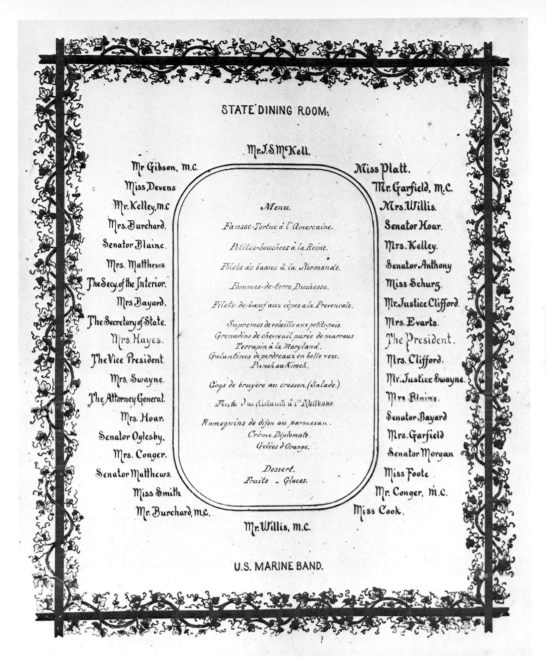

The menu and seating arrangements for a state dinner at the White House during the administration of President Rutherford B. Hayes. The original is drawn by hand, in color, and included with some fifty other leaves in a volume bound in red leather and hand-tooled with gold edges. Each guest was also presented with a gold-edged card of the seating order as a souvenir of the occasion. Despite the setting and all the goodies with French names, there was ill-natured wrangling over precedence in those days, exacerbated perhaps by the fact that Mrs. Hayes, an earnest woman anxious to do good in this world, had banished wines and spirits from the Executive Mansion.

The duel as practiced in nineteenth-century America presents a striking example of conflict between a social convention and statute law. An American contribution to the etiquette of the duel was known as "posting"—the circulation of an insulting public notice *(below)* designed to bring on an encounter.

NOTICE!!

TO THE PUBLIC!

I, the undersigned, on my own personal honor and responsibility, do hereby publicly declare G. W. BROWN, Editor of the Herald of Freedom, to be a wilful LIAR, a malicious SLANDERER, and a most contemptible COWARD; all of which charges I hold myself in readiness to prove.

RICHARD REALF.

Lawrence, July 14, 1857.

such things as are proper for men." Although she was "a godly young woman and of special parts" she went out of her mind "by occasion of her giving herself wholly to reading and writing." The *Massachusetts Spy* fired a double-shotted broadside at both male pedantry and feminine deficiencies when it recommended to the "fine gentleman," ironically of course:

"Whenever you are in company with ladies, endeavour to show your sense and learning. Select as many *hard words* as possible, and quote passages out of Horace and Homer. Praise the former as a fine Grecian, and the latter for excelling in Latin. If you meet with a lady who knows *more* than yourself, be always *of her opinion*, and exclaim 'Gad's curse, you have take *them words out of my mouth*.' "

Not every man was frightened out of his wits by the learned ladies. Dr. Ramsay adored his brilliant Martha and was proud of her achievements. Aaron Burr considered it a far more likely peril that his daughter, Theodosia, might become merely a woman of fashion rather than a bluestocking and so had her, at the age of ten, well into Terence and Lucian and starting the study of Greek. A few women broke through the barriers, not content with a bit of lace, a bottle of snuff and the drawing room chit-chat which Colonel Byrd characterized as "like whip-syllabub, very pretty but nothing in it." Jane Colden, daughter of Cadwallader Colden, Lieutenant Governor of New York, philosopher and scientist, was herself a distinguished botanist. Mercy Warren, daughter of James Otis, sister of the more famous James, and her musical friend, Hannah Winthrop, exercised their classical learning in an intimate correspondence. Mercy wrote as "Honoria," Hannah signed herself "Philomela," in Greek mythology the daughter of a legendary king of Athens who could sing like a nightingale. Mrs. Samuel Meredith, wife of the Philadelphia financier, knew European history, delighted Chastellux with her ability to compare Francis I and Henry IV, Richelieu and Mazarin, with grace and understanding; while aristocratic, fragile, romantic Elizabeth Graeme, sometimes saluted as the Philadelphia Sappho, became celebrated as a poetess, translator and patroness of the arts. Miss Graeme received special marks of favor in London from George III and returned home to preside over America's first authentic salon. Around her gathered a group that included Francis Hopkinson, Thomas Godfrey and Nathaniel Evans.

Even a brief glance at women who escaped the submissive pattern must include Anne Bradstreet, the first American woman poet, Anne Hutchinson, the seventeenth century religious liberal, and the tiny, formidable aunt of Ralph Waldo Emerson, Mary Moody Emerson, learned in the poets and philosophers, herself a diarist and stylist of such pith and force that Emerson borrowed as freely from her as from Plutarch and Montaigne. Aunt Mary's behavior, in the view of more conventional women, left much to be desired. She was "not nice in her habits," one disapproving contemporary said, but "would do for these days better than in the time when women were retired and modest in manners, and had great reverence for the stronger sex."

There were also women who managed successful business enterprises in the eighteenth century. Eliza Lucas Pinckney was not only an ornament of Charleston society, a woman who had studied law in her spare time and was more deeply read in the Latin authors than the parson of the parish, but the manager of several plantations who developed indigo as a staple crop and revived silk culture in South Carolina. Mary Salmon shod horses in Boston. The phrase "she merchants" occurs in old documents, referring to such a woman as the widow of Rudolphus De Vries of New York, who continued her husband's shipping ventures after his death and often went to Holland as supercargo on her own ships. Anne, the widow of James Franklin, managed a printing and publishing business. Madam Martha Smith of St. George's Manor, Long Island, was in whaling. She left one memorandum which said: "Jan. ye 16, 1707. My company killed a yearling whale made 27 barrels." Margaret Brent, to round off this account of women who managed their own businesses, was an aggressive accumulator of land in Maryland in association with her sisters, Mary and Anne. A historian of the province, George Alsop, said of the Brent women that they preferred "Plain wit" to "Complemental Courtships" and warned, "he that intends to Court a Maryland girle, must have something more than the tautologies of a long-winded speech to carry on his design."

The decisive battle over what women were or could become was fought out in the next century. But the natural-rights philosophy incorporated in the Declaration of Independence opened the way for a new approach. The opinion gained currency that if women had brains, and it appeared that they did, perhaps the Creator had placed them in their heads to be used. English and French conservative theorists declined in influence. Life as it was lived under American conditions was moving steadily toward legal, economic and political freedom for women. This topic has been so thoroughly explored that it is now often overlooked how many nubile young women were content to confine their sphere to the vigorous pursuit of husbands, as one may surmise from a last example of New England's distinctive art form, the epitaph:

Sacred to the Memory of Mr.
Jared Bates who Died Aug. the 6th
1800. His Widow Aged 24 who mourns
as one who can be comforted lives
at 7 Elm street this village
and possesses every qualification
for a Good Wife.

II

Manners adjust to democracy

★ ★ ★

ONCE A CAPTAIN,
ALWAYS A CAPTAIN

There is an old saying in the Hudson Valley country that a man isn't entitled to be called Colonel unless he has killed a rattlesnake.

This bit of gnomic wisdom may not greatly illuminate the subject of herpetology, but it throws a significant light upon a long-standing American attitude toward prestigious titles; as does also a report emanating from Arkansas that in the Old Southwest a man who had never sat as a magistrate could assume the style of "Judge" if his peers generally conceded that he was a good judge of whiskey. Titles of compliment flourished similarly in the Nevada mining towns of the 1870's, such as Virginia City, Gold Hill and Silver City. Mine supervisors and leading saloon keepers were universally deferred to as Colonel, and all lawyers were colonels except that some preferred to be called Judge.

There is, then, exhaustive documentation for saying that the plain, republican citizens of the United States have shown a remarkable appetite for ceremonious titles, and that they cling to them as tenaciously as molecules of water to ethyl alcohol.

"Strange indeed," exclaimed William Maclay, U.S. Senator from Pennsylvania and a philosophical democrat, "that in that very country where the flame of freedom had been kindled, an attempt should be made to introduce these absurdities and . . . pompous and lordly distinctions."

Maclay was referring to debates which took up almost the whole time of the Senate from April 23 to May 15, 1789. The issue was whether the President should have a throne with a canopy over it, what his formal title should be, how the President should be addressed, whether senators should sit or stand when he came to their chamber. John Adams, who was Vice President and presided over the Senate as its President, early showed a most meticulous concern with what men like Maclay regarded as "trivial distinctions and matters of mere form. . . ."

"When the President comes into the Senate, what shall I be?" Adams asked the members anxiously from the chair. "I can not be [president] then. No, gentlemen, I can not, I can not. I wish gentlemen to think what I shall be."

Maclay, who wrote in his journal every evening of the events of the day, said of Adams' distress, "the prophane muscles of my face were in tune for laughter. . . ."

Two opposing conceptions of the nature of man were involved in these contrasting attitudes toward social titles. One, expressed in the words of the preamble of the Declaration of Independence, represented the view that men are by nature equal and potentially good. The conservative opinion, which has a familiar Calvinistic sound, assumed that man is corrupt, selfish, passionate, and virtuous only when kept in line by a governing elite. Moved by enthusiasm for the leveling doctrines of the French Revolution, many American Jacobins came to find offensive even the ordinary polite terms such as Sir, Mister or Doctor. Objections were advanced against Reverend and the familiar Right Worshipful Grand Master used in the Masonic lodge. A New York newspaper editor announced that he wished to be addressed as Citizen. It was seriously debated whether a housewife was a "Citess," a "Civess" or a "Neighboress."

The question involving titles of honor and formal compliment which stirred up the broadest public interest concerned how the officials of the new government should be addressed. The Constitution provided that "No titles of nobility shall be granted by the

United States." But strong Federalists in the Senate, such as John Adams, Oliver Ellsworth of Connecticut and Richard Henry Lee—to the embarrassment of Virginia democrats—urged the establishment of elaborate titles for all who held high official rank. They believed the affairs of government should be conducted in an atmosphere of formality which would serve to cow what Fisher Ames, son of an innkeeper but a starchy New England aristocrat in his social philosophy, termed the "loathsome mobs." John Adams plainly had a relish for pomp and circumstance. He thought the simple term "President" entirely too common for George Washington because there were also presidents of fire companies and cricket clubs.

Adams proposed "His Elective Majesty" as a title for Washington and went on to suggest that the President's cook be called "Steward of the Household" and the Senate sergeant-at-arms "Usher of the Black Rod." Without such trappings, he urged, "neither dignity nor authority can be supported in human minds."

When President Washington made his tour of New England an incident occurred which seemed to point up the argument. The wife of an innkeeper in Rhode Island, hearing that the President was approaching, supposed that the person meant was Dr. James Manning, President of Rhode Island College, later Brown University, and sent word, "the President must go on to the next tavern."

Other titles for the Chief Executive which were mulled over included "Excellency," "Highness," "Elective Highness," "Serene Highness" and "Supreme Mightiness." John Fenno, editor of the *Gazette of the United States,* which he hoped to make the official organ of Federalism, wrote that "respect for public men depended in a measure on public titles." Fenno tried to help out on the problem of nomenclature with "Your Magistracy" and "Your Supremacy." Not every advocate of elevated titles was inclined toward monarchy; but some were. Colonel Lewis Nicola, a respectable figure in the Revolutionary generation, had been the spokesman for a clique who favored monarchical institutions. As far back as 1782, Nicola proposed that Washington be crowned King George I of America. The General rejected the idea "with abhorrence."

A Joint Committee on Titles won majority support in the Senate when they brought in a real jaw-cracker: "His Highness, the President of the United States of America, and Protector of their

Liberties." But the House of Representatives stood firm against all titles except those which were named in the Constitution. The Senate yielded. Thus the first President, clad in his suit of brown broadcloth spun at Hartford, worn to advertise American manufactures, with hair powdered, white silk stockings, silver shoe buckles and a dress sword, took the oath of office on the portico of Federal Hall in New York and heard Robert R. Livingston, Chancellor of New York, shout to the crowd, "Long live George Washington, President of the United States!" So the tradition was fixed that the American chief magistrate was simply "Mr. President" or "The President" to the relief of all who felt a distaste for courtly forms of etiquette.

During the first years of government under the Constitution a great storm blew up over the establishment of an hereditary society with aristocratical tendencies, known as the Society of the Cincinnati, which honored not Cincinnati, Ohio, but the memory of Lucius Quinctius Cincinnatus, the old Roman who was called from the plow in 458 B.C. to save the Roman army. American and foreign officers were eligible for the Cincinnati, but not the common soldiers. Members were invested with elaborate insignia and had a royal patron, Louis XVI of France. Since membership was transmitted through the eldest son, and primogeniture was dead in the United States, the group did indeed hark back to the class system of older times. According to an anecodote told by Ward McAllister, the New York society leader, he was once invited to a ball which the Austrian minister in Florence gave in honor of the Archduke of Tuscany who was marrying one of the princesses of Bavaria. The host approached McAllister and said:

"I see I have another American as a guest to-night, and he is decorated. Will you please tell me what his decoration is?"

The New Yorker said he didn't know but suggested they go together and find out. To the question put by the Austrian, the stranger replied:

"Sir, my country is a Republic; if it had been a Monarchy, I would have been the Duke of Pennsylvania. The Order I wear is that of The Cincinnati."

McAllister, not usually a man of humor, said with obvious relish that the Austrian minister withdrew "deeply impressed" with the medal of gold suspended by a deep blue ribbon two inches wide and edged with white.

Benjamin Franklin ridiculed the Cincinnati and spelled out in some detail his objections to the theory of descending honor, recommending instead the practice of the Chinese among whom "honor does not descend but ascends." He thought the members of the Society would be well advised to enjoy for one lifetime "their little badge and ribband, and let the distinction die with those who have merited it."

This issue of monarchical leanings has persisted remarkably in American life. It was used with deadly political effect as late as 1840 when the preposterous idea was successfully advanced against Martin Van Buren that "Little Van" was not only "a used up man" but that he chose the same toiletries as Queen Victoria and, if re-elected, would surely wangle for himself a crown, a scepter and a royal stole. Thousands of Chicagoans can still remember the political mileage the colorful patriot, William Hale (Big Bill) Thompson, got as a mayoralty candidate, out of his offer to "bust King George in the snoot." Thompson ruled over the Second City for three terms and many sagacious observers believe that his margin of victory was provided by a fierce determination to do battle against the King of England.

The names of several Americans come to mind who, before the separation of the colonies from English institutions, were honored with authentic titles—Sir William Pepperell, the first American baronet, and Sir William Phips, for example. Benjamin Thompson, physicist and philanthropist, was knighted by George III and made a Count of the Holy Roman Empire by the Elector of Bavaria, with the Order of the White Eagle and the title, which Thompson chose after the old name of Concord, New Hampshire, of Count Rumford. There are, as has already been mentioned, no American patents of nobility, though the eccentric Timothy Dexter of Newburyport, Massachusetts, in the 1790's styled himself "Lord" Timothy Dexter, an honor which he said was conferred upon him by the state of New Hampshire. Probably the most exalted title ever assumed by a private citizen of the United States was the one taken by Brigadier General William Alexander who gave himself the rank of sixth Earl of Stirling on the basis of a claim that was rejected by the British House of Lords but generally accepted as genuine here. Chastellux wrote once of Alexander, "He is accused of liking the table and the bottle, full as much as becomes a Lord, but more than becomes a General." Fenno, in reporting on the "American Court" in his *Gazette of the United States,* always referred to Alexander's widow as "Lady Stirling" and his daughter, who smoked a clay pipe, as "Lady Kitty."

The American army officer, retired, who followed a trade such as blacksmith or tavern keeper was a constant source of wonder to visitors from overseas accustomed to the rigid system of social stratification maintained in Europe. Edward Kimber, traveling in Maryland, Virginia and the Carolinas, heard so many colonels, majors and captains mentioned that he decided the region must be a veritable "Retreat of Heroes." At Bute County Court House, in North Carolina, later Warren County, John Davis, a British visitor, found the inn kept by no less a figure than a General—General Jethro Sumner. Davis was astonished to learn that a Continental officer and a member of the Cincinnati conducted a boardinghouse in New York and was not a little proud of the motto surrounding his badge, *Omnia reliquit servare Rempublicam*—he gave all to serve the republic. Davis found this very entertaining since "it is notorious that few Americans had much to leave." Henry Wansey, the English clothier, remarked upon having his horse held by a Major and seeing a group of captains digging a ditch by the roadside. Notwithstanding the American doctrine of political equality, it seemed to detached observers that the citizens engaged in the republican experiment clearly followed the old adage, "Once a Captain, Always a Captain." Nathaniel Hawthorne met an old Dutchman near Shelburne Falls, Massachusetts, who had his own formula for playing safe: he called everybody Captain.

Mrs. Frances Trollope, the novelist, who wrote the astringent *Domestic Manners of the Americans,* ascending the Mississippi and Ohio rivers wrapped in her shawl and prejudices, made sharp comments upon the evident fondness of Americans in the late 1820's for titles, "Lady Jackson" for the recently deceased wife of the President, the eternal recurrence of militia titles attached to gentlemen who, she scoffed, "were not of the same genus as those of the Tuileries and St. James's. . . ." One writer on the social amenities, Robert de Valcourt, was amused while traveling to see a trunk marked "Mrs. Lieutenant Sprague, U.S.A., San Francisco," and he added in his *Illustrated Book of Manners* (1866):

"Ladies are sometimes designated as Reverend Mrs. Smith, Mrs. Captain Scott; Mrs. Dr. Jones, Mrs. Judge Evans, and even the Honorable Mrs. Boodle, when their husbands have chanced to be members of some Legislature." The author disapproved of these second-hand titles as he did of the indiscriminate applying of Honorable to members of the state assemblies which he remarked "diffuses the honor rather widely."

When Mrs. Martha Washington, the General's lady, presided over the Presidential "palace" at 10 Cherry Street in New York City, she became the object of two complaints. One was that she was too royal; the other that she was too simple. Although she was known as "Lady Washington," admired for her dignified yet affable manners, compared favorably with the noble Roman matron of classical times, she confessed she felt "more like a state prisoner than anything else." In contrast, Mrs. Madison, the one and only Dolley, played zestfully her role as "Lady Presidentess," was referred to seriously as "her majesty"; but they were careful to use the small letters. Still later—we are down to the 1840's now—the beautiful and vivacious Julia Gardiner, as Mrs. John Tyler, reveled in the dressing and the dining, the steam cutter *Legare* bearing the President's flag, and herself being toasted as "Mrs. Presidentess."

Perhaps the persistence of ceremonious titles in American life should be regarded not so much evidence of snobbery as an invitation to soar if the talents will permit it.

"Is your master at home?" a visitor inquired of the girl who opened the door.

"I have no master," she replied. She was *help,* but no servant girl.

Similarly, by a liberal extension of the system of nomenclature, a piano player in a Western saloon rose to be "professor" and in Boston a whimsical man once wrote after his name on a hotel register, the mystic abbreviation, P.O.P.S.F.C. When asked what the letters stood for he explained that he was Professor of Psalmody and Schoolmaster from Connecticut.

Modern social annals continue to document the point that men would rather be known as chiefs than Indians. The Kentuckian is a born romanticist who wants to believe in "the colonel that never was." In Kentucky a man can get a military title by prerogative of the Governor, which has been exercised so generously that the Kentucky colonels have had to organize in order to keep track of themselves. The colonels wear their honors modestly. But they don't like to have their rank ignored or downgraded.

Bing Crosby, Viscount Montgomery, Louis (Satchmo) Armstrong and former President Miguel Alemán of Mexico all have a distinction in common. They are admirals in the Great Navy of Nebraska along with about thirty thousand other shipmates. Possessors of highly prized certificates, they pledge in pseudonautical language that the naval person whose name is engrossed thereon is entitled to be obeyed by "all officers, seamen, tadpoles and goldfish under his command." Texas also has its own navy; John Nance Garner, former Vice President of the United States, is a Texas admiral.

St. Louis has been the scene since 1878 of a mass fantasy called the Veiled Prophet's Ball, centered upon the crowning of a Queen chosen from the year's debutantes. A similar revel in the trappings of royalty occurs each year in Omaha, the Nebraska city which is also saluted as "The Diamond Stickpin in the Bosom of the West." At Omaha a charade is enacted each October at a ball known as Ak-Sar-Ben (Nebraska spelled backwards). Substantial businessmen dress up elaborately as princes and counts to escort princesses and countesses. A queen emerges from behind golden curtains and everybody has a fine time bowing and curtsying. A substantial businessman, such as the president of an insurance company, is chosen king, and king and queen reign in feudal splendor as monarchs of a fabled land called Quivera which is the place Francisco Vásquez de Coronado was looking for during his reconnaissance of the region in the summer of 1541.

According to the newspaper pundit, Joseph Alsop, simplicity is fast slipping away from us. A United States Senator used to be plain "Mr." Within living memory U.S. Cabinet members were still "Mr." But nowadays a Senator is always a Senator and if Brown is an ambassador he is always "Ambassador Brown." Yet one wonders if it was not always so. The same sort of lament was being made nearly a hundred years ago when Mrs. Sarah Madeleine Vinton Dahlgren, author and Washington hostess, observed the creeping advance of "Mrs. Secretary," "Mrs. Senator," and "Mrs. General"; and sharp-eyed Miss Fanny Knight of Natchez, Mississippi, daughter of a well-to-do cotton merchant, saw in the guest register, when the Knights visited the alpine hospice of St. Bernard, the signature, "The Hon. Charles Sumner, Senator of the United States." "I think it in very bad taste," Fanny wrote in her diary.

Glance for a moment at the array of titles common in business today. They have become richly variegated in recent years with dozens of delicate gradations. The acquisition of an impressive title is a part of the art of officemanship, like having a two-pen desk set or a secretary with her own private office and wall-to-wall carpeting. The New York advertising agency of Ted Bates & Co., for instance, has four distinctive handles which rate above that of president. Benton & Bowles, Inc., which is also in the advertising game, has three varieties of chairmen—honorary, founding and ordinary. Time, Inc. has three chairmen, too, but the largest single stockholder, Henry R. Luce, is chairman of nothing. The J. Walter Thompson Company, a communications empire on which the sun never sets, has a title for practically everybody with four executive vice presidents, eight senior vice presidents and one hundred and forty plain vice presidents in its U.S. offices alone. Down in Wall Street Merrill Lynch, Pierce, Fenner & Smith, the world's largest brokerage house, known familiarly in the vicinity of Broad and Wall streets as "the thundering herd," has a hundred and four vice presidents, comfortably nosing out the National Broadcasting Company which can field only fifty-eight.

Often a plain vice president outranks a fancy one. One just has to know what the appellation signifies in the particular situation. Some of the flossiest designations carry with them a measure of peril. A man promoted to the heights of Vice President for Special Assignments is probably not going to be very busy. He is being, in the argot of the management world, "ceilinged out"; or, as his dilemma is described in the scuttlebutt of the executive washrooms, the V.P.F.S.A. is headed for "the boneyard."

Happily, Americans seem to possess an ability to take the measure of pompous and self-important men. A notable instance of this technique of head-shrinking occurred when a Kansas editor said of a political opponent, Thomas J. Key, that every morning Key stuck his head into an empty flour barrel and yelled at the top of his voice, "Honorable Thomas J. Key," just to hear how nice it sounded; and it was alleged further that Key hired local urchins, when he appeared upon the streets of Doniphan, to shout "There goes Honorable Thomas J. Key."

One may infer that these pleasantries ruffled Key considerably, for he replied:

"We would gently hint to the cross-eyed, crank-sided, peaked and long razor-nosed, blue-mouthed, white-eyed, soft-headed, long-eared, crane-necked, blobber-lipped, squeaky-voiced, empty-headed, snaggle-toothed, filthy-mouthed, box-ankled, pigeon-toed, reel-footed, goggle-eyed, hammer-hearted, cat-hammed, hump-shouldered, blander-shanked, splay-footed, ignoble, Black Republican, abolition editor, to attend to his own affairs or we will pitch into him in earnest."

Americans have shown an ambivalence about honorific designations. The tradition is against it. But men of all societies apparently long for the outward marks of distinction. We have no princes of the blood, no Knights Companion of the Bath, no ribbon of dark blue velvet, edged with gold and bearing the words *honi soit qui mal y pense* and worn below the left knee. But in harmony with our history and our genius we have still a fair sprinkling of Honorables, the Society of the Cincinnati and the male descendants of Confederate army officers with their own hereditary Order of Stars and Bars. A pretty girl who walks like a Phys. Ed. major may aspire to wear a tiara as Miss Central Heating. Even a synthetic or non-person can acquire a complimentary title. Doesn't nearly every woman in the United States know that Betty Crocker is America's First Lady of Food? Now, as always, when City Hall appoints an "honorary" commissioner for services not always visible to the ordinary citizens, the recipient of the dignity—had you noticed?—wants the world to know who he is and advertises the fact by mounting a bronze medallion on his automobile to demonstrate that some men are more equal than others.

7

THE AWKWARD AGE

The years between the War of 1812 and the Civil War saw power and place pass from the nabobs of the colonial period to the dreaded "new people." While the old plutocracy gloomily predicted the early collapse of the Republic, the blacksmiths, cobblers, mechanics, freighters, shipwrights, rail splitters and coonskin voters of the new West rallied to put General Andrew Jackson in the White House.

"General Jackson," wrote Amos Kendall, who came on to the capital city from Frankfort, Kentucky, to become a chronicler of the new regime and a member of Jackson's "Kitchen Cabinet," "is *their own* president."

The old General grew stronger after every contact with the common people. They, in turn, responded with affection to a leader who smoked a Powhatan-bowl pipe with a long stem, chewed his quid with a grave and deliberate manner of spitting while conducting the affairs of state. And sometimes he got tangled up in his rhetoric, as did his supporters, too. "All Jackson men bow down," the republican freemen riding on the Erie Canal packet boats would shout happily when the helmsman sang out, "Low Bridge." "After such commands," one traveler making the tour to Niagara Falls noted, "we find few Aristocrats." Two frolicsome young English army officers, on leave from the Rifle Brigade at Halifax, found out in what regard Jackson was held by the common people when they made a joke at his expense. On their way to dine with the British Secretary of Legation in Washington, they saw an old man in a worn soldier's coat breaking stones by the side of the road; "and what should Deedes do," wrote Lieutenant George Kirwan Carr, "but stop a Yankee who was passing, and very politely ask him, '*Whether that was General Jackson,*' pointing to the old man!" and he adds, "we had to run for our lives. . . ."

Never before had Americans faced their problems with so exuberant a sense that their reach did not exceed their grasp. The nation had between 1830 and the 1850's business enough to attend to—the removal of the Indians to the west of the Mississippi River, formulation of a public land policy, highways to be built, railroads and canal systems, too, the Texas problem, the California Gold Rush, the Oregon boundary dispute and the expansion of manufactures. These tasks fell to new rulers. They represented a social stratum which had been glad to see the end of the restricted franchise and church tithes but one which, as Frederika Bremer said, "has not yet worked itself up." The mid-nineteenth-century American lived in a thriving environment of iron mills, machine shops, Otis elevators; of new sleeping cars, steam-powered ships, Colt revolvers, of Gail Borden's tinned milk and the marvels of central heating powerful enough to stifle the inhabitants, and hot and cold running water which often ran hot at both taps and could not, it seemed, be turned off by any human agency.

Public behavior, in this assertive social climate, skipped the elegancies. Since the Americans had rejected their political past, it is not surprising that there was social insubordination, too, among people groping for a new kind of relationship with each other. Observers from abroad, to whom the more exclusive circles were often inaccessible, had much to say about the slovenly dress and poor posture of the Americans, their wolfish eating habits, the incessant chewing and spitting, the heavy dramming and generally unbuttoned behavior in steamboat, hotel and stagecoach. It is from this period that the idea gained currency among the American democrats that rusty manners were less a fault than a virtue, an indication of rugged masculinity and personal integrity. Polish, indeed, and courtesy, became a kind of *lèse republicanism*.

Thomas Jefferson's sentence, "All men are created equal," might have affected American attitudes in either of two ways. The ideal of gentle is as gentle does could have been tossed into the discard, and it very nearly was; or the argument might have taken the turn that the highest standards should be aimed at since the way up was open to all. A good deal was said on both sides. Many Americans claimed that we had the refinements. Another answer was that the amenities didn't matter anyway. This fitted in neatly with a prevailing mood of Anglophobia which contrasted the plain, honest American with the ascribed dandyism and affectations of the British nobs.

It was consistent with the thought of the ordinary man to believe that the U. S. Constitution, the guardian of his political liberties, also secured to him the right to surmount the barriers to the delectable regions inhabited by people of wealth and long-established position. That was, as it came out, the direction which the main stream of American life took. Mrs. Trollope, starting out with an acescent point of view, was sure the Americans would never make the grade socially and put the blame on our Constitution; "as long as they can prevent human respect and human honor from resting upon high talent, gracious manners, and exalted station," she wrote crossly, "so long may they be sure of going on as they are."

A quite different tone was taken by one of Mrs. Trollope's young compatriots who had settled in the vicinity of Chicago. He wrote triumphantly to his brothers and sisters in England: "We have no Corn Laws—Bread Tax—Game Laws—Tythe parsons . . . no Property Tax to prevent us from getting on in the world—no Income Tax peeling the very flesh from off our bones. . . . No tipping your hat when you meet with a man a little better off than yourself. . . . Precious few of third class men . . . that is, politicians, parsons, Doctors, and Lawyers."

Those citizens who felt a lack of early advantages were free to improvise, practice, watch and learn. The alert salesman could determine by reading and observation that the vest in gaudy checks was not in the best taste; the dancing lady that it was more decorous to appear graceful than agile. The toilers of one day who struck it rich became in fact the gentlefolk of the next; for, as Vespasian said back in Roman times, money does not smell of its origin.

The ambition of the "self-made" man, a term that dates back at least as far as 1832, received enthusiastic clerical support. The Reverend Thomas P. Hunt, for instance, in his *The Book of Wealth* (1836) assured his readers that the common desire to make one's pile was in accord with the law of nature and therefore beneficent. "No man can be obedient to God's will," Hunt wrote, ". . . without becoming wealthy." The enjoyment of social splendors, "is and should be," a behavior writer assured his following in 1849, "the aim and ambition of every American."

There was, of course, still a quiet, closed society composed of those who had enjoyed a long and easy familiarity with dressing for dinner, with epergnes, girandoles, phaetons, Hungarian polkas, flirtation and whist. Since an aristocracy is always nostalgic, the conservatives extended the newcomers a gelid hand. John Quincy Adams was mortified when Harvard College conferred an honorary degree upon Andrew Jackson and refused to attend the ceremony honoring "a barbarian and savage." The patricians of Philadelphia continued to associate with those of their acquaintance who had acquired their knowledge of the polite usages through osmosis; that is, Family. It was agreed that one could have a respectable character and still not be a gentleman. There were just so many of those little things. . . .

Sidney Fisher, diarist and well-connected Philadelphia lawyer, said of Joseph Ritter that he was honest enough, but "without the slightest approach to the appearance or manner of a gentleman. This however is not to be expected in a Governor of Pennsylvania." And Philip Hone, son of a carpenter, who rose to become a zealous guardian of the genteel tradition in New York, was already mourning, as early as 1847, the departed golden age when presidents and directors of banks "were the only nobility we had," adding, "now we have none." But the higher levels of society did not reproduce themselves and had to give way before surging economic forces generated in the age of awkwardness.

It was an environment of plank sidewalks, muddy streets, lard oil lamps and outside plumbing. But stoves were replacing open fireplaces in the 1830-40 decade and camphene and various proprietary burning fluids provided better lighting and stimulated more reading. The Tremont House, which brought a new standard of hotel luxury to Boston in 1829, had eight water closets. The American House, also in Boston, provided gas illumination in halls and rooms in 1835. By the fifties gas was in general use in the cities, coal oil—kerosene distilled from shale oil—the coming light-source for the country generally. The private bath was introduced in a New York City hotel in 1844. But window screens were unknown for another twenty years. The state of communications may be inferred from a fashion note of 1849. A merchant in Decatur, Illinois, received some cotton net night caps. Neither the clerk nor the customers had the slightest idea what the dainty headpieces were for. But the store sold them successfully as the latest thing in the *grande toilette* for the ballroom.

The spirit of the times called for new male fashions to express a new attitude. Men turned to tight-fitting long trousers with a strap passing under the instep, set off with a frock coat and topped, in the North, by the stovepipe hat. Waistcoats were as flowery as a carpet bag. But the wearers were unconcerned if their linen was dirty. Once more, costume was significant of political change. When Roger B. Taney was sworn in as Chief Justice of the Supreme Court after the death of John Marshall, Taney wore trousers, not knee breeches. The women whom Mrs. Trollope observed in America had lovely faces, but slouched around no less than the men, waved fluttery hands and tottered along on feet pinched into tiny slippers so that the total effect was, she decided, that American women simply lacked *style*.

Meals eaten in public places were dispatched silently, rapidly, the diner's elbows sawing like a fiddler's, the manner of helping based upon the execution of the maneuver known as "the boardinghouse reach." There was no limit to the abundance of food. The waiters hovered, Anthony Trollope wrote, not to render service but to hurry up the business of eating. Trollope, then a high-ranking British civil servant and distinguished novelist, was more sympathetic toward the civilization of the United States than his celebrated mother had been, though he too is sometimes sharp in his comments upon republican crudities.

There was a remarkable sameness in the menu from meal to meal and day to day, with heavy emphasis upon steak, roasts, puddings and salt pork. "Made dishes," vegetables and salads were rare. A guest at the American House in St. Paul in 1855 found the meals absolutely predictable. Men ate in their shirt sleeves, helped themselves out of serving dishes with their own forks, took their desserts on the plates off which they had just lapped up the main course. Reflecting upon what he called the "morality of dining" Hawthorne remarked, "People at just this stage of manners are more disagreeable than at any other stage. They are aware of some decencies, but not so deeply aware as to make them a matter of conscience." Table etiquette could even be peremptory in a rail-head town. During the construction of the Kansas Pacific Railway, a man said "Pass the butter." When his table mate failed to respond, the diner pointed his pistol and repeated "Pass the butter."

A bell announced the meal at the principal inn at Nashville, Tennessee. The hungry crowd rushed into the hall and settled themselves at long tables on which the steaming food already stood. Noses were blown with fingers, handkerchiefs spread on knees, cuffs turned back. Then came a crash of crockery and the clash of steel. Bones were taken up in both hands for thorough stripping, knives drawn through the mouth for the final dainty bit. Replete, the patrons rose and departed without excusing themselves.

When Austin, Nevada, was a rambunctious mining town, the local newspaper, the *Reese River Reveille,* was distinguished for the candor of its reporting. One revealing item dealt with the con-tretemps which arose over a request for a napkin. "A few days ago," it ran, "a stranger at one of our restaurants asked for a napkin at dinner. The landlord refused to give him one.

" 'But,' protested the guest, 'that man at the other table has one.'

" 'That man is a regular boarder,' the publican replied, 'and just got back from San Francisco, and I have to pamper him for a day or so; but it won't be long before he will be wiping his mouth on the tablecloth, and cleaning his nails with a fork, like the other gentle-men. No, stranger, we don't allow any style here as a regular thing, but we can't help ourselves sometimes.' "

The consumption of alcohol, with American whiskey often mas-querading under the more distinguished name of imported brandy, rose steeply during the nineteenth century until the excise taxes of Civil War times and rising sentiment for temperance put some restraint on drinking. It was estimated in the 1840's that there was one retail liquor dispensary to every one hundred inhab-itants; and all the serious drinking fell upon the men. Horace

Greeley recalled from childhood days "there was no merrymaking, there was no entertainment of relatives or friends, there was scarcely a casual gathering of two or three neighbors for an evening's social chat, without strong drink." The Kentuckian of legend, when he went to some foreign land like Ohio, packed his valise with an extra shirt, two detachable collars, his pistol and a quart of Old Bourbon. A correspondent of the *New York Tribune,* looking up General Grant's antecedents, concluded that more liquor was consumed in the vicinity of Brown County, Ohio, where Grant spent his youth, than anywhere else in the North, for there, he reported, an adult male could hardly maintain his standing in the community if he didn't tie one on at least two or three times a year.

The churches and spiritous liquors lived compatibly together until the temperance crusade got rolling, as is evidenced in the phrase "Whiskey Baptist." Drinking had its own code of politeness. "Never press people unduly to eat or drink," wrote Robert de Valcourt. "True politeness consists in putting people at their ease. . . ." Early nineteenth century printed materials are awash with references to rum, whiskey, applejack, mixed drinks with highly picturesque names and the recipes for preparing them. The reasons for the heavy drinking can be understood if not condoned. They lay in the cultural heritage of a hard-drinking Anglo-Saxon and Scotch-Irish ancestry, in the life of rural hardship, exposure, disease and tedium; a climate with extremes of temperature, a monotonous diet of meats preserved by heavy salting and a firm folk belief in the medicinal properties of alcohol. Spiritous liquors were, one may add, a fair substitute for the central heating that still lay in the future.

There was a curious distinction in permitted practice between smoking and chewing tobacco. No gentleman would smoke in a parlor with ladies present without asking permission. But permission was not required for chewing and its necessary sequel, spitting. Since chewing was almost universal, every home was equipped with spittoons fabricated from sturdy brass or tasteful examples of ceramic art or embossed and decorated china. If the host didn't chew himself, his guests did and it was best to be prepared. So the convenience was set out where the visitors could, if reasonably good marksmen, project into the cuspidor the substance known euphemistically as "ambeer."

In the corridors and rooms of hotels and all public buildings the receptacles for spitters were everywhere in evidence. Down into the present century, and there is no reason to doubt but what this was typical, the County Court Room of the Greene County courthouse at Carrollton, Illinois, was liberally provided with heavy iron spittoons for the spectators, two for each row of jurors in the jury box, one at each lawyers' table and one for the judge. If the facilities were not readily available the result was quite untidy, as was observed at the Boston State House by Lieutenants Carr and Deedes, whom we met earlier in this chapter. They found "the [would be *white*] stone floor as delightfully *variegated* with the *juice,* of the Tobacco from the mouth of the illustrious Jonathans." English travelers made much of this spitting as evidence of uncouth manners in the United States; and it must be remembered that their strictures against any uncomely behavior was often given a cutting edge by their distaste for the American form of government.

Yet there is no escaping, on the grounds of prejudiced reporting, from an accumulation of evidence regarding the universal chewing habit. Philip Lindsley, President of the University of Nashville, was so thoroughly be-sprinkled at church by a fellow-worshiper "as fairly to put all devotion out of countenance." A river boatman on the Ohio, the half-horse, half-alligator type, roared that he was "Billy Earthquake, Esquire . . . all the way from North Fork of Muddy Run! . . . I can out-run, out-jump, out-swim, chaw more tobacco and spit less . . . than any other man in these localities!" Ladies in brocades, cashmeres and point lace, with fan and parasol, did undeniably have to navigate on floors wet with tobacco juice.

Even with basins abundantly present, the magnificent Burnet House in Cincinnati sluiced down its halls and steps every morning, producing as a result a "brown cataract." Members of the House of Representatives lolled in their chairs with their hats on, coughing, rattling newspapers and spitting into the private wooden box of sawdust which the government located under each legislator's chair. The senators were more decorous, took their hats off and kept their feet down. But they too possessed and used a personal spit box. They also had access to a snuff box on the desk of the President of the Senate. The duties of page boys included carrying a pinch to needy senators.

An enormous spittoon stood at the door of the White House,

which John Milton Mackie, who was not a disgruntled British
Tory, but a teacher at Brown University, described as "a perfect
monster . . . a gentle hint, this, no doubt, to the stranger just arrived from Texas, or the upper Mississippi, that he will please un-
pack his cheek. . . ." But Mackie had to abandon this idea when
he found more spittoons inside. It was all too evident that the
American freeman expected to exercise the right to chew and ex-
pectorate at any time or place. Mackie thought that it would be
appropriate if Pennsylvania Avenue was lined with cuspidors, as
the approaches to the palaces of Europe were lined with rare plants
and flowers. Today it would be extremely hard to find a young
man, north of the Mason-Dixon Line at any rate, who would know
the difference between a chaw of Red Man, Horse Shoe or the fe-
licitously named Sweet Mist. Spittoons are now being manufactured, not for spitting, but as planters for flower arrangements.

Mrs. Trollope found mixed dinner parties very rare among the
people with whom she had social relations in Cincinnati. Even at a
dance the gentlemen gathered together for a sit-down supper while
the ladies, like wallflowers, all sat around the sides of the hall sulk-
ily balancing their plates on their knees. This occurred because
"the gentlemen liked it better." In Boston a young man took his
date to a lecture at Mechanic's Hall, went later to her home, if
invited in, for oysters, crackers and cheese. In New York the great
common denominator of amusements was walking down Broadway
to see and be seen. C.F.M. Noland, humorist of the Old Southwest, has his character, Colonel Pete Whetstone, an early example
of the country yokel, put up at the Astor House which he found to
be larger than the State House at Little Rock. "Broadway," said
Colonel Whetstone, "is the big brag street of the city . . . and
then there are some of the tarnationest purty gals twixt heaven and
yearth—lord but they do look nice—the height of fashion is to wear
a slick little apurn behind. You would soon tire out here. . . ."

In Philadelphia, honored guests were taken to view the water
works. In Chicago ladies and gentlemen put on expurgated plays,
heard Clara Louise Kellogg, the prima donna, sing, and attended
the annual meeting of the Historical Society while young men in
modest circumstances saw the girls home from prayer meeting. Funerals provided not only an opportunity to express grief and respect for the deceased, but to socialize with old friends. One old
minister who had come a far piece on foot through the heat and

dust to a funeral in the middle South, was invited by the minister in charge to sit on the platform and open the service. Before he "gave out the hymn" he paused to say:

"But while I'm before you, I want to say as how my main business over here is a huntin' of sum seed peas, an' if anybody here has got any to spar', I'd like to know it after meetin'."

Our ever-lengthening calendar of holidays was not known to the American of the mid-nineteenth century. Christmas and Easter continued to be largely ignored as they had been in the previous century among a people who would have no part of saints' days. Henry Ward Beecher as a boy, reared in the spirit of Connecticut Congregationalism, never attached any joyous significance to Christmas. He remembered long afterward how one snowy night when the family lived in Litchfield, Connecticut, he paused as he passed the Episcopal Church. The door was open. Inside he could see vistas of decorative evergreens and hear the choir singing carols and he stood and marveled at "what manner of folk these Episcopalians were who took their religion gladly."

Boston marked the day of the Artillery Election and munched " 'Lection Cake," a kind of sweetened bread with egg-and-molasses on top. Thanksgiving was observed and Maine and Massachusetts shared Patriots' Day on April 19th as a public holiday. But from Maine to Georgia the day of real meaning was Independence Day. Cannon roared. Veterans of the Revolution shuffled along to the picnic grove to hear the orator of the day, and listened with moist eye to the ceremonial reading of the Declaration, an unvarying part of the day's ritual.

The churches continued to be dominant in the social life of America. The introduction of stoves into the New England meetinghouse in the 1830's threatened to disrupt the life of the churches. Congregations which once lived in loving fellowship split down the middle to become the Stove Party and the Anti-Stove Party. The latter worshipers wished for no amelioration of their physical suffering and, indeed, received spiritual refreshment from hearing the frozen communion bread rattle like marbles in the plate. But the Stove Party carried the day. Gradually it became unnecessary to bring live coals in a foot warmer to the place of worship.

On the Sabbath Day people walked softly on their tiptoes, jumped when the bell rang at nine, gathered in the church house when the "second bell" gave the final summons at ten o'clock. Meditation was upon every brow. Samuel G. Goodrich, popular author, best known under his pen name, Peter Parley, declared that the hens of New England laid their Sunday egg without cackling and that the family cat sat with her eyes half shut, as if she too was considering the ways of God toward cats. The Christian sectaries carried on acrimonious quarrels over who possessed the key to final truth. In Virginia Baptists were jailed for exhorting and Quakers were escorted to the county line by the sheriff. The Rhode Island Quaker child, in contrast, was taught at his mother's knee, as Thomas ("Shepherd Tom") Hazard remembered it, "First, that ye love one another and your neighbor as yourselves. Second, that ye hate the Puritans of Massachusetts with a perfect hatred. Third, that ye hold the Presbyterians of Connecticut in like contempt."

In the life of the church and churchly busy-work, women found an outlet for their emotional energies denied them elsewhere. Spinsters had few options. Married women had their children and the kitchen; but both had their church. The ministers were the only men, Mrs. Trollope thought, who treated women as though they were important. And in church the women were seen in full panoply.

Slowly the rigors of the catechism relaxed, so that it became possible for a Texas itinerant preacher to have this frustrating experience when he tried to interrogate a small boy in the traditional fashion:

"Who killed Abel?"

"I don't know nothin' about it. My folks has jest moved here last week."

The moral code of the thirties and forties, an age of speculation and quick riches, identified honesty with legality. But the sexual code was exceptionally strict. In general, the attitude of men toward women was chivalrous and protective. A woman of good reputation—and her own word was accepted on the subject—could venture abroad with justifiable confidence that she could trust male strangers with whom she came in contact. This gave an unexpected charm to a period which was in so many ways awkward and banal.

"An American is never rude to a woman," wrote Francis Lieber, German liberal who chose the United States as his adopted country. "Americans are essentially and substantially polite," Lieber insisted, and noted that any "respectable female" could safely travel alone in the United States. But although the men passed with high marks for their attitude toward women, the latter did not fare so well in the eyes of outside observers. Mrs. Trollope said they grabbed the best location on the canal boat, took over the backgammon board and the shady side of the cabin, looking "like hedgehogs with every quill raised . . . even the youngest and the prettiest can set their lips, and knit their brows, and look as hard and unsocial as their grandmothers." Lieber reluctantly confirms this. He found American women accepting acts of politeness as their due with never a smile or friendly glance or gentle word when a fellow-traveler rescued a handkerchief, handed a lady into the stagecoach or passed her the dish she wanted.

Possibly Lieber was idealizing the U.S. male a bit, for there is evidence that flippant girl watchers existed then as now. They were self-appointed, served out of pure patriotism under the jocular name of Hoop Inspectors, and were observed to be especially vigilant in the discharge of their duties when hoops tilted up as the wearers mounted the steps of a public hall or an omnibus. But Anthony Trollope, too, went along with the idea of Lieber's that American men had progressed further toward the social graces than the women. In New York he said that the women stared the men out of their seats, repaying them for courtesies with "no word, no smile." In the West, which he did not like, Trollope found that "The men are dirty and civil, the women are dirty and uncivil."

Women traveling alone were offered much advice as to their "unprotected situation" some of which they apparently needed. They were warned to carry a bottle of camphor in their satchel, in case of a fainting spell, and to avoid pestering the train conductor with unnecessary questions like "Where are we now?" or "When shall we arrive?" This last question is a reminder of the folklore associated with slow trains. A lady, according to one story, is supposed to have handed the conductor two tickets, one for a full fare, the other for a half fare.

"Who is the half ticket for?" the conductor inquired.

"My boy," the passenger said.

"He's not a boy; he's a man," the conductor said. "Under twelve, half fare, over twelve, full fare."

To which the mother answered:

"Well, he was under twelve when we started."

It was quite proper for a male passenger to give a lady the time of day, provided he did it in the right way. Permissible subjects of casual conversation were the Scriptures with an excursus into church work in general. Sinners might be spoken to by a gentlewoman about their souls. Introductions were not necessary for such exchanges. But if a man began to act familiar, the tactic for the woman traveler was to "lower your veil and turn from him."

Miss Eliza Leslie, "Miss Leslie" as she signed herself, a Philadelphia literary lady and authority upon things in general, gave out the word when black silk mittens became unfashionable at the breakfast table, cautioned her feminine readers against striking up an acquaintance with female travelers "who are evidently coarse and vulgar, even if . . . rich." A woman registering in a hotel was supposed to sit quietly in the hotel parlor, summon the proprietor and ask him to conduct her to a good room. In the dining hall she was always to use the butter knife, the salt spoon and sugar tongs, even though dining alone. She should appear in the public rooms with arms and neck covered and never, never play on the hotel piano unless invited to do so.

The increasing ease of ocean travel induced numbers of newly prosperous Americans to venture abroad. The intricacies of European civilization baffled Nathaniel Hawthorne. But the Reverend Lyman Beecher, in a hurry to usher in the millennium, boldly urged his lecture audiences in London to join him in the program of total abstinence from wines, spirits and malt beverages. He viewed the minster of York, climbed to the top of St. Paul's but returned home with the conviction, possibly reinforced by the refusal of the stubborn British to desert their pubs, that London was not as "pretty" as New Haven.

Most of the Americans who traveled abroad in the early national period followed stereotyped itineraries and indulged in conventional raptures. They visited the fashionable spas, made the rounds of the ateliers of Roman artists, caught an exciting glimpse of dashing Louis Napoleon in Paris and took strawberries and tea at Brighton.

The best part of a European sojourn was coming home. A varied collection of artifacts proved that one had acquired the patina of culture—new clothes, old hotel bills, archeological specimens, *cartes de visite,* perhaps a sonnet written by an amorous Italian.

There was snob appeal in travel, but substantial consolations to be found at home, too, as Miss Fanny Knight confided to her diary. Fanny, who had luminous dark eyes and page-boy curls, wrote, "I am still proud of being a daughter of America. . . . Pa has decided that we shall pass the winter in New Orleans, so I shall see HIM again!!"

For a broad cross section of the people with a rural background who were being lifted up by the factory age, the first problem in advancing beyond a feral state was to stop saying yearth for earth, to wards for towards and to drop the use of unsanctioned endings on recognized roots, such as *suddenacious*. There was the affectation of vivacity to be avoided on the one hand—remarks upon the "elegant sermon," the "smashing gown," the "awfullest fine whiskers"—and on the other the risk of committing social hara-kiri through the use of stilted expressions of exaggerated gentility, like "Where is your good wife?" Only through experience could one learn to manage the easy banter of the socially secure without incurring the risks attendant upon attempting smart answers and witty replies.

The quest was far from hopeless. With money and leisure and some aptitude for the task, it was entirely possible to storm the barricades. There was no better setting and no more encouraging prospect of success than was afforded by Washington City, where in the decades of 1800-1850 a people and a capital society were growing up together.

8

HOW TO BEHAVE IN
WASHINGTON

The social whirl which is Washington began on New Year's Day, January 1, 1801. That afternoon John Adams, first President to occupy the White House, hair freshly powdered and gathered in a queue, be-gloved, wearing a white waistcoat, black velvet knee breeches, silk stockings and silver knee and shoe buckles, received with his wife, Abigail, at the first formal reception held in the Palace. Social life in the city has revolved around "official" Washington ever since.

Like George Washington before him, President Adams bowed, did not shake hands. Like Martha Washington, Mrs. Adams, who as the wife of the Vice President had taken her station at the right hand of "Lady" Washington, believed in strict rules of precedence as outward symbols of respect toward official position. Schooled in Mrs. Washington's stately "court," familiar with the stiff etiquette of France and England, bearing the distinction of being the first American woman ever presented at the Court of St. James, no woman in the United States at the time was better prepared than Mrs. Adams for the post of First Lady.

Abigail had driven to Washington the previous November with a coach, ten horses, eight servants and the rose damask furniture which had been in the President's House in Philadelphia. Her husband had preceded her by several months. As soon as the President's wife arrived, the matrons of Washington began pushing for a "drawing room"—an official reception—while Mrs. Adams set to work dropping her visiting cards at houses scattered along the undeveloped avenues and circles of the city; and in older Georgetown, which she compared unfavorably with Milton, Massachusetts.

The handicaps for Presidential entertaining were formidable. Only six damp, newly plastered rooms of the barnlike mansion were ready for occupancy, and two of them were required for offices. There was no fence or yard "and the great unfinished Audience Room, I make a drying room," Mrs. Adams wrote of an episode which White House guides still cite, "to hang up the clothes in." The new First Lady hadn't enough lamps to light the rooms, no bells for summoning a servant. Though Washington was surrounded by deep forests, the government could not find sufficient men to cut and cart the wood for the twelve fires the building required to repel the damps of Foggy Bottom. Gouverneur Morris, home from France and filling out an unexpired term in the Senate, wrote of the vicissitudes of life in Washington at this time:

"We want nothing here but houses, cellars, kitchens, well-informed men, amiable women, and other little trifles of the kind to make our city perfect. . . ."

Nevertheless, surmounting all difficulties with New England resourcefulness, the Adamses successfully produced their first full-scale fete in the Oval Room, Mrs. Adams appearing in brocade and velvet.

Land speculators were convinced that the future lay in the direction the Capitol faced, to the East. Row houses, taverns, shops and boardinghouses were built, and "the Hill" developed a society of its own which lasted until the Civil War. Carrolls, Laws, Tayloes and Brices erected stately homes; Porters, too, and Gambles and Tingleys. There was a social tug of war between the Hill families, Georgetown and the area immediately surrounding the White House, which had in its favor the cachet of the Presidency and a popular race track. The Hill had the congressmen, an exciting sense of history in the making and an old Tayloe home converted into a hotel where John Harnett, a genial and celebrated Ganymede, would start the fixings as soon as one of the regular customers entered the taproom door. It was fashionable to go to the Capitol and visit the Chamber of the House (now Statuary Hall) about one in the afternoon, chat until two, then adjourn for a late dinner.

Thomas Jefferson, then a widower, took over the White House within four months after Adams. A period of social austerity followed. The matrons of Washington, having had a taste of ceremonial pleasures, heartily wished that the Virginia sage was back at Monticello. Under what he called his rule of *pêle-mêle,* President Jefferson insisted that there should be no precedence at White House functions, gave his arm to the lady who happened to be nearest him, ushered ladies and gentlemen en masse to the State Dining Room. He shook hands instead of bowing, introduced a circular table so no guest could outrank another. The levees were abolished, except those held on New Year's Day and July Fourth, although John Adams observed, "Jefferson's whole eight years was a levee. . . ."

Though cobblers, tinkers and Indian chiefs mingled picturesquely with the ministers of legation at Jefferson's receptions, the President's democratic social principles did not imply a plain way of living. His domestic staff was larger than the whole State Department. He introduced his guests to waffles from Holland, olive oil, macaroni, vermicelli and Parmesan cheese from Italy, vanilla and ice cream from Paris; also anchovies, citron, figs, European nuts and a dessert which we would recognize today as Baked Alaska. By the end of Jefferson's two terms it was clear that the background, temperament and preferences of the occupants of the White House would largely determine the tone of life along the Potomac.

Courtly manners and the rules of protocol were somewhat revived during James Madison's eight years. His wife, the incomparable Dolley, has generally been regarded as the most accomplished queen of official society that the nation has ever known. In recognition of her tact and charm, a biographer paid her the ultimate tribute: "She was brilliant in the things she did not say or do." Mrs. Madison called on all who called on her, held "dove parties" for Cabinet wives, provided evening receptions where the ladies came to show off their clothes, legislators to make a political bargain, office-seekers to buck for an appointment and those who simply wished to rub shoulders with an orator or a general. Dolley was also a good housekeeper. One of her first purchases was a washing machine.

Formality became still more marked during the Presidency of James Monroe. Like a sovereign, Monroe received foreign ministers standing. He wore the clothing of the Revolutionary period until his dying day in 1831. This earned for him the title of last of the "Cocked Hats." During the administration of John Quincy Adams male guests appeared in long trousers. Mrs. Adams, who had weathered a social storm involving the issue of who was required to make the first move in calling upon whom, assisted in carrying on the atmosphere of the Monroe period but, according to the Washington correspondent, Benjamin Perley Poore, the food got better.

The brilliance of the foreign legations, the official entertaining, the absence of the sounds, smells and bustle of a commercial city, the smart carriages on the broad avenues, the southern grace of the leading hostesses, all began to give the capital city a distinctive personality. Even the men found time for relaxing. Mrs. Trollope commented that the members of Congress performed little labor, got paid a handsome eight dollars a day. Captain Marryat, too, was struck by the fact that Congress never worked at night, "and do very little during the day." Yet one feels there must have been night work, or perhaps it was night life, because at a small stream called Goose Creek which ran near Capitol Hill, spanned by a wooden bridge, the members after a night session, according to contemporary rumor, sometimes missed the bridge and had to be fished out of the creek by the sergeants-at-arms. And some acquired a nose that looked like a rose-colored pincushion. Frank Carpenter of the Cleveland *Leader* thought of it as the Congressional Nose.

The tradition of congressional conviviality is a venerable one. In the 1830's, when Colonel Davy Crockett was in Congress, he once addressed the House upon the subject of free whiskey.

"Congress allows *lemonade* to the members," he pointed out, "and has it charged under the head of *stationary* (sic)—I move also that *Whiskey* be allowed under the item of fuel."

The sale of ardent spirits was illegal in the Capitol building. But there was a damp spot in the basement where a code was understood and a thirsty solon could lift a chalice of bar whiskey without unwanted publicity. Washington remains true to its traditions, even in 1965. When the Eighty-ninth Congress convened they were welcomed by a cup-bearer named Nat Gandel who advertised "Discreet Delivery" of wines and liquor which would be "Inconspicuously Wrapped."

At President Jackson's first inauguration the sons of the new democracy almost wrecked the White House. On this well-publicized occasion the jubilant guests crashed through windows, broke up the furniture, stood on satin-covered chairs in boots caked with honest Democratic mud, spilled food on the carpets and ripped down the draperies. Mrs. Margaret Bayard Smith, wife of the President of the Washington branch of the Bank of the United States, shuddered and thought of an analogy—the mob looting Versailles. The wild scene was long held against Jackson by political enemies who pointed to the disorder and damage as the inevitable fauvism of the mobocracy, though in fact faulty police work seems to have been at the heart of the matter. The second Jackson inauguration was the very pink of propriety.

Under Jackson's eye the White House interior was renovated and official Washington attended receptions every other Thursday when Congress was sitting. Great wood fires blazed brilliantly in the fireplaces. Wax tapers glowed and winked in the handsome East Room mirrors, played on the chandeliers and gilt eagles, the banked camellias and twenty new spittoons.

Members of the conservative "sets" in Washington society were bitter about the easy entrée given to spoilsmen, hungry apprentices and men who wandered about the Executive Mansion with their hats on, although at this time the members of Congress did the same thing. George Bancroft, historian and Boston patrician, complained of guests he met at the White House: "fellows," he said, "with dirty faces and dirty manners; all the refuse that Washington could turn forth from its workshops and stables." But the personal deportment of the tall, gaunt old President in black suit and black cravat was one of dignity and urbanity. Even such a diehard Whig as Daniel Webster conceded that Jackson's style was "presidential."

Contrary to the etiquette followed in other American cities, strangers in Washington were expected to pay the first call. Visiting pilgrims were encouraged by hotelkeepers and hackmen to take an aggressive stance toward the city's social opportunities.

Sometimes verdant strangers even dropped in for pot luck when a line of carriages in front of a private residence suggested that a party was swinging inside. The theory was, according to Mrs. Florence Howe Hall, daughter of the famous Julia Ward Howe, in her *Social Customs* (Boston: 1887), that "every American citizen has a right to social recognition at the hands of the rulers whom his voice has helped to elect."

There was no difficulty about getting an invitation to the White House all through the nineteenth century. Any well-mannered white stranger who bathed regularly, displayed no mourning bands around his finger nails and dressed suitably could leave his card at the door of the President's residence and expect to hover on the fringes of Society, especially if he knew Mrs. Sarah Madeleine Dahlgren, doyenne of the social coterie. Or he might apply with fruitful results to the member of the House from his home congressional district. One simply hired a hack and arrived at the White House around eight o'clock in "ball" dress. The visitors, including ex-officials with their "Potomac fever" unassuaged, passed through the Red and Blue parlors to the East Room. There either the Engineer in Charge of Public Buildings or the Marshall of the District of Columbia presented each guest to the President and his wife or official hostess, and an usher pointed significantly to the egress. "It is inelegant and annoying," wrote an arbiter of the period, "to attempt a conversation with the President or his lady on such an occasion. . . ." An out-of-town caller could also meet the heads of the various Government departments without difficulty for a chat of courtesy, though an acquaintanceship of real substance came harder.

Ladies with escorts, or venturing forth in pairs, went regularly to the Capitol where they might amuse themselves listening to a man from Cincinnati sawing the air on the subject of pork. Or the curious might visit that other fashionable attraction for casual strollers, the Library of Congress. Its treasures could be inspected on the days it was open, three times a week, if one knew the Librarian. High Government officials enjoyed their whist in private card rooms. Once Mrs. Henry Clay was chaperoning a prim young woman from Boston when they passed through a room in which a quiet game was in progress. The girl asked:

"Is card-playing a common practice here?"

"Yes," replied Mrs. Clay, "the gentlemen always play when they get together."

"Don't it distress you to have Mr. Clay gamble?" the maiden asked in Puritan simplicity.

"Oh! dear, no!" answered the wife of Harry of the West. "He 'most always wins."

What were called "morning visits" began at twelve, lasted until three, with dinner at four. The streets presented a busy and animated sight during the daylight hours. Ships from Europe that tied up at the docks of Alexandria were plainly visible from the windows of the White House. Merchantmen from the West Indies called at the port of Georgetown. Captains and crews mingled with women of position on their way to pay their calls, with pert belles, pushy newspaper writers, rustic legislators, visitors willing to accept a postmastership and "the odd mortals that wander in from the western border. . . ." Also a part of the scene were the foreign attachés, scurrying lobbyists and the merely curious who came to town to see how the country was governed. Wives of freshmen congressmen arriving from interior points were advised to buy their new clothes *after* arrival.

Faro banks ran wide open along Pennsylvania Avenue for the benefit of sporting gentlemen who wanted some action, with free liquor set out for patrons. A nine-days' wonder was a Monsieur Maetzel who exhibited a mechanical chess player and an automaton which played marches on a trumpet. The maestro also displayed a panorama called "The Burning of Moscow" with a climax of enduring interest. It showed the Kremlin being blown up.

There were no regular theaters in Washington and little evening entertainment other than subscription balls and private parties. The assemblies were very select. Gentlemen of faultless antecedents appeared in full dress, army officers in their regimentals, the ladies in the mode—"classic in its scantiness." The ball started with a country dance. Then the dancers stood up for minuets and quadrilles and, toward the middle of the century, whirled through the naughty waltz and abandoned polka, wrapping the evening up at eleven with a romp through "Sir Roger de Coverley" or "Money Musk." The guest lists for public balls were less exclusive. Cards left at the right places or a letter of introduction produced an invitation to the next "squeeze."

"Pray, sir, take your finger out of my ear," said a gentleman, mildly, at an affair given by Mrs. Asbury Dickens, wife of the Chief Clerk of the Treasury Department during Monroe's administration.

"I will, sir," came the reply, "as soon as I get room to stir." It may be added as a commentary on the crush and the company that General Winfield Scott was relieved of his wallet containing $800 in a rout held in the White House itself.

The 1840 Presidential campaign involved an issue of social snobbery which the Whigs cleverly raised against Martin Van Buren when he stood for a second term. Van Buren had endeavored to restore good feeling between the White House and Washington society, following the rupture which occurred during the Jackson period. The President, who enjoyed the amenities of good living, established a notable cuisine, a restricted guest list, a code of etiquette which some observers said rivaled that of a small German principality. This style of life delivered the New York Democrat into the hands of his enemies. Van Buren went down to a resounding defeat, administered by William Henry Harrison, the Log Cabin and Hard Cider candidate, when the Whig orators convinced the frontiersmen and small farmers that the "Kinderhook Fox" was a social swell who ate Frenchified dishes from gold spoons.

Washington hoped at each change of government that the age of brilliance, maturity and sophistication had come. But it always seemed to be delayed. No sparkling bon mots or glittering fetes are associated with the memory of President Harrison. He died within a month of his inaugural, succeeded by Tyler. John Tyler's first hostess was his disingenuous daughter-in-law who almost exploded with happy incredulity over her exalted station—"Can this be I?" President Tyler later married the beautiful Julia Gardiner. She was regal in more than appearance. The new Mrs. Tyler received on a raised dais, wore a headdress which suggested a royal diadem, surrounded herself with white-robed vestals who looked suspiciously like royal maids of honor. Most were Gardiner cousins from the fastnesses of eastern Long Island who found promenading around the East Room far more exhilarating than the bucolic pleasures of tea at Shelter Island.

Mrs. James K. Polk was a strict Presbyterian, attended the inaugural ball honoring her husband at Carusi's Assembly Rooms swathed in black and refused to dance. Her social impact during the time she occupied "the people's house" was less than moderate. Mrs. Zachary Taylor enjoyed her pipe as did "Aunt Rachel" Jackson, who had prayed nightly before the election that Henry Clay would be chosen over her husband. The Fillmores were dull, saw to it that no one threw a card on White House property, observed a tight Sunday closing, but added to the cultural facilities of the Mansion a Bible and a dictionary, both previously lacking; also an iron cookstove and a mahogany, zinc-lined bathtub. The social opportunities were sparse during the sway of Mrs. Franklin Pierce. When her husband became President she fainted.

James Buchanan, the urbane bachelor, with his ward and niece, Harriet Lane, as hostess, changed the atmosphere. Washington again wore a joyful countenance, low necks, long trains, lace berthas and elaborate headdresses. Buchanan was good for the business of florists and livery men who rented carriages, for milliners, hair dressers and wine merchants. But the hour was late for revels. The administration in its last months was falling apart. South Carolina batteries had already fired upon a United States ship when Abraham Lincoln took up the burden and Buchanan assured him:

"If you are as happy, my dear sir, on entering this house as I am in leaving it and returning home, you are the happiest man in this country."

By the time Mrs. Lincoln arrived in Washington with her dressy wardrobe, her garlands and head wreaths and the sewing machine admirers had given to her when she left Springfield, Illinois, the old Washington hands, the "cave dwellers" with states' rights sympathies, had quarantined the White House. The feeling among the hostesses with southern ties was that the Illinoisans would have to civilize themselves without outside help. The Mansion at this time was grotesquely shabby, although still not in as desperate case as it had been in the time of Tyler when Congress, in a vindictive mood, refused to appropriate sufficient funds for proper maintenance. Then the chaste white columns of the portico were splattered with tobacco juice, the carpets patched, the hangings in tatters and many of the chairs in the East Room, wrote the Washington correspondent of the *New York Herald,* "would be kicked out of a brothel."

When the Lincolns arrived the ground floor had "the air of an old and unsuccessful hotel," Elizabeth Todd Grimsley, one of Mary Lincoln's relatives, wrote home to Springfield. The interior, too, suffered from the constant depredations of visitors who snipped off the lace curtains for souvenirs, carried away bits of carpet or slit a trapezoid from the cover of a sofa.

Washington struck travelers from abroad as ungainly, presumptuous, with great but quite remote possibilities of being a world capital. Sometimes called "the city of magnificent distances," Washington was complained of because when one got to the far horizon there was nothing there but more empty earth and sky. The dome of the Capitol was unfinished. Anthony Trollope saw the Washington Monument as only an unfinished stump, was not sanguine about its early completion when he noticed a glass box set up to invite contributions. The box contained two fifty-cent pieces. Both were counterfeit.

During the years of corruption and quick riches after the Civil War, Washington acquired some of the less pleasing evidences of sophistication. A "promiscuous profanity" flourished along with locutions of excessive finickiness, such as "There has been an event in the Smith family" and outright malapropisms. Perhaps of all the women who invaded Washington the most famous for the inspired use of the misapplied word was the colorful Mary Theresa Carver, wife of the Chicago drygoods merchant, Levi Ziegler Leiter. Her memory is treasured for her remark, possibly embellished a bit by posterity, that she had "spinal staircases" in her residence, as well as "sexual bookcases"; also that her husband attended a costume party "in the garbage of a monk." That such gaffes were not unusual in the comedy of manners that made up the Washington whirligig is further suggested by an entry which Mrs. James Luther Slayden, a congressional wife, made in her journal. At the outbreak of the Spanish-American War Mrs. Slayden wrote that people were all looking at maps to find out where the Philippines were, having been under the impression up to that time that they were the subject of one of St. Paul's epistles.

It took an alert and determined woman to keep up with what was the fashion in capital-city deportment. A new kind of society bow arrived with the 1870's. It was no longer "in" to bow the head. According to accounts of the day, the lady looked you coolly in the face, smiled as sweetly as she could, and gently inclined her head toward the right shoulder, with a little backward movement at the same time. A slight, Frenchy shrug heightened the charm. A few years later the high handshake was the mode, performed at about the level of the nose. When to shake or not shake was sometimes a delicate problem. Speaking generally, a business introduction did not require the high, extended hand. As in:

"This is Mr. Belford, whom I think you can rely on to do the carpenter work of which you spoke."

In other instances, though, no matter how rich and exclusive one was, it was better to shake, as in the case of an artist about to do one's portrait or a writer preparing a biographical sketch. Even in the best society, it was pointed out, genius is entitled to deference.

Washington was regarded as a sin-city by many authorities on "impurity" including Mrs. Ella E. Kellogg, a Seventh Day Baptist of Battle Creek, Michigan, who wore rimless, gold-bowed glasses and turned out books, pamphlets and lectures almost as facilely as her husband, the health propagandist and health-food inventor, Dr. John Harvey Kellogg. Washington was a moral danger spot because so many young women were needed in the Government departments. There were already a thousand typewriters clattering in the city by 1886. These young women went astray, according to Mrs. Kellogg's analysis in *A Talk With Girls*, because of their longing to be fashionably dressed "without means wherewith to satisfy their love for adornment, save by a sacrifice of principle."

Lonely bureau functionaries, peccant congressmen living without their families in drab boardinghouses, strangers passing through, made the city a place where illicit affairs were carried on with little concealment, as one may gather from advertisements appearing in the *Star:*

WANTED—ROOM BY A GENTLEMAN of elegant habits, stranger in the city, but located here for a year; would like room or rooms and board in home of a discreet young widow, where he can enjoy all the comforts of home. Address, in entire confidence, G.R. Star Office.

Mrs. George Graham Vest, wife of the Missouri Senator, viewing the scene, or perhaps reading the personals in the *Star,* went so far as to declare that men with young families should be forbidden by law to go to Congress because of the moral effect of the city upon his children.

As late as the eighties it was possible for any bore to take up the time of the President. One simply went to the Executive Mansion, handed a personal card marked "to pay respects" to the officer in charge. After a wait which "may require some minutes . . ." the caller found himself in the presence of Rutherford B. Hayes, President Arthur or Grover Cleveland. The routine was to mention one's name and residence, offer his hand, make a respectful bow, remark that it was mild for May or that we need rain badly out around Quincy, Illinois, and give way to the next fellow.

Guests at a state dinner if not personally known around the White House presented their invitations. The men were handed a card bearing a diagram of the table, the seat of each indicated and the name of the lady he was to take in to dinner. It was suggested that those who had not had much experience at that sort of thing would do well to take the defensive; that is, watch those who knew the routine. Male guests with beards and mustaches were permitted, indeed encouraged, to use their napkins frequently and vigorously, but were not expected to tuck them in around their collars. Instances are on record in the annals of Washington dinner etiquette of congressmen who tried to eat the doilies. The improper use of the knife was common enough to call for a tsk-tsk and forks were often loaded in the style seen at the quick lunch counter. When the waiter asked President Lincoln at his first state dinner whether he would take white wine or red, the President said with great simplicity: "I don't know. Which would you?"

Some liked the life and some liked it not. James A. Garfield exclaimed, "My God! What is there in this place that a man should ever want to get in it?" Chester A. Arthur, who was born into the best circles of New York society and cut a dashing figure in the fashionable life at Newport, had a zest for the social side, the flowers, the wine, the slow pacing with a pretty woman on his arm. But he served only one term. As Van Buren was rejected in part because of his gold spoons, President Arthur, said Joseph G. Cannon of Illinois, "was defeated by his trousers." The American voter has always had a scunner against dandyism.

Mrs. Slayden, who was a Virginia Maury and linked complexly with the old aristocracy of Washington, appreciated the city as a sort of eye of the hurricane where the social forces of the nation converged. Her own position was secure enough for her to take pot shots at the over-dressed, over-fed women who talked interminably about the prevalence of la grippe at elaborate luncheons with too many courses, too many pink-shaded candles on tables invariably decorated with centerpieces of Battenberg lace. One who was not amused by the passing show was Arthur Capper, correspondent for the Topeka *Capital* and later United States Senator, who said of the social whirl as he knew it through card parties in Tacoma Park, "Too rich . . . Kansas is good enough for me."

The pattern of life was well grooved by the time the Plush Age arrived. Washington was a Vanity Fair of young women hallooing after anything male in a foreign uniform, of silk hats and frock coats, of Cabinet couples who despite high official rank addressed one another comfortably as "Mamma" or "Poppa," of servants in livery receiving a blizzard of cards on silver trays, of new recruits to officialdom who were always shaking hands with the butler, of nibbling little cakes on the parterres and so home through Rock Creek Park in the landau. Did the chargé of France go in to dinner ahead of the chargé of Switzerland, who thought he had a better claim to the distinction? That was the issue that embittered and had to be adjudicated by the Dean of the diplomatic corps, a thankless task, and one which seemed so often to fall upon the slender shoulders of the plenipotentiaries of modest powers like Nicaragua or Costa Rica.

Modern improvements sometimes only exacerbated old controversies. The Electric Carriage Call Company of New York in 1902 installed a system outside the East entrance to the White House to flash numbers which would summon coachmen in proper sequence at the end of social affairs. But—what sequence was proper? At such a moment, many a statesman felt a great surge of patriotic priority, not for himself but for the dignity of the office he happened to occupy.

As the twentieth century arrived there were many pleasant people in Washington. Yet the realization of a richly interesting society still seemed an elusive goal. The reason seems to have been the changing population and the stuffy formality of official life. Mrs. Alice Longworth, daughter of President Theodore Roosevelt, thought that was it. Writing in her reminiscent *Crowded Hours,* Mrs. Longworth remarked, "People in Washington seem as hypnotized by precedence as though they were hens with their beaks on a chalk line." It was all too in-bred. One ate the same foods, it was complained, in the same houses with the same guests. Even the waiters looked familiar, and for the best of reasons. They were the same waiters. Perhaps the social conventions were so strong because people were always arriving from somewhere else like Elkhart, Indiana, and were over-eager to fit in. They were often charming people, Mrs. Slayden wrote sadly. One got to know and appreciate them. Then they vanished, "gone back to Oshkosh or San Francisco or just Delaware."

Mrs. Johnson expressed the feelings of many who have been awed by Washington when she told reporters at the time the Vice President moved up, following the tragedy, "We are plain people . . . temporarily in a high place, and you must not expect too much of us in a social way."

The speaker was, of course, Eliza, wife of President Andrew Johnson.

Today Washington has a more informal atmosphere than ever before. First names come as easily as they do at a Rotary Club luncheon and are, indeed, equally mandatory. Nicknames are a political asset. Presidential aspirants of recent memory, after all, have included Tom, Dick and Harry; and Harry made it. A man who has both a pretty wit and a funny name, such as Hubert Horatio Humphrey, can even get valuable mileage out of the "Horatio." Ethel (Mrs. Robert F.) Kennedy drops her howdies to friends with a casual "Hi-ya kid." Mme. Nicole Alphand, wife of the recent French ambassador, tried to relax ponderous rules dating back to decisions on court etiquette made at the Congress of Vienna; and Mrs. Johnson, the former Claudia Taylor, and wife of President Lyndon B. Johnson, utters breezy "ladybirdisms," such as "See you Sunday if the Lord be willin' and the crick don't rise."

Two world wars and the telephone have pretty well cleaned up the calling card problem. The carriages and the gorgeous footmen have departed, and Mrs. David K. E. Bruce, wife of the U. S. Ambassador to the United Kingdom, has been quoted as saying that Washington is remarkably like Cranford, New Jersey. Yet there are differences. The number of unattached women in the District of Columbia is high by New Jersey standards. And in Washington, unlike Cranford, it is sometimes necessary to know how to address a queen or a Communist.

Respectable theater is now seen in the city, although the best show remains politics. The District of Columbia issued twenty licenses for sidewalk cafés in 1964 for a welcome Continental touch to its radiating boulevards; and sin now pays so poorly that a professional call girl trying to get ahead in her chosen occupation would soon find herself in need of unemployment compensation. In its steady progress toward a higher level of civilization Washington had at last count some twenty-nine exotic dancers oscillating in the lawful minimum of skimpy bra and panties. Two political cabarets have been flourishing, with eager audiences giving what one journalist on the scene calls "the traditional native treatment: when a satirist hurts, lionize him."

Washington has long since ceased to be a southern city. Now campus types from northern universities typify the scene more accurately than the string-tie senator. The men of thought who have turned activists drive vintage MG's, are knowledgeable about imported wines, can chart our economic progress to the year 2000 and have fruitful and tweedy wives who read *The New Republic* and study Spanish. Official limousines bear the decision makers to the great houses on Massachusetts Avenue and Foxhall Road where dwell the great, near-great and ex-great. There they balance a plate, lift a glass, and converse in depth with other men whose faces have appeared, or will appear, on the cover of *Time* magazine. Often they make several embassy receptions in one busy afternoon and evening. Feet, stomachs and heads may ache, the ears tuning out when people make the same old remarks about medical care for the aged and the birth control problem in India. Many, no doubt, subscribe heartily to the philosophical principle enunciated by Satchel Paige. "The social ramble," he said, "ain't restful!" Defenders of the cocktail party way of life point out, however, that the idea of the International Geophysical Year was hatched at a party in suburban Bethesda.

The District of Columbia has a well-earned reputation for a high per capita consumption of spiritous liquors. Photographers on the social beat tactfully refrain from snapping members of Congress or officials of the important administrative agencies with drinks in their fists. About twenty-five per cent of the men occupying high posts in government, who wish to be kind to their kidneys, take a ginger ale from the discreet row of tall glasses at the back of the tray. The pale, sparkly beverage looks like Scotch and soda and eliminates tiresome discussion of deviationist behavior.

"A man who may have been the life of the party in Poughkeepsie," says Robert Keith Gray, formerly Special Assistant to President Eisenhower, "is sobered here by the burdens he bears for his nation's welfare."

The excitements and tediums of the cocktail circuit do not, of course, trouble the transient ladies in Capri pants who pour into the capital to see the sights; or their sports-shirted escorts. More than nine million pilgrims of tourism visit Washington each year, according to the latest estimates, to file through the first floor of the

White House, hear the forever-new story of Abigail Adams drying her laundry in the East Room. They sit in the House gallery for a few bewildering moments, queue up for the elevator at the Washington Monument, finish off the last film on the steps of the Capitol.

It is possible now, as it was in times past, for a well-connected businessman to get a taste of the barbecue pit which is Washington society by applying to his congressman. Results will depend upon how he rates with the congressman and how the representative stands in the mysterious caste system that is Washington. Energetic women can get a peek at the social show by volunteering to perform the camel-driver tasks in an influential senator's office. There are professionals, tailored by Savile Row, who ride in Bentleys and Rolls-Royces, and for a fee can steer clients into important social circles. "There is nothing dishonest about their work," points out *Business Week,* "at least, not in a town like Washington." And lastly, for those who want a social leg up, there is the familiar ploy of supporting charity events that attract the right people. At the Washington première, for instance, of the motion picture version of *My Fair Lady,* which was held for the benefit of the new Cultural Center, the purchaser of a pair of hundred-dollar tickets could have eaten dinner in the same room with Dean Rusk and gone on to a late supper dance at the British Embassy.

The quiet civil servants who keep the store while administrations come and go, live in a self-sufficient world of their own, bound together by a common interest in crab grass, hedge clippers and the newest barbecue sauce. They wear plastic raincoats, ride in car pools, bowl and contribute to blood banks. They are not involved with Mrs. Carolyn Hager Shaw's *Social List of Washington,* or the butterflies of the partying world who glide through the glossy pages of the society magazine, *Diplomat.*

Similarly, single girls with secretarial skills who get a job in Washington are no nearer to the front-page personalities than they were back in Pocatello. They won't ever starve or have to car-hop cheeseburgers to live, since they are sheltered under the civil-service umbrella. But they won't meet Cabinet members or a GS 16—everyone has a number, one to eighteen, on the General Schedule ratings—sitting on the hard stone steps of the Watergate listening to the National Symphony. Although a well-turned-out stenographer at Agriculture has been known to crash a buffet luncheon at the Mayflower Hotel, it should be said plainly that a job with one of the departments or on a congressman's staff does not imply any hob-nobbing with Under Secretaries, Doris Fleeson or David Brinkley. As Miss Jean M. Fitzgerald, a secretary in Foreign Agriculture Service, remarked wistfully, "There are an awful lot of people I would like to meet that I don't meet."

A Hill girl can lead a life of appalling loneliness in her one-bedroom apartment in upper North West, filling her recreational time with a swim at the Skyline, dancing lessons or studying the judo technique of self-defense in a class which meets every week in the House Caucus Room. As Pin-up Girl Marilyn Jarvis, a darkish blonde with blue eyes, says, "a girl has to protect herself from the crime in this jungle!"

But while there's life there is hope that the next bachelorette dinner will produce an unmarried Administrative Assistant with a nice crew cut. Partying is useful in another respect. If social contacts do not turn up a knight on a white horse, they may still produce an interesting job opening. Jocelyn Arundel, for one, learned about a fascinating opening at a cocktail party, snagged it with her Smith College degree in French and a year on the *Washington Daily News,* and found herself writing press releases about the two-horned Arabian oryx.

The competition from other unaligned stenographers and case-workers is fierce. A good, and available, man is hard to find. For the most part code clerks at State, the Treasury auditors, Justice lawyers and statisticians at the Department of Labor, hurry off at the end of the work-day to suburban homes and their very satisfactory wives. Yet marriage remains the goal that shines and beckons. It is referred to with casual and refreshing candor by many marriageable Washington females including petite Annette Guibbord, who hails from Basking Ridge, New Jersey. "Binky" was New Jersey's Cherry Blossom Princess in 1964, loves tennis, water skiing, abstract art and the art of politics. But what she enjoys most keenly is joining with her roommate in entertaining two male friends with an oven-baked sirloin steak dinner. At present writing, she is dating a Princeton man she met while working at AID. But it is still all very tentative. Nola Pack, with auburn hair and brown eyes, to cite another instance, finds the work stimulating in the office of Joe Skubitz, a member of the House representing a Kansas district. Nola took home ec. at Kansas State, is a wonderful cook and prefers a man who keeps on developing in the after-college years.

In a special category are those men, and their wives, who were sent to Washington by a mandate which the people later withdrew. A common symptom of their predicament is a fierce determination not to go back to Lancaster, Ohio, or shuffle off to Buffalo. Those who came and don't want to return add an element of stability to real estate values in the Washington metropolitan area. Their houses are decorated in neutral colors, such as beige, not too greatly personalized, just in case they might be thrown on the market suddenly. Meanwhile, the initialed match books remind the title-holder of where he is, tell others where he has been.

Sometimes the retired lawmaker turns to the private practice of law. He may register as a lobbyist or get a job with Hill and Knowlton, the big public relations firm, with a sixteenth-floor office overlooking, but not overpowering, the White House. Attorneys-general stay. Texans stay. It's the same with the Army, the Navy and the Air Force. Officers who had their last duty at Washington catch the fever. Durable widows stay on, relicts of the Wilson, Harding, Coolidge and Franklin D. Roosevelt administrations, while lonely outlanders from the middle west, like the children of Israel, sit by the waters of Babylon or the Potomac and weep as they remember Zion, Illinois, or Mason City, Iowa, and the bandstand that used to be in Central Park, the footbridge across Willow Creek and the Brick & Tile plant.

But, one cannot help but notice, they don't go home.

When the late Senator Henry F. Ashurst of Arizona left the Senate he spoke with old-fashioned eloquence of his yearning to return to what he described movingly as "the starry stillness of an Arizona desert night, the scarlet glories of her blooming cactus, the petrified forest which leafed through its green millenniums, and put on immortality 7,000 years ago."

All that was mortal of the gentleman from Arizona, though, remained comfortably ensconced in a luxurious seventh-floor suite at the Sheraton-Park Hotel in Washington.

Nostalgic memories return to haunt a former bureau chief. He recalls how he used to drive down the ramp to the basement garage leaving his car in V.I.P. parking space. In his wall-to-wall carpeted office, if he was a GS-17, he had a flag and a bookcase, a water carafe on his desk, a choice of finishes for his wastebasket, a telephone without a dial and an autographed photograph of *his* President on the wall.

One does not part easily with such delights. But in Washington life there comes a time, as Cleopatra's attendant, Iras, said just before the asp scene, when "the bright day is done, and we are for the dark." The glitter, the stir and excitement remain. Hope remains. It springs eternal among those who have once responded to the call of the capital. *They never go back to Pocatello,* runs a local folk saying, and like many statements of the conventional wisdom, its truth is self-evident.

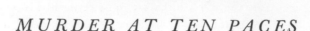

MURDER AT TEN PACES

The first American duel was fought in 1621 near Plymouth Rock by two lowborn fellows who succeeded in maiming each other with daggers so severely that they received a light sentence. They were made to lie with their heads and feet bound together for twenty-four hours without food or drink. The event created a considerable stir, chiefly because of the impertinence of servants in having recourse to the code of honor which was not included in their privileges.

A duel was more than a fight and far from a brawl. It was conducted with much bowing and fol-de-rol, all performed with icy courtesy, and may be defined as a prearranged encounter between two persons wielding deadly weapons in accordance with a set of conventional rules. The object was presumed to be to settle a quarrel or satisfy wounded honor. Obviously a frequent motive was vengeance. The custom reaches back to the feudal age in Europe, borrowing from the judicial combat the idea that an appeal to the God of battles would produce a special intervention from Heaven in favor of the innocent.

There are analogies in primitive cultures. Among the aboriginal Australians a man who eloped with a woman without the intention of marrying her, had to allow her relatives to throw spears at him. (He could use a shield.) And in Greenland the Eskimos have been observed dueling in songs barbed with abusive lyrics. An audience decided who was the victor in this musical game of name-calling. This sounds like a definite improvement over the acts of mayhem which flourished for so long in the civilization of western Europe and which Montesquieu called a prime example of foolish things conducted in a very wise manner.

Out of the doctrine of the gentleman, with its emphasis upon haughty dignity, came the notion of personal honor and the fiction that a chivalrous gentleman could not lie. It was a mortal offense, then, for anyone to insinuate that he could. Such a touchy ideal led inevitably to the high drama of the dueling field, with each contestant literally taking his life in his hands. Opponents of the duel argued that honor rested not in the world's opinion but in virtue. Therefore honor could not be wounded except by the unworthy action of the individual himself. And it was noticed that the fighting settled nothing, since public opinion on the dispute remained what it was before.

There was something in the volatile French temperament peculiarly susceptible to dueling, so that the nobility of the *ancien régime* almost decimated itself as a result of its pugnacity. The mania spread to England where in the reign of George III alone the score was one hundred seventy-two duels, ninety-one fatalities and two prosecutions ending in the death sentence. Under English law to kill one of the king's subjects was murder and a duel was clearly an attempt to commit murder. But the penalties were seldom imposed.

In the comparatively unsophisticated society of the American colonies, with few representatives of the English gentry around, the code of the duelists received less attention than in the home country. Before the American Revolution most duels fought here took place between officers in the royal service, conforming to the European traditions in which they had been trained. Puritan opinion found the whole idea abhorrent, although Judge Sewall records three such combats in Boston between 1695 and 1718. A celebrated encounter occurred at dusk on the Common near the powder house in 1728 when Henry Phillips, Harvard 1724, reputed to be the handsomest and most dashing young man in Boston's gay younger set, killed Benjamin Woodbridge over a gambling debt. The town was anguished and the General Court moved to strengthen a statute already in force against dueling, adding an ancient English penalty, the interment of both the murderer and murdered, since both were guilty, without Christian burial and with a stake driven through the corpses.

Little evidence survives of dueling in the middle colonies. Nor was it a conspicuous feature of southern colonial society, although Colonel Daniel Parke, Jr., a member of the Council in Virginia, and according to a hostile account, a "sparkish gentleman," was quick to resent anything that looked like an affront and was given to challenging "especially before Company." On one occasion Colonel Parke struck Governor Francis Nicholson of Maryland with a horse whip, but before Nicholson could challenge him, Parke got himself safely arrested.

Shortly before the Revolutionary troubles dueling had been outlawed by the American colonies. Blackstone, in his famous *Commentaries on the Laws of England,* included dueling in his discussion of malice as an essential element in the crime of murder. Lord Chesterfield and Samuel Richardson were in agreement about one matter, at least, that both Christ and the classical tradition were arrayed against the duel, and Jonas Hanway made a palpable hit when he pointed out that the Mohammedans didn't duel; they behaved more like Christians. Dueling, he declared, "is the law of fools." In America social influences produced a degree of toleration of private fighting carried on under a system of protocol. The presence of royal forces in America during the wars of the eighteenth century sustained a military atmosphere which made men more sensitive to imputations involving physical courage. The Continental Congress adopted the British Articles of War with small emendations. But the prohibition did not prevent dueling in the Continental Army, even among officers close to General Washington.

Although the American officers' corps followed the social code rather than the Articles of War, criticism was not lacking. James Thatcher, a Massachusetts surgeon who served with a Virginia regiment, wrote that the principals in a duel proved their malice, not their gentlemanliness, called the whole business "fashionable folly." Thomas Paine damned dueling as "Gothic and absurd."

Jefferson thought the duel an "immoral settlement of differences" for which the punishment should be hanging. Dr. Franklin devoted one of his felicitous anecdotes to the subject:

"A Gentleman in a Coffee-house desired another to sit farther from him. 'Why so?' 'Because, Sir, you stink.' 'That is an Affront and you must fight me.' 'I will fight you, if you insist upon it; but I do not see how that will mend the Matter. For if you kill me, I shall stink too; and if I kill you, [you] will stink, if possible, worse than you do at present.' "

The tragic climax in the conflict between law and custom came in the 1804 meeting at Weehawken, New Jersey, when Colonel Aaron Burr killed Alexander Hamilton. But dueling gave ground slowly south of the Mason and Dixon line where it was a persistent feature of, should one say polite life? until well after the War Between the States. Apologists asserted that the threat of a hole in the waistcoat improved men's manners. Indeed, it was suggested in the 1850's by Doctor (both a D.D. and an LLD.) Rufus Wilmot Griswold, influential man of letters of the period, that the celebrated politeness and exquisite courtesy associated with the men of South Carolina was due to the high incidence of dueling. It paid to guard one's tongue and keep smiling in a land of individualism and romantic posturings.

John Lyde Wilson, a former Governor of South Carolina, was deeply stirred by a slighting reference in a northern magazine to southern "fire eaters." Himself a participant in several duels and compiler of the first American "blue book" of dueling etiquette, Wilson retorted that the citizens of South Carolina and adjacent states which had been characterized as barbarous, "would feel a deep humiliation to be compelled to exchange their urbanity of deportment for the uncouth civility of the people of Massachusetts."

Men threw down the challenge for many reasons, less often over a woman than legend would have it. The most frequent cause of serious quarrels that ended upon some secluded field of honor was offensive personal remarks—name-calling or political vituperation. Choice epithets of insult included branding a man a poltroon, a white-livered coward or a dastard, all words of quaint antiquarian charm now, associated with raw melodrama and good for a laugh. But they once had a force, when uttered in anger, which led men to risk their lives.

The origins of many duels seem almost unbelievably trivial. John Randolph of Roanoke, while a student at the College of William and Mary, challenged and wounded a fellow student over the pronunciation of a word. Subsequently, when a member of Congress, Randolph refused to fight the notorious General James Wilkinson, not because of his respect for the law, but because gentlemen fought gentlemen and Wilkinson didn't qualify. Later, when Henry Clay demanded satisfaction for some searing remarks Randolph had made in the Senate, the latter was quite willing to be called out, for Clay was a gentleman. They met on the Virginia side of the Potomac so that Randolph, if he fell, might die on the soil of the Old Dominion. Randolph appeared for the encounter in an old dressing gown. There were two fires, no casualties, exquisite courtesies.

"It was," said Senator Thomas Hart Benton, "about the last high-toned duel that I witnessed."

For a blow there could be no apology. But James Jackson, a Georgia Governor and U. S. Senator, once fought a duel because a law he disliked had been included in an official digest.

On a raw, sleety, January evening in 1801, two handsome young men sat at cards before a crackling fire of hickory wood in an upstairs room at McLean's Tavern, Bardstown, Kentucky. One was John Rowan, later a judge, member of Congress and U. S. Senator, and the other was James Chambers, a physician. Over their mugs of toddy they fell into a hot argument over who was the better Latinist. Rowan called Dr. Chambers a liar and a chain of irreversible circumstances was set in motion. Early in February the two classical scholars rode to an early-morning rendezvous on the Beech Fork. As the fog lifted, they dismounted, shed their greatcoats, wheeled and fired at ten paces. Dr. Chambers died, so it was proved that Rowan was the better pistoleer. The original question remained unresolved.

Newspaper attacks were a frequent cause of offense, although opinion was divided as to whether a newspaper editor was a gentleman and therefore entitled to stand up to be shot at. Politicians and members of Congress, if it is not tautological to distinguish one from the other, fought so frequently in the early years of the nineteenth century that a certain location at Bladensburg, Maryland, became notorious as the field where differences were adjudicated under the dueling code by lawmakers who were also law breakers. A case of dueling pistols was a part of the equipment of a southern and western member, like his tickler of whiskey, and they also carried a stubby derringer in their pockets for close work in street fighting.

When two Congressmen, Jonathan Cilley, a Jackson Democrat from Maine, and William Graves, a Kentucky Whig, fought on the Marlboro Pike in Maryland, Cilley was killed on the third exchange. A British visitor in Washington asked an American how long the tragic affair would stop the practice of codified mayhem and murder.

"Well, I reckon three days," was the meditative reply, "or thereabouts."

Not every gentleman caught in the net of the system was athirst for "satisfaction" as events rolled on toward the moment when the triggers would be squeezed. The central figures often seemed like pawns in the game. Men who might have composed the differences failed to intervene. The seconds frequently appeared to be more filled with the fighting spirit than their principals. The duel itself seemed to become a kind of super organism capable of taking off on a fatal life-cycle of its own.

"I have never been your enemy, sir," said Captain Stephen Decatur as he faced Commodore James Barron, just about where U. S. Route 1 now crosses the District of Columbia line.

But no one on the ground that day moved to explore the opportunity the remark presented to attempt a reconciliation. A few moments later, Barron's bullet hit the bull's eye—the crest of the ilium—and was deflected into the groin: a fatal wound.

The etiquette of dueling involved rules which varied from region to region and elaborate niceties of how to handle an insult and shoot with cold and formal courtesy. But there was a kind of consensus about the proprieties of the dueling field. They had been digested and systematized in what was known as the Irish Code of Honor. It was adopted at the Clonmel Assizes in 1777 after much serious deliberation on the part of the gentlemen of Tipperary, Galway, Mayo, Sligo and Rosscommon. The whole of this curious document appears as an appendix in Hamilton Cochran's *Noted American Duels and Hostile Encounters* (Philadelphia: c. 1963). Captain John Newland Maffit, later famous as a Confederate naval officer and blockade runner, recalling his midshipman's training on the *Constitution*, wrote "Young officers of the Navy seemed to fancy that their status in the service was not established until they had burnt powder under the rulings of the celebrated 'Tipperary Articles'—a copy of which could be found in the preface of every midshipman's journal."

Instances of the light touch are sparse in the annals of the deadly pastime, but one California meeting produced a state-wide chuckle. Senator William M. Gwin, a string-tie southerner and a forty-niner who sought political power rather than gold, quarreled with Representative J. W. McCorkle, another forty-niner and a Democratic member of the Thirty-second Congress. They ended up on the field of honor while Mrs. Gwin waited in desperate anxiety. Harnett T. Kane tells the story well of how a courier rode to her, like the messenger in a Greek drama, except that in this instance the news was not tragic:

"Ma'am, first fire's over. Nobody hurt!"

"Thanks be to God," exclaimed Mrs. Gwin, weeping. Then another herald arrived.

"Second fire, and they're both safe."

"Praised be," said Mrs. Gwin.

Again a horseman pulled up at the Gwin home with even better tidings.

"The third's over; nobody's hurt and they've called it off."

"That's good," said Mrs. Gwin. She was asked if she didn't think the news wonderful. She gave the man a quizzical look.

"Yes, but there's been some mighty poor shooting today."

One of the most colorful secondary figures in the history of the Old South was Cassius Marcellus Clay, a cousin of Henry Clay and, although a Kentuckian, a thorough-going abolitionist and unionist in Civil War days. Clay fought several duels in defense of his unpopular opinions, customarily carried a bowie knife and two pistols and at certain critical moments in a long and wildly turbulent life, fortified his home and office with a small cannon. Clay was a dead shot, could sever a string at ten paces three times out of five. In his first duel both Clay and his adversary fired three times, missed, and shook hands. Afterwards a friend asked Clay how he could have missed when he had this marvelous ability to cut a string with a bullet.

"The darned string had no pistol in its hand," he explained.

When Clay was ninety-three years old and legally adjudged to be out of his mind, the old man lay dying on a hot day while a large fly buzzed noisily on the bedroom ceiling. Deeply annoyed, the old fighter propped himself up in bed, took aim with his rifle, blasted a hole where the fly had been, and died.

Many duels were fought in the decade before the Civil War because of sectional politics, especially the issues arising from whether the new western states should be slave or free territory. The most sensational slaying which developed out of this background was that of Senator David C. Broderick, representing the northern wing of the Democratic party. Broderick died at the hand of a rabid southerner, David S. Terry, Chief Justice of the California Supreme Court. Terry had made contemptuous allusions to Broderick and the latter retracted the view he had previously held that Terry was an honest judge. The real issue was that Broderick was anathema to his colleague in the Senate, Senator Gwin, to President Buchanan and the whole southern wing of the party because he opposed a plan to admit Kansas into the Union under a proslavery constitution. In Washington the social boom had been lowered against Broderick by the President and by Senator and Mrs. Gwin, who moved in the circles of the "chivalry." Broderick was also down-graded because his father had been a stonemason who, as a matter of fact, helped to carve the capitals and pilasters that supported the roof of the Capitol.

When Judge Terry, who was an expert marksman, challenged the northern Democrat, it was widely believed that the chivalry had decided to do away with him and that Terry would make a good job of it. Broderick acceded to Terry's demand for "the satisfaction usual among gentlemen" and they met in the early morning of September 13, 1859, about six miles from San Francisco. The weapons were Belgian dueling pistols with hair triggers. One was defective, with a trigger so light a sudden motion would discharge it. Terry had practiced with the weapons and knew this. Broderick had the choice of ground, Terry picked the sound pistol. The distance was carefully marked off—ten paces. The code duello was read, the words "Fire!—One! Two!" But not the usual "Three!" Broderick's pistol discharged harmlessly into the ground as he started to lift his arm. Terry hit the Senator in the right breast and the mason's son who had accepted the gentleman's code, died by it.

Judge Terry was arrested, but the trial was repeatedly postponed. The district attorney finally moved to quash the case. The presiding judge, a southern sympathizer, promptly granted the motion. The consequences of this duel were disastrous for the California slavery element and for Terry who could never overcome the suspicion that he had triumphed by trickery. In 1869 he came to a miserable end. He struck Stephen Field, a Justice of the United States Supreme Court, coming up from behind his back, and a U. S. marshal gunned him to death.

In the northeastern states the idea wore thin that a personal slight called for the unlimbering of cannon, and public opinion ostracized not the man who refused a challenge but the one who issued it. Dueling had never taken hold in the central west. An occasion arose in which Lincoln made a travesty of the aristocratic code. He was later ashamed of the incident. When an army officer attending a reception at the Executive Mansion asked the President if what he had heard about Lincoln dueling was true, he got this answer: "I do not deny it, but if you desire my friendship, you will never mention it again." Mrs. Ruth Painter Randall, biographer of Mrs. Lincoln and widow of the late Lincoln scholar, J. G. Randall, calls this episode, a non-duel which took place on a sandbar in the Mississippi River, "Lincoln's most embarrassing moment."

In this potentially dangerous meeting, vigorously pumped up by inept hotheads, the comic spirit was present and triumphed. Here is the background. James A. Shields, Democratic State Auditor of Illinois, was an attractive bachelor, thirty-two years old, who came from Tyrone County, Ireland, where he had received a good classical education and instruction in sword play. His manners were ornate, which made him seem pompous, and his fiscal measures following the Panic of 1837 sent the Whigs ravening after his political scalp.

A series of four letters appeared in the *Sangamo Journal* of Springfield in August and September, 1842, discussing from the Whig point of view the current situation with regard to state bank paper, which Shields had ruled was not acceptable as a medium for the payment of taxes. In addition, Shields' manners, dress and the figure of somewhat exaggerated gallantry he cut in Springfield society, were throughly worked over. Lincoln wrote the second and most personal letter of the series. The first and third were, conjecturally, from the pen of Simeon Francis, editor of the newspaper. The fourth was the joint production of two merry young ladies of staunch Whig principles, Mary Todd and Julia Jayne, who later became the wives of Abraham Lincoln and Lyman Trumbull, U. S. Senator from Illinois. It is not unlikely that Lincoln saw these other effusions before publication and took at least a benevolent interest in their effectiveness.

In his own letter, Lincoln assumed the character of a backwoods wife, "Rebecca," It was a droll lampoon filled with humorous strokes. "Rebecca" reports how her neighbor, "Jeff," a Democratic farmer, insisted that Shields was a Whig because he smelled like one and, anyway, "Jeff" saw him strutting at a fair in Springfield last winter where "They wouldn't let no Democrats in for fear they'd disgust the ladies, or scare the little gals, or dirty the floor."

"All the gals about town was there," Lincoln wrote, "and all the handsome widows and married women, finickin' about trying to look like gals. . . . I looked in at the window, and there was this same fellow Shields floatin' about on the air, without heft or earthly substance, just like a lock of cat fur where cats had been fighting. . . ." Finally, "Jeff" exclaimed, "Shields is a fool as well as a liar. . . ."

Springfield "roared with laughter," according to A. J. Beveridge, the historian who gives the most detailed account of the Lincoln-Shields embroilment. Shields wrote a peremptory and menacing letter to Lincoln believing that Lincoln was responsible for all the letters as well as a "saucy jingle" which was printed after the letters. It celebrated in mock-heroic style the imaginary marriage of the fictional "Rebecca" and the angry state auditor. Shields challenged. Further communications flew back and forth. It is evident from the correspondence how Lincoln felt about dueling. A man representing Shields came to Lincoln and said that honor would have to be satisfied, adding: "As the challenged party you will have the choice of weapons—what will your weapons be?"

Lincoln is supposed to have replied:

"How about cow-dung at five paces?"

However, the preliminaries moved on toward a fight with cavalry broadswords. Dueling in Illinois was a prison offense. So the parties adjourned to a sandbar on the Missouri side of the Mississippi River, across from Alton, Illinois. The resolution of the controversy came when Lincoln acknowledged authorship of one letter, asserted it was written as a political, not a personal comment—a nice distinction!—and disclaimed the other efforts which held

Shields up to ridicule. Shields accepted the explanation and the combat was off.

A shooting scrape was not necessarily a duel. When a volley of shots rang out in the State Treasurer's office in the Georgia State Capitol in 1879 and gunsmoke eddied along the ceiling as Edward Cox and Robert A. Alston lay on the bloody floor, that was simply a gunfight without preliminaries or formalities. Its style was that of the southern stomp-and-gouge fighting in which two enemies roamed the town, expecting an encounter in the barbershop or barroom, each maneuvering to obtain an advantage over the other which would enable him to kill his opponent, as Professor Frank Lawrence Owsley has pointed out, "but which would not be so obvious as to turn public opinion against him or preclude the plea of self-defense." This is the kind of affray in which William Cowper Brann, Brann the Iconoclast, died on the streets of Waco, and of the shootings and stabbings of the mining and cowtowns of the West.

The shoot-out was not governed by written articles of agreement but, barring outright assassination, there were some ground rules which were understood and observed. They ran about like this: "Don't never shoot a man in the back. If you come a-gunnin', notify him proper. If he reaches for his artillery, then you got license to shoot." These were the minimal conditions which were observed when Jim Courtright, ex-marshal and "protector" of gambling in Fort Worth, called Luke Short, an honest gambler with no taste for paying for unneeded protection, out of the White Elephant saloon. Short appeared, thumbs in the arm holes of his vest, coat negligently unbuttoned. But when he dropped his hands to adjust his flowered vest—Luke was always a bit of the dandy—Courtright reached for his scabbard. Short slicked his Colt .45 out of an unique leather-lined hip pocket and got off five shots at point-blank range. Courtright's body pitched, oddly enough, into the door of a shooting gallery.

Instances of women dueling are rare as dust in March. There have been plenty of episodes involving ordinary barroom fighting, without rules of polite usage, recorded in the pages of the frontier press, usually reported with tongue in cheek as another "cat fight." The Dodge City *Democrat* said of such a battle, staged between Ollie Hart and Mollie Hart, "both, as we understand it, claim the right of possession to the heart and necessary appendages of their 'lover'. . . ." One reasonably well authenticated feminine duel did occur in Colorado, although even this incident is entwined in hearsay and legend. This much is known. Mattie Silks, who often pointed out "The girls who work for me are prostitutes but I am and always have been, a madame," and always insisted upon making the distinction, exchanged fire with Katie Fulton, also the operator of a commercial boudoir, over the affections of Mattie's knight.

The gentleman in dispute was Corteze D. Thompson, an accomplished hell-raiser. Professionally, if he could be said to have an occupation, Thompson was a foot-racer who "trained only on the choicest bourbon." His two admirers made a rendezvous in a cottonwood grove just beyond the authority of the Denver police, took their assigned positions and fired at the count of three. Neither was harmed but Cort was hit in the neck, unfortunately not fatally. Whether he was winged by intention or poor shooting has never been determined.

One resort to the code duello by women can be thoroughly documented. A tall, blonde Alsatian actress of no great distinction, Mlle. Marie Muller, who displayed her generous charms at the Théâtre Place Royal in Paris, decided it would be a profitable stunt to challenge the American star and leading sex symbol of the sixties, Adah Isaacs Menken, because, Marie or her press agent alleged, Adah had snatched one of her lovers. To make the challenge stick, Marie also slapped Miss Menken's face in front of the Hôtel Suez before a party of gentlemen. Mlle. Muller was suitably attired for the incident in a scarlet gown and feathered hat. She was obscure; it was all a put-up job. But Adah got her mad up and declared ". . . if she wishes a duel, she shall have one."

Two delighted English boys in top hats and tail coats and not long out of public school, represented Adah's interests, called upon Marie's seconds "with the mock dignity," says Paul Lewis, la Menken's biographer, "that the English achieve so well on such occasions." The boulevardiers licked their chops at the notion of two beautiful actresses hacking at each other, in the French fashion, with swords. But this was not to be. Miss Menken, as the challenged party, chose pistols under "the American code." This was interpreted as meaning that the principals would fire alternate shots until honor was satisfied. The affray was looked at askance by Adah's friends, as a comedy by the press, and the gendarmerie, who had no appetite for being made to look foolish, viewed the business with professional torpor.

The scene of the meeting was a clearing in a wood near Versailles. The well-advertised event was attended by bevies of ladies and their escorts fortified with hampers of food and wine who arrived in elegant carriages and high spirits. Marie looked bewitching in emerald green velvet and matching hat. She graciously gave the press every assistance they could ask for. Adah was so tardy as to raise the ugly suspicion that she had bugged out. But she came, bare-headed, without make-up. Her costume was a pair of old boots and worn breeches topped by a man's shirt. She told the reporters that she had nothing to say. Old Alexander Dumas, *père,* loaded the pistols, then asked formally if the ladies would be reconciled and embrace each other.

"My honor makes it impossible," Marie declaimed.

"No," said Miss Menken, shortly.

Adah gave Marie the first shot without bothering with the customary toss of a coin. Some of the men began to feel distinctly nervous. As they watched the caper they gained the distinct impression about Adah from the way she stood, the way she looked, her handling of her weapon, that she knew something about the use of a hand gun.

The two actresses, as instructed, stood back to back, then paced off fifteen steps, Marie swinging her hips, milking the audience. She turned, fired wildly into the ground in front of her, screamed and started to decamp, but was sharply commanded by the Menken seconds to stay where she was. Adah slowly raised her pistol, took deliberate aim.

"At that instant," wrote one of her seconds later, "I realized this was no charade."

The bullet went through Marie's hat, less than one inch from her temple. Adah apologized, promised to do better on the next exchange. But Mlle. Muller knew the jig was up, fainted, and when she recovered got out a faltering apology.

Marie Muller would not have been so bold, nor the French police so relaxed, if they had been familiar with a bit of American theatrical history. In May, 1862, Adah Menken was appearing at the Broadway Theatre in New York. The war had not been going well, although Admiral David G. Farragut had just captured New Orleans. Adah was a native of that city. The audience, in a peculiar mood, hissed when she appeared on stage and someone shouted "Hang the Reb!"

The next night Miss Menken walked on in her street clothes, declared that any man was a liar who questioned her loyalty to the United States and offered to fight "here and now, on this stage, with swords or pistols, as he prefers." There were no takers. But to back up her offer to duel, Miss Menken arranged for an exhibition of her proficiency with the pistol at the Bowery Academy. The verdict of the committee who inspected her targets after the shooting was that few sharpshooters in either the northern or southern armies could do as well.

Democracy, which eroded class distinctions; immigration, which made the United States the melting pot; the powerful middle class, which resented aristocrats immune to the consequences of an illegal act; a more sensitive public conscience—all these discrete influences had their part in the decline of dueling. The ounce of lead gave way to legal redress or a good punch in the nose. John S. Wise, Virginia lawyer and scion of a long line of duelists, who became adept with the foils as a little boy and learned to shoot with either hand at the silhouette of a man drawn on the garden wall, gave up personal combat in 1883. No one could question his courage when he inserted a "card" in the Richmond newspapers stating that the dueling code was uncivilized, illegal and foolish. He declared that he would abide by it no longer. Wise's resolve was a turning point in southern social history. There were no more duels in the Old Dominion.

Crusading editors had a reputation for carrying a pair of big horse pistols and being willing to back up their pungent comments on the field of honor. It was a man of this class, William N. Byers, a Denver publisher and champion of the regular processes of law, who notified potential challengers through his columns "You are wasting your time in sending us challenges. You may murder us but never on the so-called field of honor under the dignified title of a duel." The brilliant George D. Prentice, who acquired a towering reputation in Louisville, Kentucky, as an able and fearless journalist during the crises of the middle nineteenth century, rejected dueling as a "miserable code" requiring "two men to go out and shoot at one another for what one of them may consider a violation of etiquette or punctilio in the use of language."

An etiquette book issued in 1855 discussed seriously the methodology of demanding satisfaction for an insult and the ceremonious details of politely killing a man. Ten years later, in a booming industrial society which had no room for a medieval faith in adjudication by personal combat, a newly issued guide to good form informed its readers that the habits of good society no longer required familiarity with the politesse of murder at ten paces. But the pseudonymous author of *The Habits of Good Society* did suggest that it was handy to know how to box. To the extent that sectional attitudes toward dueling diverged as between the North and the South, the custom may be regarded as another "peculiar institution" along with slavery, whose elimination was necessary as a precondition of genuine national unity.

10

⫸⟦══════════════════⟧⫷

THE CYCLE OF THE BEARD

Politics, moral issues, religious polemics, sex and aesthetics clash or blend in the various choices men have made about wearing their hair and beards—long or short, natural, false or none at all.

The American Atlantic coast was explored and colonized by men who wore whiskers—Cabot, Champlain, the first Lord Baltimore, John Endecott with his soldierly "stiletto" beard. Edward Winslow wore a mustache and thick, pointed beard. In Virginia, Captain John Smith was full-bearded at the time of the Jamestown settlement. Dominie Everardus Bogardus, a mirror of fashion in New Amsterdam, who perished in the wreck of a Dutch ship on the coast of Wales near Swansea—an event piously characterized by John Winthrop as "the observable hand of God against the Dutch" —met his end full-bearded.

In the seventeenth century the western world was dominated by French fashions. When Louis XIII began to lose his hair, wigs were "in" and facial hair ceased to be à la mode. Wigs and whiskers together seemed to be too much of a good thing. In England Van

Dyck painted his aristocratic sitters with beard and ringlets falling shoulder-length, often with the lovelock, a long curl worn over the left shoulder, tied with a ribbon ending in a rosette. The barber-surgeons in the days of the Stuarts left only a tiny lip beard and mustache—the mustache a thin, mannered line, like that of a modern film star. The cascading ringlets and well-disciplined facial hair had political significance; they were associated with the principles of the court party. So the New England Puritans, being Parliament men, went "crop-headed." Yet often enough, among those who were not fanatic in their outlook, custom had its way. It would be inaccurate to say that all Puritans removed the hair from their faces or followed St. Paul where he says in First Corinthians, "Doth not even nature itself teach you, that, if a man have long hair, it is a shame unto him?"

The Airedale look comes and goes in long, swinging surges and recessions. Whiskers burst into bloom, then yield ground, disappear completely, persistently return again. The eighteenth century would have nothing to do with facial shrubbery. Gentlemen removed all hair from the face, clapped wigs upon their heads, then found it necessary to clip or shave the head, too. The first wigs were made of human hair, described by William Prynne, the English Puritan pamphleteer, in an angry little book, *The Unloveliness of Love-Lockes* (London: 1628), as "the hairie excrements of some other person. . . ." Such wigs were intended to look like the hair of the wearer. Later an artificial effect was deliberately cultivated, including a massive piling up of—horse hair.

French fashion ascendancy made the formidable "full bottomed" wig the vogue. This noble top-piece stood high over the brow in double peaks, parted in the middle with curls, sometimes powdered, falling to the shoulders. Indoors, the toupee was laid aside, the shorn head protected from the chills by a little skull cap or a turban. This style lasted for about a century.

Terming himself "the Wonder of the World, an honest Barber and Peruke-maker," John Still, late of London, arrived in New York in 1750 ready to supply wigs of all shapes and sorts. Among those he specified were "Tyes, Full-bottoms, Majors, Spencers, Foxtails, Ramalies, Tucks, cuts and bob Perukes, also Ladies Tatematongues and Towers after the manner that is now worn at Court." The tie wigs had a puff or roll over the ears, were succeeded again by natural hair, gathered behind, sometimes placed in a little bag or tied with a ribbon into a pig tail. But the hair was powdered so it would look like a wig. Powder, it was felt, flattered the face and hid gray hair.

In Revolutionary France, the National Assembly banned social distinction in dress. Short hair became the republican mode, crossed the Atlantic and was promptly adopted by the followers of Thomas Jefferson, eventually if reluctantly by tie-wig Federalists. It has been with us ever since. At the end of the eighteenth century Americans who were linked in sympathy with French radicalism wore neither wig nor queue. The United States Army surrendered its wigs in 1808. The Reverend John Marsh of Wethersfield, Connecticut, never gave in until his dying day which came in 1820. Marsh always put on a wig when he made the annual journey to Commencement at the College in Cambridge. For it was by the wig that the people knew him, bowed low along the route and saluted him with a respectful "How d'ye do, Dr. Marsh?" English portraiture and the illustrations in the literary histories of the Age of Enlightenment have made us familiar with the bewigged heads and uniformly smooth faces of Defoe, Swift, Steele, Pope, Dr. Johnson, Goldsmith, Sheridan and Burke. When the second Lord Rokeby (1713-1800) was the only peer of England to wear a beard, the people thought him mad.

An early leader in the new fashion in the American colonies was Sir William Berkeley, colonial Governor of Virginia. Although a man of the seventeenth century, he adopted the full shoulder wig and the smooth chin. William Randolph, Speaker of the Virginia House of Burgesses, shaved his face, deviated slightly in keeping his natural hair. George Washington and his generals couldn't muster a whisker among them. No Signer of the Declaration of Independence or the Constitution wore either a mustache or a beard with the possible exception of Edward Rutledge of South Carolina. Rutledge wore his hair unusually long and brushed forward over his forehead and cheeks so that the hair is visible in front of his ears. Whether this forward-thrusting hair should be considered a rudimentary beard or a part of his hair styling is a close technical question. But his chin and cheeks were clean-shaven.

No President of the United States before Lincoln wore a full beard or a mustache. The national symbol, Uncle Sam, was depicted without whiskers until about 1858. Dr. Franklin considered it an eccentricity that Keimer, his first employer in Philadelphia, insisted upon wearing a beard, and Elizabeth Drinker wrote in 1794 that she had seen an elephant and two bearded men on the streets of Philadelphia, curiosities which called for equal notice.

Small side-bars of hair began to become elongated early in the nineteenth century. U.S. naval officers in the War of 1812, men like Decatur and Perry, wore sideburns, but a half century had to pass before the luxuriant full beard shrouded the face of every respectable American citizen. In the 1840's the beard continued to be unpopular. When Andrew Jackson was President, the only mustaches seen in Washington were those of the foreign ministers and their suites. Louis Agassiz, the great naturalist, was clean-shaven, though he adopted side whiskers before his death in 1873. The ubiquitous "razor strop man" who peddled shaving requisites through the back country and the paintings of George Caleb Bingham delineating folk subjects demonstrate clearly that beards were scarce among farmers, artisans and the rough men out on the settlement line in the early 1850's. The nude chin continued its dominance in 1857 when *Harper's Weekly* made the waggish suggestion that New Yorkers were smooth-shaven because they didn't have the strength required to produce a beard—a consequence of their social habits which included too many cigars, midnight suppers and a distaste for exercise.

Exceptions always intrude to complicate neat generalizations. In July, 1843, Cadet Ambrose E. Burnside entered the United States Military Academy equipped with what came to be called later sideburns or "Burnsides," the short, bushy whiskers reaching from the hairline to below the ears, with smooth chin, which he continued to wear throughout his life. His whiskery panache is as likely to keep the General in the American pantheon as his services as soldier and statesman. Hamilton Fish and Walt Whitman were ahead of their day with wreath beards in the 1840's and Sam Houston, who grew a beard in times of great emotional stress, let his whiskers grow when his second wife was pressuring him to join the church. In contrast to these instances of vanguardism, however, are three resistant presidents of Harvard College. Although they lived well into the period when, as Lewis Gannett, leading pogonologist, has observed, "Beards were in the air," all clung to their eighteenth century look—Edward Everett, Cornelius Conway Felton and Jared Sparks. The latter did have tufts in front of his ears. This suggests that college presidents of a hundred years ago were cautious men, happier to be last than first.

If a man shaved himself, he required the do-it-yourself equipment offered for sale in 1801 by James Ingols in the *Hampshire Gazette* of Northampton, Massachusetts. "Improved Windsor Soap, peculiar for shaving and softening the skin . . . shaving boxes, Raizers." "I reckon it among my felicities," Benjamin Franklin once wrote, "that I can set my own razor and shave myself perfectly well; in which I have daily pleasure, and avoid the uneasiness one is sometimes obliged to suffer from the dirty fingers or bad breath of a slovenly barber." Neither halitosis nor sanitary procedures were mentioned by a barber who advertised in 1813. But he did make this poetical pitch for patronage:

No unbid tears adown the cheek will steal
No Torturing pain, his customers will feel.

A few of the virtuosi of the times shaved themselves or were barbered for six cents a shave; less if they hired the service on a quarterly basis. Some shaved twice a week. More usual was the once-a-week mowing of the bristles on Saturday or Sunday morning before church. The day of the week could be told with considerable accuracy by the length of men's beards.

The barbershop early achieved institutional importance, comparable to that of the livery stable or the village general store. Well-worn chairs lined the walls. A cigar case, cuspidors and the *Police Gazette* provided club comforts in an atmosphere of tobacco smoke, bay rum, witch hazel and hair tonic.

"Seen the *Police Gazette?*" runs the old joke.

"No, I shave myself."

The barbershop was the refuge of the male when the world was too much with him. The customers ogled the girls on the street and offered reminiscences of past gallantries, entertained themselves with democratic debate and rustic hoaxes. Barbershop quartets, although not specifically mentioned in the Bill of Rights, enjoyed the protection of the right of peaceable assembly, rendering in close harmony such period favorites as *Mandy* and *Dear Old Girl*. Privately owned shaving mugs of regular patrons, each emblazoned with a design representing the owner's occupation or lodge affiliation, stood in a rack along the wall. The decorative motifs represented, Professor Lewis W. Atherton has noted, "the only coat of arms which democracy permitted."

In the larger cities the barbershop interior was one of opulent pier mirrors, marble-topped stands, plush fittings. Political and business leaders met at the barbershop, enjoyed an intimate privacy while submitting to razor, scissors and comb. Thus, George A. Myers of Cleveland, Ohio, the Negro proprietor of what Elbert Hubbard called, "the best barber shop in America," knew Mark Hanna, James Ford Rhodes, iron master and later famous American historian, and eight U. S. Presidents who sat for Myers' ministrations. It was, said Dr. Harvey Cushing, "a mark of distinction to have one's insignia on a private shaving mug in George A. Myers' personal rack, and to receive his addresses, both intra- and extra-cephalic," referring to the barber's accepted status as sage and authority on eschatological subjects as well as stropping, trimming and the correct location of the part.

Various ingenious explanations have been advanced for the sudden mass phenomenon of beardedness. There was, as a possibility, the interest in the Great West and the influence of the gold diggings where a man found it difficult to shave regularly; the arrival of European liberals which made the beard a political badge; the example set by Abraham Lincoln; the soldiers' problems with shaving during the Civil War campaigns. There was an aesthetic factor. It was observed that mutton-chop whiskers filled out a thin face. Perhaps the beard was a part of the romantic return to nature, a rediscovery of the picturesque. In any event, the full beard typed the period of *Weltschmerz,* sentimental poetry, melancholy ballads arranged for the melodeon, graveyard urns and weeping willows. A full beard made a fat face seem leaner. A psychological hypothesis has been made that men turned to beards in unconscious protest against the restlessness of the New Woman. This was the time of deep popular involvement with the pseudo-science of phrenology, when the findings of the head-feelers had all the cachet attached to psychoanalysis in the middle of the present century. A luxuriant beard could serve in concealing a weak chin. How reasonable it was, then, in a generation which believed that the shape of the skull revealed character and aptitude, or their absence, to choose the prudent course and retire behind male plumage.

For whatever reason, around 1859 or 1860 American men switched to goatees, imperials, the spade, the box, the brush, the fan, the mutton chop, the sideburn, the full, flowing panoply of the patriarchal beard. President Pierce's Cabinet in 1853 possessed not a single beard. Buchanan's in 1857 contained only one, a spade worn by Aaron V. Brown. Lincoln and Douglas debated with clean-shaven faces. John Brown was shaved clean in 1858 but when he was hanged in '59 he wore a magnificent long Moses-style beard and the noose was adjusted in order to spare it.

So the United States went hairy on a national scale, the mountain men, the railroad builders—Huntington, Leland Stanford with his connected short beard, Hopkins and Crocker; the professors with Longfellow and Lowell, the theater with A. E. Sothern and his "Dundrearys"; and there was the pointed chin-tuft with mustache of Napoleon III, strongly favored by military figures like General Custer and William F. (Buffalo Bill) Cody. The young doctor raised a beard as soon as he emerged from the pest house. It quickly became an occupational badge, a sign of professional competence. Quacks affected the "doctor" beard, men like Dr. David Hostetter of Hostetter's Bitters and Dr. S. Andral Kilmer, who gave the world Autumn Leaf Extract for Females and the power-house laxative happily christened Prompt Parilla Pills. Bankers found that a respectable face-fringe was equated with probity. Outdoor men discovered the utility of long facial hair: the bearded man escapes sunburn. Economical men discovered another advantage: the full beard worn *au naturel* saved the cost of a necktie. The author of *The Illustrated Book of Manners* plunked for the full Santa Claus beard as against the topiary effects. The natural beard was, he said, "most comfortable, most healthful, most expressive, dignified and beautiful. . . . Nature gave man a beard for use and beauty. . . . The gods and heroes wear beards. . . ."

And so did the villains. In the copious literature about shop girls, there was always a seducer with mustache and side-whiskers. The plot also provided an honest clerk or bookkeeper who appeared in the nick of time to rescue the maiden in distress. He, too, was well-equipped with ornamental hair. "The heroine, by some method or other," wrote Edmund Pearson, who studied the sociology of the subject some years ago, "is able to differentiate the side-whiskers of infamy from the side-whiskers which are enlisted in behalf of the celestials."

Abraham Lincoln, who acquired his rounded beard with shaved upper lip and a patch below his mouth between the time he was nominated and elected, read the Emancipation Proclamation to a Cabinet who wore grandfather beards, except for two holdouts, Stanton and Seward. According to a charming story, Lincoln grew his beard because a bright and dedicated little girl named Grace Bedell who lived in Westfield, New York, wrote him a winsome letter. Grace urged that he would look better with a beard. "All the ladies like whiskers," she wrote, "and they would tease their husbands to vote for you and then you would be President." Lincoln answered the letter promptly in his own holograph suggesting gently to "My dear little Miss" that people might consider it an affectation if he started a beard "now."

Time passed and the train that carried Lincoln to Washington and his first inaugural stopped at Westfield to take on wood and water. The President-elect called out over the heads of the crowd for his little correspondent and she was led to the train platform. Lincoln stepped down, shook her hand and gave her a kiss as he said: "You see I let those whiskers grow for you, Grace."

The crowd cheered, the train whistled, then disappeared over the eastern horizon. Grace Bedell ran all the way home, looking neither to the right nor the left, ducking and dodging between horses and buggies, crawling under a wagon, speaking to no one. Alone in her room with her glory she looked down, saw in her hand the tattered remains of a bouquet of yellow musk roses. She had intended them for Mr. Lincoln.

The exchange of letters is an historic fact. Lincoln specialists have received with some skepticism the idea that the President did grow his beard because a little girl asked him to. There is no direct evidence either way. Lincoln never discussed his reasons with any-one for making this change in his appearance. Quite possibly he had determined to do it at the precise moment when Grace Bedell addressed him with the winning frankness of a clever child: "I have got 4 brothers and part of them will vote for you anyway and if you will let your whiskers grow I will try and get the rest of them to vote for you. . . ."

Ulysses S. Grant had the bushiest beard of all the Presidents, Hayes the longest. Grant's Cabinet was the hairiest in American history. This was the day of the beard triumphant. Periodicals were filled with advertisements promising a thick beard in six weeks. If white hairs appeared, gentlemen were urged to use Ayer's Hair Vigor or Buckingham's Dye for the whiskers.

Etiquette manuals introduced new rules for dining, directed at those who were inclined to snarf down their goodies. "Never allow butter, soup or other food to remain on your whiskers," said *Hill's Manual of Social and Business Forms* (1879), adding "Use the napkin frequently." Signs that the tide had passed the flood could be read in the political events of 1885 when beardless but heavily mustachioed Grover Cleveland defeated James G. Blaine for the Presidency, despite Blaine's full complement of whiskers, trimmed to a rounded point. Only one man with a beard was elected after that, Benjamin Harrison in 1889, and he failed to get a majority of the popular vote.

The Yale and Harvard football teams of the same year, the squads consisting of eleven and thirteen iron men, respectively, were beardless. The mustache score was a tie—5-5. In the decade of 1880-90 a small mustache was retained, as distinct from the record-breaking kind one Leonard Jerome developed at Hays City, Kansas. It had a wingspread of nine inches, tip to tip. In 1896 the American District Telegraph Company issued a decree forbidding its messenger boys, some of whom were pushing seventy-five, to wear any version of the hairy ornaments favored by convention since before Civil War days. Beards became not merely unfashionable, but sinister, a part of the cartoon stereotype of the anarchist, the wobblies and class warfare.

Explanations as numerous and far fetched have been advanced for the decline of whiskers as for their spectacular rise. Perhaps one influence was the male figure in the famous Charles Dana Gibson drawings, the clean-shaven, strong-chinned escort of the delectable Gibson Girl. The man, a Richard-Harding-Davis type, was obviously successful in both love and business since he was able to go courting in a dress suit. And then came Gillette, the safety-razor man. Gillette made the self-shave quick, easy and safe. Yet he was more beneficiary than prime cause. The turn had already come when King C. Gillette latched on to the idea of the disposable blade.

The beard tradition held on longest in the arts and among charlatans, showmen and promoters who found it useful in creating an impression. For more than forty years, the intense, professorial face of Sherman W. Cody, embellished with a splendid black beard, peered from the advertisements of the Sherman Cody School of English and asked an intriguing question: "Do you make these mistakes in English?" In 1961 the professor and his beard disappeared from the public prints. The answer lies not in any attitude of hostility toward beards but rather in the new, casual approach to the English language. It is no longer commercially profitable to try to whip up anxiety among those who say "Leave them lay there," or "Between you and I, Mary was invited as well as myself." So the bearded portrait of Cody, the old grammarian, was finally turned to the wall.

Yet a certain titillation clings to the subject of beardedness. Men who shave like to flirt with the idea of whiskers, betraying a suppressed desire for escape from banal uniformity. This yearning reveals itself in connection with retrospective events managed by local chambers of commerce. When Deadwood, South Dakota, re-creates the West, beards sprout again. When Hutchinson, Kansas, staged a grand Pow Wow on its seventy-fifth anniversary, two hundred and fifty patriotic citizens grew beards to mark the most spectacular event in Hutchinson history since the great grasshopper plague of 1874. Similarly, Northfield, Minnesota, reenacts annually the attempted bank robbery of the James-Younger gang in 1876 and does so in full whiskers, with beard-judging contests and a hot-rod show. Thousands of visitors come to dance in the streets and see the ear of Charlie Pitts, one of the robbers who was shot in a swamp, the ear removed and preserved by a physician with an unusual sense of history.

Another phenomenon, which may rise from the male unconscious, is the protest beard: "I won't shave until . . ." This is the spirit in which Jerome H. Taub, a New Jersey poultry raiser living near New Brunswick, vowed a few years ago to let his beard grow until the price of eggs went up; a project which, if he persevered in it, must have produced a beard rivaling that of Valentine Tapley of Frankford, Missouri, whose beard reached a length of twelve feet.

The late Ben Hecht, as a member of the working press in the early years of this century, learned the value of a beard in perking up a newspaper story when his boss instructed him to go to the Chicago Beach Hotel and interview a fellow named Wilhelm Stekel, who claimed to be a professor from Vienna and "the colleague of somebody named Sid or Sam Freud. . . . Ever hear of anybody named Frood or Freud?"

The question was asked by the city desk of the Chicago newspaper Hecht worked for. He didn't recall the name either but he got the assignment.

"Ask him what the hell psychoanalyzation is. There may be a little feature story in it. And don't forget to notice if our boy has a beard," concluded the man giving out the day's assignments.

As the *Doktor* talked to young Hecht, the latter heard "the first trumpet peals of the Freudian conquest," from a man with a splendid Van Dyke. That day's work helped Hecht to formulate a valuable journalistic maxim: a beard always belongs in the lead.

How do women who have no personal history of hypertrichosis feel about beards? This is an important question since in the United States aesthetic values are determined by women. The testimony is conflicting. For the negative we have Beatrice in *Much Ado About Nothing:* "Lord, I could not endure a husband with a beard on his face. I had rather lie in the woolen." On the other side stands the regal, beauteous Miss Julia Gardiner, of the pedigreed New York Gardiners, who as the celebrated "Rose of Long Island" and future bride of President Tyler, promenaded at a White House reception on the arm of Colonel Thomas Sumter, whom she described as being "sumptuously equipped—whiskers brushed to a turn—[in] a dashing vest of black velvet." Havelock Ellis has said in the language of the scientist that the beard is a prominent indication of virility and sexual allurement. The same idea about the male's most noticeable secondary sexual characteristic has been expressed in a more natural idiom by a bearded man of letters, the late Ernest Boyd, who declared, "Blondes go for them."

Watchers who scan the horizon for signs of social change are always announcing, prematurely so far, the return of the beard. It is doubtful, however, if the Civil War Centennial celebrations have produced anything more than temporarily bearded soldiers. Despite the wide influence of fascinating, bearded Peter Ustinov or Mitch Miller or the littérateur Rex Stout, who strongly favors self-expression in this matter, most men when tempted think of Fidel Castro, of the ordeal of dining out while growing a beard, of cornball jokes, of fleas and fire hazards—and decide to pass up the oriflamme. Even Ustinov, who has worn a beard since 1956, concedes that risks are involved. "A man who eats carelessly should not grow a beard," he has said, "as he may find himself pursued by pigeons." In non-bohemian circles, a feathered face remains a social and economic liability. An Assyrian spade beard may be dandy for Al Hirschfeld, the caricaturist. But if a bristly bank teller appeared for work looking as though he spent his nights in an old bingo parlor called The Place, his boss would undoubtedly start auditing the books.

Institutions of higher learning seem to take a dim view of whiskers. A Seton Hall University senior was given the choice of keeping his scholarship or his beard, which was ruled by the authorities of the South Orange, New Jersey, institution to be incompatible with "university dignity." He chose the scholarship. A University of Pennsylvania student, Bruce Dern, proved to be made of sterner stuff. Dern, a promising runner on the Penn two-mile relay team, and grandson of the Secretary of War in Franklin D. Roosevelt's first Cabinet, turned in his suit rather than obey an order to shave off his sideburns, which the coach regarded as non-ivy.

"It doesn't make you a hoodlum," Derm said earnestly if ungrammatically, "just by wearing sideburns."

Alexander Bisset took vigilante action under similar circumstances. When he was a junior at Colorado School of Mines at Golden, Bisset was reported as standing on the old western tradition of the right of self-defense. Faced with an order from the seniors that all underclassmen were to display bare cheeks, Bisset got off four shots from a hand gun in defense of his beard, seriously wounding one senior. In 1963, General Francisco Martinez Peralta, head of Mexico City's traffic police, issued a shave-it-off order. Ten indignant policemen went to court, filed an injunction to set aside the order. A federal judge granted it. And in the same year, a vintage one for pogonophobia, a teacher of political science at Pasadena, California, achieved national prominence when he went to court to uphold the tradition of Lincoln, Walt Whitman and Santa Claus. Told to remove his hirsute ornamentation by the principal of the John Muir High School under a regulation that required teachers to "practice the common social amenities," Paul S. Finot, who wears a Van Dyke and sideburns too, pointed in vain to a bust of John Muir that stood in the foyer of the building named in his honor. The naturalist and famous explorer wore a beard.

The beard of the Prophet is sacred in the Moslem world; but no less so is the facial hair of Jefferson Davis in the Old Confederacy. The United Daughters of the Confederacy stand guard *semper fidelis* over a lock of President Davis' hair. These historic filaments repose today under tight security at "Beauvior," the Davis shrine on U.S. 90, midway between Biloxi and Gulfport, Mississippi. Another fibril structure, a Davis whisker, which a wily traveling salesman once sold to a Confederate veteran, also rests in the vault of the library-house at the University of Kentucky.

"Yes, we have a capillary appendage alleged to be from the

beard of Jeff Davis," the Keeper of the Whisker, Lawrence S. Thompson, wrote recently to an inquirer. "In December, 1951, I bought a beautifully tooled case in Istanbul with two or three enclosed cases, the last one supposedly embalming one of Mohammed's whiskers. We preserve both reliques, but we do not vouch for their authenticity. I think the latter is a cat hair."

For the man who has everything except hair on his face, and prefers the appearance rather than the reality, a shop on the Champs Élysées may herald a new swing in the mode whereby a man may shave and have his mustache too. It offers a false mustache made of genuine human hair in three different shades and styles, the "Guardsman," the "Toothbrush" and the "Dali." A British magazine goes even further. *The Tailor and Cutter* visualizes the well-dressed man as possessing a whole wardrobe of false beards as a sort of virility symbol, to counter the Freudian notion, no doubt, that shaving is part of the castration complex, the desire of the male to effeminize himself. The idea of removable human vibrissa has come into the news here in an odd connection. Two bandits wearing white trench coats and false beards snatched a payroll of the Ball Export Packing Co., Inc., in New York, and warned the clerk-typist as they left, in authentic beatnik prose, "Don't call the fuzz."

Of one thing we may be sure. There are deep subterranean currents in the human psyche which move men at divers times to become barbate. Beards are definitely cyclical. Eighty years have now passed since bearded James G. Blaine went down to political defeat. Who wears the beards today? *Young* men. It may be later than you think.

11

THE GELDED AGE

During the last half of the nineteenth century the comfortable middle class in the United States seemed to have found all the answers. Revealed religion pointed the way to what was right and what was wrong, while the traditional American faith in progress gave assurance that the world was moving in the right direction. Such maladjustments as came to notice were regrettable but unavoidable and were recognized as a mysterious part of "God's own plan." Social justice consisted of sending turkeys to the poor at Thanksgiving time. Edward Everett typed the gentility of the period in draping his copy of the Apollo Belvedere; and when Miss Fredrika Bremer approached the piano to demonstrate a point about Swedish music Mr. Emerson forbade it:

"No, Miss Bremer, this is Massachusetts, and Sunday evening! I can't have it!"

The full-blooded generation which lived bodaciously before the Civil War, recited with gusto the barrack room ballads of the time, laughed at "Sugartail's" account of a "knob dance" in the mountains of Tennessee, took no offense at Henry Clay Lewis' ribald sketch, "Cupping on the Sternum," based upon a fledgling medical student's misunderstanding of the location of the sternum. After the War new recruits joined the polite world bringing with them an anguished uncertainty about social bench marks and a great eagerness to conform. The word which expressed the banal aspirations of the epoch was "genteel."

Now used by the educated classes playfully or in a derogatory sense, genteel first appeared in the seventeenth century as an English adaptation of the French *gentil*. Then in good repute, the term referred to persons of cultivation or good breeding; as when Cotton Mather said that the colony of New Haven was governed by holy, prudent and "genteel" men. In a long descent genteel passed through the sense of outward polish to hit bottom by the 1830's as a catchword for whatever was à la mode. When Mrs. Samuel Harrison Smith, wife of the publisher of the *National Intelligencer and Washington Advertiser,* wished to honor Miss Harriet Martineau, she called in a fashionable caterer and asked him to plan "a small, genteel dinner." His suggestions were so elaborate that she reminded him that she was not a Secretary's lady. What was wrong with having some ordinary vegetables on the menu, like potatoes and cauliflower? "Why, ma'am," he objected, "they will not be genteel," and went on to explain that pies and plum puddings were definitely out of style while nuts, raisins and figs "are quite vulgar."

An excessive refinement introduced a parlor culture which avoided all that it was inconvenient to observe. The result was an era of unparalleled dullness. E. L. Godkin called it "a chromo civilization." There was something about being complacent over one's racial, social and religious circumstances, while toying with aesthetic values, which produced a delicacy lapsing easily into a denial of the life of the senses and of the natural man. Mr. and Mrs. William Hunter Kendal of the stage were especially approved of when they performed in Shakespeare's comedies because they were husband and wife and so the "embarrassment" of the courting scenes was avoided. Authors arranged their plot sequences so that such an indecency as birth took place between the chapters; and when Charles Brockden Brown alluded to an illegitimate pregnancy, he wrapped it up in periphrasis:

"My companion's situation now appeared such, as, if our intercourse had been sanctioned by wedlock, would have been regarded with delight."

The Victorians set up standards for what men and women should be and developed ingenious means for stimulating the desired characteristics. The man of substance, whose ample residence was set on a generous plot surrounded by an ornamental iron fence, its lawn adorned with an iron stag, was an impressive social figure. With whiskers well combed, he appeared in public in a swallow-tailed coat and starched shirt, carried such impedimenta as a cigar cutter, a gold toothpick in its own little case and a heavy gold watch chain draped across an ample "corporation." The romanticism of the domestic architecture provided a becoming background for ladies with flirty fans and tiny parasols. They cultivated the wedding-ring waist, sublimated their brains and their bodies, played the ivy to their husbands' oak. Fainting came easily as almost the only form of pleasurable exhibitionism through which a woman of position could express her humours.

The practice and appreciation of the arts was associated either with melancholy or poor health. Sylvester Graham, the propagandist of the vegetarian diet, wrote lachrymose poetry seated at the door of the Public Tomb in Northampton, Massachusetts. In his verses the decaying vegetables of an October garden suggested, by an insensitive metaphor, the vanity and brevity of human life. Gerty, the long-suffering heroine of Maria Cummings' popular novel, *The Lamplighter,* shared Dr. Graham's partiality for lugubrious meditations. She spent her happiest hours, smiling through the tears, in a cemetery. Every village had, it seemed, an authoress who supplied tales and poems of sensibility to the local press. Those dove-eyed darlings who were less gifted painted on velvet, copied verses into albums, picked out pathetic refrains on the rosewood piano, such as "Whisper Softly, Mother's Dying." Magazines of polite literature, for example the *Ladies' Visitor* of Boston, assured the reading public that their pages were closed to "politics and obscenity"—an interesting association of ideas—or anything "which might cause the crimson fluid to stain the cheek of unaffected modesty."

Women were females and expressly called that as though to draw attention as prominently as possible to their biological functions. The students of Louisville Female College, to cite a convenient example, published a monthly paper, *The Female Student.* "Never call me a female," Margaret Fuller sternly instructed a correspond-

The arm of the law reaches for the Tiger on the Tandem. The scene was captioned when it first appeared in print, "The Speed Limit—a Last Warning." Note the expressions on the faces of the other wheelers.

These cautions as to musical manners for the gifted amateur are both timely and timeless. Never exhibit anxiety to sing or play. Don't attempt something beyond your skill and above all don't overstay your welcome.

The song cover (left), dating from 1915, indicates that the newspaper expert on doing The Right Thing was already a fixture on the national scene as a guide to social success and personal happiness.

The cotillion was a sprightly square dance of the eighteenth century, based upon an elaborate series of steps and frequent change of partners. The polka took over in the middle years of the next century. The *New York Herald* declared that it had vulgarized American fashionable life and Queen Victoria forbade the dance when she was present.

If a gentleman joined a lady of his acquaintance on the street in the 1880's he of course threw his cigar away. But customs change and we change with them. Groucho Marx, for one, is not a man to discard an expensive cigar, even when dancing with Kathryn Murray.

The costumes *(above)* are of another era but the manners of the show-off are very familiar. *(Below)*, the indomitable American tourist who takes his culture and flag with him when he ventures abroad is delineated by the gently satirical pen of the late John T. McCutcheon as he watched his countrymen scalp the Alps.

The Landauer Collection, The New-York Historical Society

The hasty engorgement of indigestible meals by Americans was rated a national trait as far back as stage-coach-and-steamboat days. The gulp-and-run dining continued in the bedlam of railroad lunch rooms where sweating waiters bawled out code words to the short-order cook: "two ship-wrecked" (two eggs over) ; "soaked bums" (pickled beets) ; or "one in the dark" (coffee without milk) . While they "slung the hash" the customers scraped, dunked, sopped and were still struggling with their food as they sprinted for the steam cars.

Handwriting can be a useful social indicator *(left)*, making it known in a well-bred, understated way that a young woman has a good family background and attended a proper school.

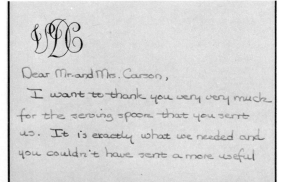

Dear Mr. and Mrs. Carson,

I want to thank you very very much for the serving spoon that you sent us. It is exactly what we needed and you couldn't have sent a more useful

From the author's collection

"Hello"

From the earliest days of telephony, "Mother Bell" and all the companies in the chatter business have spent millions of dollars teaching the principles of courtesy. Speak in a low voice, directly into the mouthpiece. Identify yourself. Be attentive. Sound interested. Don't interrupt. Put the instrument down gently, without slamming. In sum, phone as you would be phoned to. The industry's stake in courtesy: Impolite Americans tie up expensive equipment, and *time is money*.

There was Bridget in the kitchen of a well-ordered New York brownstone, and on the parlor floor a fresh arrival from Ireland who resisted fiercely the cap and uniform of domestic servitude. Upstairs, Nana "knew her place" which was a frigid little room with a china bowl and pitcher of cold water for the amenities. But there was great rejoicing in Nana's cubicle up under the cornice caves when her wages were increased to $18 a month, from $17. And at the end of ten years she received in addition the material for making a black silk dress.

ETIQUETTE.

MR. HOLWORTHY.—" Is Miss Roseleaf at home?"

RECENTLY ACQUIRED TREASURE, (who has been carefully instructed in regard to callers.)—" Yis; but I can't let ye up stairs till ye've put ye'r name in the dish."

In the days of the humble nickelodeon and the plush ten-cent cinema palaces, the audiences of recently-arrived immigrants, as well as native sons and daughters, were introduced to American styles and fantasies, advertising, film previews, popular music, speech patterns and standards of behavior through graphic messages thrown on the screen "while the operator changes the reels."

Bertha Honoré Palmer, wife of Potter Palmer, Chicago merchant prince and real estate figure, was the unquestioned social leader of the Second City in the 1890's and early years of the present century, ruling her demesne from a stately pleasure dome at 1350 Lake Shore Drive. As a member also of what would now be called the International Set, Mrs. Palmer maintained a social position in Europe, too, and counted among her brilliant successes playing hostess to the Prince of Wales (Edward VII) at the Palmer ranch in Wyoming. A less happy event occurred at the ranch when Mrs. Palmer unwittingly received Mattie Silks, a madam from Denver's notorious Holladay Street. Mattie turned up incognito as the blonde and beauteous traveling companion of a railroad president. "I showed those Newport society dames I was as good as any of 'em," Mattie declared later. "But not a one of 'em could make the grade as a boarder in my parlor house."

The mountain women of Appalachia once puffed at their cob pipes, and "fast" women such as actresses essayed the Turkish cigarette. The older generation still recalls the famous but cautious advertisement of the 1920's *(below)* in which a girl who looked to be every inch a lady beseeched her male companion to "blow some my way." Today the Cigar Institute, Inc., boldly asks: "If a man enjoys smoking a cigar, why shouldn't a woman?" The new etiquette: A gentleman should always offer his lady fair a cigar before lighting his own.

Cigar Institute of America

Pictorial Review, February, 1931

"You Didn't Say a Single Word All Evening"

"HOW could I? I didn't even know what they were talking about."

"Well, Ralph, I wouldn't brag about that."

"But how was I supposed to know that they were going to talk literature and art? If they had discussed real estate, I could have chatted with them easily—all evening. . . ."

"Business, always business! If you were a big enough real estate man you'd know how to forget business and talk of other things in company!"

"I never felt so uncomfortable in my life," he said ruefully. "Couldn't even follow the drift of things. What was all the discussion about some poet who was killed in the war?"

"Really, Ralph—you should keep more abreast of things. I was surprised that you didn't contribute at least one idea or opinion to the whole evening's discussion."

He turned to her, curiosity and admiration mingling in his smile. "You were certainly a shining light tonight, Peg! You made up for me, all right. Where did you ever find out all those interesting things?"

Many Wives are Keeping Pace with Successful Husbands —This Pleasant Way

Peg was grateful for her husband's praise.

But, instead of answering his question, she smiled enigmatically.

He moved closer, glad to have diverted attention from himself. "You were the prettiest and cleverest woman at that dinner, dear!" he said.

"Just for that," she beamed, "I'm going to tell you why I was able to join in the conversation tonight—and you were not."

"Oh, that's easy," he said, man-like. "You get more time to read than I do."

"Is that so!" she retorted. "I don't get the chance to read a good book from one month to the next. But I've solved *that* problem. I have a copy of Elbert Hubbard's Scrap Book."

"What's that?"

"It's a whole library condensed into one fascinating scrap book. It contains only the best thoughts of the best minds of the last four thousand years—the 'high lights', you know."

"That sounds interesting. Tell me more about it."

The Famous Elbert Hubbard Scrap Book

By the time they reached home, she had told him all about the unique Scrap Book. How Elbert Hubbard, many-sided genius, began it in youth and kept it throughout life. How he added only the choicest bits of inspiration and wisdom—the ideas that helped him most—the greatest thoughts of the greatest men of all ages. How the Scrap Book grew and became Hubbard's chief source of ideas—how it became a priceless collection of little masterpieces—how, at the time of his death, it represented a whole lifetime of discriminating reading.

"Imagine it! This Scrap Book has now been published and anyone can have a copy. Do you know what that means? You can get in a few minutes' pleasant reading each evening what it took Elbert Hubbard a whole lifetime to collect! You can get at a glance what Hubbard had to read days and days to find. You can have the finest thoughts of the last four thousand years in one wonderful volume. If you read in the Scrap Book occasionally, you'll never be uncomfortable in company again. You'll be able to talk as intelligently as any one."

May We Send It to You for FREE Examination?

The Elbert Hubbard Scrap Book radiates inspiration from every page. It contains ideas, thoughts, passages, excerpts, poems, epigrams—selected from the master thinkers of all ages. It represents the *best* of a lifetime of discriminating reading, contains choice selections from 500 great writers. *There is not a commonplace sentence in the whole volume.*

This Scrap Book is a fine example of Roycroft book-making. The type is set Venetian style—a page within a page—printed in two colors on fine tinted book paper. Bound scrap-book style and tied with linen tape.

Examine it at our expense! The coupon entitles you to the special five-day examination—if you act at once. Just send off the coupon today, and the famous Elbert Hubbard Scrap Book will go forward to you promptly. When it arrives, glance through it. If you aren't inspired, enchanted—simply return the Scrap Book within the five-day period and the examination will have cost you nothing. Otherwise send only $2.90, plus few cents postage, in *full payment.*

We urge you to act now. We want you to *see* the Scrap Book, to judge it for yourself. Mail this coupon TODAY to Wm. H. Wise & Co., Roycroft Distributors, Dept. 331, 50 West 47th Street, New York City.

How to talk interestingly has long been recognized as a part of the human predicament. But the owner of Elbert Hubbard's Scrap Book, it was promised, would astound the wits and highbrows and become Assistant District Sales Manager of a nail and screw corporation.

ent. But the odious word was used everywhere. Rufus Wilmot Griswold, the anthologist, published *The Female Poets of America* (1848 and after). Genesee Wesleyan Seminary had its Female Department. The wide currency of the word may have expressed an unconscious form of male subversion designed to keep women under control in their allotted sphere of wife, mother or impecunious spinster relative so useful in connection with mending and unpaid baby-sitting.

Mrs. Sarah Josepha Hale, editor of the important *Godey's Lady's Book,* found the term "female" as objectionable as did Margaret Fuller. When Mrs. Hale's friend, Matthew Vassar, wrote to her from Poughkeepsie, New York, on the stationery of the college he had endowed, Vassar Female College, he always tactfully drew his pen through the word in the title which he knew offended her with its suggestion that women were something less than full partners in the human race. Later the degrading word was removed from the name of the college by legislative action and from the façade of Main Hall by vote of the college trustees, leaving an empty space which aroused much curiosity. The marble slab bearing the repugnant word was dumped in a swamp on the Vassar farm and disappeared from human view.

A major theme of a vast Niagara of patent medicine advertising was addressed to a pathological condition known as "female weakness." Under this catchall phrase was gathered all the ills of feminine physiology, especially of the reproductive apparatus. In language of Elizabethan frankness, this propaganda advanced the idea that women were poor biological specimens to begin with and that, in some way not altogether clear, they had experienced a further decline due to higher education and the brutality of men. The recurring suggestion of a Camillian fragility seems to have had definite erotic overtones. Some of the most mendacious advertisements, incidentally, appeared for years in the religious press. Even Miss Catherine Beecher, of the celebrated New England Beechers, who labored so long and fruitfully for the higher education of women, fell into the prevailing mode of thought about woman's inferior biological inheritance, conceded that the health of Vassar girls often broke under the weight of a curriculum competitive with that of the men's colleges plus what she termed the "excitements so frequent at Vassar." And she criticized the faculty sharply for keeping the girls so busy they had no time to do their hair.

Humorists and satirists discussed "the Girl of the Period" as a topic of unflagging interest. She was said to be scheming, cold-hearted, frivolous. And she laced. An outraged dairy farmer sitting in the Wisconsin legislature, Assemblyman Henry L. Daggett, from Bear Creek, shocked at what the women were doing to the thoracic cage, tried to organize the friends of natural waists behind an anti-corset resolution which he introduced. Daggett's colleagues refused to take the crusade seriously, referred his resolution successively to the Committee on Public Health, the Committee of Agriculture and the Committee on Public Improvements. The Bear Creek statesman went down to defeat in the next election under the crushing nickname of "Corset" Daggett.

Woman was, of course, what the times made of her. Her intelligence, the skills of the previous century, were not in demand. Supported increasingly by the factory economy, the well-placed matron had at her disposal an abundant and cheap supply of hired help to wash, iron, clean and prepare—although not very well—the overpowering dinners which put on the pounds. The woman who earned her living lost her standing as a lady. The assigned role of the woman of some social station was to stay at home where she never, in the old phrase, lifted a finger. Yet she incurred censure if she was idle. So she kept busy with her sewing and china painting, achieved social approval for her industry, provided that it was directed to a useless objective.

"Nice" women packed barrels for the foreign missions, which gave them a fleeting, tantalizing contact with exotic peoples whose women lived a carefree life without multiple petticoats, japanned trays and acres of doilies. So many instances of false delicacy and outright pruriency occur in the Gilded Age that one might fairly call it the Gelded Age for its determination to emasculate the language. Yet the Girl of the Period exposed an extraordinary knack for finding double meanings in the commonest expressions, judging from the frequency with which she was warned against the practice.

James Laver, a British expert on Victoriana, has defined the repressions of the age as "a psychological device for keeping up the temperature of eroticism in cold climates." Interest has always tended to shift around as to what constituted an erogenous zone. In the early 1800's it was definitely the elbow. Who would have thought that joints could be so exciting? The pleasure which gentlemen took in observing the bosom in its natural development, moved one authority on decorum of the sixties to grant his fair readers this indulgence: "If Nature has not bestowed the . . . budding form, let art supply the deficiency," but, he insisted, "with caution and moderation."

Although it was considered indelicate for ladies and gentlemen to sit down together on the grass, Mrs. Trollope overheard a merry colloquy between a young man and a girl who was making an undershirt, their badinage filled with indecorous overtones. He teased her to tell him what she was making, an article so intimate that it could not even be named. Both understood this very well and were convulsed with laughter. One is reminded of Swift's biting line: "The nicest people have the nastiest ideas."

A famous instance of prudery in action during the Gelded Age was the publication by Mrs. Nathaniel Hawthorne after her husband's death of the *American Notebooks,* which she cleaned up in accordance with her ideas of propriety. Passages relating to sex were pruned or omitted entirely. Two rather luxurious descriptions of bosoms got the ax. A man's "animal desires" became his "temperament." Some eighteenth century church records which Hawthorne had transcribed were cut out, probably because of references to fornication and seven-months' babies. Bellies became bodies, backsides was softened to rear. Mrs. Hawthorne also excised references to phases of life which she considered unpleasant—the extraction of a tooth by a rural dentist, the novelist's observations upon the corpse of a girl who had been drowned. For the sake of social elegance filthy became dirty, sick was changed to ill. A smell was, of course, an odor. *Went to bed* was crossed out in favor of the affectation of *retired*. Where Hawthorne had referred to a social inferior as "Amasa Richardson," Mrs. H. moved poor Richardson down the scale still farther by writing into the manuscript, "the man Amasa Richardson." Completely eliminated were such interesting details as the fact that Hawthorne smoked cigars, liked to take a drink and had a zest for observing and mingling with ordinary humanity in the places where people were to be met with—in railroad stations, inns and the public rooms of the Parker House in Boston.

Even in the backwoods of the Old Southwest, once the source of coarse humor, hearty and unashamed, an astonishing system of verbal taboos arose under which the names of male animals could not be mentioned in the presence of women. This made it necessary for an Ozark preacher to tell his congregation that Pharaoh's daughter found Moses in the *flags*. A stallion became a *stable-horse*. *Bitch* was avoided altogether. *Parts* acquired an obscene implication and poultry were categorized as *girl-birds* and *boy-birds,* while the word *peacock* was not said at all. It must have been quite inconvenient, especially if one owned a flock of peacocks. Mrs. Trollope expressed the shrewd suspicion that "this ultra-refinement was not very deep-seated." It occurred to her, indeed, that the ladies who were "ready to faint at the idea of a statue," were really guilty of a not very well-veiled grossness. She was much astonished when she visited the gallery of antique sculpture at the Pennsylvania Academy of Fine Arts to have an old crone, who appeared to be connected with the staff, bustle up to her and whisper:

"Now, ma'am, now: this is just the time for you—nobody can see you—make haste."

The custodian explained, to Mrs. Trollope's astonishment, that there would be no gentlemen watching and that it was the custom to separate the sexes before admitting visitors to the room. In the age of the draped ankle, the unclothed body was obviously too much to take in mixed company. At the Corcoran Gallery in Washington, mothers nervously hurried their daughters past Hiram Powers' literal nude, "The Greek Slave." When the Diana of Augustus Saint-Gaudens was placed on the tower over Madison Square Garden in New York in the autumn of 1891—not on the old Madison Square Garden, but the *old,* old Garden—she immediately became a subject of controversy upon the score of indecency. Envious models gossiped around town about the identity of the goddess' human counterpart, as though Dianas were as thick as huckleberries, until the professional beauty who had posed for the sculpture became genuinely annoyed. She was Miss Julia—"Dudie" —Baird who received three dollars a day from "serious workers" and scorned the society fellows who were always talking about having lunch or a quiet little supper.

"I'm the Diana of the Garden," she stated flatly. "Did I object to posing for Mr. Saint-Gaudens. . . . Not at all. I have often posed for artists in the 'toot and scramble,' if you choose to call it that."

At almost the same moment there was an uproar of a similar sort in Boston. A bronze sculpture was at the center of the hurricane, the "Bacchante and Child" of Frederick MacMonnies. In what appeared to some prominent Bostonians to be an attempt on the part

of wicked New York to undermine the morals of the youth of the
Hub, Charles Follen McKim, the New York architect who had designed the Boston Public Library, wished to give a fountain for the
Library's courtyard as a memorial to his wife. His offer of a statue
by the distinguished MacMonnies was gratefully received and accepted. Then the acceptance was rescinded in haste and with considerable acrimony when it was discovered that the half-dancing
classical figure held a bunch of grapes in her left hand high above
her head, while a naked child gazed with considerable interest at
the grapes. A committee of the most respectable and genteel men
of Boston, including Charles Eliot Norton, a weighty man where
aesthetic and moral judgments were concerned, looked, shuddered
and reported to the Library trustees that the woman of the sculpture was in the barrel and furthermore her clothes had been stolen.
Even the extraneous question of the identity of the model in-
truded itself. Other cities laughed. The *New York Sun* observed
that bacchantes always cast off their clothing in the good old days
when there were bacchantes and remarked unkindly of Bostonians: "Some of them are very wicked; but they are not joyful in
their wickedness." The *Boston Globe*, wincing under the unfavor-
able press the city was getting, suggested whimsically that the Library settle for a statue of a Sunday School teacher. But the preach-
ers, who clearly favored dumping the statue where the patriots had
buried the tea in 1773, carried the day with the help of the
Woman's Christian Temperance Union, the Y.M.C.A., the
Y.W.C.A., the Massachusetts Kings' Daughters and Sons, the old
reliable Watch and Ward Society, the Law and Order League and
the Bethel Total Abstinence League. Erect a memorial, if you
please, cried the Reverend James B. Brady, to Benedict Arnold,
John Wilkes Booth or the luscious and notorious Josie Mansfield,
but do not place this arrant hussy on a pedestal! The Library trustees buckled under the heat, McKim withdrew the gift in disgust
and the original was promptly accepted by the Metropolitan Museum of Art in New York. Today, the times having changed somewhat even in Boston, a replica may be seen in the courtyard of the
Museum of Fine Arts in Boston, enclosed by the Decorative Arts
Wing on Huntington Avenue. And in the Sheraton-Plaza Hotel in
Copley Square one may buy today a box of cigars named Bacchante
Longfellows, ornamented with a lithographic reproduction of the
insouciant statue.

The theory that the true function of art was to strengthen the moral fiber of the people had long held sway in Boston, for back in the 1820's when Hiram Powers' "Chanting Cherubs" was exhibited there it was deemed necessary to put the cherubs in pants, a treatment similar to that accorded at about the same time to the *parts* of a visiting orangutan. But the practice of this kind of delicacy—or should one say, indelicacy?—was quite general. "The Greek Slave" was exhibited in Cincinnati dressed in a calico blouse and flannel drawers. The A. T. Stewart department store in New York was denounced for displaying corsets in its show windows, and Captain Marryat claimed personally to have seen a square piano in the reception room of a seminary for young ladies whose *limbs,* the piano's limbs, were dressed up "in modest little trousers, with frills at the bottom of them!"

When the parlor was fading out, but the living room had not yet arrived, the room for general family living, whatever its name, was filled with bric-a-brac and art objects collected to enhance social prestige. The story may be entirely apocryphal that Mrs. Potter Palmer, wife of the Chicago multimillionaire, once explained, "People of our position would naturally be expected to have a Corot." But circumstantial evidence exists which makes it possible that she may have said it. The Palmers did acquire a good Corot in Florence in 1889. Soon after they bought it there appeared a Chicago novel, *With the Procession,* written by Henry B. Fuller. In the story a rich Mrs. Bates, very conscious of social values, appears as Mrs. Palmer's literary counterpart. Fuller, who was not known for sweetness and light, has Mrs. Bates say, in addition to the quotation already cited:

"We haven't got any Millet yet, but that morning thing over there is a Corot—at least, we think so."

The word "lady" looms large in the vocabulary of The Gelded Age. It carried a heavy burden of snobbish associations. A lady was one who had the time and the occasion to practice fashionable fribbles such as a kind of kangaroo walk known as the Grecian bend. The operative word in the titles of many works on manners and the proprieties was *Ladies'*. These treatises told the reader how to walk, talk, remove freckles and warned that any man was potentially dangerous who had not passed his grand climacteric. The usage of the word lady was a complicated business. Sometimes it was simply a synonym for woman; as in saleslady, the Ladies' Aid Society, Ladies' Day, the Ladies' Entrance. A Nashville jailor told Miss

Martineau apologetically that he did not have any ladies in the watchhouse at the time of her visit. The word did not, of course, carry the musty connotation that it does today.

"When we use the word 'Ladies,' " wrote E. M. Woods in *The Negro in Etiquette* (St. Louis: 1899), "it is generally understood by colored people to mean white women. . . ." Martha Washington was the first, First Lady. But Eve was the First Woman, and not a lady at all. Anthony Trollope was amused when he heard a hotel chambermaid referred to as "that young lady" and Mrs. Harriet Beecher Stowe observed that the United States was the only country where it would be possible to speak of "the lady who does her own work."

Ordinarily a woman would refer to herself in speech as a woman, not as a lady. An exception was Belle Starr, a pistol-packing mama of Dodge City. Belle was married to an Indian called Blue Duck. While on a horse-stealing safari in Oklahoma Territory, Belle lost her hat. No one coming to her assistance, she pulled her revolver and addressed her husband:

"Get down there and pick it up, you ignorant bastard. Haven't you got any manners when you are with ladies?"

In the years when a "nice" woman might summon strength to meet a crisis by uttering the prayer "Help me, God or Frances E. Willard," an antiseptic culture and the coarsest vulgarity existed side by side in a curious co-existence. A Reverend New England gentleman named William L. Gage was appearing on the lecture platform in Shakespearian readings which tidied up *The Merchant of Venice,* eliminating from the text what his advertisements termed the blemishes of a less refined age. Yet the Victorians displayed a keen appetite for grotesque and often cruel practical jokes, gross witticisms about corpses, drunkenness and ladies' undergarments. The public eye was filled with advertisements on every rock and cliff, every brick wall and elevated railroad platform, offering electric belts which would make old men sexually young again, bottled "cures" for urethal stricture and other "diseases of men." And the "ladies" were candidly offered French Female Pills which were declared to be "infallible" by Madame Restell, who was listed in the New York city directory as "midwife" and occupied a handsome brownstone mansion at the northeast corner of Fifth Avenue and Fifty-second Street. Madame Restell, the city's leading abortionist, had an alternative procedure by which she guaranteed "a cure at one interview"; while the gifted charlatan, Dr. H. T. Helmbold, made a fortune in the Civil War period out of his Extract of Buchu. What it would do for those who had indulged in indiscretions was described clinically in frightening tracts distributed in hotel and public toilets, bound in pink paper.

When Mark Twain got off the line "I was born of poor but dishonest parents," he parodied the middle class convention that it was disreputable to be poor. The humor of it had shock value, George Santayana commented, because most of Mark Twain's readers themselves shared the conviction that poverty was dishonorable. On a lower literary level George W. Peck pilloried the age in vulgar but imaginative terms when he wrote his widely read *Peck's Bad Boy* (1883). Here is a parade of pratfalls, cupidity, uncouth pranks, hyprocisy and sadism, all mixed together in a merry burlesque of the sacred institutions of respectability—Family, Church, Business and the sentimentality represented by *Little Lord Fauntleroy* with his long curls, his improbable cheerfulness and his tedious friends, Mr. Hobbs, the grocer and Dick the bootblack.

Newspaper paragraphers racily explored the obverse side of the prevailing gentility. Louis Timothy Stone, for one, became nationally known for his columns about entertaining but improbable natural marvels he encountered in the otherwise undistinguished little city of Winsted, Connecticut. Stone told of a cow, milked for years by a maiden lady, that was so modest that when she was sold to a man the cow had to be completely clothed before she would give down her milk. And a Kansas editor reported, apparently as an artless social note:

"A couple came from Ohio, arriving in Leavenworth a few days since, and were married about noon. At 8 o'clock in the evening a bouncing boy weighing ten and a half pounds, was born to the blooming bride of less than ten hours. This is only another evidence of the fertility of Kansas, and a proof that the drought is not so general and fatal in its effects as some of our eastern friends suppose."

Sheltered women were fenced off from knowledge of their fallen sisters whose professional activities may have been more than a little a result of the oppressive refinement which governed the attitudes of respectable women toward sexuality. But the "pure"

women of Leadville, Colorado, could scarcely have been unaware
of Laura Evans on one occasion when she, with a friend who also
believed in spectacular promotion, staged a Ben Hur race in two
circus chariots down decorous Harrison Street where "the girls on
the line" were forbidden to promenade. Laura later rose in her
profession to have a plush house of her own with brothel beauties
who "wore silk garters embellished with ten dollar gold pieces,
locked on their thighs with a gold lock and chain."

Newspaper men took a patronizing rather than indignant attitude toward prostitutes, probably because they were a source of
news. Describing them as soiled doves, calico queens, nymphs du
prairie and other euphemisms, the press recorded such incidents as
the time a gust of wind removed seven dollars from the stocking of
Alice Chambers on Front Street in Dodge City, Kansas. The services of all the tramps in town were enlisted in the search for the
missing currency, but only a single dollar was recovered. The editor of the local newspaper expressed regret that the Kansas wind
would be so larcenous and lecherous: "even the wind can be found
feeling around in and by forbidden paths."

A full and reliable account of this submerged aspect of American life has never been written. Perhaps it cannot be written. At
any rate, whiskey-hungry, woman-hungry miners flocked to the
dance houses and saloons in the camps of Montana, Colorado and
California. It was the same way in the army towns like Hays and
Leavenworth, or the cattle towns. The men were young, single,
with no opportunities to marry because there were no suitable
mates available. So they turned for solace to the girls called in the
census records milliner, laundress, housekeeper or as one candid
enumerator of the census wrote it down at Ellsworth, Kansas, in
1870, Harriet Parmenter "does 'horizontal' work." Pangs of community conscience were felt from time to time about the double
sexual standard, sharpened perhaps by the knowledge that the fines
levied against the houses of ill repute were so nicely adjusted to the
ability to pay that they constituted in effect licenses to operate.

Societies have always, so far, reacted healthfully against their
own excesses. The stuffy outlook on life of the Gelded Age was
ameliorated by various liberating influences, among them the bicycle, which shortened the skirts and got women out of doors,
women like Mrs. Julia Archibald Holmes, a sturdy bride in bloom-
ers who out-climbed her husband in scaling Pike's Peak, and

Charles Dana Gibson's brilliant invention of the serene, high-spirited and queenly Gibson Girl. Gibson's drawings entitled "His Move," "You Are Going on a Long Journey" and others of an anecdotal nature, replaced the colored chromo on the walls of American parlors in the 1890's. There were "Gibson Girl" clothes, hats, spoons, plates, wall paper, glove boxes and umbrella stands. "Fifth Avenue is like a procession of Gibsons," declared Joseph Pennell, the illustrator. As adaptable young women came to look like the well-born Gibson Girl they also felt her influence in another way. For she shaped the manners and attitudes of a whole generation.

12

THE PIANO GIRL

The old-fashioned parlor was a room of lace curtains, valances and stiff furniture nobody ever willingly sat on, where families of median social position put their claims to "refinement" on display. Framed wax flowers hung on the wall. Hand-painted china stood on the whatnot. The marble table held the albums and stereopticon. On the piano stood a gray plaster copy of John Rogers' genre statuette, "Coming to the Parson." The greater the clutter the higher the culture. The parlor was also a place where Mabel could have a word with a gentleman.

When the modern living room succeeded the parlor, there was no place left for the china and the whatnot. The creative arts drooped. Only the piano held its sway. *She* still played and sang while *he* turned the pages and, in some way, marriageable girls continued to get married.

When James Parton declared in 1867 that the piano was only less dispensable to the American home than the kitchen stove, he was pointing to a significant social phenomenon. The sale of twenty-five thousand pianos per year at the time, not counting imports, clearly indicated that the piano was the basic instrument for diffusing musical culture in a pioneer country. Its influence in shaping the genteel tradition appears very early. "Almost every home between the Delaware and the Schuylkill," said the Philadelphia *Mirror of Taste and Dramatic Censor,* long before Parton made his observations, "has its piano or harpsichord. . . . Almost every young lady . . . can make a noise upon some instrument or other . . . we take it for granted that we are a very musical people." Even at that date—1810—the perceptive commentator set forth a truth which has stood fast for all the generations since. He noted that the attractions of amateur pianism among marriageable young women dropped off sharply after mating. Or, as Grover Cleveland put it more sentimentally: "In many an humble home throughout our land the piano has gathered about it the most sacred and tender associations . . . with its music each daughter . . . touched . . . the heart of her future husband. . . ."

Even when it stood silent, the piano had a dynamism which set it apart from other furnishings, the onyx tables, the slippery horsehair-and-walnut sofas. The piano, first luxury big-ticket item to reach the mass public, expressed family values and social aims. Its usefulness as the mark of a family with cultural standards lasted well into the ken of people still living.

The pianoforte crossed to America in the eighteenth century. Thomas Jefferson saw a "Forte-piano" in 1771 and was charmed with it. Brissot de Warville observed an occasional piano in Boston drawing rooms in 1788. All were London-made. By 1840 the "piano girl" was a recognizable type. To the democratic conviction that every nubile maiden had the potentiality for at least a partial conquest of the instrument, was added the Christian conception of man as a free agent, moving ever closer to perfection, although the diarist, Philip V. Fithian, called what he heard from a good many harpsichords under the hands of the young ladies of Virginia "the musical phase of original sin." Precocious Margaret Fuller began her formidable day with a brisk walk from five to six in the morning, piano practice from six to seven. More piano was later sandwiched in between philosophy and Greek, and in the evening she sang to her own accompaniment after her Italian and before she wrote in her journal.

"A lady," wrote Florence Hartley in *The Ladies' Book of Eti-*

quette, published in 1860 and frequently reissued for the next twenty years—"a lady without her piano, or her pencil, her library of French, German, or Italian authors, her fancy work and tasteful embroideries, is now rarely met with. . . ."

American inventiveness contributed many improvements to piano construction which made possible a successful resistance to the extremes of our climate and the punishment the instrument received from healthy girls with a wholesome farm background, who were working out on one of the popular battle pieces, represented typically in James Hewitt's *The Battle of Trenton.* This work was a supreme test for any piano, a period piece which undertook to depict musically such matters as Attack, Cannonading, Flight of the Hessians, General Confusion, Trumpets of Victory and Articles of Capitulation Signed.

A composition which enjoyed an even greater vogue was Franz Kotzwara's *Battle of Prague,* a show piece which Huck Finn heard with astonishment when the young ladies of a distinguished family —Colonel Grangerford's—performed on the "little old piano . . . that had tin pans in it, I reckon." The American piano appeared in the gold diggings when Leadville, Colorado, was still a tent city. It withstood Kansas cyclones in numerous authenticated instances, to say nothing of the abuse which Jimmy Durante was destined in our time to visit upon the sturdy instrument. According to an estimate made in 1887, there were half a million pupils studying the piano in the United States. This meant that about eight per cent of American youth was engaging in what was often a compulsory accomplishment, if one subtracts those who had "taken" but stopped.

The more serious or affluent students read the advertisements of German conservatories and sighed, in agreement with the reports of Amy Fay who had preceded them to Germany, that "there *is* something interesting and romantic about being a Pole." The theory upon which the popular approach to musical studies rested was pleasure and self-improvement. But the pragmatic test was public performance, if not on the platform then at least in the family parlor. Papa, who paid the bills, wanted to see results, even if the repertoire consisted only of what one father sadly appraised as "the thousand-dollar piece."

Catherine Beecher turned the ladylike accomplishment to good purpose, as one would expect of a good Beecher. She learned to play well enough to teach in a New London school and to play the organ in an Episcopal church. At that period, she remembered long afterward, "very humble performances . . . gave satisfaction." And at the very end of her long and useful life, Catherine sang in a quavering voice to her own accompaniment, the old hymn whose words articulated her faith in American life—"It's better farther on."

A few of the piano girls made it to Berlin, living decorously in Königgrätzer Strasse, practicing five and six hours a day, searching for the magic touch, the passages that pearl, the octaves performed from the lightly held wrist. "Let the fingers fall naturally," *Der Musiklehrer* roared, *Spielen Sie mit dem Gewicht*. There was so much to think of—the chord, the well-sustained trill, the broken octaves, the chromatics, rhythm, pedal work, the task of refining *die kleinen Passagen*.

The climax of four years of hard work and expenditure of several thousands of dollars was a modest debut in the *salle* of a quiet hotel at some spa, the folding chairs occupied by an audience whose attendance the maestro could command. There was a bouquet, a little champagne supper after the concert, congratulations, and Fräulein returned to Ohio or somewhere to disappear forever from the pages of history. She had, at least, strolled in the Tiergarten, heard Clara Schumann play, caught a glimpse of Bismarck once, all spangled with stars and glittering orders, and attended Mrs. George Bancroft's Washington's Birthday party at the American legation to which all American citizens were invited.

Amateur performers have ever been charged with the fault of coyness. "All singers," Horace wrote in a passage which has been often quoted, "have this fault, that they never can be found ready to sing." As the diffusion of musical education through the United States increased, the books on decorum took notice of the problems in behavior which arose in connection with musical performances. Lady singers were admonished to sing or not sing, but they were not to complain about their cold or hint that acquiescence might place an intolerable strain upon delicate and valuable vocal chords. If they did sing, songs should be avoided "descriptive of masculine passion."

The piano girl was cautioned not to show up at a social occasion with her music or indicate that she expected to be asked to perform. Do not display anxiety to play, the authorities on refined behavior said, yet do not insist upon being coaxed. If it is your unalterable intention to play, then play. The nearest gentleman offers his arm, escorts the pianist to the instrument and holds her bouquet and gloves while she plays, turns her music if he is a good sight reader. The musician is further advised that it is impolite to compare the hostess' instrument unfavorably with another or point out what may well be true, that it badly needs tuning. In her performance she should avoid dramatic tricks or whimsicalities, the attempt to startle with showy execution. The listeners, on their part, had the obligation to be quiet and attentive. Otherwise, they risked and deserved the fate of a woman described by Mrs. Stowe. When the music unexpectedly dropped to a *pianissimo* a voice rose over the music: "I always cook mine in vinegar."

Oddly enough, a search through an extensive collection of books dealing with the conduct of life did not produce any sage counsel on the important topic of when to stop, although Mark Twain made some suggestions upon this subject and Jane Austen touched it lightly when she had Mr. Bennet in *Pride and Prejudice* gently dissuade a daughter from further effort on the ground that she had "delighted us long enough."

Between 1890 and 1900 the number of pianos in use in American homes increased more than five times as fast as the population. At the beginning of the new century the general public owned a million instruments. This deep yearning for our primary musical instrument must be seen in the context of life as it was lived by a predominantly rural people. Few Americans traveled as much as a hundred miles in the course of a year to visit a city. There was no telephone, no phonograph, no movies, radio, automobile or newspaper, except the local weekly. Amusement, then, relaxation and reverie, emotional release, came in the short time between supper and bedtime, when the lamp was lighted and the daughter of the house played the old, well-loved hymns and such parlor pieces as "Hearts and Flowers" or Ethelbert Nevin's "A Day in Venice," out of which popped, when the music was first opened, a supply of doilies.

The family piano became the basis for the melody business which sold sheet music in enormous quantities after 1900, always in arrangements made for piano accompaniment. Gradually a new musical idiom—gayer, more proletarian—reflected a new national tempo. "Silver Threads Among the Gold" gave place to "Bedelia, I'd Like to Steal Ya," and Mabel was delighted to discover that she had an instinct for finding keyboard combinations, said good-bye with a sense of relief to Ethelbert Nevin and the doilies, concentrating thereafter upon developing a wicked base for her interpretation of "Maple Leaf Rag."

Pianos of the highest grade were produced in the cities of the eastern seaboard. But the great inland center for the quantity production of the $200 piano was Chicago, home of the Bush & Gerts, the Crown, the Washburn and the Kimball, whose name was once as well-known in the farming states as General Grant's. These were the pianos, together with many others in the medium price class—the Wing, the Everett, the Vose, A. B. Chase, the Weber—which became the pivot of the parlor. There was a recognizable "Piano Row" in most large cities. Here the dignified showrooms were all serenity and red brocade, the epitome of "class." Grands with noble names on the fall board—Steinway, Sohmer, Chickering, Henry F. Miller—were displayed with the elegance and austerity of a Cartier necklace. There were busts of Rachmaninoff, Liszt and Hofmann scattered around on pedestals, and a painting of Schubert in the very frenzy of musical creation. Imitating this rarefied atmosphere, most piano dealers in the smaller communities affected to be handling *objets d'art,* though many doubled in embalming.

The refining influence of music did not extend to the traveling agents who peddled pianos through the heartland of America and uncharitably referred to all competitors as thieves and robbers. The piano peddlers, who also often sold a five-drawer, drop-head sewing machine, epitomized the aggressive salesmanship of the 1890's. Drawn to a prosperous granger by a kind of built-in tropism, the salesman sometimes pretended his dray had broken down in front of the farm home of his intended victim. Could he just store the piano in the parlor for a few days? He knew it would never leave the house. Once George P. Bent, who learned the selling game when he was in sewing machines, moved a Crown piano into a farm house while the family were away. Watching until he saw them returning the callid agent began to sing reverently to his own accompaniment on the shiny, new Crown, "Lead, Kindly Light." Needless to say, under such circumstances, the girls cornered their pa, whispered tensely, "Git it, pa, git it, pa." And so another Iowa hog went into the spring wagon as a down payment, the farmer's note was quickly discounted at the nearest country

bank, while the piano peddler went on his way rejoicing and singing the hymn of his trade:

> *For a farmer who had money and a girl, we'd unload*
> *From our office on our wagon, from our wagon on the road.*

The piano agent was as aggressive at collecting as he was at selling, and he knew the law—what constituted a valid order, how to
attach a debtor's property, the rights and remedies of a holder of a
bank check, the statute of limitations. And in parts of the West not
yet pacified he traveled with a gun across his knees. Chester Ellsworth, for instance, who worked out of Boise, Idaho, always carried
a rifle after he learned how a party of marauding Sioux had relieved a colleague, Ben King, of his Kimball piano, and didn't even
sign the installment contract.

In the more stabilized life of the Eastern states, the piano traveler cut quite a dashing social figure. He wore mutton-chop whiskers and a high celluloid collar, a silk hat and a preacher coat, with
a great linen handkerchief billowing from his breast pocket. He
was a good liver, appreciated a Havana cigar and was reputed to
have a sweetheart in every town. Sometimes the piano drummer
liked to lift a flagon in some alcoholic shrine. A western retailer
once said to Colonel Edward Saxton Payson, who later became
President of the Emerson Piano Company, "Do you drink whiskey?" To this the urbane Colonel replied, genially:
"Well, well, is this a trial or an invitation?"

Using such dubious merchandising techniques as the "Special
Sale," the "Going Out of Business" gambit and fictitious price re-
ductions, backed up by glowing endorsements from obscure institutions like the *Kentucky Confederate Home* or such oddly as-
sorted celebrities as A. Conan Doyle and Lillian Russell, the piano
agents spoke with a rough tongue. When the time came to spring
into action they went for the jugular. A. A. Fisher, father of the
famous cartoonist, "Bud" Fisher, and an expert in the piano business, once distributed his hand bills in Fort Wayne, Indiana, announcing "The Slaughter Begins Monday" at the Arcade. The local piano retailers were prompt in their response. They called
Fisher's descent upon the city a "false clothing sale" and asked
publicly where Mr. Fisher would be in thirty days "when the piano
is warped, the glue cracks off, the action falls to pieces, the case

splits down the back, or the strings snap into a jumble with every change of weather?"

Music teachers were often retained on the quiet to push a particular piano or upset the sale of a rival. The piano tuner as the confederate of the touring sales agent could also spot a promising opportunity. A few days after the tuner worked over an old piano, a personable young man greeted the lady of the house at the door by name and complimented her on the remarkable musical gifts of the twelve-year-old daughter. It was not unusual for him to give a musical aptitude test on the spot to the little brother. Invariably, he uncovered a prodigy in the same range as Josef Hofmann and pointed out how nice it would be, when grandmother came down from Wisconsin for Thanksgiving, for Matilda to have available a new piano worthy of her interpretation of *The Robin's Return*.

The man who showed the firmest grasp of the fundamental fact that a piano was a piano and nothing more to a public which could not tell one from the other, was William Wallace Kimball. The Kimball Piano Company perfected what was called, not always in admiration, the "Kimball system" of providing "Music for the Multitudes." Kimball's operation in the music trade was sometimes compared to that of John D. Rockefeller, Senior, in his ruthless elimination of competitors in the early petroleum industry. But money does not smell of its origins. Kimball lived to become one of the Chicago millionaires who lived on fashionable Prairie Avenue in his own version of a twelfth century French chateau. An admirer, after saluting in home-grown verses the great men of all ages, continued when he got to the subject of merchandising:

> *No greater merchant prince e'er lived*
> *Than William Wallace Kimball.*

In 1905, before the bathroom emerged as the shrine of the American home, there were more pianos and cottage organs in the United States than bathtubs. In that year the Sears, Roebuck & Company catalogue offered four versions of their Beckwith, all described with carefully regulated hyperbole according to the price-ticket. Decoratively, the Beckwith was in the main tradition of what has been called "piano ostentation," looked like a wedding cake with its heavily carved music desk and a keyboard supported by four Grand Rapids caryatids.

The piano, the piano girl and the aspiration for culture and the graces of life called into being an army of music teachers, usually women. The teachers burned to find another Liszt, but had to settle for pupils who repeated the same old clinker ad infinitum, playing the downbeat of the fourth bar one-half tone too high, on on into eternity. Such a patient instructor must have been Miss Louise Forest, who charged fifty cents a lesson and eventually taught Fred Allen, later the star of literate satire on the radio, to play *Pitter, Patter, Little Rain Drops* on Fred's Aunt Lizzie's Emerson upright. Allen later, on a slight commercial detour on his climb to fame, became the nemesis of delinquent installment purchasers who owed money to a piano store on Boylston Street in Boston. The collection procedure centered upon a bit of theater which called for two husky piano movers, a one-horse wagon, a large coil of rope, a block and tackle and Fred Allen to cue the dramatic action. When this entourage clumped up to the door of an unfortunate debtor, the bluff was that the Colonial Piano Company wanted its piano back. But Colonial, as the script for this charade always provided, would graciously defer drastic action if the payments were promptly brought up to date.

Teresa Carreño could read any music at sight at the age of fourteen. But what most girls hoped for was a more modest accomplishment, the ability to do cross-hands work with easy nonchalance in the "Miserere" section of a medley of arias from *Il Trovatore*. When the weather was warm for May and vacation fever set in, the wise teacher bowed to the inevitable, made the last lesson a review of what was optimistically called the pupil's "repertoire," and Junior Miss departed joyfully for the summer hiatus with nothing to do musically for three months. It was the hope of dedicated women like Miss Taletta Williamson, of Quincy, Illinois, that the young artists under her tutelage would at least keep up their finger exercises and pass the leisure hours of the good old summertime reading the lives of the great composers. Miss Taletta never had the great happiness to produce a Madame Bloomfield-Zeisler. But she does figure in an authenticated incident wherein she explained, with some excitement on her own part, "Perhaps I shouldn't give you the 'Barcarole' from the *Tales of Hofmann,* because the music is often considered to be passionate."

To which Miss Braids replied, with round eyes: "What is passionate, Miss Taletta?"

There was another way to learn to play the piano. One could "recite . . . through the Postoffice" to the Seigel-Myers Correspondence School of Music. Siegel-Myers chivvied its prospective scholars into answering its advertisements with the nagging question: "Do you Know How Paderewski Holds His Hands at the Piano?" Sears, Roebuck & Company also taught the piano by mail as did a Dr. Quinn, who announced from his conservatory in Boston, "I'll Teach You Piano in *Quarter* Usual Time." The Easy Method Music Co. did even better. It promised "Play the Piano in One Evening."

It was one of these mail order firms, the U. S. School of Music, which published the famous advertisement about Jack, a deceitful little exhibitionist who, after a turn as a social clown, so deeply moved his partying friends with a magical rendering of the *Moonlight Sonata*. Men pumped his hand in congratulation. Beautiful girls languished. And before the autistic reader of this little fantasy in *Physical Culture* magazine could lick her lips she was in the iron grip of the Free Booklet and Demonstration Lesson. You will recognize the advertisement from the celebrated headline which John Caples wrote to introduce us to Jack: "They Laughed When I Sat Down at the Piano—but when I started to play . . ." and so on to the thrilling triumph of music-without-effort.

The World's Columbian Exposition in Chicago, visited by twelve million people, stimulated piano sales, helped send the little old reed organ to join the spinning wheel in the attic. Vernacular music, in particular, benefited. The itinerant piano clan from the level of life inhabited by sporting gentlemen and hip-swaying girls, introduced the new syncopated melodies which became ragtime, preeminently piano music. Almost everybody, it seemed, wanted to learn to rag. There was a *Rag Time Instructor* published in 1897. Soon after, Chicago-born Axel Christensen advertised "Ragtime Taught in Ten Lessons." With his ragtime magazine and ragtime piano contests, Christensen's conservatory became the alma mater, by 1935, of half a million syncopated old grads.

The wide diffusion of the piano through the country was further stimulated by the invention of the first practical player piano by Edwin S. Votey. The mechanical player was equipped with such refinements as the Phrasing Lever, Melody Button, Tempo Control, a soft-pedal mechanism and ivory keys made from the tusks of selected ranch-grown Indian elephants. The manufacturers of player pianos directed their promotional attention to gifted music lovers whose time was too valuable for the mastery of the hand-played piano, but who enjoyed pumping air through apertures which activated the perforated paper rolls to perform, say, *The Light Cavalry Overture,* with some individual variation in dynamics, speed and accentuation. "You," said the Pianola people, "can play the piano as well as anyone," thus moving the discussion of pianistics to a simpler domain where "Even Pop Can Play the Pianola."

The mechanical player was only one of many anti-piano influences at work in the 1930's. Soaring phonograph sales popularized the habit of passive listening. Radio then followed as a better reproducing device than the old paper rolls, eliminating, in passing, both the player piano and the amateur performer. "Thousands of American parlors," remarked a Cleveland music dealer, "contain that shining monument to a past girlhood—a silent piano."

Today, pianos fitted to small homes and small incomes, harmonized with current decorative trends in furniture, have stimulated a new appreciation of the instrument. But its day is over as a social showcase. "*One* generation passeth away," as The Preacher wrote, "and *another* generation cometh. . . ." The roving piano agent has gone to join the lightning-rod salesman in the seventh circle of Hell, while the Piano Girl has dissolved into the mists of time, to the tinkling accompaniment of Tosti's *Goodby.*

13

IT IS ALL IN A BOOK—
OR IS IT?

In the flush times of the post-Civil War years a new commercial and industrial middle class emerged in the United States, puzzled about the proprieties and weighed down by the burden of Calvinism. Its members knew the fear of sex, of God and of the wrong fork. There had been "new people" before. But this time there were so many of them, who held a touching faith that salvation in this world depended upon an easy nonchalance in disposing of cherry stones after the butler had passed the fruit bowl that there was a need for a new enculturating device to do the buffing and polishing of the rugged individualist who had been born in a log cabin, cradled in a sap trough and was inclined unpredictably to rip open his shirt to show his scars of war. The need brought forth the nineteenth century etiquette book. It was not a work on civility in the old, established sense, but rather a collection of rites and shibboleths, a sort of rule book of behavior in the fashionable "sets." Fat, gilded, for a slight extra fee "stamped in gold with your name," these hack works were often outrageously padded with miscellaneous and bizarre information, such as the year that Solomon's temple was begun, the source of the water supply at the White House and how to clean kid boots.

The importance of knowing the ground rules of polite usage was frequently urged by writers in the etiquette field. For example, in a work of collective authorship, the *American Etiquette and Rules of Politeness* (Chicago: 1882), the authors pointed out that the rich needed to practice courtesy "because of the finish and the éclat thus given to their wealth and their homes." The middle classes could advance themselves through acquiring familiarity with what was good form and gain "admission to the houses of the rich. . . ." The poor in their tatters would find in the social refinements a solace for "the stings of poverty."

A large corpus of how-to-do-it writings flowed from the industrious pens of such littérateurs as Miss Eliza Leslie, Mrs. Lydia Maria Child, Catherine Beecher and her sister Harriet, William Andrus Alcott and Orson Squire Fowler. They treated such disparate topics as regular bathing, quilting, management of stoves, evening parties, straw bonnets, kitchen economy, parlor games and homilies on "the oil of civility" and the gaucherie of women who crossed their legs or clasped their knees with their hands. When cautions are repeatedly offered upon a specific point, such as drinking the lemon water from finger bowls, the error must have been widespread.

The history of the etiquette books does not, of course, end with the last century or even with the Edwardian years. Who that has heard of Emily Post and Amy Vanderbilt—and who has not?—can doubt that the problem of normlessness, the need for a rule of thumb, has lost its urgency? Commercially, the books which pointed the way to grace and sophistication in the last century were a staple of subscription publishing. Hard-eyed peddlers canvassed through hamlet and countryside with fancy specimen bindings, glowing prospectuses and hog-tight contract forms from which, once signed, there was no escape, not even death.

Some of these volumes were written by authors who had personal knowledge of the world of social privilege. Mrs. John (Mary Elizabeth) Sherwood, author of *Manners and Social Usage* (New York: 1887), for example, was a conservative and proper arbiter, daughter of a congressman and wife of a New York lawyer. Mrs. Sherwood had served as her father's official hostess after her mother's death, traveled abroad extensively, and had been decorated by the French government. She knew many people of prominence—Daniel Webster, the historians Prescott and Bancroft, Julia Ward Howe, the reigning New England poets, and many British figures in the arts and politics. Another New England woman, of different antecedents but limitless energy, also entered the field with her little *Guide to Health and Etiquette* (Lynn, Mass.: n.d.) containing a remarkable mélange of material upon the qualities of the gentlewoman, intertwined with frightening case histories of prolapsed uteri and the usefulness of Lydia E. Pinkham's Vegetable Compound. Mrs. Pinkham herself was the author of the *Guide* as well as originator of the patent medicine it advertised.

In the last half of the last century the compilation of books giving advice on deportment was sufficiently profitable to attract such popular writers as the cultivated and gently bred Catherine Maria Sedgwick of the old Stockbridge, Massachusetts, family; the "female bard," Lydia H. Sigourney; the moralist, T. S. Arthur, who had granted in 1852 that woman could reason and be reasoned with. Also of this company was Mrs. Dahlgren, wife of the Civil War admiral, who knew Washington social life well, and Miss Rose E. Cleveland, official hostess for her bachelor brother, President Cleveland.

Another group of writers retired behind pen names, calling themselves "Count D'Orsay" after a celebrated French dandy, the "Marquise de Fontenoy" or just plain "Aunt Matilda." The how-to books turned out by all these writers, named and unnamed, were aimed at "those who have not had the educational advantages of polite society." Mrs. Mary Virginia Hawes Terhune, better known as Marion Harland, said she was addressing people "of humble lineage . . . who yet have longings and tastes for gentlehood." And Robert de Valcourt exulted that the young American "unlike the citizen of almost every other nation, has no barrier of caste or order, but is free to rise to the highest place of social distinction" in what he called "this land of Freedom, of Ambition and of energetic Self-hood."

The etiquette manuals got right down to hard-pan on such themes as uncomely habits. "No lady is ever seen to spit," wrote one compiler, and added that the rule applied also to gentlemen "as far as possible." Advice on bathing has to be seen in its historical setting. A bath was a major production when there was no running hot water and no tub to climb into. Not until the administration of James Monroe did the President of the United States have access to a simple copper tub, and it had to be filled laboriously by hand. Not until 1877, when Rutherford B. Hayes was Chief Executive, was the White House equipped with a running-water tub.

Quoting Solomon, Lord Chesterfield and each other, the social mentors enforced their dicta with appeals to literature, custom, folk proverbs, the sanctions of religion and often reflected the unconscious elements implicit in prevailing attitudes. They exhibit, therefore, considerable anthropological interest as a paradigm of the age they were written for. Casters, we learn, were being removed from smart dining room tables in the 1880's. Birds were in vogue. No home of refinement was complete without a canary. The woman's rights movement did not get much aid or comfort from the essayists on deportment. They were traditionalists and labored manfully, or womanfully, to keep things on an even keel and accepted the assumed fact that man had a larger cerebrum than his mate. The only suffragist who staked out a claim in the manners field, as far as the present writer knows, was Florence Howe Hall, daughter of the revered and majestic Julia Ward Howe.

The demand for books consulted in secret by those seeking social sheen was so strong that between 1870 and 1917, according to Professor Arthur M. Schlesinger's estimate, some two to three hundred volumes dealing with domestic culture were circulating information about the Victorian proprieties. And this does not take into account the periodical articles and etiquette departments of such household companions as the *Cottage Hearth, Peterson's* magazine and *Godey's.*

Speaking in general terms, the writers advanced an optimistic theory that gracious manners could be acquired through discipline and drill until raising the hat, smiling a greeting, rising in the presence of ladies became automatic responses to the social situation. The consensus was not so clear as to whether courtesy should be its own reward or practiced as a form of self-interest. Should a young man, for example, be mannerly because kind hearts are more than coronets or because if he was polite he would in the fullness of time be admitted to the firm?

"Etiquette," wrote a ten-year-old disciple of Machiavelli, Virginia Carey Hudson in 1904, "is what you are doing and saying

when people are looking and listening. What you are thinking
. . . is your business. Thinking is not etiquette."

A matron who took literally what the handbooks said on the ritualistic side of social usage, such as the subject of afternoon calls,
had her work cut out for her. It was a game as stylized as the Japa-
nese kabuki. First, she had to establish a day when she was "At
Home" and stock up with an abundant supply of personal cards, of
the fashionable shape, size, thickness and style of engraving. Sometimes the card said "Mr. and Mrs. Charles Sprague." Again, husband and wife had separate cards. "His" might list his club affiliation. "Hers" indicated in the lower left hand corner when she
received calls, as "Thursdays until May." After May, if she went to
Saratoga Springs, she received the first call from other summer visitors if she was installed in the main building of the hotel but was
expected to make the advances if she was domiciled in an annex.

Social calling involved a burdensome amount of record-keeping.
Marion Harland suggested compiling the "At Home" days of all
one's acquaintances and keeping the score as to credits and debits.
Punctuality, which has been called the courtesy of kings, was
stressed. The penalties for laxness could be severe. As an instance
of this, Miss Ellen Harvie of Frankfort, Kentucky, was walking
along the street one day when she saw that Mrs. Watson's chimney
was on fire. Her first impulse was to dash across the street and notify her. Then she remembered that Mrs. Watson had owed her a
call for some time and regretfully continued on her way.

It was hard to shoe-horn in all the calling since many women had
the same day at home. But an experienced veteran of the social
marathon, setting forth with her small, "elegant" card-case in one
hand, an embroidered cambric handkerchief in the other, could
ring a doorbell, enter, drop her cards in the receiver, walk into the
parlor, greet, chat, take a cup of tea and be out in fifteen minutes.
If there was a slight wait, the counselors cautioned, don't peek at
the cards on the salver to see who has been on the social ramble
lately or play chopsticks on the piano. But it was quite correct to
leaf casually through an album on the center table or examine the
steel engravings on the wall.

The consumption of cardboard must have been stupendous.
The married visitor left a card for her hostess, one for the man of
the house, two from her own husband, and an energetic caller
could cover between six and ten "At Homes" in a good afternoon.

If she knew there was a house guest, there went another card. A visit from a new caller required a call-back within three weeks. A bride was initiated into this folkway as soon as she established her own day at home. The dinner guest paid a *visite de digestion* within a week; a guest at a large reception within a month.

The *Home Library of Useful Knowledge* (Chicago: 1887) presents some of the finer points through the device of introducing the reader to a well-placed St. Louis family, created for purposes of illustration. We learn through their pasteboards a good deal about the Charles Corey family. Mrs. Corey, 19 Olive Street, had her At Home days on Tuesdays. She was assisted at the tea table by a no-doubt reluctant "Miss Anne Corey" or an elder sister who was just "Miss Corey." But there came a rift in the family. At least Mr. Corey's card gave a different address, 119 Olive Street; and sometimes his card placed him at the St. Louis Club which certainly does suggest that the marriage had, as Walter Winchell would say, splituated. Then, later, we find all the Coreys together again, farther out on Olive, at 1753, where the couple formally requested the pleasure of Mr. and Mrs. Charles Somers' company at dinner "from 4 until 6 o'clock." The Coreys didn't care when they ate or else they were becoming increasingly fashionable, for they had the Somerses in again, this time for dinner at eight.

Even death could not stay for long the blizzard of visiting cards. Following a funeral there was the visit of condolence (leave card). The arrival of a thank-you note was the signal to resume the dizzy, corseted round of ceremonial visitations.

A young man who circulated in good society, wishing to see an attractive girl home, spoke up in this kind of language if he went by the book: "Miss Ella, make me happy by selecting me for your cavalier." If Ella accepted his "protection" she called him mister, for she had been warned by Emily Thornwell in her *Lady's Guide to Complete Etiquette* . . . (Chicago: 1888) that addressing men by their first names "opens the way to unpleasant familiarities." It did not occur to anyone then that the familiarities might on occasion have been pleasant. If the couple took a streetcar home, a slight touch on Ella's arm was all that was necessary from her temporary guardian in helping her on or off the car. Both refrained from the "extremely bad form" of reading a fellow-passenger's newspaper over his shoulder.

In crossing the street, if it was muddy, Miss Ella raised her dress a little on one side only, gracefully, with her right hand. But not on both sides with both hands. Double elevation was definitely vulgar. When her escort of the evening met Ella on the street the next day he raised his hat. Only coachmen touched their hats with a finger. The cavalier did not put his hat on again until Ella had twice remarked that if he didn't he would catch his death of cold. He had, of course, removed his cigar from his mouth at the moment of recognition, holding it as inconspicuously at his side as he could. There were two situations in which a gentleman did not tip his hat to a feminine social acquaintance. An elderly man with a touch of neuralgia, standing in a cutting wind, was excused. And a young society man if he was in the company of a woman of questionable reputation would not raise his hat to a girl in his social set. Even though he was interested in welfare work and may have been engaged in a rescue assignment, he did not tip and Miss Ella would have been justified, if he did, in giving him the cut direct.

A special problem in manners is presented in *The Negro in Etiquette*. The author refers to a widespread discourtesy, the failure of Negro men to lift their hats to white women because they were afraid of being tagged by their peers as "white folks' niggers." Equally to be censored was the "representative (?) colored man" who tips his hat to a pretty white girl, then leaves it in place when greeting an equally pretty colored girl. Such a man, the author suggests, practices not politeness but "hypocrisy."

All this business with the hat seemed so fatiguing to James C. Boyle of Spokane, Washington, that he invented the Boyle Derby Tipper, a labor-saving device with wheels and levers within the hat. The Derby Tipper met the criteria of the patent examiners. The idea was novel. It was Boyle's own origination and it was presumed to be useful. The inventor was, accordingly, granted U. S. Patent Number 556,248 for eliminating the exertion required in manually saluting ladies, flags, cathedrals and other entities and monuments entitled to such a mark of respect. But there was a lag in culture or politeness in America for Boyle's effort to promote affable manners through automation never found its market, and remains only a curiosity of the U. S. Patent Office.

During the passing years the graceful old custom of a woman's curtsying gave way to "a slight but gracious inclination of the head and body." It was ill-bred for her to shake hands with a man unless they were close friends. For men, too, hand-shaking was described as obsolete "except in some country towns," as one writer stated somewhat snobbishly, noting that next to being presented to the Grand Jury was the ordeal of meeting "some Americans, indeed, who . . . will seize your hand . . . and visit it pretty roughly before you recover it."

Introductions were performed best when they were accompanied by a bit of information that would serve to cue in the other person, as "Miss Cameron, you must know Miss Fordyce who can tell you all about the art-student life of Paris"; or "Mr. du Pont, from France." This latter fill-in would be especially useful since without it one in the United States would assume, not unnaturally, that Mr. du Pont was from Wilmington, Delaware. The head of a college department was properly presented as "Professor"; but not public exhibitors, mesmerists or jugglers. The fact that the introduction was made gave it the full weight of a social endorsement, as in the instance of the Texan who declared, "if he steals anything I will be responsible." Among persons of unequal social levels the quasi-introduction was recommended as a polite evasion of the real introduction. Suppose you were talking with an upholsterer when a woman friend enters the room. This could be sticky. But an awkward situation may be avoided by informally including her in the conversation: "Mr. Brown thinks the couch should be covered with a puce brocade."

Funeral folkways are fully reflected in the etiquette books which treat with loving detail the decorum of death. The rigid position of the body, the crossed hands, are giving place—the time is 1891—to something more lifelike. The shroud has been replaced by garments worn in life. Flowers in the shape of anchors, crowns or broken columns were no longer considered smart. But the manners of mourning remained elaborate and the instructors in the decencies would certainly have rejected the suggestion of H. L. Mencken, the iconoclast of the 1930's, who asked his friends, if they wished to remember him, to forgive some sinner and wink an eye at a homely girl. The suspicion arises that the elaborate ritual of death was a kind of expiation, a compensatory gesture for failures in family relationships. Furthermore, a display of grief provided an effective answer to the question, important in a closely knit community, What will the neighbors say?

Some of the ancient customs associated with death were falling into disuse in the decades immediately after the Civil War, when commercial travelers swarmed over the countryside selling factory-made caskets with model names suggesting the upper-class social world, such as "The Princess" or "The Grand Duke." The sexton no longer tolled the bell, one stroke for each year of the decedent's life. But the men of Cripple Creek, Colorado, and les girls clung to an old custom when they went *on foot* to the cemetery to say farewell to the nymph, Grace Devere, and then marched back in recessional to the bar, assisted by the Elks Band which struck up "There'll Be a Hot Time in the Old Town Tonight."

The arbiters of good form dodged the difficult question of pre-scribing definite periods for wearing the garments of grief. The rule was that there was no rule, but it was occasionally hinted that the degree of display was not a reliable indication of the depth of the survivors' sorrow, and indeed meticulous observance was rec-ommended as most useful "where the sorrow is not so great." But down well into the twentieth century families of respectable social position were expected to follow a routine of lavish good-byes to those who had gone to their long home. Close the blinds. Draw the shades. Muffle the bell. Fasten the crape to the door; or, if the de-cedent was young or unmarried, intertwine a white ribbon with the flowers. Send out a hurry call to the dressmaker to come with yards and yards of bombazine or delaine or some other lustreless, black, heavily clinging material. Prepare the veil and cap, insigne of the widow, or the conspicuous crape weed which a man wore on his hat. If a widow was in what was called "deep mourning" she was swathed in black except for a border of white *lisse* on her wid-ow's cap. The black veil with heavy border was worn over the face, swept to the ground. All pins and buckles were of black jet. There were no bows or flounces. Black gloves and a handkerchief with a black edging completed the costume. The width of the border was determined by who had died—husband, father, mother, brother, child, uncle, aunt, and so forth. There was a prescribed width for each, if one followed the niceties. Deep mourning lasted up to two years, and many American widows, wrote Eliza M. Lavin in her *Good Manners* (New York: 1888), never put aside the garments of grief.

Other outward signs of dolor included black-edged note paper, envelopes with the mourning border, sealed with black wax, visit-ing cards with mourning-band edges. By a series of carefully regu-lated steps, a lady lightened her burden, threw the veil back from her face, cut off its tail, wore diamonds in moderation, but set in black enamel. Then she moved into what was called "second" or sometimes "dressy mourning." In this stage custom permitted white collars and cuffs and a net or tulle veil. Then came a succession of purple, violet, lilac and gray shades and a bit of ruching at the neck and wrists. After the first three months a widow could visit an art gallery, but not a fashionable exhibition. She could attend a concert but not the theater or opera. She could go to a wedding provided she sat where the bride could not see her and presumably encounter the disagreeable idea that death is a part of life. A widow in mourning would not wish to go where there was gaiety so the question of attending balls and parties did not come up. It was customary for the widow to keep her piano closed.

In New York fashionable life the servants also put on mourning and the male members of the family adjusted the degree of their blackness—the suit, scarf, gloves and armband of crape—to the carefully paced emergence into normal life of the women of their households. Miss Cleveland, in her enchiridion of decorum, describes the male costume for all the degrees of consanguinity, but acknowledges sadly that many men are unconventional and apt to resist these finely drawn distinctions. In the eyes of the ladies of the 1880's, though, the trappings of woe were proof of one's sensibility. There was a sense of luxury to be found in the expression of grief. No greater compliment could be paid than to have it said admiringly, "She has been a great sufferer."

A standard chapter in the literature of nineteenth century politeness dealt with how to write a letter, illustrated with examples covering a wide range of possible relationships, social, business or erotic. These presumably typical letters, designed for the use of the inexperienced, have flowed from the presses for hundreds of years, as has already been noticed (Chapter 3). The same letters appear and reappear, filled with exhortations about building character, instruction in duty to parents and warnings against marrying a fool. The hackneyed material demonstrates that the compilers were lazy, unimaginative, or both. One model which first appeared in 1805 was still circulating in the early 1900's: "From a Young Gentleman, in Expectancy of an Estate from a Penurious Uncle, to a Young Lady of Small Fortune, Desiring Her to Elope with Him." The wealthy uncle objected to the romance; but Maria, for that indeed was her name, refused to meet her suitor on Sunday evening at the bottom of the garden. She had some advice for him: hang on to the uncle.

Just when one gets interested in an unfolding situation in these letter writers, the authors have an annoying way of dropping the subject of love and introducing some little scion of the Main Line gentry who is going out for a row on the Schuylkill next Wednesday and writes to invite Charles Ellwood, Esq., of Pine Street to join the expedition because "You're a jolly fellow and a good steersman." But back to love: Henry Lewis of Cincinnati sent a ring, he called it a "little circlet," to Miss Lizzie Atkins who lived on West Thirtieth Street in New York, as "an emblem of esteem and affection." But Lizzie, although she signed herself his "faithful well-wisher," fired the circlet right back, with the tart message, "I make it a rule never to receive anything in this way from gentlemen." Perhaps Henry should have tried mink. We never learn how he made out after that rebuff because the subject of the author's candied prose changes to, of all things, Lord & Taylor, whose amiable business practices never showed to more advantage than in the pages of *The Home Library of Useful Knowledge*. There we find this estimable store writing to Mr. Julius Sickel, who was in Wall Street, asking the financier to furnish a Mr. Smith with all the information he needed and, as though that was not enough, "Should Mr. Smith have need of any money for his expenses, you will be good enough to let him have what he may ask for and charge the same to our account." That's Lord & Taylor for you, with a concept of service that included information, merchandise and a quick loan.

Over the years the letter writers tended to catch up slowly with the real world. The flowery school of "I enclose a little rosebud, Harold dear, which I have kissed," gave way before a style that was more natural and carried the conviction that the patterns might conceivably have been written and mailed to a real correspondent. The use of the third person, once the very pink of stylish formality, as in "Mrs. Theodore Brown presents her compliments, and begs to ask . . ." came to seem stuffy. An exception to this general rule is a business complaint where the more formidable the communication the better. An example of this genre might go as follows: "Mrs. Theodore Brown presents her compliments and wishes to inform the Home Heating Division of The General Electric Company that the oil burner has conked out again."

With the welcome abandonment of implausible examples the letter models shifted to more generalized advice such as the mechanical details of the salutation, the closing, the form of address. An unconventional address that came not from books but the heart once showed up in the Fayette, Missouri, post office:

"Swift as a Dove *your course pursue,*
Let nought your speed restrain,
Until you reach Miss LUCY DREW,
In Frankfort, *State of Maine."*

The hostess at evening parties was deluged with counsel about the details she must see to, the arrangement of washstands for the ladies, the pin cushions and pins on the bureau, a bootjack for the men. She was cautioned against trying to outshine her guests: "It is not good policy to say every clever thing one thinks of." The husband was to refrain from addressing his wife as "my duck" or "Mrs. C." If there was to be music, don't omit inviting all who sing or play to favor the company with a number; but one is enough. The possibility was raised that hearty applause could be interpreted as relief that the performance was over.

Merry charades or monologues by a good elocutionist were in style in 1860, but if a woman guest attempted to mimic the Irish chambermaid, she was warned to remember that "you are a lady" and not to play the part too convincingly. Afternoon receptions were known as kettle-drums. Miss Cleveland suggested that it was a pretty caprice at these informal affairs to have a tiny drum beaten at intervals near the tea table, and the young woman who did the serving costumed as a vivandière. A guest who departed from a kettle-drum with her reticule filled with cakes and bonbons raised the suspicion that she was either hungry or unaccustomed to society of good *ton*. The practice was discouraged.

The best possible way for a bachelor to repay his social debts was to give an afternoon tea, perhaps focusing the occasion upon the display of a portrait. Or he might unveil a bronze. First he should clean up his quarters, bring in some flowers, provide for a man or maid in livery. He would need tea things and a Russian pianist; for music "breaks up the monotony." It was the host's further responsibility to keep the conversational ball rolling. Women with a social position did not make the customary party call at a bachelor flat. But they would soon invite him to their dinners, the shortage of presentable men being what it was.

The writers on manners and minor morals handled as standard topics such matters as weddings and christenings, dining and dancing, with information on how to dance the waltz modestly; proper dress for all occasions, the fine points of riding and driving etiquette; for example, a man sat in a carriage facing the ladies. Mrs. John Farrar, wife of the mathematician, physicist and astronomer, even prescribed in her *The Young Lady's Friend,* a Boston manual which stayed in print from the 1830's to the eighties, the correct behavior for a woman who found herself in a carriage about to be wrecked by a runaway horse. It was undignified to jump up and down and scream. The correct procedure, when the vehicle turned over, was—relax and roll.

Other recurring themes were New Year's calls and proper deportment "for elderly girls." There is plain talk about the ever-present knife and fork difficulties, strictures against immoderate laughing, touching unnecessarily the person of a lady and the use of such solecisms of speech as "Pardon my glove," "pants," "gent," "beaut," or "had not ought to."

A curious feature of the rule books directed to an audience which needed to be cautioned about such matters was the introduction of information about such wildly extraneous subjects as how to address a vicomte or the ceremonial connected with being presented to Queen Victoria. This was not so much evidence of the encyclopedic comprehensiveness of the treatises as of sloppy borrowings from works issued by London publishers.

Writers who moved in the best circles, or said they did, when addressing the plain people laid great importance upon good manners at the family table so that correct techniques would be easy and unselfconscious when the occasion arose for dining in company. Children seated at the table should be instructed that their supply of conversation should never exceed the demand. Fathers were to be permitted to tell their stories without interruption or juvenile comment. Parents were allowed the initiative in selecting the subjects of conversation, the younger members of the family striking in occasionally with "some variations of moderate length." Table manners were to be closely watched.

"Gilbert," said the old Quaker, Dr. Gilbert Titus Pearsall of Dutchess County, New York, "use thy fork," when he saw Gilbert Junior pick food up from his plate.

"Fingers were made before forks," replied the Doctor's pert off-spring.

"Thine wa'nt," said Dr. Pearsall.

There are a few foods where no satisfactory substitute for fingers has ever been found, among them chicken wings, corn on the cob and spareribs. "There's just no nice way to eat a sparerib," Mrs. Lyndon B. Johnson once told the press. A good deal has been written about how to eat corn on the cob while observing the proprieties.

"It is not elegant to *gnaw* Indian corn," wrote Charles William Day in his *Hints on Etiquette and the Uses of Society* (New York: 1844). "The kernels should be scored with a knife, scraped off into the plate, and then eaten with a fork. Ladies should be particularly careful how *they* manage so ticklish a dainty, lest the exhibition rub off a little desirable romance."

But Eliza M. Lavin permitted gnawing under some circumstances; that is, if the diner took the ear daintily by the stalk end, onehandedly, and nibbled without dribbling grains of corn, sticking the elbow out at right angles or leaning over the table. Otherwise, it was better to score and cut, as Day recommended. The author permitted the use of little metal spikes at each end, but says it was "very inelegant" to take the ear up in both hands.

Perhaps the best accommodation was to behave with plasticity, according to who was present at the table. Corn served on the cob was essentially a family dish. On a Michigan farm, for illustration, where the hired men sat at the family table and sopped up the gravy with their soda biscuits and used their coffee spoons to finish the gravy, the advice quoted above would, if followed with exactness, have betrayed a lack of a sense of nuance and situation. Therefore the observance of one social canon would require the violation of another and perhaps a more important one. The late, great pomologist, U. P. Hedrick, son of a pioneer farmer located in the Little Traverse Bay area of Michigan's lower peninsula, looked back when he was full of years and honors to the sweet corn season and the way the Hedricks handled their succulent Country Gentleman and Stowell's Evergreen.

"We paid little attention to etiquette when eating corn in our family," Hedrick wrote. "We did not break the ear in two and hold a half in one hand, daintily eating two rows; we held an ear of corn in both hands and covered rows in accordance with the sizes of our mouths."

If corn on the cob seldom appeared at formal dinners neither did the Hedricks. Perhaps the most winsome remark ever made on the subject came from Harriet Martineau, the British learned lady who faced the corn-on-the-cob dilemma in 1835 in Massachusetts. "It looks awkward enough," she admitted; "but what is to be done? Surrendering such a vegetable from considerations of grace is not to be thought of."

Place settings came in around the middle years of the last century. Carving was done at side tables, the various dishes served to each guest, one course at a time. This was the new service *à la Russe*. It continued to be bad form to spear the olives or gig a biscuit, lean on the table, draw pictures on the cloth or make bread pellets. There were at least two tablecloths spread, an upper one, removed before the dessert, the under linen taken away, if the bare table was handsome, when the fruit and nuts were brought in.

There is confusion among the counselors as to whether the ladies and gentlemen did or didn't separate, according to the English fashion, after dinner. De Valcourt declared that they didn't because women had advanced to the place where they could carry on a conversation as well as their lords and the men had become weary of their stale after-dinner stories and much preferred the flirtations of the drawing room. A contrary view comes from Mrs. Sophie Johnson. Writing under the name of Daisy Eyebright, she said that in the years immediately after the Civil War the usual custom was for the men to remain in the dining room with their cigars and wine. *The Ladies' Book of Etiquette* split the difference, saying that the ladies and gentlemen should separate, but only briefly. Eliza M. Lavin concurred, and suggested a separation of from twenty to thirty minutes. She called it an instance of "social courage" when the host indicated the men would adjourn to the drawing room along with the women guests and regretted that the American dinner party did not provide the intellectual pleasures of the French salon.

The hardest time was just before dinner when the resourceful hostess needed "all the armor against stupidity that you possess." The blessed cocktail had not yet been invented and the hour was early. Dinner moved slowly forward during the century from two or three o'clock in the afternoon to about six o'clock. The departing guest who lived by the book was gracious but not effusive, urbanely concealed any surprise he may have felt in case he enjoyed the occasion.

The well-stuffed guests at a formal dinner had to face oysters, fish, roasts, punch, game, salad, dessert, fruit, bonbons, liqueurs and cordials, *café noir* with cognac. During the repast the waiter poured red and white wines, whispering the names to each guest, unless, that is, the hostess was a follower of Miss Frances E. Willard, the Great Spirit behind the Women's Christian Temperance Union, or "Lemonade" Lucy Hayes who as First Lady barred all alcoholic beverages from the White House. Three servants in the dining room were enough. The butler usually chose two waiters from among the footmen, or even the parlor maid could assist. The times were becoming more casual. A servant behind every chair was quite unnecessary; and on a Sunday evening the waitress on duty in the kitchen simply sent up supplies and the mistress cooked the hot course on a silver chafing dish. It was possible, of course, to get a meal on the table in the homey American style with only one well-drilled waitress and the cook. This was often done with unpretentious charm by "people living in suburban or inland cities."

Above all, the host and hostess were charged with the responsibility of being calm, serene, chatty and nonchalant even though there was an emotional storm in the kitchen or a crash of glass or china in the butler's pantry. One host, cited for gallantry and urbanity, had a clumsy servant who dropped a boiled tongue on the dining room floor. The host capitalized on the mischance by remarking easily, " 'Tis a mere *lapsus linguae*."

Down to the early years of our own century, the essayists who discussed social procedures assumed that their readers had a domestic staff of from six to ten servants. The butler and coachman were addressed by their surnames. The others were referred to in the third person according to their job description; as, "the up-stairs girl" or just "cook." When spoken to directly they responded to their first names. Nurses and governesses always called their little charges by their given names. The other servants, in speaking to the children directly, said "Yes, Miss Gladys," or "No, Mr. Henry." They followed the same style if they had need to mention the children in the third person, remarking, as was apparently often necessary, "Miss Gladys did not eat her oatmeal."

But where there were servants there was also the servant problem. One writer shuddered at "the household reign of terror, which follows the entrance of the 'new girl' on the scene of devastation . . ." and simply chopped off the subject as one requiring not a chapter but a whole book. A New York matron who found each new arrival more incompetent than the last finally burst out with exasperation to her latest acquisition, a Finnish girl:

"You can't cook, you can't make beds, you can't sweep, you don't even open the door for visitors. Is there anything on God's earth that you can do?"

"Yes, ma'am," the Finn replied, "I can milk reindeer."

The native domestic appears in memoirs of the period with a Western setting as a sturdy democrat who ate up most of what she baked or cooked, expected to be asked to sit down when there were guests for tea and put her head in the door of the parlor to shout, "Mrs. Clavers, did you holler? I thought I heered a yell!" The situation on the eastern seaboard was not more comfortable. A Boston Brahmin like Henry Adams could appreciate from a safe distance the aesthetics of the European Catholic civilization without taking the local Irish to his bosom and it was not until the 1890's that Irish obituaries found their way into the pages of the Anglo-Saxon *Transcript.* So, while Henry Adams was finding a philosophy of history at the shrine of the Virgin at Chartres, Mrs. Adams continued to prefer well-scrubbed Protestant maids.

Miss Beecher, who believed in counting the clothes pins and sweeping under the beds with *short strokes,* wrote that success in handling servants depended upon the manners of the lady of the house toward them. Severity was to be avoided. "Few domestics, especially American domestics," she said, "will long submit to it." Yet the mistress had to be watchful also that the servant did not become the mistress. Miss Beecher suggested that it was a good idea to call the staff together and offer friendly counsel along this line:

"The duties committed to you by God . . . are indeed most solemn and important." Alluding delicately to future tangles which might occur on the job, Miss Beecher explained that "trials are sent by God, not for evil, but for good, so that we, by patiently bearing them . . . may grow wiser and better. . . ." Try to look at them this way, she urged: vexations are "designed for your good."

Dip anywhere into the literature produced by the guardians of gentility and it is apparent that the subject which received the fullest treatment was how to talk. The ability to converse was the test of social sophistication. Slang was to be avoided and cant phrases such as the tiresome repetition at one particular time of the word *splendid.* The traveling, the potatoes, the gin, were all equally splendid. Social nuisances were itemized: punsters, scandal-mongers, tellers of tedious tales. Men in the professions were especially admonished to avoid anecdotes of learned counsel, the muster roll of dead colonels, majors maimed or retired. Merchants should break away from shop talk, medics from their preoccupation with disease. Speak to a pretty woman of the beauties of her mind, not her face; for, says the astute author of the *Art of Conversing* (Boston: 1846), "if she is pretty, she already knows it." Be tolerant. Be considerate. Help your interlocutor to be pleased with himself. Remember with a long patience that triviality comes naturally from trivial people and do not follow Dr. Samuel Johnson, who recommended gracious manners for others but was not a conspicuous practitioner of suavity himself, being quite capable of saying, "Sir, you are a fool."

Authors should not be cross-examined about their work unless it becomes all too evident that they cannot talk of anything else. Nothing handsomer was ever said of the poet, Cowley, than that he did not direct the conversation to poetry. On the other side, nothing is less agreeable to an author than to be told that you have not read his recent book but have sent to the circulating library for it. All of this reminds the humanist that the more we see of change the more it is the same thing; for back in the sixteenth century Castiglione sketched the uncouth conversationalist who entertained a fair lady with an account of how he had killed so many men, how he handled the sword with both hands, the different ways of grasping the battle ax, until the poor woman was affrighted lest he might slay her too.

There was more than a touch of Polonius in the compilers of social by-laws in the Red Plush era. The sententious cliché had a fatal attraction for them, such as "The boy is father to the man." But after allowance is made for other times, other ways, this humble branch of popular literature did convey much sensible counsel which no doubt served as good cement to bind the social structure together. It is the little snobberies, the stuffy style, the saying of accepted things in such a solemn way that have moved later generations to laughter and parody.

There is an element of pathos, too, in the implicit idea that with the elimination of gross behavior the aspirant for social recognition would find the doors of a glittering society swinging hospitably open. To the extent that the manual writers offered such entrée they promised something they could not deliver. The elite have always established a set of cues by which members may recognize each other. And the countersign changed too frequently to be caught in the pages of a book. The conflict of interest between those safely within the charmed circle and those on the outside wistfully looking in was not spelled out by the learned authorities. Yet clever and aggressive persons of iron will who could get near enough to the admired models to shape themselves into a replica have often been rewarded by an invitation to come in out of the cold. In such instances the successful push-up occurred because the aspirants for recognition have had genuine charm or beauty, the power generated by great financial resources and perhaps a political feeling for playing the social angles. The satisfactions of being accepted by those who revolved decorously, or ostentatiously, in a milieu of aristocratic privilege could be had at a price; but not at the price of an etiquette book.

14

※==================================※

MANNERS IN THE REAL WORLD

The French maid comments to the footman in Mrs. Anna Cora Mowatt's play, *Fashion* (1845), upon their employers:

"Monsieur make the money—Madame spend it. Monsieur nobody at all—Madame, everybody altogether."

The new lady of quality of the nineteenth century created and staged the social show. Her husband acquiesced in the arrangement, supported it with his prosperous abattoir or patented pill-rolling machine and faded into the familiar stereotype of the Tired Business Man. It was largely woman's work, then, to devise the patterns, codes and mechanisms of social differentiation such as the precise moment when the spoon tumbler that formerly stood in the center of the family dinner table became gauche and therefore "now rarely used."

Mrs. Robert Greaves McGann, whose father helped to found the exclusive suburb of Lake Forest, Illinois, encountered perplexing distinctions when she was a little girl. Why did not her mother have a sewing machine in the dining room, she wondered, and a nice dish of rosy apples centered on the table as did the wife of their coachman? But her mother, Mrs. Charles B. Farwell, wife of a successful operator in Chicago real estate, marched to a different drummer. "I never had a satisfactory answer," the daughter confessed.

Derogatory names for religious, racial or ethnic groups have often provided a convenient handle for social typing; for example, "bran-eater" a pejorative reference to socio-religious vegetarian tenets, "mackerel-snappers" for Roman Catholics, "spics" for Spanish-speaking groups, "wop" for Italians, "cloak-and-suiter" and many others. According to a "Social Distance Scale" devised by the sociologist, E. S. Bogardus, which expresses the outlook of the dominant U. S. ethnic body, the white, Anglo-Saxon Protestants, the order of social quarantine descends in this sequence, with the most favored at the top:

> *Canadians*
> *British—English, Scotch and Irish*
> *North Europeans (non-German)*
> *Germans*
> *South and East Europeans*
> *Jews*
> *Spanish-speaking peoples*
> *Orientals*
> *Negroes*

Just how stratification and mobility coexist is well illustrated by the Greek-letter college fraternity system. The fraternities have reflected perfectly the style of life, standards of dress, attitudes, speech mannerisms and the gregariousness of the "regular guy." The type most in demand has always been the youth who was already socially poised, with the firm handshake and the confidence that shows he sees his own personality in the right light. The rushee who wins the pin usually has had financial substance behind him. But not always. An attractive candidate who comes from a working-class background, is obviously no grind or meatball, who places a high value on the non-academic aspects of college life, sometimes is chosen for brotherhood. If so, he must pursue the values of the chapter he has entered, rejecting in his social transition those of his parents and less facile siblings.

People who are pushing to the front in a social sense have traditionally turned to their ancestors to validate their own worth, placed crests on their harnesses and coats of arms on carriage doors. Noting the busy department of heraldry in a large New York jewelry store, Price Collier, in his *America and the Americans* (New York: 1897), ridiculed the "American idea that pellets, or carpets, or furs, or ready-made clothing, or reaping-machines, or dry-goods, or patent medicines . . . confer patents of nobility on their possessors or their legatees. . . ." But ritualistic nuances could always be invoked against infiltrating parvenus to enforce standards of caste. The Chestnut Street ladies, Miss Martineau noticed during her visit to Philadelphia, would have nothing to do with the Arch Street ladies because the latter had fathers who had made their own fortunes while the Chestnut families possessed capital that had been accumulated a generation earlier. There was another observable distinction. The Arch Street ladies rose twice on their toes before curtsying; but the Chestnuts rose three times.

The family of a man who sold merchandise in quantity for resale, a wholesale merchant, that is, was a part of the social scene, while the man who made the merchandise, the manufacturer, was not accepted. With the arrival of mass production the manufacturer rose to the top, so that a man whose father had lived in a log cabin could, if he got up a successful new composition for blacking stoves, or a dyspepsia tablet, expect to see his daughter enter the smart set in due time driving her own pony cart. A new class appeared which raised delicate social problems—artists, musicians and "persons connected with public journals." One writer commented with sympathy that these professional people were apt to be hypersensitive, since they "do not know precisely where they stand." For them, along with the possibility of rising in the world, came an unlooked-for consequence, the tensions and anxieties of mobility.

Appearances can deceive, but not speech. The inflections of the voice, its tone and cadence, provide the indicators of those who "belong," for the spoken word connects the speaker with his natural environment. Anyone who started out in life pronouncing *merry, Mary* and *marry* all as *merry* will continue always to do so unless he or she hires a speech therapist or attends a charm school. Family crests and over-mantel portraits were obviously fraudulent if the master of the house or his lady said *gempman*. Voice pitch ranked with pronunciation as a clue to social placement. A girl of the early 1900's said of some of her contemporaries: "You can almost say 'Smith' or 'Wellesley' from the mere tone of their voices. They catch their manners from one another."

Regional accents are not necessarily limiting. The southern accent is often admired for its lazy charm and vague overtones of patrician forebears and social expertise. A pretty and ambitious girl from a Cajun parish in Louisiana coming up to New York for a career in television commercials would, of course, have to go to a speech school and stop saying "couzain" for cousin. These things can be learned. "Lyndon B. Johnson," wrote the late Stanley Walker from his retreat in Lampasas County, Texas, ". . . is an almost perfect example of what can be done with an unpromising Texas voice with a little attention to elocution." Geographical subareas have to be rated individually on the social scale. Some are quaint, like the Western slow drawl; others, like the slurred singsong of the Delaware Bay area, are simply unacceptable. The Boston intonation and the broad A of Long Island, recognized as early as 1870 as a sign of social nurture that began in the bassinet, are the nearest speech style that we have to the mannerisms of the British upper classes; and as hard to endure, in one way, as the "join" or "oyster" of "Brookalino" English is in another.

Emily Post maintained that provincialisms such as "guess," "figure," "folks" for family, "cute" for pretty, were preferable to mincing pretense, as in "Will you permit me to recall myself to you?" A hundred years ago most women said "sir" constantly when in conversation with a man. Mrs. Lincoln did it so incessantly that John Lothrop Motley, the historian and diplomat, complained to his wife, wishing that Mrs. Lincoln "would not, like all the South and West, say 'Sir' to you every instant, as if you were a royal personage."

"You all" got by in southern cultivated speech, but not the dialectal "we uns" and "you uns." When blonde, blue-eyed Anna Evans, daughter of a blacksmith in Franklin, Pennsylvania, announced with a happy shriek, "Dad's struck ile!" the whole country chuckled and took it up. Later the oil heiress explained that she had uttered the famous exclamation as a joke. But the neighbors knew better and probably Anna did too.

The taboos of speech have always been more important than the sanctions. The trite phrase was a particular hazard for the unwary, and still is; like "by and large," which Harry Hansen recently called "a delaying phrase" used by those whose ideas are lagging behind their words. And malapropisms have always been a sure way to achieve an unenviable fame. To move forward in time for a moment, one may cite the linguistic entanglements of a living statesman, Mayor Richard Joseph Daley of Chicago, the pride of the Illinois Democracy and the joy of the working press whose pleasure it is to quote him accurately and in full. His Honor has engaged in a long, gallant but losing struggle with the English language which has marked him as a sort of cultural watershed. It was Daley who, waving expansively in the direction of Carl Sandburg at a dedication ceremony, once declared: "We are proud to have with us the poet lariat of Chicago!" He also once concluded a campaign speech with the stirring pledge: "What we have got to do for Chicago is to restore to Chicago all those good things it never had!"

Periodical literature in the nineteenth century devoted itself anxiously to the improvement of the manners of a society not far removed from prairie, forest and farm. The press took up such subjects as smoking, swearing and slang. Many terms familiar today, such as "racket," meaning a swindle, or "dizzy blonde" date back to the 1880's. Mrs. Stowe wrote about the life she observed around her. So did the urbane George William Curtis and Charles Godfrey Leland, the Philadelphia author and editor. Leland's literary instrument was irony. He recommended that the reader by all means charge forward to take the best seat in an opera box; or, if a Protestant attending the service at a Catholic church, that he "mutter, in an expressive tone, 'humbug,' from time to time." Leland dealt in similar fashion with the conduct he observed at evening parties, behavior in public conveyances and at summer resorts where it was quite the thing, he wrote, to complain of the table d'hôte and to demonstrate aplomb by abusing the dining room staff.

Much anxious thought was expended upon what is now known as Gracious Living. When Chicago was getting ready for its World's Fair in 1892, which included, among other preparations, the erection of a factory for the manufacture of roulette wheels and the laying down of two hundred barrels of whiskey, Ward McAllister, the New York society leader, became worried. What was going to happen when the polite world judged the United States by what could be seen in Chicago, a city run by cottolene manufacturers and dry goods princes who could not be expected to understand the finer points of cosmopolitan living? So McAllister forwarded some suggestions from New York for the guidance of the undisciplined Chicagoans, recommending the employment of French chefs and explaining how to chill a bottle of wine. To this the Chicago *Journal* ungratefully replied that Mrs. William Astor's chamberlain need not concern himself about Mayor Carter H. Harrison frappe-ing the wine too much because, as a matter of fact, his guests would simply blow the foam off their schooners while they enjoyed "Irish quail," which the *Journal* helpfully translated as pig's feet.

Although unlearned about wine coolers or duck bigarade, the ordinary American in real-life situations often practiced the kindliness of a true aristocracy as the "hired girl" and the lady of the house exchanged courtesies in this wise:

"Your bakin'-powder biscuits is always just a *mite* lighter'n mine, Miz' Eddy."

To which the employer generously responded, ". . . if they are, your piecrust's flakier'n mine." And few indeed were the Americans so insensitive to the feelings of others as to greet an undertaker with a witty, "Hi ya, digger." This general statement holds true on all levels. The latest chronicler of the moral history of San Francisco has written that when Abe Ruef, the political boss who picked the city's pockets, was finally jailed for it, his cell mates paid him the highest compliment within a convict's power. They insisted that he take the bottom bunk. Railroad history, too, offers illustrations of the sincere application of what is, after all, simply the Golden Rule. According to a news account of the seventies the engineer on the Kansas Pacific's morning train always drove slowly across a trestle in the present Logan County, Kansas, so the passengers could see if anyone had been hanged during the night.

Following the instincts of a warm and generous nature, John L. Sullivan did not need a handbook to tell him how to be polite. On one occasion the pugilist charmed authentic royalty. The Boston Strong Boy met Edward, Prince of Wales, in London in 1887. Bored with protocol, His Royal Highness greeted the holder of the diamond-studded belt with a gracious informality which proved to be contagious.

"Prince," said John L., "if you ever come to Boston, look me up. I'll see that you're treated right."

Sullivan said afterward, "Anyone can see he's a gentleman . . . the kind of man you'd like to introduce to your family."

The champion always defended Edward VII after that, even when the Irish question came up. "He has to keep his job," the fighter would explain to the boys deployed along the brass rail. King Edward had to follow British policy or "he wouldn't last as long in the king business as a ham sandwich at a Jew picnic."

The ordinary American could be direct and forthright when firmness was needed to discourage social offenses. The methods were less subtle than the double-whammy administered by the lorgnette and icy stare, but wonderfully effective, according to a report of how a man was dealt with who interrupted a dance in Cherryvale, Kansas. "They do not allow any protracted disturbances at dances in Cherryvale," reported *The Commonwealth* of Topeka on a May day in '75. "Mr. Hollifield lately invaded a scene of revelry by night in that place, and went to shooting off his light fantastic mouth, when he was promptly knocked down by a skillet in the hands of a floor manager."

In the days of Chicago's lusty youth, just about the time when McAllister was offering instruction in French cookery and the proper decanting of wines, a gracious American woman demonstrated her breeding in a celebrated social dust-up. The episode occurred in connection with the Exposition whose ostensible purpose was to commemorate the four-hundredth anniversary of the discovery of America by Christopher Columbus. But it had other objectives, too—to advertise Chicago and provide the setting for some rare social didoes. The most important guest of the nation present when President Grover Cleveland pressed the button, the gonfalons were broken out and the fountains began to play, was Her Royal Highness the Infanta Eulalia, who represented the King of Spain at the festivities. The Princess, accompanied by her husband, Prince Antoine, arrived in George M. Pullman's own private car. The royal couple were installed by the City of Chicago at the Palmer House and there was much excited speculation among the socially eligible as to whether one shook the Infanta's hand or not. One of the brilliant functions arranged for her was a reception at the turreted mansion of the society leader, Mrs. Potter Palmer, who was also the able and hard-working President of the Board of Lady Managers of the Fair.

Eulalia created a furore by refusing to go to Mrs. Palmer's home since Bertha Honoré Palmer was the wife of an innkeeper, as such matters were understood in Spain. The Infanta finally yielded, went late, left early, sat crossly on a small dais prepared for her, sullen and unbending, while the beautiful hostess, Mrs. William J. Calhoun remembered, stood at the side of her icy guest "offering martyred Chicago society at her altar . . . that night, it was she who was the princess."

The prejudice against women trying to support themselves continued down to the close of the century. But changing circumstances were offering young women alternatives to their "circles"— Shakespeare, Browning or sewing—or the modest degree of self-expression attained in doing something new with crétonne. The typewriter, cash register, adding machine, addressing equipment, duplicating machines and especially the telephone opened up new opportunities for women to achieve economic independence. The office, assisted by the bicycle, produced what the dress reformers had demanded but failed to get for generations—shorter, less voluminous skirts, sensible tailored suits and shirt waists for street wear. At Vassar College an early undergraduate, Ellen Henrietta Swallow, wore her gymnastic suit all day long one memorable October day when the geology class went to Rondout. Ellen found the freedom of the unconventional costume "so suitable," and wondered with a shiver "if the *Poughkeepsie Journal* will chronicle the wonderful sight." But even liberal Vassar, haven for the spirit of free inquiry and social innovation, balked when Professor Farrar arranged to take some of the girls down to West Point to see the Cannon Factory. The college administration would not permit such a field trip; "it might get into the papers."

Women of the theater who were not afraid of what the newspapers would say, and indeed rather favored their saying something, or anything rather than nothing, threw their influence against the conservative standards of the times. Adah Isaacs Menken, according to her most recent biographer, was the first woman on either side of the Atlantic to bob her hair or smoke her cigarette in public. When her husband objected to her experiments with the sophisticated habit, Adah reacted violently to his "badgering me with his sermons on cigarettes. . . . I will not submit to dictation of any man."

Another stage figure who exerted a deep influence on the manners of the emerging new type, the American business girl, was the French actress, Anna Held, who helped to popularize the pleasure of chewing chicle. Anna Held was a woman of little dramatic talent, but no one denied that she was extremely decorative—and all the world knew that she took milk baths as a beauty treatment. For years Miss Held's career was promoted by William J. White, a man of bold enterprise who made a fortune by softening Mexican chicle and adding mint flavor. Once an obscure popcorn and candy peddler, White became known internationally as the Chewing Gum King and made his home city of Cleveland the Gum Capital of the World with his peppermint-flavored Yucatan. Anna publicly chewed the new confection, for which she was well rewarded. Worldwide headlines told the story when Anna's grateful friend gave her a $120,000 necklace of matched pearls.

The gum tycoon also made sensational news for his delicacy when he once handed a stick of Yucatan to Edward VII, sometimes known as "Edward the Caresser," and White saw to it that the American newspapers were aware of the King's "gracious acceptance." Although Edward laid the packet aside with the polite remark that he would not chew "just now," the clever Clevelander had established the atmosphere that he wanted. The King of England, traditionally the First Gentleman of the World, had joined the brash Americans in their rhythmic enjoyment of the dainty which millions were chewing for its long-drawn-out sweetness and then discreetly discarding in convenient spots under piano keyboards, tables, sofas and chairs. So thoroughly did the gum habit establish itself that today a professional gum-exterminator working full time harvests a seven-pound wad of used gum every weekday in New York's Grand Central railroad station and double that amount on holiday weekends. But the cud no longer comes from the sapodilla tree. It is polyvinyl acetate, most of it supplied by the Hercules Powder Company, the big explosives manufacturer.

The overfastidious woman who conducted her life in light of what the neighbors might say and regarded such exclamations as "bother" and "the Dickens" as demi-swearing, was probably unaware that a sometimes coarse familiarity and frankness had been for centuries one of the marks of the aristocratic posture. King Henry VIII stretched his gouty leg upon Catherine Parr's lap, and his daughter, Elizabeth I, exclaimed to Sir Roger Williams, who had fought so gallantly in the Low Countries against the Spaniard, "Williams, how your boots stink!" to which the knight replied with spirit, "Tut, Madame, it is my suit, not my boots which stink."

The eighteenth century, like the twentieth, to which it bears some resemblance, had a taste for plain-speaking and robustious anecdote. William Byrd II, while reading the sermons of Tillotson one afternoon, wrote in his diary, "I gave my wife a flourish . . . the flourish was performed on the billiard table." Dr. Alexander Hamilton, when he dined in the family circle of a Robert Hogg in New York City, heard his host speak "good neat bawdy before his wife, who did not seem to be much surprized att it." There was certainly nothing repressed about Ann Willing (Mrs. William) Bingham, the beautiful and fascinating society leader of Philadelphia in Federalist times. A lady of the nineteenth century did not hear a double entendre; or if she heard it she pointedly did not understand it. If something ribald was said, "not the shadow of a smile should flit across the lips." But it was otherwise with the gay Mrs. Bingham. She could swear as picturesquely as the contemporary Duchess of Devonshire and was known among the fashionables of her social set for her relish of sophisticated innuendo.

Dixon Wecter tells of Mrs. Bingham being at dinner with an intimate circle of friends when "someone mentioned the Duke of York, a gentleman so embarrassingly rotund that 'he was compelled to cut a semi-circle out of his table to give access to his plate,' whereupon Mrs. Bingham demurely solicited the company's sympathy for the plight of his new bride, the Duchess of Württemberg."

There was a far closer correspondence between the frankness of the privileged classes and the free-and-easy manners of the proletariat than existed between the upper levels of society and the middle class with its fastidious reticences and almost pathological attachment to the concept of "respectability." Mrs. Bingham would have treasured equally with any hard-rock miner, one feels, the anecdote of the young lady of Austin, Nevada, who was disappointed in the gifts her suitor presented to her and asked for "something binding." Whereupon her cavalier immediately dispatched to her a present of seven pounds of cheese.

Edmund Quincy, second son of President Josiah Quincy of Harvard, who followed the arduous profession of being a Boston gentleman, did not consider himself bound by the proverbial "of the dead say nothing but good" when in his judgment funerary tributes clashed with the truth.

"We have at last succeeded in burying Mr. Choate," Quincy wrote soon after the event, referring to Rufus Choate, a clever barrister who had filtered more rascals through the interstices of the law than any other lawyer in America; "but he is now fairly at rest in Mount Auburn. We began the wordy sacrifice as soon as the news came of his death . . . we brought together an infinite quantity of words and heaped them together over his body. . . . What had Mr. Choate done in his lifetime that so many men should glory in making themselves fools over his grave?"

Strong social taboos existed against gossip, but human nature kept breaking through when Mabel spent the afternoon with Florence. The record spoke for itself: "We talked everybody over & ate nuts." But the effects of gossip have not been as destructive as generally supposed. Sentiments uttered in private, such as "He'd skin his own grandmother for a buck," do not usually enter into public situations. Since the victim is not confronted with what has been said about him, there must be present in these private revelations some element of consideration for the feelings of others; either that, or ordinary prudence.

Some three thousand terms of denigration exist in the English language. Americans have contributed generously to these ample resources for name-calling. Only a few can be noted here. Colonel William D'Alton Mann, publisher of the scandal-mongering society magazine, *Town Topics,* printed his social notes from Chicago under the heading "Skunkville." William Goebel, Kentucky legislator and governor, who had a talent for biting invective, described a man he didn't particularly care for as "Gonorrhoea John." An editor in Emporia, Kansas—not William Allen White! —wrote of a man he regarded as a lout that he was a New Englander but had "spent *all his manhood* in Illinois," and asked, "Is that the reason he brought so little to Kansas?"

William Barclay ("Bat") Masterson, frontier peace officer, was as formidable an adversary with a pen as a revolver. A specimen of his prose runs as follows:

"Horace Greeley once said that 'politics makes strange bedfellows.' The old sage comes very near hitting the nail on the head, judging from where we saw Col. Prouty and Perry Wilden last night. Gentlemen we advise you to disinfect yourselves this morning."

It is impossible in a discussion of the American facility in verbal assault and battery to omit the prayer of a plain-spoken Missouri preacher who was called upon professionally when a young man was bitten by a rattlesnake. According to Ozark tradition, the parson offered up the following petition:

"We thank Thee, Almighty God, for Thy watchful care over us

and for Thy goodness and tender mercy, and especially we thank Thee for rattlesnakes. Thou hast sent one to bite John Weaver. We pray Thee to send one to bite Jim, one to bite Henry, one to bite Sam, one to bite Bill; and we pray Thee to send the biggest kind of a rattlesnake to bite the old man, for nothing but rattlesnakes will ever bring the Weaver family to repentance. . . . We pray Thee to stir up Missouri, and, if nothing else will bring the people to repentance, we pray Thee to shower down more rattlesnakes. Amen!"

Plain-speaking on a higher level of society comes into view in a lively incident in the tutorial life of Dr. William Everett, son of Edward Everett, clergyman, diplomat and orator. Dr. William, known to his contemporaries as "Piggy" because of his slovenly dress and careless personal habits, was headmaster of Adams Academy in Quincy, Massachusetts, and suffered acutely over a stupid boy in the Virgil class. As Samuel Eliot Morison tells the anecdote, the student "insisted, despite frequent correction, on pronouncing the name of the hero of the Aeneid as 'É-ne-as.' Finally Piggy could stand it no longer. He jumped up and down, banging the desk with his fists, exclaiming, 'You goddam little fool do you suppose that Dido would have fallen in love with a man who accented his name on the antepenult when the penult was long?' "

Amusements in the later nineteenth century were governed by economic resources, social cohesiveness, the degree of isolation and the prevailing morality. In the rural areas, which meant most of the United States, the characteristic relaxation continued to be making farm work into play—husking bees, barn raisings and the like. Or in a small town, if the town was Marshall, Michigan, the bearded oldsters tilted their chairs back against the front of Seaman's Drug Store on Main Street and exercised their unappeased imaginations in gossiping about Kit Billings' breezy new milliner.

Urban relaxation in the 1880's, recorded in the letter of a young girl describing the simple pleasures of a Sunday outing in Rochester, New York, started with "Pop" hiring a carriage with a "gaily fringed top" and driving the family in style to Maple Park. Most people took the nickel ride on the horse cars but the Erie Canal had brought prosperity to many businessmen in Rochester including "Pop's" clothing store. And so they walked and trotted—the family name is not given in the letter—to the Glen House, marveled at the majestic falls of the Genesee where silent Tuscaroras once glided in the pools below the cataract in bark canoes, enjoyed the hearty seventy-five-cent lunch in the beamed dining room and a lazy afternoon on the piazza chatting with the resident guests of the resort who "spend their whole week's vacation here." And perhaps the young correspondent, Louise Florence, and her friends and "Pop" explored their teeth after the spareribs and sauerkraut, fluffy rolls, hot chocolate and pie with the new wooden toothpicks which stood in a holder. This technological advance in gracious living had become widely available since Silas Nobel and James B. Cooley of Granville, Massachusetts, had patented the first machine for making wooden toothpicks a few years before.

Recreation and inspiration came through the spoken word in Victorian times as delivered from the lecture platform by literary figures, humorists, orators, whiskeyphobes, celebrities of the moment and a generous sprinkling of insignificant nobodies. The residents of a town like Beaver Dam, Wisconsin, for instance, went to the Town Hall to hear Frederick Douglass plead the cause of the Negro people, listened to Barnum argue the temperance question, stare at Tom Thumb, laughed with Artemus Ward and resolved to dig for riches in their own backyards after hearing Russell H. Conwell, the Acres-of-Diamonds man.

In the states of the Old Confederacy the orator of the day at a speakin' had only to say "Comrades of my father" to get an ovation, rising to his climax with a reference to "the Lost Cause which could never be lost so long as Americans reverence valor and devotion." The audience would cry and stomp and some would give the Rebel Yell. The band struck up "Dixie" and in imagination a ghostly army with sacred battle flags and guidons snapping to the breeze passed in review once again.

It is significant of the cultural values of the epoch that the legitimacy of any pleasure was certified by such thought leaders as the Beecher tribe, only if it prepared the mind for the life of duty. Hunting was approved if undertaken for meat but not if engaged in for amusement. Horse racing was disapproved, like the theater and all games of chance, because the associations were apt to be evil. But here again one must look for the reality beneath the appearance, for the golden age of poker was from 1870 to 1920 and every generation which has lived since the surrender at Appomattox has understood the terms of the pastime as used in metaphor— *ace in the hole, in the chips,* and *put the cards on the table.*

Dancing was never more in favor, although the Methodists outlawed round dances as "hugging set to music" and entered the further objection that young women who went to assemblies wore dresses that were too tight, overloaded their stomachs and did not have enough vitality left after such indulgences to resist the "miasms." In the coteries of some social pretension the colonial custom of gentlemen calling upon their feminine acquaintances on New Year's Day spread westward from New York where it had originated back in Dutch times. The ladies received in their Sunday best and provided hospitality in the form of food and beverages for those who dropped anchor near their sideboards.

"Every woman, that *is* 'anybody,' stays at home, dressed in her best," wrote Lydia Maria Child, in describing the ritual as it flourished among the burghers of New York around 1842. For the convenience of the fashionable world, the *Cincinnati Gazette* printed the dialogue which was all that the occasion required:

"Good morning (or evening) Mrs. (or Miss). I wish you a very Happy New Year.

"Thank ye. May you have a countless number of them. Will you take a glass of wine, Mr. ——?"

So, said the *Gazette,* "you sip, nibble, bow and depart."

If the ladies were not receiving, they hung out beribboned baskets supended from the bell pull. It served as a depository for the callers' visiting cards. The gentlemen bragged on the number of calls made, the ladies on the number received between ten in the morning and the nine P.M. closing. New Year's Day was a great day for the wine and spirits trade. By the time a gentleman of the old school with a wide acquaintance had reached the home stretch on his social rounds, why grandfather smelled wonderful, his presence announced by the unmistakable bouquet of the ethyl acetate esters which develop in whiskies of mellow age and integrity. Mayor Harrison of Chicago recalled fondly the alcoholic overtones of New Year's Day in the Chicago of his youth: "Great bowls of egg-nog of the good old kind, made of genuine Bourbon, and 'with a stick in it,' and no mistake, stood on every sideboard. In some homes port and sherry, a rare bottle of champagne, but many a jug of an especial distillation of Kentucky corn-juice, were at hand to add their potency to the egg-nog in rendering the callers *hors de combat.* . . ."

The custom of New York's calls was well known in the West in 1867. A newspaper in Emporia, Kansas, listed it as one of the major blessings of the times, along with the laying of the Atlantic cable and the triumph of the Republican party. The observance peaked out locally when the society men of four prominent families made their calls in an illuminated omnibus drawn by six white horses decorated with plumes and rosettes and preceded by a brass band. The temperance movement struck a powerful blow at the moist visiting. The world was growing larger. Uninvited guests crashed the gates. Invited guests moved to Staten Island and were heard of no more. The custom declined sharply after the eighties, was only a memory, laid away with the lavender and old lace, by 1900.

Along with the restless mobility of life in the United States, there exists also in our people a stubborn, affectionate and sometimes pugnacious attachment to the places where they were born or have chosen for their adopted homes. When Julia Ward Howe wrote the greatly admired lyric for the "Battle Hymn of the Republic," Ralph Waldo Emerson mourned because she had been born in New York: "I could well wish she were a native of New England." Catherine Beecher's first impressions of Cincinnati were favorable because she found the women there "New England sort of folks." But even New England was not monolithic. Timothy Dwight, a New Haven man, thought that the Seminary in Cambridge suffered because of its proximity to Boston, whose splendors were too powerful an allurement for youths who had matriculated at Harvard presumably to learn to be Christian gentlemen. Even today, well-placed citizens of southern California look at distant educational institutions with reserve.

"What's the matter?" a prominent oil man is said to have asked a graduate of Harvard. "Couldn't you get into Stanford?"

We are all caught up in the distinction which the French language makes between *patrie,* the whole nation, and *pays,* one's immediate and beloved homeland. When Soviet Ambassador Anatoly F. Dobrynin and his wife called upon former President Harry S Truman at Independence, Missouri, Mrs. Dobrynin asked whether Mr. Truman had grown some corn that was lying on his desk.

"No," Mr. Truman replied. "That's Kansas corn. We raise better corn than that in Missouri."

Yet Mr. Truman's remark would have been considered incomprehensible if not libelous by a good Kansan who, if placed on the Champs Élysées and asked to look toward the Arc de Triomphe,

would think instinctively of another wide street he knew and loved
—Kansas Avenue in Topeka.

This same loyalty to *pays* could work in obverse, as when such a
distinguished and sagacious citizen of the world as John Quincy
Adams was vastly amused at the idea of a railroad being built from
Boston to Worcester because, as he saw it, "Who wants to go to
Worcester?" But for sheer naïveté it is not easy to match the response of a Philadelphia girl who was being presented at Court.
When asked by Queen Victoria where she lived, she replied simply: "The Main Line." To those who love it, Coles County, Illinois, is "The Buckle on the Corn Belt," and Kentucky, according
to the late Alvin F. Harlow, is "the finest essence of America; the
sugar in the gourd, the honey in the horn, the sort of country that
the rest of America ought to be but can't. . . ."

Americans who like it where they are say so in poetry, in song, in
humorous exaggeration and sprightly quip and in solemn, statistic-
studded Chamber of Commerce handouts. Perhaps the national
shrine for ethnocentric sensibility is Chicago's Forty-third Ward.
This garden spot of the universe is presided over by Mathias
("Paddy") Bauler, himself a real museum piece of a saloon alderman, whose political aphorisms include the astute comment, "Chicago ain't ready for reform." Voters who live west of Clark Street
love Paddy, who still provides beer and bratwurst with open-
handed hospitality and sometimes delights the local Democracy
with a ballad celebrating warmly the spirit of *pays*. It was composed and is often sung on ceremonial occasions by Win Stracke,
minnesinger of the North Side. The song begins:

> *First you head north till you get to the Park*
> *Then you go a few blocks west of Clark*
> *When you start feelin' better you can thank the Lord*
> *That you're back home in the Forty-third Ward*
> *In the Forty-third Ward*
> *The Forty-third Ward*
> *I'm feelin' great and I thank the Lord*
> *That I'm back home in the Forty-third Ward.*

"Great song," wrote Herman Kogan, watchdog of culture in the
Second City, after Bauler's seventy-fifth birthday party. "Pure Chi-
cagoese."

III

Patterns of change since the turn of the century

★ ★ ★

15

THE PAPERS—THEY PUBLISH HER FACE

It is a truth universally acknowledged that most people find it pleasant to see their own names in print. The next best option is to read about the affairs of those who live a fashionable and public life, especially if the tale is spiced with jaunty anecdote.

When the first tabloid newspaper appeared in New York it promised its readers a bountiful feast of news and gossip about the rich and powerful because, as volume one, number one, of today's mighty *Daily News* put it, "the doings of the very fortunate are always of interest." Even the murders were classified by tab editors as "classy cases" and "cheap cases." What constituted class? When a vivacious blonde was fatally shot, if the story involved beauty, yachts and racing stables—it was a classy case. The new journalism of the 1920's rediscovered the values developed earlier by Colonel William D'Alton Mann, whose *Town Topics* went about as far as it was possible to go in gossiping about "the fun of distributing an apparently endless income," or the husband of "frisky disposition," identified as a member of an Old New York family and a graduate of Princeton who "belongs to all the clubs."

In the day of the two-line joke, HE asked, "Don't you like to read that column in one of the daily papers called 'Live Topics About Town?' " To which SHE replied: "Yes; but I like better to read *Town Topics* about Life."

Keeping up with the society chatter about the fascinating follies of the idle rich was, to be sure, purely a spectator sport for the purchasers of the *Daily News*. But their paper, handy for folding in the crowded subway, was brilliantly edited to carry out the spirit of its flip slogan, "Tell it to the Sweeneys and the Stuyvesants will understand." There were beneficial side effects. It was possible to pick up from such reading occasional clues about what was permissible in social usage and what was forbidden; the perplexing fact, for instance, that it was quite all right to swear but not to call a dinner coat a "tux." And the suggestion that the devil was lurking behind the hydrangeas at Newport or Southampton was set forth in sufficient juicy detail to provide material for wholesome moral reflection.

Newspaper attention to conspicuous coteries known at various times over the last hundred years as the *beau monde,* the bon ton, the recherché, the Smart Set, the international set, café society and latterly the jet set, has ranged from a dignified "court gazette" style of reportage to backstairs revelations, pungent satire and a certain amount of parody, known in current argot as "the put on." In the course of these diurnal duties, the newspapers have done much to accentuate a sense of pageantry and aristocratic privilege by publishing accounts of the balls and parties of selected groups, repeating their names and ascribing to them an awe-inspiring authority. Society has been our best substitute for royalty.

The news items about those who symbolize some form of chic has been read by two different publics, those who are or conceivably might become a part of the ballet, and those who knew well enough that the world of the fashion-plate ladies and their suave escorts was beyond their grasp. But the commonalty could stand near the marquees with the photographers, watch beside the steps of smart churches and enjoy the obsequious prose of the society columns where they met in a Roseland of the imagination those who live out the fairy tale.

The notion of introducing into a newspaper a department devoted to the life of glitter was the invention of the clever but raffish James Gordon Bennett, who founded his penny newspaper, the New York *Herald,* in 1835. The *Herald* was bold, piquant, filled with Mephistophelian laughter. It printed accounts of the pomp and circumstance of New York's worldlings, including lavish private fetes, marriages and deaths, but not births. Complete candor as to biological events awaited the arrival upon the journalistic scene of Walter Winchell.

Bennett described his coverage of society news, possibly with tongue in cheek, as being designed "to bring out the graces, the polish, the elegancies, the bright and airy attributes of social life . . ." and coyly printed only the first and last letters of proper names with intriguing dashes in between. But the mailed fist was always potentially present in the form of barbed paragraphs capable of making a hostess think twice about brushing off a *Herald* reporter. And the newspapers had other weaponry in their arsenals if they cared to employ them—overt abuse, ridicule and, worst of all, silence.

The publisher of the *Herald* set a pattern by revealing intimate details of his own life. Bennett described lyrically the charms of his prospective bride, her mind, heart, figure, manners and net worth. The *Herald* was a pioneer in noticing the arrival of ships carrying newsworthy passengers, took the names of guests off the register of the Astor House "since obviously," Dixon Wecter wrote, "anybody able to pay $2 a day for a room must be a person of consequence."

A peculiarly lush, finger-in-the-mouth style was invented to heighten the drama of the social scramble. It was unidiomatic and decorated ornately with elaborate euphemisms. Sons of wealthy families were scions. French phrases were used with abandon to add a note of exclusiveness. A reception became a *soirée*. The ladies' attire was always *soignée*. Meade Minnigerode in his *The Fabulous Forties,* culled an ecstatic report from a New York newspaper of the period, not identified but quite probably the New York *Herald,* dealing with an event honoring a Miss C., whose last name was too exquisite to be disclosed, but her address was 473 Broadway. There she lived in an elegant granite mansion, revolving genteelly in a social circle which was "one of the richest and purest in town." The affair being described was a private dance. The reporter, almost overcome by the charm and solvency of the women present, could only convey the social atmosphere by writing "At a fair valuation about $4,500,000 of property in stocks and real estate at present prices were represented by the fair ones present."

Editors in other cities experimented with the new conception that the entertainments of the rich were of wide general interest. They began with descriptions of weddings and anniversaries. When Nicholas Longworth, father of Ohio viticulture, and his wife celebrated their golden anniversary on Christmas Eve, 1857, the Cincinnati *Commercial* published an account of the event, but apologized nervously to its readers, justifying the intrusion on the grounds that the event possessed "serious historical interest."

Rudimentary beginnings of society journalism may be discerned in manuscripts which were passed around discreetly at the court of Louis XIV, a kind of forerunner of the "Washington Letter" technique of distributing reputedly inside information and wild surmise. In the London of the eighteenth century the news sheets circulated in the coffee houses reported respectfully upon the movements of the royal family, hinted at high jinks among the lords and ladies. Early news sheets of our own colonial period, when mentioning those who practiced the graces, introduced the stock phrases which were later, through hard usage, to reach the stage of complete exhaustion.

After the Civil War the new "comfort" classes in prosperous towns and small cities imitated the manners of the elite of the metropolitan areas. The weddings and anniversaries of a popular druggist or leading grocer, for example, were reported in flowery detail with full lists of the presents received and names of the donors down to the last pillow sham, toothpick holder, pickle fork and napkin ring. Often the personal items and the advertisements were commingled and had to be sorted out by the alert reader; as when a couple, just married in southern Michigan, might find the account of the nuptials appearing in the Battle Creek *Daily Moon* entwined with the news that "Scrofula lurks in the blood of nearly every one, but Hood's Sarsaparilla drives it from the system and makes pure blood." Since scrofula was a medical term popularly used to refer genteelly to venereal infection, the newlyweds might have felt understandably annoyed.

The reader appeal of the social news was essentially feminine. Once this point was established, the more important newspapers usually, but not invariably, employed women editors in their society departments. Women were found to be accurate in describing costumes, apt in dealing with local genealogy, alert as to the existence of feuds and scandals. Best of all, the sisters of the press had a feeling for when to pull out the stops and sound the lark notes.

When the West was wild, rough-hewn editors often published burlesques of conventional social reporting. A Missouri wedding was reported as having taken place "between a hazel thicket and the wagon" and the same editor reported in the next year—it was 1858—that "a society of Free Lovers has been organized on the Neosho, in the Southern part of Kansas. . . . They all take the New York *Tribune*." Similarly, the Dodge City *Times* gave a facetious account of a pair of the town's B-girls: "Miss Frankie Bell and one of her associates were deposited in the dog house this afternoon." The writer went on to identify Frankie as the lady who earlier in the summer had used language which so offended the chaste ears of Wyatt Earp, the notorious gunslinger, that he had felt obliged to box her ears. It cost him a dollar in police court, but was undoubtedly worth it.

The same newspaper, in the rowdy days of the cattle drives, entertained its readers with a parody of the descriptions of the ladies' costumes at exclusive affairs. The take-off shows that the stereotyped story was understood—as when the *Post*, back in Washington, D.C., wrote with bated breath of the wife of John Wanamaker, the great merchant and postmaster general in the administration of President Benjamin Harrison: "Mrs. Wanamaker wore a gown of silver gray satin and velvet, with silver passementeries forming a deep bertha to the square-neck corsage, on which the vest of white lace was outlined in sable." This kind of reporting was understood, then, when a "hop" was held at the Dodge House where a Mr. I.G.J., the paper said, "wore his elegant blond moustache a la gin sling, and was tastefully arrayed in arctic overshoes with collar buttons and studs."

A certain malaise has often assailed the American male when he found himself clawing his way upward in the society game. A case in point is the visit Mary Garden, the diva of the Chicago Opera company, paid to Amarillo, Texas, in 1930. It was announced that Gene Howe, the publisher of *The Amarillo Globe*, would entertain with a tea for the artiste at his home. Male guests, it was made known, would not be admitted unless they were turned out in proper style. As a consequence, there wasn't a frock coat to be had in the entire Panhandle and one clothier telegraphed to Chicago for forty-two more of the long, preacher coats. Howe wrote candidly that he would high-tail out of Amarillo if he dared on the afternoon of the event, but that Mrs. Howe regarded the tea as the highlight of her social career. "She is fearful that Miss Garden will not come to our tea," he said. "I am fearful that she will."

"Mary Garden knows everything as to etiquette," Mrs. Howe assured her husband; "she knows class when she sees it." This declaration did not add to the peace of mind of the master of the Howe ménage and Gene sneaked off to Emil Myers' night school to bone up on staccatos, arpeggios and cadenzas, but realizing all the time, he said, that he was small game to the great singer and vibrant woman who had her own villa in the south of France, was a sell-out when she sang at $7.50 a seat in New York and chummed around with such figures of the great world as the Prince of Wales, Mayor Jimmy Walker of New York and the cowboy philosopher, Will Rogers. But there were no fireworks at the tea. Miss Garden was charming, stayed for an hour and a half, drank two cups of tea and kissed the publisher, known as "The Tactless Texan," twice as she was leaving.

In small town America, the social news was usually regarded as too important to be trifled with. So it was long ago when a country scribe wrote "The Knights of Pythias received thirty new uniforms for their grand parade on Easter Sunday." And so it is today when it is still a matter of keen interest locally to know that the Walkerville, Montana, Volunteer Fire Department met at Community Hall, gave the pledge to the flag and recited the official prayer. For a hundred years the heart-beat of the "country correspondence" has not faltered. Modern social ramifications, even the rise of the union labor movement, have only served to strengthen the interest in neighborly social news. Announcements about the Sewing Club and the Hobby Club appear regularly in the regional publications of the AFL-CIO unions, of potluck suppers with bingo afterwards, of bake and rummage sales, of engagements and items reporting distinctions, such as the news reported in the *Kansas City Labor Beacon* of how Mrs. Anita Kirby, Milgram Food chain checker and a member of the Retail Store Employees Local 782, was named "Checker of the Year."

"When the girl at the glove-counter marries the boy in the wholesale house, the news of their wedding is good for a forty-line wedding notice, and the forty lines in the country paper give them self-respect," wrote William Allen White, of the Emporia *Gazette*. "When in due course we know that their baby is a twelve-pounder, named Grover or Theodore or Woodrow, we have that neighborly feeling that breeds real democracy . . . when we see them moving

upward in the world . . . out toward the country club neighborhood, we rejoice with them that rejoice."

"Our social activities," White continued, "tell of real people.
. . . We know a gown when it appears three seasons in our society columns . . . it becomes a familiar friend." "Boston people,"
he said, "pick up their morning papers and read . . . without that
fine thrill that we have when we hear that Al Ludorph is in jail
again. . . . For we all know Al. . . ."

And so it was, and is, with the joys and heartaches of this life,
and the little meannesses, too. The subscribers could read between
the lines. They understood who was snubbed when the list of wedding guests was made up, who stood outside the bereaved home
after the funeral service "waiting to see the mourning families, and
to be seen by them." Readers could make an educated guess as to
how much insurance the dead man carried. Often it was not necessary to speculate upon the matter. The local press supplied the
information as a matter of legitimate public interest.

Daily newspapers in the 1880's did not observe the standards
which mark their society pages now. The *Cincinnati Enquirer*, for
one, was definitely the tribune of the people, and mixed in items
about Mrs. Washington McLean's gown when she entertained ex-
President and Mrs. U. S. Grant with the news that "Mr. Thomas
Flaherty, foreman of the Little Miami Railroad shops, will give a
birthday party to his friends on the 20th." Similarly, the *Chicago
Tribune* kept an eye not only on the Farwells and McCormicks,
but also noticed the grand ball of the Liquor-Dealers' Protective
Association at the North Side Turner Hall where G. L. Ritzhaupt,
popular salooner, and wife led the grand march, followed by alder-
men Rowalski and Costello, Ernest Hummel and T. Hogan.

When Joseph Pulitzer took over the languishing *New York
World* and instilled new vigor into the society department, there
were no telephones, no press agents on hand to supply, as Ishbel
Ross has said, "the poundage of the wedding cake." It called for
reportorial enterprise to tell the *World's* feminine readers about
who wore an emerald tiara or a diamond choker at the opening of
the opera season. William Randolph Hearst, invading New York
in 1895 with the purchase of the *New York Journal*, made the society columns increasingly pert. His staffers portrayed the society
world as one inhabited by ordinary, fallible people. But they had
steam yachts. Hearst began the now-familiar custom of first-naming
social figures. Mrs. Herman Oelrichs became "Tessie." Thousands

knew Mrs. Stuyvesant Fish as "Mayme." The mass media had made a valuable discovery—that tales of frivolity, social jockeying for position and "conspicuous waste," as Thorstein Veblen put it, were excellent bait for inducing readers to part with their penny.

Most society editors have labored in anonymity, but Anna Bolton Ellis is remembered in New Orleans for her years of service on the *Times-Picayune.* At the turn of the century, Mrs. Marshall Darrach, writing under the *nom de plume* of Lady Teazle, gave a distinctive touch to the *San Francisco Chronicle's* reports on the activities of the descendants of the old bonanza kings. It was in conversation with a society writer that Ward McAllister remarked, "There are only four hundred people in New York that one really knows." The term "the four hundred" caught the public's fancy, became a part of the American language at a time when great stress was laid upon the competitive entertainments of rival social leaders. The top layer were few enough in numbers so that it was possible to publish the names of the boxholders and their guests in the parterre at the Metropolitan Opera House, not only on opening night but on every subscription night throughout the season.

The czarina of all society editors, past and present, she who reigned and ruled, was Miss Marion Devereux of Cincinnati, eulogist of the well-born, whose embroidered rhetoric was merely the outward expression of an extraordinary drive to power. Miss Devereux was the Dun & Bradstreet of Cincinnati society. No young girl was an authentic debutante unless the tiny, frail woman, whose office was the clearing house for society's business, said she was. By the time Miss Devereux slipped into the editorial chair at the *Enquirer,* the newspapers of the United States had learned that a little judicious buttering-up of a prominent matron created goodwill among valued advertisers. And hostesses had learned the power of the press to chastise.

Miss Devereux understood how to capitalize these opportunities. Her father, originally from Boston, was Arthur Forester Devereux, a Civil War brigadier and a Government engineer stationed at Cincinnati after the war. The editor of the *Commercial,* Murat Halstead, persuaded Mrs. Devereux, the mother of Marion and a woman of education and cultivation, to handle the society news for his newspaper. Called Madame because of her French-sounding name, she survived several newspaper consolidations, perfected her own technique of praise and punishment, edited *Mrs. Devereux's Blue Book of Cincinnati, a Society Register and Convenient Refer-*

ence Book. Mrs. Devereux handed her portfolio on to her daughter when she retired in 1910. Marion, burnished in two fashionable schools, with a fluent command of ladies' seminary French, became adept in the art of gush and in skirting the law of libel when she wanted to enforce discipline. Mrs. So-and-So, she wrote "appeared in a lovely bead necklace." She would bring a young matron down the pole fast enough by noticing her absence from the social scene, and explaining, "But of course she is not going out in any large way at present." Or she could give just a playful little tap of warning: "Mrs. B—— wore the green dress in which she always looks so well."

When an important ball or wedding was coming up on the social calendar, Miss Devereux set the date, named the hotel or country club where the function would be held; and her word was final. If society reporting is, as some newspaper men have privately defined it, "the art of saying the least in the most possible words," then Miss Devereux was the champ. A competitor, the *Cincinnati Post,* once paid her the tribute of saying "When better participles are dangled, it is safe to say Miss Devereux will dangle them." She caroled and she twittered. Debutantes were "rosebuds." If there were two in the same family they were "twin rosebuds on the parent stem." A table was "the mahogany." Mrs. Charles Dana Gibson, who was in Miss Devereux's good graces, was always "very distinguée," and Mrs. Henry Probasco, "very Grande Dame." The Hinkle box was "a scene of constant *va* and *vient.*" The ladies who made up Cincinnati society were, collectively, Femina: "For this supreme occasion, Femina had resplendently arrayed herself in some of the most scintillatingly exquisite creations evoked by the couturier's wand of enchantment."

When Miss Devereux died in 1948, the *Enquirer* remarked retrespectively of the tiny ink-queen's contributions to the subliterature of the United States:

"Her endless sentences, complex processions of high-flown writing in which modified modifiers were modified by modified modifiers, compelled the awe of the shop girls and dowagers, college professors and high school students, who read her column. The spangles of phrases in French and exquisitisms in English which glittered through paragraphs added dazzle to opulence."

But the women of Cincinnati ate up what has been called "Devereux English" and asked for more. All limitations on space ceased so far as Marion Devereux's department was concerned. Often a single weekday's society news might run to sixteen full columns or two pages of coruscant prose which Alvin Harlow once said tinkled like "small, sweetly attuned bells in a mauve-tinted, heliotrope-scented atmosphere." Perhaps one specimen culled at random from an abundance of riches will suffice to demonstrate what this indefatigable chronicler of the Best People could pack into one sentence:

"Saturday night's affair was therefore a tribute to this long friendship, the plans for it having been made before Mr. Blank left last spring for Washington and, later, for London, where he was best man at the wedding of the daughter of the Count and Countess Széchényi (Gladys Vanderbilt), a brilliant event in the English capital, where the bride's father holds the distinguished post which, until the last year or so, he filled with such distinction in the United States—that of ambassador of his native Hungary, of which his house is one of the most ancient in that land of the Magyars."

Marion Devereux was, obviously, a character. She created an unique role for herself. A whole city accepted it, sometimes to the considerable inconvenience of Very Important People. Upper-class Cincinnatians, one can speculate, enjoy anecdotes about Miss Marion, but would not willingly look upon her like again.

With the connection between publicity and Position well established, the endorsement of commercial products by women of social consequence reached its fullest expression after World War I. The idea was old enough. A hundred years before, an advertising throwaway was distributed in New York by a dry goods store on lower Ninth Avenue, with a picture showing the exclusive Miss Julia Gardiner of the Long Island Gardiners, strolling along Ninth Avenue carrying on her arm a small sign, shaped like a lady's hand bag. It carried the commercial message:

"I'll purchase at Bogert and Mecamly's, No. 86 Ninth Avenue. Their goods are Beautiful and Astonishingly Cheap." There was a caption identifying the endorser as "Rose of Long Island" on this possibly first sale of her name by a New York lady of quality. The Gardiner family shopped, as a matter of fact, at A. T. Stewart's. But Professor Robert Seager II, biographer of Julia's future husband, President John Tyler, thinks there is no doubt but that Miss Gardiner posed for the picture or authorized its use.

Other instances come to mind of similar arrangements later in the nineteenth century. The famous preacher, Henry Ward

Beecher, lent his name and prestige to the promotion of sewing machines, pianos, Pears' Soap, a patent medicine and a truss. Mrs. James Brown Potter, wife of a nephew of the august Bishop Henry Codman Potter, spoke up for Harriet Hubbard Ayer's Cold Cream on her fashionable Tuxedo Park notepaper. On the contrary, Mrs. Potter Palmer of Chicago was definitely unhappy when a brewery used her photograph to cheer up a calendar advertising beer.

Bertha Honoré Palmer, whom we have met before in these pages, had brought big-time Society to Chicago and ruled her demesne from a glass-domed mansion on Lake Shore Drive. She had attended the coronation of Czar Nicholas II in Moscow, entertained the Prince of Wales at the Palmer ranch in Wyoming. Presidents Grant, Garfield and McKinley had eaten off Mrs. Palmer's gold plates. Mrs. Palmer drove the golden nail at the dedication of the Woman's Building at the Fair in 1893 while a vast concourse gave the Chautauqua salute and all sang "America." Yet Mrs. Palmer could not escape the beer calendar since Illinois had no statute covering the right of privacy. The reply to her protests was that her face and name were a national resource: "Greatness is death to privacy . . ." affirmed *The Western Brewer.*

Pond's Cream moved into high society in 1924 when Mrs. O.H.P. Belmont agreed to do an advertisement. By the end of the decade a long list of names carrying associations with the great world—Roosevelt, Astor, Gould, du Pont, a countess or so, the Lady Iris Mountbatten—were appearing regularly in the advertisements, from *Harper's Bazaar* to *True Confessions*, revealing that Pond's was a necessity of life among the exquisites. History came full circle when a Mrs. Potter d'Orsay Palmer, grand-daughter-in-law of *the* Mrs. Palmer, posed with her Camel cigarette. It was a brand preference she shared in the slick magazines with Mrs. Rufus Paine Spalding III, who was seen everywhere at Pasadena, in Mexico, in the West Indies or at the exciting opening nights of the New York shows; also with Mrs. Anthony J. Drexel III of Philadelphia for whom emphysema held no fears, and Mrs. Nicholas G. Penniman, also a IIIrd, of Baltimore. Other Camel enthusiasts were Mrs. Louis Swift, Jr., of Chicago, Mrs. J. Gardner Coolidge II, of Boston, and Mrs. Thomas M. Carnegie, Jr., of New York. It may be observed that the young women who leased out their photographs and their husbands' prestigious family names had often acquired them through marriage to juniors, seconds or thirds.

In the 1920's and the thirties, the testimonial became a potent enculturating device as manipulated by the far-flung J. Walter Thompson Company, an advertising agency which maintained a fully staffed "personality" department for entwining potent names with potent products. "Get the Pope!" Sam Meek, a Thompson vice president, once said to Miss Lucile Platt, head of the Personality Department. Miss Platt failed. But it was a glorious failure, for she procured a legal release from the Most Reverend Samuel A. Stritch, Archbishop of Chicago, the Archbishop of Canterbury, the philosopher John Dewey, and George Bernard Shaw.

Changes in the world and in our national life since the 1940's have depreciated the value of the old society names on the testimonial bourse, while the rising market on show-business personalities has beat the Dow-Jones averages. But there was a flutter in 1960 when Mrs. Alfred Vanderbilt modeled a nightie for *Harper's Bazaar* with a sleepy-time hairdo. It was all very ladylike; "about as naughty," commented the New York *Herald Tribune's* Eugenia Sheppard, "as a potato sack." The appearance of this photograph may not have been a shattering event in our social history. But it did provide something to talk about at formal dinner parties and had the professional models, who customarily double their fees if asked to pose in lingerie, batting their false eyelashes over the unexpected competition.

There is now in existence a code of ethics to guide those who are socially important and may wish to turn intangible values into hard cash. It has been spelled out by the authority on what is mannerly, Miss Amy Vanderbilt.

"Many of the most conservative people in the country," Miss Vanderbilt says, "now consider it acceptable to endorse a commercial product for either money or publicity" but "the boundaries of good taste should never be overstepped." Miss Vanderbilt offers an example of where to draw the line. Parents and grandparents may be brought in—tastefully—"but preferably not without their knowledge and consent if they are living." If dead, they can just whirl in their graves. Miss Vanderbilt might, as a matter of fact, have put the case for notifying the living even more strongly than she did. In this instance good taste is backed up by legal penalties. In a number of states, New York to name one, there are tough statutes covering the commercial exploitation of living persons without their consent. The products which people who move in the best company may praise for a consideration without loss of face include: foods, liquors, cosmetics, cigarettes, home furnishings, cars, radios, musical instruments and various means of public transportation. Still considered canaille are depilatories, mouth washes, tooth pastes, foundation garments, underwear, stockings and patent medicines.

"If you endorse products, use them," Miss Vanderbilt cautions, "or at least possess them for possible use."

Here ordinary prudence comes to the aid of a refined sense of the proprieties. For there is always the possibility of some patrician lady finding herself mixed up in a quite unpleasant Federal Trade Commission proceeding conducted by an ungallant examiner who often permits government attorneys to pursue a perfectly horrid line of interrogation.

Somewhere in between Family and Money lies American Society, or what is left of it. And publicity has come to exercise a profound effect among the fashionables since they have absorbed the lesson that family and money mean little unless generally recognized. But Society has adjusted to the facts of life and found them rather fun. Marie Manning, who originated the Beatrice Fairfax column of chat, states flatly, "It was all bluff, we knew, about these people not wanting accounts of their Belshazzar feasts written up in the papers."

As long ago as 1898, a book of etiquette laid down the rule that it was better to see a reporter than to order a servant to kick him downstairs. "If the errand is inoffensive," the pseudonymous author of *Etiquette for Americans* wrote, "remember that the person bearing it is, after all, only earning an honest living in a disagreeable way." This counsel of toleration was hardly necessary, for at almost the same time Price Collier, who viewed the social scene from the perspective of Tuxedo Park, New York, noticed sadly an "evident love of publicity," which he deplored as "very *bourgeois* indeed."

The Edith Wharton and Henry James kind of society long ago disappeared from the gossip columns. There is a new elite, talented young men and women from the amusement field who have become celebrated because of their accomplishments and deft publicity. They possess no great fortunes but are attractive and amusing. If they entertain professionally at some high-level event, they also mingle afterward as honored guests while the names and faces of the stars now appear even in the *New York Herald Tribune's* carefully edited party pages beside those of Mrs. Lytle Hull or the Ambassador of France. Notable for exercising an unusual restraint is Miss Angie Dickinson of the movies who has never hired a press agent and has said that she doesn't want the whole world to know it every time she says hello to the President of Bolivia.

It is significant of the shift in emphasis which has occurred that the first issue of the *Daily News* devoted its front page to a picture of the present Duke of Windsor sitting on a horse, captioned "Newport to Entertain Prince of Wales in August"; while today the paper's social orientation is toward vignettes from nightclub life: "Upstairs at the Downstairs girl-watchers got an eyeful when Shirley MacLaine, Chita Rivera and Monique Van Vooren ankled by on the same evening." And that iron man of Broadway and television, Ed Sullivan, makes his daily omelet from such exotic ingredients as gambling news from Las Vegas, Orson Welles's gall bladder ("acting up in Madrid") or a romantic interlude between Alice Topping and Roy Cohen who are, or were, "blazing in Acapulco."

Far removed from the personalia of the Manhattan bistros, the staple social news across America has remained the wedding, frozen into a form so rigid that only the names and pictures need to be changed. The young girl ready for marriage is the center of American social life. It is a moment of effulgence for the bride and groom and the newly allied families. The spotlight is on the bride, her costume, attendants, the mother's costume, the father's occupation, if noteworthy. The community rating of the families can be understood by the knowledgeable reader without a glossary. The marriage ceremony will not be performed at City Hall but in a church, preferably a Protestant Episcopal Church. The contracting parties are likely to be listed in the *Social Register*. If one is not, it is a "mixed" marriage. If the families are not in the *Register* they share at least the outlook and position in life of those who are. If the grandparents of the bride were residents of New York City and pretty well fixed, that fact will be indicated in the story, which suggested to a team of sociologists who have studied the society pages of *The New York Times* "the recency and impermanency of any aristocracy."

The bride's ancestry, if linked with early American history, will get a thorough combing-over. Preference is given to colonial governors and Revolutionary War heroes. Her memberships in genealogical and patriotic societies will be enumerated. The specific gravity of the Colonial Dames is considerably heavier than that of the Daughters of the American Revolution. But one must watch for a trap here. There are two rival orders of Colonial Dames. Both are impeccable. But one is more impeccable than the other. The importance of Old Family, however, has recently been called into question.

According to dashing young Mrs. Richard Savitt of New York, who had a year at Briarcliff College and possesses an *avante garde* fashion sense, the important points today among those who consistently maintain a high degree of visibility as social symbols are how one talks, dresses, handles make-up and the hair. "Family and that stuff," she says, "really doesn't matter today."

This bulletin detailing the essentials of the society woman in contemporary practice may have beneficial side effects in saving ambitious families from committing improprieties in the hot pursuit of escutcheons. The invention of ancestors or their embellishment has in the past produced some classic blunders. The instance comes to mind of how one American family's vaulting ambition o'erleaped itself. These people installed a brass tablet, well antiqued, honoring a reputed progenitor in a rural parish church in England, only to have their monument exposed as spurious when an English family of the same name revealed that the plate bore the imprint of the manufacturer and the date 1879. Another cautionary tale in connection with the manufacture of ancestors attaches to an indiscreet Duc de Levis who hung in his gallery a painting in which the Virgin was represented as graciously saying to his forebear, who bowed before her, hat in hand, *"Couvrez-nous, mon cousin."*

If a New York bride is of social consequence, her parents will have multiple homes. Location is important. The town house, for instance, will not be situated in the Bronx. Country residences are subject to similar restrictions: Southampton, yes; Hampton Bays, no.

The educational background of both bride and groom is part of the tribal story, provided that they attended private preparatory schools and the groom graduated from an Ivy League college. College background for the bride is permissible but not required. Information regarding the bride's debut is important, the date, place and auspices, if a public group affair, because some presentations are more significant than others. If the bride was presented to society at the Colony Club and the wedding reception was given at the Union Club, *The New York Times* will photograph the couple after the ceremony at its own expense and publish a two-column cut under a three-column head at the top of the page.

Although the wedding story is a stereotype, it is surprisingly revelatory. There in print stands a record from which caste can reliably be inferred. New York is not peculiar in this respect. Similar clues exist for other cities. In St. Louis the bride will have attended the Mary Institute and been a maid of honor at the Veiled Prophet Ball. If a Washington reception is held at the Sulgrave Club, if the bride has been presented at both the Debutante Ball and the Baltimore Bachelors Cotillon (spelled just that way) and if her grandmother honored her at the F Street Club, even the out-of-town papers will understand that these nuptials are practically dynastic. Any marriage throughout the United States is socially important if the bride brings to the union prestige (Her people have held on to ancient riches); economic power (Father of the bride is president of an insurance company); or important function (Father is chairman of the Republican State Committee). If the family of the groom qualifies under any one of these categories and the bride's family does not, the marriage is still newsworthy. But the story will be shorter and there will be no picture.

Certain contingencies sometimes arise in which a wedding is newsworthy, all right, but the city desk channels the story into the general news section far from the chaste pages concerned with "Family," as the *Los Angeles Times* calls it. For example, when Harry Leeb, a rich but little-known Chicagoan, who wears green-tinted glasses and a sharp, continental-cut suit, had his press representative distribute to the newspapers a news item prepared for their use headed "Gray-Haired Prince Charming Gets His Princess at El Morocco," *The New York Times* was sufficiently impressed to send a reporter interested in sociological phenomena to witness the first marriage ever solemnized in the Champagne Room of the well-known night spot. There was a double-ring ceremony, *The Times* reported. The bride wore both rings, one a 20-carat diamond, the other an emerald which Mr. Thomas Buckley, the representative of *The Times,* declared "was just as green as and only slightly less noticeable than Lever House."

After the knot was tied, Mr. Leeb packed up his money and flew his bride and fourteen friends to Paris where the wedding party occupied a whole floor at the George V Hotel. To assuage any ennui which might occur in the City of Light, there were side trips arranged for everybody to emplane for London, Rome or Majorca. Later, "alone at last," as Mr. Buckley expressed it, the Leebs cruised among the Greek islands in a chartered yacht.

The question of ostentation inevitably came up.

"It's really not being ostentatious," the bridegroom insisted, "because our normal way of living is on a comparable scale."

Strangely enough, the very next day after the ceremony at El Morocco another unusual wedding occurred, this time in River Forest, Illinois, which is a nice residential suburb of Chicago but not to be confused with Lake Forest. The *Chicago Tribune* gave the River Forest story a real play but kept it far, far away from Society, Home and Family. After a church wedding, a thousand guests jammed into the lavish suburban night club, Villa Venice, which is located actually in Northbrook. Each guest carried a white envelope stuffed with the most popular gift in the world—cash. The fete was held to compliment Anthony R. Accardo, Jr., son of Anthony (Big Tuna) Accardo, patriarch of living Chicago mobsters, and the junior Anthony's bride, Marie Hawley, also well-known as Miss Utah of 1961.

Among those attending were a squad of Chicago detectives and the Federal Bureau of Investigation, both mingling in their professional capacities, pointing cameras and popping flash bulbs as the interesting guests arrived in their big, black limousines, covering their faces as they cornered sharply into the club driveway. The guest roster included Jackie (The Lackey) Cerone, the loan shark, and Paul (The Waiter) Ricca, the latter a bit glum because he was under a Federal deportation order; also Felix (Milwaukee Phil) Alderisio, trigger man, Sam Battaglia, gambler and juke box racketeer, two gentlemen who operated a floating crap game, Murray (The Camel) Humphrey, as survivor of the old Capone mob and Albert (Obbie) Frabotta, terrorist and the syndicate's "beatnik poet," who almost carried three detectives into the clubhouse on the bumper of his car when he nearly missed the turn. Observers acquainted with underworld society noted with raised eyebrows the absence of Sam De Stefano. Sam had been convicted as a rapist and bank robber and was snubbed by the father of the groom "because of his conduct in recent months."

Some Los Angeles, or at least Hollywood, parties are also rated as general rather than social news, since it is only to be expected that at such affairs, no matter how posh they are, the conversation will turn to business and some fortunate guest may go home with a good capital-gains deal. It was before such a gathering that Art Linkletter called across the street to Ray Stark, the producer and host, in what may be regarded as the Hollywood equivalent of neighborliness:

"Hey, Ray," he shouted, "can I borrow a cup of money?"

Later Stark took pains to dispel the idea that the whole thing was tax-deductible.

"Part of it," he said ruefully, "I am stuck with as a party for my friends."

Mr. Merriman Smith, in his witty *The Good New Days,* provides an illuminating key to understanding the society sections of the Washington papers, which suggests how invaluable it would be if such exegesis was available for all major U.S. cities. These pages of social intelligence have, as Mr. Smith says, "a language of their own; a language for which there is no Berlitz save experience."

"If a woman is *attractive, vivacious* or *charming,*" the veteran United Press International correspondent explains, "chances are that she's a wee bit plain, fiftyish but important. To mention her *attractive silvery locks* means that she has one foot in the grave. To say that she has *prematurely gray hair* can be quite catty.

"Should a woman be said in print to be *ravishing* or *beautifully tanned,* her dress showed everything. She was half-naked if the gown was *stunningly cut.* . . .

"If a man is described as *courtly* or having *charming Old World ways* and a *still-erect figure,* watch for an obituary soon. He's on his last legs and . . . talks endlessly about Senator Borah and how they quit making good cars when they quit making the Reo . . .

"The experienced Washingtonian . . . also pays attention to descriptive detail. If the affair was *gay* . . . there was only punch. . . . When the gathering was *très gai,* things are looking up—a few got looped, others went on to finish the job at a quaint gin mill. The hosts were a bit above par. . . .

"*Bubbling gaiety* is a dead giveaway. The writer may have been a shade socked-in. It was fun, though. . . .

"Should an affair be referred to as *daringly different,* this may require inquiry. Either the decorations were shockingly bad or the historian dropped in on so many affairs the same day that he or she isn't too clear on detail. Or possibly, the hostess lived up to her not-so-public reputation." *

The charity ball is a social fixture in which the pursuit of prestige or pleasure is justified because the event raises money for good works and the costs are tax-deductible. Such occasions have taken the place of the big, expensive private party. For the lady who desires to escape from the "monkey fur" set and establish herself as an Old Guardswoman, the charity ball gambit continues to be the best bet. Carefully managed altruism pays off in a chance to meet the old families and in social recognition. The field is large. "Name a disease," goes the epigram, "and there is a ball for it"; or if a disease is not involved, the benefit may be a fund-raising device for underprivileged children, or the members of the Association of Former Russian Cavalry and Horse Artillery or just for Wellesley. Often the expenses of the gala are assumed by a cosmetic company, a furrier or a whiskey firm seeking to trade up, if you will forgive the catchword, its "image." The admixture of fun and benevolence has become a folkway on all social and financial levels, so that one finds also the sisterhood of the Ladies' Auxiliary of the Brotherhood of Maintenance of Way Employees in Spokane, Washington, working for the Muscular Dystrophy drive while they play whist and exchange recipes for chicken curry.

The social gains which accrue in working for a given charity are very hard to assess. The names of the committee may be top-drawer, but sometimes they are only window dressing. A personal press agent, for a fee ranging upward from a hundred dollars a week, can spot worthwhile opportunities, gently propel a client toward a fashionable charity, sometimes even place her on the committee. A woman loaded with new money must really work at the treadmill tasks and the cause must be carefully chosen. In New York it could well be the Judson Health Center or the Boys' Club. A good extension ladder into the social heaven in Chicago is the Art Institute or the Illinois Children's Home and Aid Society. In Boston the debs of the exclusive Vincent Club act and dance for the cause of gynecology.

The socially mobile family which actually undertakes the struggle must be able to grasp the subtle standards of the admired group

* From *The Good New Days*, copyright © 1962, by Merriman Smith, reprinted by permission of the publishers, The Bobbs-Merrill Company, Inc.

and conform as to address, dancing classes, correct schools and an approved style in interior decoration, vacation spots and conversation. The nimble aspirant quickly senses that one drives an old, beat-up Bentley or Mercedes rather than a shiny new Cadillac. If her setting is Boston, she may own mink but will publicly express a preference for tweeds. She would be well advised not to attempt immediately to follow the example of Mrs. Jack Gardner in scrubbing the steps of the Church of the Advent during Lent, toying with Buddhism or appearing in Boston streets with a lion cub on a leash.

In Seattle a small but conservative inner group keeps its nose to the civic grindstone. Service is the key word. Any woman pushing for social attention in that empire of fish, shipping, timber and airplane manufacturing should be prepared to hustle for the Seattle Symphony, the art museum and the new repertory theater, participating, if eligible, in organizations restricted to descendants of pioneers who arrived before 1870. This approach would not work in Philadelphia, where Biddles, Cadwaladers, Chews, Morrises and Rushes were dancing minuets and quadrilles two hundred years ago. The way to mount the barriers in Philadelphia is, well—perhaps it would be better to try some other city.

"I should not like to be a newcomer in Philadelphia," a member of one of the old families has said quite simply.

The modern exemplars of the shop girls who devoured the saucy tidbits in Bennett's *New York Herald,* the granddaughter of the housewives from Dullsville who quivered with excitement over the international marriages of the early twentieth century, still seek social gods to worship. Theirs is the special satisfaction to be derived, in Edmund Wilson's phrase, "from imagining the enjoyment of glamour and power and from immolating oneself before . . . the dwellers in these privileged places." So duchesses, countesses and Frank Sinatra pass in review in "Suzy Knickerbocker's" column of chat in the *New Jork Journal-American* where we can also eavesdrop on the luncheon-table exchange of airy nothings at the Colony—the restaurant, not the Club. Mrs. Clarence Busch, "known as Polly to all" is—had you heard?—"a terrific photographer." The Countess of Camerana who is married to Cinzano, the aperitif fellow, travels to Paris once a week to be coiffed because no one in Rome or Milan understands her hair.

"I don't know about you," comments Suzy, "but just knowing these things helps me get through my day."

Exactly. And who doubts for a minute but what these busy actors in the social pantomime each of whom is, in Professor Daniel J. Boorstin's pleasant phrase, "a person who is well known for his well-knownness," occasionally glance at the public prints, too, and live more successfully with their neuroses because they can exhibit press clippings about their glamorous selves.

"People out here are lonely on a gala scale," according to Mr. Martin Manulis, the television and move producer, commenting upon the social whirl in the Los Angeles area. "They have parties because they don't know what else to do with themselves. The big thing is to put up a tent and invite everybody you know." This motivation is explained by the late psychiatrist, Karen Horney, who noted the psychic satisfaction to be found in prestige "as a means of overcoming fears and inner emptiness. . . ."

With almost everybody in America having access to the good things of life like Ovaltine, dentures and *The Reader's Digest,* our great danger now is a monotone of proletarian affluence. Let us pray, therefore, that the clever rich will grow richer still. Otherwise we may find that there is no one around to wear the new black sheath by Rodriguez and no one to describe the effect. What did Mrs. Perle Mesta whisper to Carol Channing when the stars of the theatre and Washington officialdom mingled so delightfully at Mrs. Mesta's party? The people, caught between the ironing and the peanut-butter sandwiches, have a right to know. Men, and especially women, need to believe in a Land of Cockaigne where the escorts are rich, handsome and suave, the women glossy and blond-tressed, where privileged couples have a home in Virginia, a castle in Ireland, a ranch in California, a purple helicopter and a luxurious yacht anchored in Florida waters while Hialeah is in action. These fascinating possessions of the very fortunate deserve the attention of some less acerb institution than the Bureau of Internal Revenue. There is a good one ready at hand, the woman's-interest page, which keeps the line open to the world of sophistication and in addition can always come up with a good recipe for custard pie.

If the society page did not exist, it would be necessary to invent one.

16

FROM CHAPERONE TO SALOON

When the calendar said the twentieth century was about to arrive there was great public interest directed toward the question: exactly when did the new century begin? January 1, 1900, appealed to the imagination of the average American, to the eye and the ear and to common sense, as the great bench mark which divided what had been from what was to come. But mathematicians and purists held that the new century began at midnight as December 31, 1900, gave way to January 1, 1901. Otherwise the previous century would consist of only ninety-nine years and not really be a century at all.

So on New Year's Eve, 1901, the Reverend Edward Everett Hale stood on the pillared balcony over the front entrance of the State House in Boston and recited the Lord's Prayer in a sonorous voice. The moon hung in a starry sky, the sea of upturned faces filled Beacon Street, Hancock Avenue, Mt. Vernon Street, Park Street down as far as Tremont and lapped over into the Common. There were massed choruses and a blare of trumpets. A cannon boomed as the midnight hour struck at King's Chapel. And there was merry-making at the clubs.

The general cultural level, the *Transcript* said next day, "is coming up, coming up fast"; but "We are not better than our fathers, and as regards personal behavior we don't want to be better. We are bluntly, confessedly worldly. . . ." But there was widespread confidence that the twentieth would be a soaring century. Bryan had been twice defeated. Victoria was still regnant, but a relaxation of the puritan concepts of total virtue, total evil made possible a more genial climate for comfortable living. It did not seem extravagant when Walter Hines Page, prominent editor and journalist, announced that the United States "is, in fact, changing the character of man."

Incautious though Page's exuberance seems sixty-five years later, it only reflected the optimism of the ordinary man who enjoyed access to comforts and conveniences never known before. Novelties and luxuries became familiar needs and reasonable expectations. The typical American was an artless countryman, according to enduring legend, who stuffed his pants into his boots and, when he visited a city, blew out the gas before he went to bed. Yet in 1897 Sears, Roebuck & Company were selling four suits a minute, a buggy every ten minutes, a watch a minute, a revolver every two minutes with the important assistance of a new extension of the postal service, the Rural Free Delivery.

At the same time, the pull of the city was evident as the farming population continued its migration—still unended—to the industrial centers and their higher standards of living. In 1898 indoor plumbing was a novelty and *The Ladies' Home Journal* was reflecting life as it was actually lived when it offered hints on "The Washstand as a Thing of Beauty." Yet by 1925 the Crane Company, manufacturer of plumbing supplies, was asking: "Has Your Family Outgrown One Bathroom?" The pattern can already be discerned here for the second automobile, radio and television set.

Lines of social differentiation changed slowly. "There were the Negroes and the working people," Henry Seidel Canby wrote of the nineties in Wilmington, Delaware, "and the 'plain people,' and Us." If there was an oppressive respectability, there was also little vulgar display, plenty of time for affability. Formal manners were put on for formal occasions. "The pretense of being an aristocrat," Canby wrote, "was hard to keep up."

The older generation had confidence in its civilization. Edward Bok's *Ladies' Home Journal* was the popular authority on the amenities, urged young women to take more exercise and think kind, happy thoughts that would make their faces look pleasant. Rice powder could be used discreetly because it didn't show. Perfume scents were lightly floral, used for a feeling of luxury, not as a man-trap. Sex meant the altar and the stork. Samuel Eliot Morison, admiral, scholar and Boston gentleman, who knew the best society *circa* 1900, recalls that he never saw a cocktail served in a private house until around 1910 and what he got then wasn't very good, being mostly vermouth.

The musical culture of the average American consisted of the current popular ballads, either boisterous or moist with sentiment, and hymns. The latter were sung under circumstances not necessarily religious. People simply knew and loved them. So they sang "Rock of Ages" on moonlight hay rides. A housewife in her kitchen might hum "Work for the Night is Coming" without any application to her own situation. Widely known, too, was Paul Dresser's "Just Tell Them That You Saw Me" ("and they will know the rest") which warned of the dangers surrounding country girls who went to the city. The song won such acclaim that its title was printed on buttons and worn as a sight gag. It was a staple on the stage and in the newspapers and became part of the latest patter used in casual, daily contacts like our present, wearisome *good-bye now*.

In the West and in small communities generally the institution of the chaperone was unknown. But there was a certain amount of informal surveillance. The mother of a young girl receiving male callers looked them over in the parlor, fed them toothsome suppers in the dining room and waved them on into a social life which was largely church-centered. Formal chaperonage appeared in proper social sets of eastern cities as early as 1855, took root in the eighties as traveled Americans became acquainted with the nuances of upper-class European life. Cotillions and chaperones seemed to go together. The writers of etiquette books pushed the idea hard. Mrs. Burton Harrison would concede only this, that "elderly girls" of twenty-five and above did not require the services of a duenna, with one notable exception. Under no circumstances could an unmarried woman, even if pushing thirty-five, visit an artist's studio alone.

If no matronly relative or friend was available, then a girl who was careful about the proprieties, said *The Designer* in 1902, must "perforce secure the good offices of some cultured 'gentlewoman in reduced circumstances'" to shield her from the world's wicked ways. The burden upon a young man's pocketbook and patience can be understood, with roast beef costing sixty cents a portion, lobster Newburg a dollar a plate and all intimate topics barred, making conversation a sticky wicket. A young New York society man, for example, in order to take a nice girl to dinner and the theater would be compelled to underwrite the costs of three or perhaps four tickets, dining at the new Waldorf on Thirty-fourth Street before the play, returning for an after-theater snack, and so down Fifth Avenue to the stately homes of Washington Square for a total outlay of some thirty-six dollars.

One of the very few places a young man could take a gently bred girl without supervision was the Mall in Central Park where, in fine spring weather, the horse-car lines provided free musical entertainment. But the couple could not enter the Casino to have an ice cream or the girl would be the talk of the town. At a formal ball, the young dancers were expected to include the chaperone in their conversation, "at least occasionally," as one writer puts it. If that proved to be too fatiguing, there was always a refuge in some shady corner behind the palms. No rules existed covering visits by young women to the dormitories of men's colleges. The situation did not arise.

In urban life the "bachelor of society," whose social obligations were discussed briefly in Chapter 13, became an interesting *fin de siècle* phenomenon. He lived in a smart apartment or studio and had the liberty, indeed the obligation, to entertain in view of the social attentions he received. "No entertainments," said the *New York Herald* in 1898, "seem so alluring to women as those bachelors give in their own apartments." Feminine curiosity ran high concerning the sitting room over which no woman ruled. The walls were covered with sage green denim, hung with tasteful pictures, the divan decorated with "embroidered eastern stuffs"; it sounds like the Casbah. And there were interesting curios picked up in foreign lands, *objets d'art* and cushions "pyrographically embellished . . . by wishful hands."

Whether the occasion was a tea, reception or chafing dish supper offering novelties and dainties "rarely placed before women," the host was expected to provide himself with a competent chaperone who poured "with a pretty air of assuming responsibility." Or perhaps the girls brought their own. In any event, tête-à-têtes were interdicted. "The whole proceeding," wrote Marion Harland, "is delightful, informal, and Bohemian in the best sense of the word."

The complacent bachelors of 1900 who lived so pleasantly, with the gleam of old mahogany and silver, dining room walls covered with dark red paper and cretonnes of a warm red shade, were in no hurry to alter their way of life and came in for a good deal of public disapproval. The *New York Tribune* called them the "obstinate unmated" and a state assemblyman from New York City, representing the district known to its citizens as "de Ate," actually introduced a bill at Albany to levy a special tax on bachelors. The statesmen, after profound meditation, were unable to decide what committee should open hearings on the bill. But there were many facetious suggestions. The measure was finally amended to provide that the proposed law would affect only the assemblyman who introduced it.

The freedom of American women to go anywhere without thought of molestation had to be modified in the early years of the present century, according to the Travelers' Aid Society.

"Up to a comparatively recent time it has been a justified boast that pure womanhood was its own sufficient protection anywhere in the United States," said the Society in its *Annual Report for 1907*. But it was determined that this was no longer true. Social mutations cited included the enormous influx of immigrants from countries where freedom for women was unknown except as license, changed economic conditions which moved millions of girls from the home to shops and factories and a relaxing of standards which accompanied a growing cosmopolitanism.

Yet the duenna system turned out to be unsuited to the American taste, situation or sense of humor. It represented one aspect of the mores of the metropolitan centers which the rest of the United States had no intention of imitating. But the chaperone remained on duty for several decades in Eastern upper-class coteries. When *Town Topics* said some nasty things about Alice Roosevelt, including the innuendo that she was "flying all around Newport without a chaperone," gallant young Robert J. Collier published an editorial in *Collier's Weekly* comparing the editor of *Town Topics* to a horse thief and second-story man. This thrust became the subject of a celebrated libel suit. The jury, as it turned out, believed that *Collier's* had told the truth.

When the new nickelodeons flashed a slide on the screen saying "Ladies without escorts cordially invited" the end of the chaperone was clearly in sight. The whole idea collapsed in the rebellious twenties. Emily Post's book on the proprieties, first published in 1922, devoted a chapter to "Chaperones and Other Conventions." Five years later Mrs. Post admitted that the chaperone was "vanishing." Ten years later a further revision in Emily Post's classic exposition of the principles of decorum and good form made it clear that the cultured gentlewoman in reduced circumstances had disappeared from American life.

A few vestigial chaperones occasionally surface in connection with the travels and activities of pretty young women who have entered or hope to into a public life. Sedate guardians are appointed to watch over the lovelies who compete for the Miss America title at Atlantic City each September. Miss New York State 1961, for one, was accompanied to the Beauty Pageant by an elderly, cousinly type who spent the whole time talking about chiropractic. The Miss Universe contestants, too, have their duennas. But the show girls of New York and the girls who work the strip in Las Vegas do not. They can dispense with genteel protection since they are experienced in handling the wolves. And their time is so filled up with taking lessons and improving their personalities that, according to soundings taken by one investigator who inquired along the Rialto, they act "as chaperones for one another."

Critics of social change in the century that was supposed to soar found many targets to shoot at before World War I. Decadent manners were blamed on the Kodak which transformed demure maids into show-offs. The quidnuncs denounced the bloomer bathing suit and the bachelorette who earned her living and carried her own latch key. They condemned Dr. Sigmund Freud's theories, the suffragists, the hemline and the new dances. But the mood of youth was gay, buoyed with a sense of liberation, with overtones of bravado, caught by a Victor Herbert song which asked "Dear Beatrice Barefacts, am I in love or not?" The reference was to the well-known Beatrice Fairfax department in the newspapers and the popularity of heart-clinics-in-print which told shy men that they need not kneel in proposing and to hold off on buying the ring until she said yes.

The belles of Revolutionary days had taken their snuff and the mountain ragtail women puffed on their clap pipes all through early federal times and down into the nineteenth century. These indulgences were, if not wholly accepted, at least indigenous. It was definitely something else, an imported style from Europe and the Latin countries, when Adah Isaacs Menken received the reporters stretched out on a tiger rug in front of the fire, feeding bonbons to a French poodle and smoking a cigarette. Ladies of the theater, indeed, led the way to feminine puffing. A New York magistrate committed an actress to the psychological ward at Bellevue Hospital in 1900 because she smoked cigarettes. When lovely Mrs. Patrick Campbell lit a cigarette in the Plaza Hotel in 1907 the dining room shivered and she was asked to cease and desist. Then society women took up the habit, with its cachet of cosmopolitanism. The resistance was spirited. Arthur Brisbane, pundit of the Hearst newspapers, wrote on Sunday that cigarettes destroyed the hair and on Monday morning the papers quoted from the Sunday sermons preached against the new vice. Literary women smoked, too, women like Gertrude Atherton, Agnes Repplier, Jeannette Gilder and Mrs. Edith Wharton, who was literary and high society, too; also Alice Roosevelt, who was authentic society but not literary.

A rumor even filtered down from Boston that the well-placed women members of The Country Club at Brookline, a social enclave which required no other identification than *The* Country Club, were smoking. Although the club membership represented "the nearest thing to the sporting element in Boston" the canard was given little credence. A social crisis did occur at the White House when the wife of the Russian ambassador asked President William Howard Taft for a drag. Taft's military aide, Major Archibald W. Butt, scrounged a cigarette from a musician. Taft was plucky about it and even held the match. The following year— 1911—so slowly did the warders of convention yield the field, a Russian danseuse and a real countess, too, was tossed out of Chicago's Blackstone Hotel for lighting up. But feminine smoking had caught on, obviously, when a newspaper quipped:

"You folks are being taken up by society, aren't you?"

"Well, we don't believe in bragging, but we know three ladies who smoke cigarettes."

All barriers fell during the 1920's when the makers of Chesterfield cigarettes posted the billboards of the nation with a shocker showing a nice girl sitting on a moonlit river bank with a young man—in itself once a serious offense—and saying "Blow Some My

Way." Then things picked up. Within three years, Pebeco Tooth-
paste was nationally advertised as a specific for removing tobacco
stains from women's teeth; and at a dinner dance which marked
the formal opening of the Hotel Kansan in Topeka, a geisha girl in
yellow satin pajamas offered the guests cigarettes at the end of the
dinner and a woman took one which, runs a contemporary account, "added greatly to the 'swankiness' of the occasion."

The First World War is often cited as the great divide between
two long slopes, the first an Arcadian age of innocence, the latter
the epoch of disillusionment which, sadly or gaily or defiantly, rejected the standards of the past and came in some degree to rue it.
All such neatly pigeon-holed eras, epochs, periods and ages, convenient as they are for historians, are dubious "epigrammatic sum-
mations" in which, Mark Sullivan observed in writing his multi-
volume archive summarizing twentieth century social history,
"much of the truth falls outside the walls of the form." The tendencies associated with the days of whoopee and flaming youth were
in fact all in motion before 1917-19. Sham civility, for one instance, was being mocked in the funny papers early in the 1900's
by Frederick Burr Opper whose characters, Alphonse and Gaston,
bowed and scraped and got into spectacular difficulties which
"made excessive courtesy forever ludicrous." It is an oversimplifi-
cation, then, to ascribe the revolt from old conventions entirely to
the War. Signs of the times appeared in preceding events—in
bobbed hair, the bushy permanent wave, the fox trot and the
turkey trot, a cleaned-up version of the tango as danced in the dives
of Buenos Aires.

The National Association of Masters of Dancing tried to placate
the Methodists by creating a very circumspect dance and naming it
in honor of John Wesley. Predictably, the dance pleased neither
the dancers nor the Methodist General Conference which rejected
the gesture with contempt. Yet in the day of the jazz baby and the
shimmy (*I Wish I Could Shimmy Like my Sister Kate*) older, traditional ways of life were by no means swept away. Country girls,
all primped and pressed and shining-clean, were standing up to
dance the Portland Fancy while Uncle Ed called the sets. Teen-
agers in middy blouses also shared the excitement and practiced
the steps for Money Musk over in a corner; and tired horses still
pulled the surrey homeward as the morning birds began to stir.
The American scene could only be painted with a palette of vio-

lent contrasts. While swift launches armed with machine guns were freighting Canadian whisky across the Detroit River and "Texas" Guinan was greeting her cabaret customers with "Hello, Sucker," the burning question for millions of palpitating young hearts remained whether to invite the boy up on the front porch when he hadn't yet said anything about going to the movies.

Of all the influences playing upon life and manners in the first quarter of this century the most dynamic was, beyond question, the automobile. In 1899 the problem was what to call it. The word *automobile* had been introduced but it had to compete with *motocycle, motor wagon, horseless carriage, autocycle, autocar* and other entries. Automobile, which some pronounced au-tom'o-bil, was finally adopted for formal reference. But the polysyllabic word was clearly too long for daily use. Cabriolet had already been cut down to cab, telephone to phone, pantaloons to pants and the *Boston Herald* thought that automobile would shrink down to *mobe,* "to mobe or not to mobe—that is the question." But mobe didn't make it. When mother looked at the big thermometer on the front porch and said, "It's thirty-two outside, Will. You'd better throw a blanket over the hood of the Stearns-Knight," she was not alluding to a mobe but to the family auto. Eventually the auto became a *car,* a *jalopy* or a *heap,* depending upon the age of the speaker and the condition of the vehicle.

The automobile was a European mechanism with aristocratic sponsorship. Before the end of the old century the modistes of Paris were designing gowns for fashionable women permitting the free use of the legs in driving an auto in the Bois de Bologne. Oliver H. P. Belmont imported a French automobile in 1899, which made motoring, it was noted at the time, "good form." "Automobile red" became a high fashion note. In fact, so many men and women in Newport's gilded set turned to the new sport of automobiling that it was reported their horses were neglected and the grooms exercised them since they were not being ridden by their owners. In 1900 a plaything of the rich, by 1913 the automobile had become democratized and a popular song of the year "He'd Have to Get Under" dealt with a well-recognized experience of the ordinary American motorist. In duster and overalls he faced cheerfully the inevitable breakdowns, expected to make his own repairs on the spot. The invention of the electric starter introduced the woman driver with many interesting sequelae. Skirts got shorter than ever. As legs became visible, the word for them also became permissible in casual talk, in song and in the written word.

The exciting machine called for the practice of new amenities since, as Marion Harland wrote, "automobiling has so increased in popularity that it is almost a national pastime." There was, it seemed, something about the speed or the smell of gasoline that introduced among "motormen" a "flourishing crop of bad manners . . . the sense of superiority over slower vehicles, that robs many an otherwise well-bred automobilist of all consideration." Among points of etiquette for the road, Mrs. Harland mentioned that a driver should always stop to assist a disabled auto, offer the loan of tools, gasoline or a tow. "Do not stare at another's car," she said, "nor, if at a standstill, examine the mechanism. . . . The fact that you are so lucky as to be an automobilist gives you no license to investigate the workings of another man's machine. . . . When passing an auto of inferior horse-power, do not choose that moment to exhibit your own greater speed. . . . Be careful also not to give such a car your dust. . . . Do not boast of phenomenal runs. . . . Do not violate the speed ordinance. . . . Do not frighten animals."

The thoughtful automobilist provided linen dusters and goggles for his guests, arranged the top and side curtains for their maximum comfort, transmitted all instructions to the chauffeur; or, if a driver himself, he was careful not to turn around when at the wheel to converse with friends seated in the tonneau. The host avoided the stiffly visored cap and leather puttees since they were the badge of the hired driver. An owner who steered, it was pointed out, must differentiate his dress from that of the professional or embarrassing mistakes would ensue. Children were told to keep their hands off the window glass and not to nibble in the back seat. The professional driver who bathed and shaved every day, kept the lap robe neatly folded, tuned the motor up and did not impose his conversation upon family or guests followed an honorable occupation and was often remembered in the will.

The 1920's, rejecting older moralities, especially in the area of sexual freedom, regarded sexuality as "the wisdom of the flesh." At Atlantic City, where women once wore corsets when they entered the water, bathing suits became so brief that the city employed viewers equipped with tape measures to check on the legality of the exposed epidermis. The lyrics of Tin Pan Alley shifted from the traditional theme of idealized love toward sex in the biological sense and gave the young, as Sigmund Spaeth said, "complete and detailed information concerning the Facts of Life." The most spectacular and inane event of these years was the experiment with Constitutional Prohibition which brought the hip flask, the speakeasy, a new familiarity with law-breaking, a mingling of the upper and underworld which had never occurred before. Young women of good reputation drank hard liquor of unknown provenance in illicit saloons, unchaperoned and undamaged in social position. New types of somewhat disreputable citizens became familiar, the big butter-and-egg man, the Daddy, the playboy. In New York there was a white trade from downtown which went uptown to Harlem to listen to a five-piece stomp outfit and drink Chickencock at the Cotton Club. Or they went to Mexico's place where the patrons sipped and splashed in Old 99. This was hooch made right on the premises. Duke Ellington remembered that Old 99 never came out exactly as planned. So Mexico "decided to be honest and admit that 99 per cent right was the best he could do."

In retrospect, the year when the spirit of the twenties topped out may well have been 1926, a year of many memorable escapades. The religious spellbinder, Aimee Semple McPherson, was on trial for conspiracy and perjury in connection with her alleged kidnapping. Earl Carroll, the theatrical producer, was being tried as the host at a party where Chorus girl Joyce Hawley was believed to have indulged in a nude champagne bath on the stage of Carroll's theater. This was the year of the December-May marriage of aging but spry Edward W. ("Daddy") Browning and his buxom, blonde and sexually precocious fifteen-year-old bride, née Frances Belle Heenan. Daddy pet-named her "Peaches," a stroke of onomastic genius, the first time he laid eyes on her.

The romance was conducted with all the calm and sobriety of a calliope concert. The word *peaches* tickled the popular fancy. The *Chicago Tribune* launched a contest to pick the "Prettiest Peach in Illinois," but closed down the contest hurriedly when Daddy filed suit for a separation. Peaches cross-filed, and the case was on at the White Plains, New York, courthouse with salacious overtones and pitchmen hawking a little number on the steps of the house of justice called *Who Picked Peaches off the Tree?*

It caught the spirit of the times—or was it a middle-western device to gig the "effete" East?—when a Chicago newspaper published a dispatch from New York which revealed, "It is now possible in certain New York society circles to send a new form of polite, conventionally worded card of regrets courteously announcing that one is exceedingly sorry one spanked one's hostess while a guest at one of her charming affairs.

"Handsomely engraved cards, couched in the approved language of well-bred etiquette, are being circulated in New York by means of which one can express his apologies for any one or all of fourteen social errors, including striking one's hostess with a bottle, throwing glasses, indiscreet petting, and excessive destruction of the lady's tasteful furniture."

A valuable archive and one still underestimated by scholars is to be found in the advertising pages of the mass magazines which appeared between the two great wars. The text of these commercial exhortations often equaled and sometimes exceeded the candor and vulgarity practiced by the sophisticates. Advertisers discussed in clinical detail "Athlete's Foot . . . that unpleasant moistness between her toes," the problems and consequences of bad breath and difficulties associated with the other end of the digestive tract (California Sunsweet Prunes for regularity). "B.O." (body odor) was invented to promote a soap with a heavy carbolic odor of its own, extremely unpleasant but suggesting to susceptible minds that Lifebuoy Soap possessed remarkable antiseptic powers. Odo-rono, the perspiration suppressant, led the way in the creation of what Hal Stebbins, a Los Angeles advertising man with a reflective cast of mind, has called "The Armpit Industry." A new silk-shirted middle class was listening and buying, including many "hyphenated" Americans just emerging from an older culture.

Between 1900 and the First World War an average of about one million immigrants entered the United States each year, many of whom were eager to shed their beards and step into a ready-made business suit with an Eversharp pencil in the jacket pocket. They groped for a new scheme of life derived not from the authority of an entrenched upper class of which they knew little, but rather adjusted to a code of usage which would put them into harmony with the manners of the level immediately above them. It was also true of the native-born who were moving up that the search for the "right thing" had a good deal more to do with consumption standards than with the cultivation of inner grace.

These restless classes, new and old, provided an audience of several millions for a literature of self-improvement which handled such matters as how to speak standard English, deal with menu French, acquire social ease, discuss whatever came up in polite conversation—companionate marriage, the Pianola, or *Elbert Hubbard's Scrapbook*. Eager Americans, persuaded that they could acquire a cultivated mind by spending fifteen minutes a day with *Dr. Eliot's Five Foot Shelf,* purchased a set of books. They studied the saxophone by mail upon the assurance that the ability to play *le jazz hot* was the new form of chic, and tried to develop a memory like the wizard in the advertisements.

If you can remember when men wore watch fobs and women's shawls were called "fascinators" and necklaces were "lavalieres" then you should be able to remember the advertisement about Addison Sims—"Of course I place you! Mr. Addison Sims of Seattle." The text explained how two men met by accident in the corridor of the McAlpin Hotel in New York. One was the memory expert. He came right up with the most amazing details of a casual encounter which had taken place ages ago: "Mr. Burroughs, the lumberman, introduced me to you at the luncheon of the Seattle Rotary Club, three years ago in May. This is a pleasure indeed. I haven't laid eyes on you since that day. How is the grain business? And how did that amalgamation work out?"

Just why this improbable feat of memory was so important was never explained. But it became an article of faith in the success literature of the United States that the wide-awake hustler never forgot a name or a face and that this was the secret of the successful push-up. Some of the advertising catering to the hunger to be admired, to win money and status, gnawed cruelly at the confidence of the inept and the lonely with the narration of little horror stories of frustration and humiliation. One of Nelson Doubleday's *Book of Etiquette* advertising headlines became a classic, "Again She Orders—'A Chicken Salad, Please!'" There it was. No matter now that she had worn her prettiest frock for him. She was dead as far as he was concerned because he saw that she didn't know how to pronounce the French words on the menu.

Thousands of matrons who had already achieved the wedding ring remained apprehensive over their cultural shortcomings. So they purchased Ridpath's *History of the World* and were prepared, in the unlikely event the subject ever came up, to discourse upon Napoleon's advance on Moscow. Probably the most famous single advertisement aimed at readers of this general character was John

Caples' fantasy written for the U. S. School of Music, selling piano lessons by mail (See Chapter 12). But Caples had a similar triumph with a variation upon the same theme: "They Grinned When the Waiter Spoke to me in French—But Their Laughter Changed to Amazement at my Reply."

The nature of this little parable can easily be surmised. For years afterward, joke writers, vaudeville comics, cartoonists in need of a gag, refreshed themselves at Caples' well. One example:

"They grinned when the waiter spoke to me in Greek, but their laughter changed to astonishment at my reply:

" 'I wanna roasta bif san'wich, str-r-romberry pie, two cup skawfee!' was my simple and clear answer."

A manual of decorum which won the confidence of the new postwar public appeared in 1922 and rose in esteem through the years to become, like the Cadillac motor car, the "standard of the world." First issued as *Etiquette in Society, in Business, in Politics, and at Home,* the book was written by Emily (née Price) Post, a former Baltimore society beauty. Mrs. Post had had an unhappy marriage which ended in divorce. To support herself and her two boys she became a writer of sprightly novels of fashionable life here and abroad in a setting awash with titles and liveried servants. The spirit of the times was favorable for a new manual written with wit, sense and humanity. Mrs. Post produced 250,000 very readable words in ten months.

"The War had acted," wrote Mrs. Post's son, Edwin, in a memoir of his mother, "like a big spoon in stirring up the contents of the American melting pot! . . . a lot of people previously submerged had come to the top. Many of these quite honestly and sensibly wanted to improve themselves . . . to give their children more and better than they had had."

It all started when a Mr. Duffy telephoned Mrs. Post about the encyclopedia. She thought with annoyance that he was a book agent. After this was straightened out, it developed that Richard Duffy of Funk and Wagnalls wanted her to write a book, not buy one. He had in mind a popular but authoritative manual on how to live and move in polite society. Mrs. Post sniffed at the suggestion. She remembered how in her girlhood her mother's friends had laughed at Mrs. John Sherwood for writing her *Manners and Social Usages,* a work they heartily disapproved of as being aimed to boost the ambitious into the Smart Set.

A day or two after she talked with Richard Duffy, Mrs. Post received in the mail a packet of advertisements touting the reigning etiquette book of the time and a copy of the book. She was furious with the advertisements and the book for their condescending tone. Before she quite knew it she was at work on a book of her own. It was to make its author a legend in her own time, and change her own attitude toward etiquette so that at the end she could scorn the form—"nothing is less important than which fork you use"—and sum up the substance: "Etiquette is the science of living. It embraces everything. It is honor. It is ethics."

Emily Post's book pushed to the top of the best-seller lists, shouldered Papini's *Life of Christ* out of the first slot. Everybody called the book "Emily Post." So it has remained in the popular vocabulary. Eleven editions have been published, with the title shortened in 1931 to *Etiquette: The Blue Book of Social Usage.* Total sales are estimated at well over a million copies.

Mrs. Post was re-educated while she educated others. Thinking originally of the New Rich, she wrote of servants and great houses, the protocol of joining an exclusive gentleman's club, casting her illustrations in the form of little storiettes about people or types she had met. Her gift for fiction was evident. At the top of her class structure were the Worldlys who had the right "social credentials" and were loaded. There were Mr. and Mrs. Gilding (she was the former Lucy Wellborn). Lucy played bridge for high stakes and "smokes like a furnace." Somewhat apart, not exactly frowned on but not included in the Eastern set, were Mr. and Mrs. Spendeasy Western. But from the staggering correspondence which she received, Mrs. Post learned that her anguished readers were not trying to squirm into high society like that Mr. Richard Vulgar she had been writing about. What they were concerned with were the tribal customs of normal American neighborhood life—the bridge luncheons, the various kinds of showers, the sewing circles and evening weddings which filled the lives of feminine readers who aspired to ladyhood but had also to be the cook and waitress.

This was an America which Emily Post had not encountered. Meeting gamely for the first time the folks who liked a hot pastrami on rye, she started explaining how to eat a sandwich (with fingers), enter a drawing room (walk in). She wrote of a Mr. and Mrs. John Appleyard, whom she visualized as hailing from Iowa, going abroad on their one great fling and told them and the kibitzer-reader how to arrange for deck chairs on the steamer, how to get their table assignment in the dining saloon and how much to tip.

Mrs. Post's text was under constant revision for years, for she was astute enough to follow in order that she might lead. It worked out well for all. The book stands as an unique commentary on changing manners and mores, spanning the distance between the formal dinner party and such homely topics as Going Steady and Paper Plates for Outdoor Parties, which are, incidentally, just what the guests get today when the First Couple of America give a cookout at their ranch on the "Purd'nalis" River. Whether or not, as has been suggested, Emily Post's *Etiquette* deserves to stand with *Uncle Tom's Cabin* as an influence on American society, an estimate of its authority may be made from the fact that for a generation the public libraries of the nation found that more copies of Emily Post were stolen than any other book except the Bible.

Emily Post was no longer young in those feverish years of jazz babies, racketeers and bathtub gin, gate crashers, collegiate rug-cutters, Stutz Bearcats, raccoon coats, flagpole-sitters and other celebrated phenomena of the times. As she looked out and pondered upon a generation ambivalent about its own values, divided between a sense of liberation and of confusion, Mrs. Post must have looked backward with nostalgia to gentler days when the Old-names lived in a low, white, shingled house, and talked in a low, cultivated tone of voice and the door was opened by a maid in a silver gray taffeta dress with organdy collar and apron, white stockings and silver buckles on black slippers—a maid who would not say "Dinner's all ready!" or deal the plates out like cards from a well-shuffled deck. Despite the social ferment, America was steadily advancing, Emily Post thought, in the remarkable task of creating people of gentle manners within the space of a single generation. We were, she declared, "a wonderful nation."

But, she cautioned, in a low, well-modulated tone of voice, this was something "not to be talked about to anyone except just ourselves!"

17

THE JOINERS

Loneliness is harder to bear in a fluid society than in a carefully graded community life where there is a niche for everyone. Here in the United States where it is a truism to say that everyone came from somewhere else—another city, another geographical region, possibly another level of society—labels and certificates of merit are useful for purposes of identification. Hence the extraordinary strength of the impulse to join, to affiliate, to become known, to eat ceremonially with new people and acquire the privilege, which is easily done, of calling them by their given names. All of this was foreshadowed long ago by Tocqueville who observed: "The Americans of all ages, all conditions and all dispositions constantly form associations."

It is not surprising, then, that no other civilization can show so many orders, associations, fraternal lodges, sodalities, trade groups, booster clubs, garden clubs, women's clubs, relic societies, service and veterans' groups where it is possible to "meet people," "make contacts" and find a place. "Not to belong to a *we* makes you lonesome," as the young girl explains in Carson McCullers' play, *The Member of the Wedding.*

The need for something to tie to has propelled both the frontiersman and urbanized man toward social groupings which distill loyalties and dramatize ethical attitudes. Above all, clubbing together eases the impersonality of American life and relaxes the tensions associated with the struggle for a place in the sun. And so men take oaths in secret orders as buffaloes, elks, moose, eagles, nobles, red men or owls. They gather in temples, grottoes, nests, droves, hives, shrines, shelters, commanderies, encampments, wigwams, leagues, herds, parlors and mystic circles. They join genealogical societies and pin medals or glittering badges upon themselves, invigorated by the knowledge that the principle of inclusion acquires its value because of the existence of its corollary, exclusion. Veterans' organizations serve to recapture youth, preserve the recollections of dangers shared. And they chivvy the Government for gratuities. In rural areas, the Order of Patrons of Husbandry, with local chapters called granges, romanticize farm life, relieve the tedium of existence at the crossroads with exotic ritual and watch over practical issues in Washington affecting farm subsidies.

Sophisticates have laughed at these phenomena. Yet the intellectuals are not immune from similar motivations. They, too, yard up together, for it has been reported there are more academic organizations in the United States than in the whole of Europe. These scholarly sodalities of archivists, professors and learned bibliographers gather by tradition between Christmas Day and New Year's in New York, Washington or Chicago to hear erudite papers delivered and relax discreetly in upstairs hospitality suites. They do not parade along the avenues in fez and burnoose. But they do have professional mysteries of their own which associate them with the trade association movement.

John Buchan, the British author who became Lord Tweedsmuir, has called American friendliness "one of the wonders of the world" while observing also that it "has its fake side. The endless brotherhoods . . . into which people brigade themselves encourage a geniality which is more a mannerism than an index of character, a tiresome, noisy, backslapping heartiness." But, he adds in extenuation, "The native genius is for overstatement."

The development of the gentleman's club in colonial North America paralleled the evolution in England of the coffee houses into the institution of the London club. In the colonies men of leisure and cultivation met in private houses to dine, talk, sing and push the bottle briskly around. Dr. Alexander Hamilton, Scottish physician and fun-loving bachelor, was easily admitted to the Maryland tobacco aristocracy when he emigrated to Annapolis, became the central figure in the Ancient and Honorable Tuesday Club which was "dedicated to raillery." When Dr. Hamilton journeyed north to New England he enjoyed the civilities of similar groups of sparkish gentlemen in Philadelphia and Boston. At the Philosophical Club in Newport the Doctor noticed that punch and tobacco were staples and the talk ran to shipbuilding and privateering, but "no matters of philosophy were brought upon the carpet."

The American city clubs, developing in the nineteenth century, were patterned after the clubs of London's West End. The club became the place where the male, white Christian could retire from the buffetings of the world, the women, the ochlocracy, and enjoy hearty, protein-rich meals, heavy cigars, choice liquors and throw a card in the company of congenial peers. If the member needed a room overnight, a pleasant but impersonal chamber was at his disposal along with the lingering aroma of previous occupants—a mingling of toilet water and used cigar smoke. The oldest social club in the United States with a continuous history is the Philadelphia Club, dating back to 1834. Ladies were admitted to the premises only three times in the first hundred years of the Club's existence; for a ball in 1851 and again in 1869. And there was a centenary tea in 1934. Since the autumn of 1953, women have been permitted in the clubhouse after six o'clock in the evening.

The Union Club in New York, which harbored similar ideas about guests wearing petticoats and "glossy ringlets," dates from 1836. Even its mascot was a tomcat. Both the Philadelphia and the Union developed a set of club characters and the cartoon stereotype of the starchy old member about whom legends, sometimes but not invariably affectionate, cluster.

The clubs whose members represent a fair cross section of The Establishment, which are well financed and encrusted with tradition remain still, as they were in times past, conservators of the outlook of the Frightfully Nice People. A splendid example is the Somerset Club in Boston. The Somerset never lowers its guard, even in an emergency requiring the presence of the Boston Fire Department. Once when the clubhouse was on fire the porter on duty at the front door stopped the firemen and directed them around to the service entrance.

By 1900 a hundred-odd social, political and athletic clubs existed in New York, occupying clubhouses along Fifth Avenue. Their massive façades and heavy oak paneling reflected the power structure of New York's merchants, bankers, lawyers, corporation officers and stock brokers, while the practitioners of the arts found companionship in more modest structures between Gramercy Park and Herald Square. Many of these clubs have passed from the scene, among them the Quill, the Cosmos and the Aldine. About thirty are left today. The Players still stands in Gramercy Park. And further uptown are the various college clubs and the "prestige" clubs such as the Metropolitan, Union, Century, the small but important Brook, and the Union League where, as a member once said approvingly, there are "no dogs, no women, no Democrats, no journalists." All this has changed, however, with the possible exception of canine visitors.

Today the click of spike heels on marble floors is heard in most men's city clubs, either daily or on special occasions. The reason is based on simple economics, the financial perils endured during the Great Depression, the flight to the suburbs from the central city and the nagging servant problem. Club dining rooms are nearly empty at night. But they overflow at the noon hour with broad-shouldered, conservatively dressed men bearing attaché cases who come together to eat lightly, compose a controversy or swing a deal. It has been reported that ninety per cent of the meal checks at the Chicago Club are tax-deductible as a business expense under the Internal Revenue Code, which indicates that the gesture of the host has little connection with old-fashioned "club life."

In Washington the stature of journalists may be gauged from the fact that diners at the Metropolitan Club, meeting place of those who decide and govern, include Walter Lippmann, James Reston, Arthur Krock and the Alsop brothers. The Cosmos Club has attracted men of achievement in science, education and the arts. The Army and Navy, the capital city's largest club, has a membership of retired officers who chat, snooze and grouse among the trophies of many a splendid little war. According to a favorite Washington anecdote, a visitor, being shown around the city, made an inquiry of his host about the club when passing the Metropolitan. "All money, no brains," he was told. At the Cosmos the explanation was "All brains, no money." And at the Army and Navy the guide remarked, "No brains, no money."

Every large American city has one or more men's clubs of impressive architecture and membership—the Pacific Union in San Francisco, the Denver Club in Denver, the Maryland in Baltimore, the Duquesne in Pittsburgh—and most cities have their own university club which requires a college background and a modicum of social credentials. All these clubs keep alive in some degree the courtly traditions of the Gentleman of the Old School.

The country club, with its concept of family togetherness, is quite a different thing. Strictly an American improvisation, now about eighty years old, the country club is an expression of the idea of outdoor recreation for the whole family. It provides a rough equivalent of the English weekend, adapted to American conditions. Such an institution was not needed in England where a gentleman lived in his country box, put up when necessary at his London club. The man of the same general social stratum in America lived in the city, needed some way to get a breath of fresh air. Between the 1880's and early 1900's, the country club altered profoundly the social pattern of urban life in the middle-to-upper classes, led to a rediscovery of play, provided a way of escape from the boredom of the old-style boardinghouse or summer hotel. The country clubs widened the interest in tennis, created generations of swimmers and divers, made golf the dominant gentleman's sport. Women had taken up golf, too, by the late nineties and in Cleveland John D. Rockefeller, Sr., had become involved in his long love affair with the game.

The country club first appeared in the *faubourgs* of Boston when coaching and the old road houses had fallen from social favor and men of position felt the need for a more private form of hospitality than a publican could provide; although the last surviving member of The Country Club in Brookline disputed this explanation. His version was that the purpose of the Club was to provide "a place for the men of Massachusetts to get away from their women-folk." This reminiscence undoubtedly reflected the climate of opinion as recollected by one man. But it was not factually accurate. The club's yearbook for the first year, 1882, mentions privileges extended to wives and families.

Hunting clubs had existed before this time and Charleston, South Carolina, had had a golf club in 1795. But the golf club did not last and the hunt clubs, while good for red cheeks and the liver, did not meet the same broad purpose as the country clubs with their spectrum of sports facilities plus the taproom and the weekly Saturday night dinner-dance. Presumably atypical was the country club described by Forbes Parkhill in his *The Wildest of the West* whose location on the outskirts of Denver was not far from Anna Gould's establishment which she called a "young ladies' boarding house," a facility so popular with some of the country club membership that it was commonly referred to as the "club annex."

There were a score of country clubs in the New York area by the end of the century, and new ones always forming, for, wrote a commentator, "Not all the 'sets' have been as yet taken in, and new clubs are easy to found." Men of limited means "but of course of good social position" often had a weekend at a total cost of not exceeding six or seven dollars. Soon the pattern was being repeated from coast to coast so that almost every man in the local business community of any small city was also a clubman. An indication of the standing of the country club in the United States at a comparatively early date appeared in the San Antonio *Express* in 1908. An obituary notice of the passing of a Texas matron included as pertinent information the statement that she was survived by a sister who "lives in El Paso and belongs to the Country Club and the Episcopal Church and often entertains the social set."

Today the country club is a nucleus of social activity in most suburbs and satellite cities, its membership a ready-made list of the local elite who support community drives, proper dancing classes and cotillions where marriageable young women "bow" to society in a replica of the debutante balls of the metropolitan cities. Admittance to country clubs, like that of all social clubs, depends upon manners, appearance, business connections and style of living. To meet the regular annual deficits, fierce but well-disguised recruitment drives are pressed by suave membership committees who canvass the area for charming and solvent families of suitable ethnic origin able to adorn the club parking lot with another Cadillac not over three years old.

In Los Angeles there is an interesting deviation. Families of good position belong, of course, to the best country clubs. But they use the facilities infrequently. Their homes are in effect all-purpose, self-contained country clubs with swimming pools, tennis courts, exotic gardens and patios with built-in rotisseries. In contrast, Texas country clubs were never so popular. Society has turned to them because of the servant scarcity and the trend toward smaller houses, many of which, despite the twenty-seven and one half per cent oil depletion allowance, lack a cocktail lounge, juke box, walk-in fireplace, soda fountain and dining room seating two hundred. Another factor has been cited by a gentleman from Dallas:

"It's all the fault of the goddam women," he groused. "They've gotten so bone-lazy they won't even spend time managing the help who do the work."

In another development, the country club is becoming democratized. "Industrial recreation for the many," says *Business Week*, "is now an established tool of management." The International Business Machines Corporation operates three luxurious country clubs for employees. The Frigidaire Division of General Motors offers a golf driving range for employees who wish to eliminate their slices and hooks, while the Eastman Kodak Company has a recreation center in Rochester, New York, that can handle seven thousand people at once. The OnIzed Club of Owens-Illinois Glass Company, with headquarters at Toledo, Ohio, claims 32,000 members, draws whole families into its varied activities.

"You take a young man with a family who isn't able yet to travel in the country club circle. For him the broad scope of OnIzed activities is a real benefit," says M. C. Byers, employees services supervisor at Toledo.

It has been mentioned that a large Fifth Avenue jewelry store finds it profitable in this officially democratic nation to maintain a department of heraldry which puts together coats of arms memorializing the luster of putative ancestors. Social groups of similar origins also club together for mutual warmth and security by preserving through hereditary associations the cachet which attaches to prior immigration. And so we have the Mayflower Society and the Descendants of the Signers of the Declaration of Independence, the Order of Colonial Lords of Manors in America, the Order of Founders and Patriots, the St. Nicholas Society of New York, the Society of Colonial Wars and countless others, each with its specialized and difficult qualifications for admission, its ribbons, buttons, medals and badges. "In no country of Europe," said Price Collier, "do you hear so many titles, or see so many insignia worn."

The basis of association for the Native Sons and Daughters of Kansas is their common attachment to their state and its history. They preserve landmarks, dedicate flags, listen to talks about sod houses, grasshoppers and Indians, sup together on pioneer mush and milk, choke down dried apple pie for dessert. The Native Sons and Daughters of the Golden West, however, differ in being a fraternal society with benevolent features. They perpetuate the memory of the Argonauts through local chapters called "Parlors," which blanket California like the Bank of America. The members revere the date, July 7, 1846, when Captain John Drake Sloat raised the Stars and Stripes at Monterey and annexed California to the United States. Nor do they forget the founders of their own order and how they paraded so picturesquely their first Fourth of July in 1875, swinging past Lotta's Fountain on San Francisco's Market Street with pick, pan and shovel on their shoulders, bowie knife and revolver strapped at their sides, and the sacred Bear Flag at the head of the procession.

A rival association, which once placed heavy emphasis upon the social side of belonging, is the Society of California Pioneers. They descend in the male line from ancestors who were in the state before 1849. This confraternity rose from humble beginnings in Delmonico's Saloon on Montgomery Street, to celebrate New Year's Day and Admission Day with great elegance in champagne toasts to "the first digger" while a band played "Oh, California." The Society once attempted to give balls. But extraordinary complications arose. There were two kinds of women in California who insisted upon attending—the "virtuous" and the "depraved." The latter were not without friends and protectors. The effort to allot invitations to the feminine contingent upon the basis of virtue proved to be not only impossible but a source of bitter contention and appalling deficits. The Society continues today to honor the memory of the Bear Flaggers, of General John C. Frémont and the state's romantic history. But social exclusiveness has been subordinated to historical responsibilities—the collection of historical materials and the display of such artifacts as a little brass cannon once owned by John A. Sutter, old guns, watches and the dispensing equipment of the Bank Exchange Saloon.

The memory of old wars and past valors provides a powerful adhesive to bind together the feminine descendants of the front fighters of long ago. A remarkable enterprise is carried on by the ingenious United Daughters of the Confederacy. The Daughters specialize in liberating the loot removed in 1861-65, a silver teapot which has been tracked down in New England, old books which can perhaps be pried from the hands of "repentant Yankees." The return of the garrison flag of Memphis, for example, which had been whisked away to Indiana in '64, required the services of the entire corps of United Daughters, two poets laureate, a luncheon, a parade, flag escorts, girls marching, speeches and a requiem by a male chorus.

The Daughters keep the society editors of the newspapers in the old Confederate states jumping with their luncheons, teas, conventions, historical birthdays and pilgrimages to historic shrines of the Old Confederacy. Jefferson Davis is always referred to as "President Davis," as though he was alive and the occupant of the Executive Mansion at Richmond. The torch will be passed on. Thousands of little members are drafted into the Children of the Confederacy. They open their meetings with a ritual built around the Confederate flag, write prize essays on "The Part Kentucky Played in the War Between the States" and similar topics, memorize "The Bonnie Blue Flag" and the pathetic verses of Father Abram Joseph Ryan's "The Conquered Banner." Recitations of the Gettysburg Address are discouraged. Rebel sentiment now runs so strong in Kentucky, indeed, that a distinguished native son well versed in the state's history and attitudes, has declared that although Kentucky remained in the Union during the War she seceded afterward.

Of all the embattled groups of women patriots who stand watch over our national security, the most numerous and bellicose are the Daughters of the American Revolution. They descend directly from one or more male ancestors who, if caught by the British between 1776 and 1783, would have been hanged. A Daughter must also be personally acceptable to the Society which gives its membership committees a comfortable degree of latitude. In recent years the D.A.R. has specialized in alerting the country to the enemy within. The Daughters found, for instance, that the school children of Wichita, Kansas, were directing traffic with red flags, placed in their hands presumably by the Soviets. The chapters also unearth old cannon balls, erect plaques, back teachers'-oath laws, place American flags in Negro schools, nibble away at the United Nations and UNESCO. Southern chapters model the costumes of the Confederacy and sing "Dixie," followed, with no sense of incongruity, by the Pledge to the Flag of the United States and a collation of punch and cookies.

Of whatever value to the nation these vigilant ladies may be, the psychic profit which accrues to them for manning the ramparts hardly needs to be spelled out. The Daughters hold garden parties and style shows, followed by an Indian War Dance. They listen respectfully to thunder on the right from such personages as the arch-conservative and now ex-representative Katherine St. George, the godly Norman Vincent Peale, our durable *Schutzmann* J. Edgar Hoover, and the doormat was always out welcoming the late U. S. Senator Pat McCarran of Nevada, opponent of immigration. There is much ceremonial. Corsages are presented, State Regents honored, flanked by the chairmen of committees on Americanism and the Correct Use of the Flag.

The Daughters like to meet in Washington and let their light shine out from the nation's capital. "The tide of battle rolls on in the D.A.R. convention," Mrs. Slayden once wrote after attending a reception for the visiting delegates. "All those able to leave the firing line came . . . mostly very modish in high-waistline frocks, peach-basket hats, and generally a miniature of a distinguished ancestor on their manly bosoms. But they fought their battles o'er again. . . ." Mrs. Slayden hoped that some day, but without much conviction, they would "mend their manners."

The emergence of the fraternal lodges in the last half of the nineteenth century expressed a need of the urban man for a social center which would provide a substitute for the lost friendliness of small town life. The mystic brotherhoods provided, moreover, a romantic opportunity to soar above the humdrum affairs of life as members of societies loaded with regalia and liturgy and bearing such exotic names as The American Order of Druids or the Prudent Patricians of Pompeii. Official titles carried the same aura of fantasy—Grand Keeper of the Records and Seal, Venerable Patriarch, Exalted Ruler, Esteemed Knight, and there were trumpeters, votaries and one ladies' auxiliary called Nomads of Avrudka whose members wore "rakish Oriental attire." This spirit of make-believe transforms life into a wonderland, as Mr. Charles W. Ferguson has remarked sapiently, without requiring us to give up the practical advantages of "a single piece of sanitary plumbing."

The Fraternal Order of Eagles meet in Aeries. New members

are nestlings, full-fledged members are beaks. The Loyal Order of Moose, founded at St. Louis in 1887, have chapters called Watering Places, a credo written by Elbert (Fra Elbertus) Hubbard. They operate an institution for orphaned children at Mooseheart, Indiana, believe in the brotherhood of man, flowers, good books, good women and their own Loyal Order. There are many Negro societies which parallel the white lodges, to name one—the Grand United Order of Antelopes. Negro fraternalism embellishes life and provides sanctuary. Antelopes enjoy sepulchral chanting, wear fezzes, brown gloves and a badge which has a "mourning side" for funeral use. The lowest degree among Antelopes is white.

Most visible on the surface of American life of all the resplendent lodge brothers are the members of the Ancient Arabic Order of the Nobles of the Mystic Shrine for North America. The Shrine, a luncheon club when it was started in 1872, is a kind of spin-off of the Ancient and Honorable Society of Free and Accepted Masons. Shriners parade at the drop of a fez, wear Egyptian or Arabic costumes, turn out by the thousands for their conventions which have a distinctly carnival atmosphere. The Shriners drop water bombs out of hotel windows, annoy the local constabulary with boyish horseplay, boost the demand for cracked ice to unprecedented levels. Their philosophy: "Dignity must be unhorsed."

In Shriner imagery death is "the call of the Black Camel." Trips are pilgrimages. Chapters—temples, that is—of which there are now one hundred and sixty-seven, have Arabic names like Kismet in Brooklyn, Sphinx at Hartford, Connecticut, Alzafar in San Antonio, Texas, or Elf Khurafed at Saginaw, Michigan. The head man is called Most Illustrious Grand Potentate. Some temples own real camels. Three Presidents of the United States have been Shriners— Warren G. Harding, Franklin D. Roosevelt and Harry Truman. It is an old dream of the Shriners to have their M.I.G.P., mounted on a live camel, ride up the steps of the White House to be received by the President. So far, permission has been refused. The chief purpose of the Shriners is whoopla, though they also raise substantial amounts of money for crippled children and other welfare purposes.

Inclusion implies also exclusion in fraternalism no less than in other social mechanisms. The excluded have frequently been women. The ladies reacted resentfully against the poor man's club —the saloon—by bringing down Prohibition on their unfortunate country and then, changing their minds about the Great Experiment, made sure when Prohibition was repealed that the saloon came back with a new name and policy as the coeducational cocktail lounge, taproom, café, tavern or piano bar. The men, one must admit, have not been gallant. When the Sons of the American Revolution was formed in 1883, it voted to exclude women. So the Daughters of the American Revolution came into being. The United Confederate Veterans also barred the ladies and very nearly expired in the early 1900's until the United Daughters got organized and carried on. The barbershop choristers of North America, to be noticed later in this chapter, love to sing "Oh! What a Pal was Mary," but Mary was conspicuously absent from their woodshedding sessions of harmony and song. When a platoon of Chicago women tried to pry their way into fellowship, even resorting to legal remedies, the males fought back saying, in effect, "Wait Till the Sun Shines, Nellie." The judge, a man, naturally ruled in favor of segregation. Wives of members of the Society for the Preservation and Encouragement of Barbershop Quartet Singing in America may attend the Society's competitions as audience. But women who want to harmonize have to do it by joining their own Sweet Adelines, a society no men have yet tried to crash so far as is known.

The Order of the Eastern Star, popularly thought of as an affiliate of the Masons, has only this tenuous connection with freemasonry, that members must be wives, daughters, mothers or sisters of Masons. The Eastern Stars long hoped wistfully that the famed masonic signal of distress would some day be disclosed to them. This dream has never materialized. The Eastern Stars are not consoled by the view held by some modern historians that William Morgan of Batavia, New York, the renegade Mason who was kidnapped and presumably killed in 1826 for having published the secrets of the lodge, was really done in because he had committed the most monstrous crime possible: he showed how little there was to reveal. But the Eastern Stars developed rites and rituals of their own which have fed the emotions of white and black and has provided a partial answer to feminine curiosity about what goes on behind the doors of men's lodges.

It was, in fact, an ill-considered male snub that started the whole, massive woman's club movement in the United States, a social instrument which has made its weight felt on many occasions in the last sixty years. Here is how it all began: a tremendous literary lion turned up in New York in April, 1868. Charles Dickens had come over to mollify the touchy Americans for his painful observations upon our culture on his previous visit. The New York Press Club issued invitations to the banquet. Everyone was to be there except the city's clever professional women. The discrimination made Mrs. Jane Cunningham Croly, highly successful in journalism as "Jennie June," so indignant that she founded her own club, Sorosis, the first woman's club of any consequence, and went on with Julia Ward Howe, Charlotte Wilbur, Mary A. Livermore and others who had felt the quickening of the times, to bring all the women's clubs of the country together in 1890 as the General Federation of Women's Clubs.

Women first learned to associate in church, foreign missions and charitable activities, for which they sewed and collected rummage. To this mix was added, after the Civil War, the ladies' literary club devoted to self-development. Earnest women in Quincy, Illinois, were reading Plato, while at Skowhegan, Maine, under leaden skies that so often promised snow, the cultivated women of the town gathered to consider together the Ruskin theory of art, ancient mythology, Ireland and the Irish. In Grand Rapids, Michigan, "The Furniture City," which James G. Blaine once called "the biggest city of its size in the country," The Ladies' Literary Club erected the first building in the United States designed as a clubhouse for women. Incised on the oak of its paneled library appeared these words in praise of books as a spur to the intellectually hungry: "Round these our pastimes and our happiness will grow."

The women's club movement, which has touched all levels of society during the last sixty years, has done much for the diffusion of knowledge about song birds, Duncan Phyfe furniture, gardening, flower arrangements, for social welfare and the advancement of consumer interests. And it brought forth an institution for which there is no analogue, the male lecturer on culture, extending from the pioneering Hamilton Wright Mabie to the reigning John Mason Brown whose platform triumphs have been facilitated by the vacuum cleaner, dishwasher, electric pig and all the mechanisms of the new leisure.

Somewhat similar to the Elks and Odd Fellows, but with more sheen, are the Greek-letter fraternities which have long been a prominent feature of college life in the United States. The system, mentioned briefly in Chapter 14, dates back to the founding of Phi Beta Kappa which, like James Pepper Whiskey, was "born with the Republic" in 1776. Admiral Peary placed the flag of Delta Kappa Epsilon just beneath the Stars and Stripes at the North Pole. Grover Cleveland accepted membership in Sigma Chi while in the Presidency. Like the Order of Hoot Owls, the college fraternities have spent breathless hours on solemnities and banalities in their sacred chambers. By the 1880's the social fraternities had come to occupy a place of assured power in student life. Their members learned the art of politics and the values which sometimes could be salvaged in addressing a professor deferentially as "Sir." The knowledge the brothers acquired of the survival value of conformity has doubtless proved of inestimable worth to many fraternity members in the great world of After College.

Since the contribution of the fraternities has become an issue from time to time, the accomplishments of distinguished alumni have not gone unsung, such as the achievement of the Greek-letter man who trade-marked borax; the brother who put over "Say it with flowers"; the artist who designed more *Saturday Evening Post* covers in one year than any other illustrator; the life and values of Hubert Prior (Rudy) Vallee, a member of *both* Sigma Alpha Epsilon and the Elks. "The emotional overhead of fraternities is enormous," says Mr. Ferguson, who quotes one elderly joiner as saying, "I hope I shall never live to see the day when my college fraternity ceases to make demands upon my material resources." He is not likely to be disappointed.

A notable instance of the retreat into the womb occurred when George Kerr Edwards, Princeton '89, felt such devotion to his eating club that he returned to it to die. He attended the Annual Dinner and passed away most appropriately during Commencement Week. A twist on the fraternity idea has been the marked expansion of professional fraternities. They have appropriated such features of the social fraternities as grips, passwords, jeweled pins, colors and ritual. Eight have osteopathy as the basis for fellowship. Pharmacists unite under the banner of Kappa Psi. Delta Sigma Delta is for nascent dentists. The brethren of Alpha Delta Sigma are votaries of the muse of advertising.

Exploding college enrollments, public policy emphasizing higher education for all qualified to receive it, the concern among college and university administrators over discriminatory practices, all suggest that the heyday of the social fraternities is over. Yet one cannot be sure. The joining instinct is endemic. The pleasures of being on the right side of a barrier are not given up without a struggle.

It would be difficult to imagine American civilization in the twentieth century without the service clubs which meet for luncheon every week across the continent and in the islands and subcontinents of the world. In these consociations the leaders of the local business community, the employer group—realtors, embalmers, the fire-extinguisher distributor and automobile dealer, taking a breather from his wheeling and dealing—come together to boost community projects in an atmosphere of compulsory joviality and eat what John Gould, the Lisbon Falls, Maine, gourmet has described as "a squeeze of chicken à la king on a patty shell of wallpaper paste . . ." which he has found depressing when followed by a heavy speech on the national parks program.

Rotary came first. The Club was founded in Chicago in 1905 by a lonely lawyer, Paul P. Harris. Rotarianism has been called a way of life, an ideal of service, a quasi-religious movement, a state of grace. One preacher told the Hartford, Connecticut, Rotary Club "If Mark Twain were alive today, he would be a Rotarian." A president of the Schenectady, New York, club raised the bid: "Lincoln," he declared, "was a born Rotarian." But the Reverend W. F. Powell took the pot when he assured the Kiwanis Club of Columbus, Mississippi: "God was the first Kiwanian." Kiwanis arose in Buffalo in 1914. The Lions whelped in 1917. "Lionism," it has been said, "is caught—not taught." All of these brotherhoods express a degree of idealism and render useful social service in a setting of somewhat pumped-up good fellowship.

The characteristic American blending of business and social intercourse extends to trade and occupational clubmanship, providing endless opportunities for indulging a taste for liberty, fraternity, empathy and a night out on the town. The Baby Ramblers are a social unit within the American Association of Nurserymen. The Concatenated Order of Hoo-Hoo has a tenuous Egyptian atmosphere. A black cat is its symbol. The leader is known as Snark of the Universe, the name borrowed from Lewis Carroll's nonsense poem, "The Hunting of the Snark." The order was founded to indulge the playful proclivities of lumbermen, but is now so respectable that it has a magazine and helps members with their "lumber problem." The Asparagus Club draws to its roster men of distinction in the area of food distribution. The name signifies a bunch of good fellows bound together by mutual interests.

On the distaff side there is the Kiwi Club. Marriage, which automatically grounds American Airlines stewardesses or "stewardi" as Shelley Berman insists is the plural form, leads to membership in this club. Kiwis recall old memories and hold fashion shows for sweet charity. The Club derives its name from an almost extinct bird found in New Zealand. It does not have wings.

The various state societies have done much to knit the uprooted into social groupings, notably in those great gathering-places of the transplanted, Washington, D.C., where the migrants are mostly young, and in southern California where they are mostly old. Washington secretaries employed on The Hill affiliate with their state societies as a way of getting into circulation. In Los Angeles, the last Valhalla of the American Dream, the Ohio Society closes its meetings on a note of nostalgia. The ex-Ohioans stand and sing, "Should Old Ohio be forgot and scenes we left behind?" The answer is a resounding *no*—"we keep them still in mind."

Iowans were among the first to form a state society in California. They were retired farmers, Ford dealers, shoe merchants solid, sensible, lonely people, the salt of the earth, with small competencies and an unshakable attachment to the old-time religion, union suits, early rising and the Saturday night bath.

A hundred and fifty thousand persons have at times answered the call to the Iowa picnics. There was a special location reserved for every county and an official button—an ear of corn and a fat pig on a white ground, bearing the legend "Hog and Hominy." Closely connected with the state societies was the self-service restaurant or cafeteria which appeared in Los Angeles around 1912. For temperance people the cafeterias rendered the social services of the old-time saloon. There the state groups held their meetings, elected officers and admitted new members whose qualifications for membership were to have been either a native or long-time resident of the home state and the ability to push a tray around the rail of the steam table.

Harry Leon Wilson once referred to the region as "Sunny Cafeteria." Strangers queuing up with their trays, silverware and paper napkins were supposed to inquire courteously of the next fellow, "What part of Iowa are you from?" The first generation of immigrants is passing on and the home-grown Californian takes less interest in family origins back East. But these folk festivals will remain a part of the California scene for many years to come.

Loneliness remains endemic in the land of sunshine which has been recommended for being "Italy without the Italians." Here people draw together for human warmth or to practice Yoga, follow the vegetarian regimen, meditate with religious cultists like the Rosicrucians, hear the Foursquare Gospel, Aimee Semple McPherson's spiritual legacy, or find solace in the flourishing Self-Realization Fellowship. Licensed find-the-companion-of-your-choice clubs exist in substantial numbers in the Los Angeles area. They provide "dignified introductions" for a weekly fee, addressing both the elderly and "singles" through the classified advertising columns of the _Los Angeles Sunday Times_. "Are you WON-FER-FULL?" (sic) asks one club operator. "You will be . . . to someone." Appeals are rifled directly at the widow, at Catholics, Germans, Orientals, Jews or those attracted by the idea of what are called "European bachelorettes."

Food and drink have always provided a basis for congenial associations. Eighteenth century gentlemen of New York came together under the name of the Social Club at the famous tavern kept by "Black Sam" Fraunces. The oldest gourmet group of this sort which exists today is the Fishing Company of the State in Schuylkill, or the Fish House Club, of Philadelphia. In its castle on alternate summer Wednesdays generations of proper Philadelphians have put aside the cares and responsibilities of running the Quaker City's banks, trusts, hospitals, the Symphony and "the Railroad," that is, the Pennsylvania Railroad. Members still happily don aprons and peculiar straw hats called boaters, learn the mastery of the spit and oven for epicurean feasting. The Fish House joined the United States voluntarily in 1781, even before the Treaty of Paris had been negotiated, and its ritual still requires a toast to General Washington. Fish House punch is now a part of our national alcoholic culture.

Since 1769 the Old Colony Club at Plymouth, Massachusetts, has commemorated the landing of the Pilgrims with a roll of drums, the discharge of a small cannon and, while wearing tall silk hats, the members hold a flag-raising with "an elegant silk flag." Silk hats are, of course, somewhat scarce articles today. But not in Plymouth. An Old Colony member explains, "Oh, in Plymouth we _have_ our silk hats!" Following the patriotic devotions, members fall

Warren G. Harding *(right)* is one of three Presidents of the United States who have worn the red fez of a lodge brother in the Ancient Arabic Order of the Nobles of the Mystic Shrine of North America. The others: Franklin D. Roosevelt and Harry S Truman. Shriners support good works, such as hospitals for the treatment of children's diseases, blow off steam at annual conventions, march in mammoth parades, dropped an estimated $15 million when they gathered 100,000 strong in Washington last year for fun and games. Equally devoted to the carnival spirit but harder to join is the International Order of Alhambra (10,000 members) and the very exclusive (60-70 members) Society of the Descendants of the Illegitimate Sons and Daughters of the Kings of England.

Library of Congress

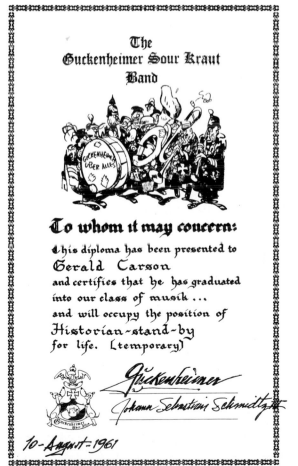

The Guckenheimer Sour Kraut Band

To whom it may concern:

this diploma has been presented to

Gerald Carson

and certifies that he has graduated into our class of musik ...
and will occupy the position of **Historian-stand-by for life. (temporary)**

Guckenheimer

Johann Sebastian Schmidtz

10-August-1961

Nine brave and whimsical business and professional men joined together a few years ago to form a very brassy band, the Guckenheimer Sour Kraut Band, which has flourished remarkably in the musically-sophisticated San Francisco Bay area by playing a little Wagner, a little Strauss, a little Bach and a little off-key. Wearing the musical comedy uniforms of an old-fashioned German village band, the zany Sour Krauts, under the leadership of *Kapell-meister* Richard Gump, have performed for lodge picnics, wakes and weddings, charity drives, church socials, veterans' hospitals. At the Sonoma Wine Festival the musicians were solemnly awarded a medal "For Valor." The group has given up the arduous business of rehearsing because, as George Lichty the cartoonist (he's on the drums) says: "We were getting too smooth."

The girls once called "typewriters" added dictation to their skills, learned to handle the telephone, mastered accounting machinery. From the shy miss clacking away at her period typewriter, descends the confident career girl of the sixties. Today's important secretaries receive distinguished attentions, such as a long-stemmed rose every Monday from United Airlines, are courted in advertisements which say: "Secy 'Queen Bee Spot' $125. Take minutes at board meetings. Be accustomed to hi-level execs." Under the Civil Rights Act of 1964, a woman may yet drive a locomotive, steer a tugboat or pitch for the Mets. Meanwhile worried Government officials, labor leaders and personnel officers wrestle with discrimination in reverse: What happens when a male applies for a job as a "bunny" in a Playboy Club?

The business girl was armed against the office wolf *(above, left)* by a frightening and minatory pamphlet literature, illustrated with pictures. This one was headed in the 1880's: "The Insulting Proposal. Young Hilton tempts the virtue of Miss Beatrice Claflin, and is indignantly spurned." *(Above, right).* By the 1900's the progressive National Cash Register Company was encouraging employees to learn to cook, sing, think and enjoy sun and surf.

Women employees of sixty years ago at "the Cash" in Dayton, Ohio, relaxing during the noon hour. The Company provided free umbrellas and rubbers, introduced hot lunches and encouraged the twice-a-week bath. *The National Cash Register Co.*

There is nothing like a dame to draw favorable attention to milk, meat, the glories of the Empire State or baton twirling. Therefore we come to know "Miss Rego Park, L.I.", her diadem and interesting measurements; or *(above)* the queen who reigns during Colorado Beef Month, backed with the full faith and credit of the State of Colorado. Humor too *(below)* is a valuable business stimulant, especially in connection with convention life, service club luncheons, restaurant promotion and personal salesmanship.

with good appetite upon clam chowder made without tomatoes, a point on which the 196-year-old club is inflexible, escalloped oysters, a dish of codfish and "an apple Pye." The Club celebrates Forefathers' Day on December 22nd instead of December 21st when everybody else in Massachusetts honors the Pilgrims. This arose in a curious way. After the Julian calendar was succeeded in 1752 throughout the British world by the Gregorian, which conforms more closely to the astronomical data, the Plymouth clubmen got confused by the innovation of New Style and commemorated the wrong day. This was not discovered until 1832. Since they had been wrong for sixty-three years the men of Plymouth decided not to change the day again. As one member has explained, "We much prefer established error to novel truth."

The Americans, who feel happier in having a written constitution and by-laws regulating every activity, have even organized their caprices. A society which combined dining, nostalgia and a mad vein of waggery was, and one uses the past tense regretfully, the Guild of Former Pipe Organ Pumpers. Its motto was "Pump, for the Wind is Fleeting." The Organ Pumpers, who antedated the introduction of the electric motor as a source of power for ecclesiastical music-making, once had a thousand card-carrying members. Started in 1925 by a merry-andrew, Chet Shafer, a humorist from Three Rivers, Michigan, the fellowship pursued many worthwhile cultural objectives. The members sought to preserve the cast-iron deer which once ornamented the lawns of respectable mid-western homes and the dappled wooden horses that stood in front of harness shops. Shafer was called Grand Diapason and handed around official titles derived from the stops on a pipe organ, such as Vox Humana and Tibia Plena. Meetings were conducted with boisterous hilarity. At one convention of Pumpers, held in Boston, the Guild staged what is believed to be the shortest parade in history— out the School Street door of the Parker House and in the Tremont Street door.

The roster of members read like the pages of *Who's Who in America*. At one meeting of the Chicago Loft of the Guild, the President of the Chicago Stock Exchange delivered a scholarly address on "A Neat System for Picking up Old Razor Blades" and Julius Rosenwald, philanthropist and Chairman of the Board of Sears, Roebuck & Company, pumped an organ while the members sang "Onward, Christian Soldiers."

Chet Shafer, to whom life was a jest, died in 1951, leaving only a few grizzled survivors who had personal recollections of the fun and deviltry to be had in letting the air collapse just as the collection plates were being marched in triumph to the altar. The Guild faded away with the passing of its moving spirit, though at least one biographee appearing in *Who's Who in America* continues to list membership in the Guild among his distinctions.

Best-known of all clubs which have combined musical interests and good fellowship is undoubtedly the Society for the Preservation and Encouragement of Barber Shop Quartet Singing in America. This expression of popular musical culture erupted in 1938, now maintains an international headquarters in Kenosha, Wisconsin, and always whimsically uses the letters, S.P.E.B.S.Q.-S.A., a tongue-in-cheek comment upon the proliferation of odd-sounding agencies in the Federal Government. Two men from Tulsa, Oklahoma, became acquainted in the lobby of the Muehlbach Hotel in Kansas City, recalled the days when the hair-cutting emporium was the club and Palladium of the average American male. They decided that what the United States needed was a revival of barbershop harmonizing. Adjourning after a rendering of "I Had a Dream, Dear," they returned to Tulsa to start the first chapter, and S.P.E.B.S.Q.S.A. was in orbit. Today there is a barbershop quartet in a U.S. atomic submarine. A Chicago group, the "Mid-States Four," sang for the Fifth Marines in the front lines in North Korea with shells flying overhead, which supports the view held by many that barbershopping is a powerful weapon for combating Communism. On one occasion President Eisenhower had a District of Columbia outfit sing at a state dinner honoring Vice President Richard M. Nixon and the Cabinet, which must have been the social apogee for the four-part musicologists who huddle lovingly over "Mandy Lee" and "Dear Old Girl."

More than twenty-nine thousand barbershop enthusiasts in the United States, Canada and abroad joyously keep alive the musical tradition of the tonsorial parlors of the 1890's and compete with other warblers wearing picturesque costumes and performing under such group names as "The Four Renegades" (Chicago), the "Chord Busters" (Oklahoma City), the "Sidewinders" (Riverside, California) and the "Four Hearsemen" (Amarillo, Texas). All of the members of the last are in the undertaking business. The "Buffalo Bills," from Buffalo, New York, turned professional and became famous for their work in Meredith Willson's musical comedy hit, *The Music Man.* There is even a "Mainliner" quartet in the conservative Philadelphia suburb of Bryn Mawr which held its organization meeting at the Bryn Mawr firehouse; and "The Khyber Four" practice their "swipes" in Pakistan.

The S.P.E.B.S.Q.S.A. discourages odd-ball types. But the Guckenheimer Sour Kraut Band of San Francisco tolerates no other. The organization, which heisted its name from the label on a whiskey bottle, consists of nine mad musicians who play Bavarian *Bierstube* melodies in a mouth-puckering village-band style. The members are actually staid business and professional men from the Bay area, led by Richard Gump, third-generation head of the well-known store that bears his family name. Gump is, in addition to being a highly successful businessman and fun-time *Kappelmeister*, an artist, author and serious composer. Costumed in what has been described as "Franco-Prussian war surplus" uniforms, the Sour Krauts play, if that is the word for it, in the interest of worthy causes and for the sheer pleasure of tootling.

"We play happy music," says Gump, who believes that the musical escapades of the Sour Krauts have cut deeply into the sale of tranquilizers in northern California. On one enchanted evening, just as the doors of the San Francisco Opera House swung open and the homeward bound music-lovers emerged, they paled at what they saw and heard—the Guckenheimers on the curb in firing position. Herr Guckenheimer's arm swooped down, foot slapping the pavement. *Eins, zwei, drei,* and the Guckenheimers' challenge to the San Francisco Opera Company was air-borne as the Band gave out with a polka beat *Kommst ein Vogel geflogen,* a Bird Comes Flying.

"Gentlemen, gentlemen—what in Heaven's name are you playing?" exclaimed an agitated woman deep in diamonds and décolletage.

"The March—from Dimes," explained the leader, passing around his spiked helmet while green folding money for the victims of poliomyelitis showered softly down. The Sour Krauts had made a hit in their own peculiar way.

Cincinnati had a Society for the Suppression of Music back in the eighties whose members pretended to oppose all music except the whistling of the winds and especially, so they said, the famous Cincinnati May Festival. The Anti-Superstition Society dines on Friday the 13th in Chicago. Members walk under ladders, smash mirrors, open umbrellas indoors, light three cigarettes from the same match, once crossed without harm the paths of thirteen lovely models costumed as black cats. From New Jersey come reports of an association of minute men, a group of rabid patriots known as The Friendly Sons of Molly Pitcher. The Sons exist for the *ad hoc* purpose of snatching the remains of Molly Pitcher, Revolutionary War heroine, from the cemetery in Carlisle, Pennsylvania, where they now rest, and returning them to Freehold, New Jersey, site of the battle where Molly won enduring fame. But the Carlisle police check the grave through the night hours, assisted by voluntary patrols carried out by The Loyal Fraternal Brotherhood for the Preservation of the Final Resting Place of Carlisle's Glorious Patriotic and Ancestral Heroine, Molly Pitcher.

The panorama of American club life suggests the reasons which impel men and women to gather under a banner and adopt a constitution: creature comforts, insulation from life's bruises, social exposure, snobbery, fun and games, business advancement, a hunger for a pageantry which life does not provide, the search for tradition. All this demonstrates, it is suggested, that the United States is not so tightly regimented as despairing social critics would have us believe. If no people are so quick as we to fly to parliamentarian works like *Roberts' Rules of Order,* it is also true that we have enriched our national life with imaginative and zany social structures which reduce inflation through cleansing laughter.

No satisfactory register exists of these fellowships which lend vivacity to our club life. But George L. Moore, of Wellesley Hills, Massachusetts, a man who knows a good tangent when he sees one, has made a start. Moore has turned up recently the Pecor Hollow Venison Eating and Ridge Running Society in Vermont, and the SDNN and GGPSO which represent, respectively, the Society for Defrauding Nieces and Nephews and the Guild for General Preventing and Stamping Out.

18

SOME FOLKWAYS OF BUSINESS

"Men, as a whole, do not take polish readily," declared the mother-and-daughter team of experts on good behavior, Marion Harland and Virginia Van de Water. The tycoon who started life in humble circumstances was apt when he was fifty and had made his bundle, they said, to speak of dinner as "supper," cut up his salad, say "Sir" to his equals.

Since, as Calvin Coolidge said, "The business of America is business," any uncouthness on the part of the titans of industry was definitely conspicuous. Yet politeness was identified as only a moderately important characteristic of those who were successful in pushing to the front. In the folklore of business the great success principle until quite recently was *character*. Character meant hard work, going to church, putting up with a Waterbury watch, avoiding evil companions. The lack of early training in social usages was a slight handicap but it could be surmounted. A man with good powers of observation could learn even in the one-arm restaurants how to conduct himself when he had "arrived." So ran the argument in the rags-to-riches literature.

The self-made man, the rough diamond who graduated from the School of Hard Knocks, has faded from the scene as the businessman has become professionalized as the managerial employee, more presentable if not necessarily more interesting than the hardbitten entrepreneur who once dominated the business landscape. Today's young executive, and everybody, it appears, wishes to be one, looks clean, wholesome, wears his hair short, avoids eccentricities of every sort, takes his wardrobe cue from the narrow lapel and unpadded shoulder. As a man earning a good salary working in a big company but with no large personal capital at his command, the management type thinks about his "image" and is polite to everyone. And he understands what Emily Post meant when she wrote, speaking of manners in the business world, "One advantage of polish is that one's opponent can never tell what is going on under the glazed surface of highly finished manners. . . ."

National firms are interested today in the grammar of manners, according to Miss Vanderbilt, as an aid to efficiency and better public relations. A man with a private office is not expected to rise every time a secretary enters, or a woman applicant for a non-executive position. But for other women callers he does. He stands for male callers, too, and shakes hands, except for the non-executive applicant. When the telephone rings, he excuses himself for the interruption. Even the chairman of the board steps aside at a door for women employees, carrying over the custom of social life of giving women precedence. Thus he has to have only one set of manners. Knowledgeable company men do not call their secretaries by their first names. The prettier the secretary the more necessary it is to treat her with polite objectivity. Once the situation involves a personal element, it is difficult for the woman, Miss Vanderbilt points out, "not to show that she has her boss under rather special control." It continues to be good usage in a large concern for a junior executive to say "Sir" to his seniors, especially if he bumps into an elder statesman in the corridor.

A businessman can hardly be said to have a manner until he has eliminated his mannerisms. They may include some, but presumably not all, of the following gaucheries: ear-pulling, pipe-twirling, tie-adjusting, fidgeting, blinking, lip-smacking. Eyebrows should not be messy, the posture slouchy or the executive speech filled with hems, haws and harumphs. The voice should be well-modulated, the words fluent. It is assumed that the officer of a company is also a gentleman or at least a good facsimile. Franklin D. Roosevelt, Jr., once referred to the value of making a shining impression as "turning on the old schmoo." In this utterance one sees, rather uncomfortably, the businessman as a work of art, his nails clean, his voice control perfect, his all-enveloping friendliness superficial but all-conquering as he lays siege to the bitch-goddess, Success.

There is danger in this emphasis upon the seeming rather than the being. This is clearly apparent in the exegetical writings of some of the modern authorities upon personality development. In their admiration of the accomplishments of the real charmers of history who cast a fascinating spell—figures like Cleopatra or Leonard Bernstein, Perry Como or Billy Graham—they will lead our young men to become what Professor Orrin E. Klapp has labeled "a bumper crop of polished hypocrites."

"Actually there are few real gentlemen to be met with in business," declares Aimee Buchanan, author and business woman, in her *The Lady Means Business* . . . ; "gentlemen . . . in business, because they are so rare, loom up like lighthouses, and they shed an undeniable distinction on their surroundings. You know them by their voices . . . their infallible and unconscious manners. . . . You do not have to be on guard against them."

A good deal too much has been made of the sumptuous character of the business lunch in the United States with its vodka gimlets and veal parmigiana. Actually men in the higher brackets of the business hierarchy eat almost as austerely as the clerks and stockroom boys in the push-button cafeterias, though the décor is different. Lunching with top management provides no revelry, often resembles a meeting of the Women's Christian Temperance Union so far as the consumption of alcohol is concerned. This observation does not include the gasoline aristocracy of Detroit who are in this as in many other matters, *sui generis*. In the thirteen private dining rooms of The Chase Manhattan Bank's home office in New York the visitor faces an inviting menu. But as a warning the calorie count is shown in parentheses: Gumbo Creole (150), sliced corned beef sandwich (220), chilled cantaloupe (50), cream chiffon pie (460). The Bank is satisfied there is a causal connection between expanding waist lines and mental fat. In the higher circles, waist-watching has become as important an ingredient of success as reading *The Wall Street Journal*.

If Whistler's mother types the Victorian age, the trim, young

miss at the typewriter is a paradigm for the woman of the twentieth century. "It's a woman's world," exclaims a New York employment agency at the head of its Sunday listing in the classified advertising pages. The world is her oyster, a girl with good office
skills must feel, as she hefts the want-ad sections of the metropolitan newspapers and sifts the opportunities, the call to be secretary
to a vice president, to sell insurance over the telephone, to go to
"Stewardess College" and learn at the expense of an airline "professional tricks of poise and grooming," to be a Bunny Mother for
Playboy Club Bunnies, Girl Friday in a glamorous setting with exciting opportunities for "client contact" or, to quote literally,
"RECPT, Lingerie . . . $75. Good looker to decorate front desk,
Typing. 5 Ave office." With the typewriter, the letter filing system
and the telephone in her charge, the office girl sits at the center of
the communications network of a complex civilization.

Washington probably introduced the business woman into the
office. During the manpower shortage of the Civil War years
women entered Government agencies, especially the Treasury Department. There they operated printing presses and folded the
folding money, receiving under an 1864 law one-third of what a
man was paid for doing the same work. The date when the first
young woman stenographer entered the State Department can be
definitely pinned down. On a hot August morning in 1868 Mrs.
Isabel C. Barrows, who had studied the pothooks and curves in one
of Andrew Jackson Graham's textbooks on shorthand, substituted
for her ill husband as "phonographer" to William H. Seward, U.S.
Secretary of State. The young wife sat in a little alcove at the head
of a staircase in the old brick building on Fourteenth Street until a
little bell tinkled. She entered history as a "first" when Seward
summoned her, gave her a comfortable chair, a footstool and began, "To the minister in St. Petersburg." All her notes in those pre-
typewriter days had to be transcribed later in longhand on wide-
ruled dispatch paper.

A business office of the eighties was a dark, untidy place. Its atmosphere and occupants were entirely male. Hats were worn, plug
hats, set off by a stiff-bosomed shirt and showy stickpin. Cuspidors
were spat at. The floor was bare about the rolltop desk, the ash
trays overflowing, the air heavy with cigar smoke. At noon the
working force adjourned to the nearest saloon, gave the house
some business at the bar which entitled the patrons to dive into the

free lunch. Unknown were drugstore lunch counters or sandwich shoppes. There were no salads, no parsley, no chocolate walnut sundaes topped with whipped cream. And, obviously, no girls.

The independent business girl owes her career opportunity to bearded, gentle-looking Christopher Latham Sholes of Milwaukee, Wisconsin, whose typewriter was the first to be manufactured and marketed commercially. Sholes even came up with the appropriate name for the machine—"type-writer," spelled with the hyphen. Soon the young women who operated the machine were nick-named "type-writers," too. The name sounded flippant and was undoubtedly intended to be slyly familiar. But "stenographer" wasn't right. The ability to take Gregg or Pitman didn't necessarily include typing skills. A "secretary" might be a man. It might refer to a desk. It didn't come to work in a peek-a-boo shirtwaist and black cotton stockings. So the two meanings of typewriter, the machine that could print and the girl who operated it under the same name, provided a rich field for the purveyors of native humor.

The typing machine made its way first among court reporters, lawyers, editors, professional writers and the clergy. The big break came when the Central Branch of the Young Women's Christian Association in New York began to teach typing. The connection between stenography and typing had at last become clear. By 1888 there were sixty thousand girls in high button shoes and pompadours clacking away in the commercial offices of all American cities and keeping that natural look by sprinkling a discreet amount of rice powder on a piece of chamois and lightly patting it on for a mat finish. By 1900 almost one-fifth of all American women were reported to be working for a pay envelope outside the home. The figure had risen to nearly one-fourth by 1910, with the greatest increase among office workers, and the figures soared higher between 1920 and 1930.

The woman in business created many social ripples. Hatracks became necessary in offices, fresh air and light. Tearoom food was invented. The fashions of the woman of leisure were modified to the needs of the woman of business. The office wolf became a stock character with his hopeful search for feminine "companionship." A sharp difference of opinion on the relative attractions of blondes and brunettes has always existed. But only since about 1840 has feminine hair coloring come to symbolize types of character. After the typewriter appeared, there was a general pretense that young women had a special finger dexterity and could keep a business secret better than a male secretary. But in 1904 the *Typewriter Trade Journal* reported that nine out of ten requests to employment agencies stressed a quite different characteristic: "Have you got a pretty blonde?"

The employment of women alongside men represents an economic and social change without parallel, reflecting the shift of population away from the farm, the development of labor-saving devices in the household and the faster expansion of clerical jobs in relation to other occupations. The role development gave new importance to the feminine traits which men objected to in office life: fluttering, dropping things and saying "All righty." A male belief, hard to put down, still lingers that women are handicapped by the estrous cycle. Aimee Buchanan calls this part of "the famous menopause myth," asserts that male workers have more sick leave than women.

The modern girl who understands office manners avoids tight skirts, low-cut necklines, sweaters, dirndl effects, blue eye-shadow and endless sagas of the boy friend. Smooth careerists shun the dangling ear-drop and ankle chains, always look immaculate and have mastered the art of rising from a sitting position without girdle-yanking. They avoid remarks that sound icky, like: "Elaine, honey, have you got the folder?" And they do not believe the narratives of office lifemanship they hear from Fran, the receptionist, in the washroom.

"O.K." is used so widely that it is acceptable as one of the small coins of idiomatic speech exchanged in business intercourse. But this lenity does not extend to "swell" or "okey-doke." "Madam" is disappearing as a business salutation in the North, fading even in the southern states. "Lady" is not a very useful word in business relationships. A couth secretary might conceivably say to her employer, "There's a lady to see you from the Grolier Society." But before she ushers in the visitor, she has learned the caller's name and uses it. Certainly she does not say: "You may come in, lady." But when the same secretary stops in at the butcher counter on her way home from work, she may quite properly say, observes Amy Vanderbilt, "I am the lady who ordered the turkey last week." Lady continues to be, as it was in the past, a tricky word.

If a girl has a Rolls-Royce accent which she came by legitimately, it is a definite asset. But it cannot be faked. For most business girls a low voice, standard English and an interested but impersonal manner are more to be treasured than frilly devices for acquiring status.

It probably doesn't come up very often, but here is the way to introduce a working girl to the President of the United States: "Mr. President, I have the honor to present Miss Brown of Brockton." Miss Brown, of course, will be wearing hat and gloves, a conservative hair-do, girdle, unsculptured stockings with seams straight, nail polish unchipped. And Miss Brown will not wave her long eye-lashes at the Chief Executive.

After Dr. Alexander Graham Bell stood in that attic in Boston and uttered those immortal words: "Mr. Watson, come here, I want you!" the usefulness of telephony to commerce had to wait upon the genius of another man whose name remains unsung outside the communications industry. Yet without him we might have the telephone as a scientific toy but no telephone system. Charles E. Scribner, whose name and achievements do not appear in the most recent and most scholarly American biographical dictionary, devised the multiple switchboard, which one admirer described as a greater accomplishment than building the Panama Canal. The switchboard made possible the telephone exchange. The exchange made possible the skyscraper, creating a new kind of city. The switchboard brought the girl once known as "Central" who responded to the flashing lights on the board. Telephone operators spoke with quiet voices, good humor, good sense. The hello girls have probably done more for public courtesy than any other figure ever connected with our business structure. "Central" appeared about 1882, freed from home labors by the sewing machine, but restrained by the mores of the time from working side by side with men. In the telephone exchange women could work with other women in decorous seclusion; or, in sparsely populated areas, Central worked alone, knew the names and personal problems of all subscribers, and at night had a couch and a gong connected with the bell circuit in case it was necessary to respond to a call.

And the subscribers knew the telephone girl, too. Dick Snider, former managing editor of the *Topeka Daily Capital,* remembers how his father, a druggist in Britton, Oklahoma, never could read the prescriptions scribbled by a local doctor, and how the elder Snider would give the crank on the old wall phone a vicious whirl and yell, "Pearl, ring Doc Watson."

In 1898 Boston, New York, Washington, Pittsburgh, Chicago

and Milwaukee could all talk to each other by telephone and the anonymous "Woman of Fashion" who wrote *Etiquette for Americans* found in that year that social rules were needed to civilize the chatter business. Servants were monopolizing the telephone. Oral invitations were being issued which should have been tendered by a written note. (The "Woman of Fashion" quickly lost this battle.) Hostesses were ringing up and saying: "What are you doing tonight?" before giving any indication of the purpose of the call. With an average of 262,081,000 conversations taking place every day on the Bell System alone (1964 figures) it seemed possible that the telephone, assisted by the automobile and the jet airplane, would make obsolete one of history's most treasured resources, the confidential and important letter. Today's letters merely record decisions made verbally, say in substance, "Confirming our telephone conversation. . . ." The overtones are lost. *Litera scripta manet.* The written word remains. But the telephone has sharply reduced its scope.

The commonest annoyances of office life concern the use of the telephone. The office pest conducts her intricate social life on the telephone and, of course, on her employer's time. When she is tending to business, she is apt to say, "A man called." And if the voice on the other end is not immediately familiar, she has been known to inquire brusquely, "Who is this?" Because the telephone bell is urgent and commanding, the telephone companies have an understandable interest in telephone manners. Their files bulge with data about the subject. They encourage, they exhort, they educate their subscribers in the techniques which save time and make the use of their equipment a pleasurable experience. They urge the slow, clear, *interested* voice, point out how much better it would be if people would lift the handset and say, pleasantly, "Rug Department, Mr. O'Brien speaking." "Thank you" and "I beg your pardon" are jewels, says The New York Telephone Company, whose late officer, Howard G. Stokes, coined a phrase in 1912 which has been quoted and copied throughout the world—"The Voice with the Smile Wins."

The phone companies have identified the following as telephone sickniks: shouters, mumblers, chewers of gum and gnawers of pipes, paper clips, cigars or pencils. We still have number-guessers who remain allergic to the use of directories, party-line hogs, operator baiters. If it is any consolation, we are not alone in our shortcomings. Randolph Churchill was once heard dressing down a Russian operator who so strained the patience and imagination of the Briton by understanding only her native tongue that he burst out upon her:

"I say, it's no good your speaking to me in that foreign gibberish."

One Russian professor has given Americans high marks for polite telephone habits in contrast to what he is used to at home. Professor Vladimir I. Tereshchenko wrote in *Izvestia,* "Suppose you call an office, and say:

" 'I'd like to talk to Comrade Ivanov.'

" 'He's not around,' the girl says and slams down the receiver." And that's another uncivil habit, too.

"One tries again," the professor continues. This time the caller gets a stinging rebuke:

"I told you he's not around."

On the third try the girl reluctantly divulges the information that Ivanov is on vacation and will be back in three weeks. In contrast to this, Professor Tereshchenko found that in the United States when one calls the General Electric Company a calm, trained voice answers:

" 'General Electric, Miss Jones speaking.'

"You ask, 'May I speak with Mr. Smith?'

"The laconic answer is, 'Mr. Smith is out of town. Mr. Courtney is taking his place. His extension is such and such. Shall I connect you?' "

The telephone as boon and bane has also brought upon our heads the telephone salesman. His nuisance value may be estimated at fifty cents a month since 411,000 phone subscribers in the New York metropolitan area pay that much extra for the privilege of having their phone numbers unlisted. A lawyer in Palo Alto, California, brought suit recently to force the Pacific Telephone and Telegraph Company to place an asterisk after his name in the directory to indicate that no salesmen were to call him on the telephone. The companies are on the squirm seat about such subscriber attitudes since telephone selling is a multi-million-dollar business. Outright fraud can be a prison offense. But the typical call is simply a pitch to sell a magazine subscription. Or a cheery voice announces that the subscriber has won a course of unwanted free dance lessons. There are interesting possibilities of a counter offensive. One ingenious man keeps a shrill dog whistle by the telephone, blows it when salesmen call. Another keeps calling the salesman at midnight. This ploy is known among the pitchmen as a "phone sweat." It will be instructive, if the incident ever becomes a matter of public knowledge, to hear what happens if a voice with a smile calls LEhigh 5-3221 in New York to tell Socrates Lovinger that he has just won a course of dance lessons. Because Socrates is a dog, the only miniature schnauzer in Manhattan with a telephone number of his own.

For millions of members of the U.S. labor force the job provides a ready-made social life as well as a pay envelope. When one of the girls at the office gets engaged there will be a luncheon and a corsage; or a shower with crepe-paper decorations; or light refreshments may be served during the coffee break accompanied by congratulations, inspection of the ring and presents of washable place mats, sachet bags or leather doilies. Employee publications follow the standing of the girls' bowling teams, analyzing how the Morning Glories stack up against the Cutter Dusters. Retirements are celebrated. Old-timers who have run the clock out are welcomed back, guardedly and on carefully specified occasions. New babies and new automobiles receive congratulatory or humorous notice in the plant papers: "I hope everyone has seen Jerry Stever's new Chrysler—it's only a block and a half long."

For those who are moving ahead in business new social horizons open up through the organism known as the trade association. Association affairs peak out in the effulgence of the annual convention and exposition held in some city which Americans like to visit. There are over four thousand organizations of businessmen in the United States representing interests as diverse as the Association of Asphalt Paving Technologists and the California Lima Bean Growers Association as well as all manner of recondite bureaus which reflect some facet of our complicated technological society. To keep the local units solvent and the membership growing, it has been noted by those who watch association workings, that it is necessary to provide festivity along with the hard-nosed agenda. Thus there occurs the ceremonial of the Annual Banquet with a "reception" before the dinner and a bar nearby to get the thirsty through the dinner, and sometimes there are musical interludes by a wandering minstrel with an accordion.

The business meeting includes the presentation of an award to someone for something and the well-loved routine of the treasurer's report, the report on the membership campaign, the report of the nominating committee, the proposal to amend the by-laws, discussion of the date and place of the next meeting and the frequent colloquial use of contact as a verb. The presiding officer at long last announces that the business of the evening is over and urges, "Have fun, everybody." As an account typical of thousands covering such gatherings has it: "all sordid and venal thoughts (were) transmuted into a warm and rosy atmosphere of sincere good fellowship, comradeship and friendliness" while "exotic jungle music was dispensed by an orchestra of swarthy experts."

The office party at Christmas time, which amounted to an annual brawl fifteen years ago, has been steadily losing its effervescence. Corporations shudder at the prospect of middle-management men, with a concentration of .05 per cent alcohol frisking through their arteries, chasing the junior file clerk down the hall. The National Safety Council, concerned with the drinking-and-driving problem, campaigns now for "fun without the hard stuff." Corporate emphasis has shifted to kiddy parties, more generous amounts of time off for shopping and free turkeys. If the employees want the traditional slambang party, they hold it off-premises. This has been good news for the Little Woman at home, who formerly trimmed the tree alone because her commuting husband was delayed by a bad case of office-party tanglefoot.

About a generation ago a new economic opportunity opened up for personable young women when it was demonstrated through beauty contests and bathing girl parades that girls with measurements approximating 35-23-35 could be put to work as sales agents for American goods and services. The results were so impressive that today the services of thousands of pretty creatures are in demand for arousing and then transferring the public ardor to Gum Spirits of Turpentine, Enriched Corn Meal or Correct Posture.

This alliance between cover girls and business has made it possible for a well-endowed working class girl to fight her way up in the princess business and acquire an education in dress, make-up, charm and social poise not otherwise available to her. With a bit of luck, she enters the dream-world of jet flight, glossy surroundings and a crowded engagement book. Beauty finalists meet such interesting people—the U.S. Secretary of Agriculture, for example, because of a common passion for fluid milk, or Wilbur H. Glenn,

President of the Royal Crown Beverage Company, Inc., to dramatize the slimming effects of Diet-Rite Cola.

Most of the entrants in the cutiepie sweepstakes win their tiaras through some system of competition which whips up public interest, generates publicity and prolongs the build-up. The girls pick up a good deal more than walking-around money, miscellaneous free merchandise and the hope of becoming a dramatic actress. The last is illusory. But there is always the substantial example of Jayne Mansfield, a fixture at ribbon-cuttings and supermarket openings and one who has been well fed for spending a pleasant afternoon in New Jersey functioning as Miss Cantaloupe. The game is well worth the candle. A girl starts at the bottom as Arkansas Poultry Princess, earns a few dollars and gets maybe some frozen chickens. But the principle of the thing can sweep her right on to the Miss America crown and a hundred thousand dollars for a year's work.

These "mannequin parades of the working classes," as *The Economist* (London) calls them, phenomena now as well-established in England as they are here, got their start in 1921 when a beauty pageant was staged at Atlantic City. The purpose was tourism—to extend the summer season beyond Labor Day. The term Miss America was not used until 1940. After the 1940's, with prodding from the Y.W.C.A., the Lutheran churches and the catastrophic consequences of a boudoir scandal, the rules were changed so that a svelte figure was not enough to score with the judges. The winner was required to have talent and personality, wear high necklines and match Ivory Soap for purity—99 44/100 per cent pure. Today the physical measurements retain their traditional interest but other factors are heavily weighted, such as the ability of an entrant to tap dance or play the bassoon; and intellectual accomplishments were rewarded when a queen toured the country last year for the New York World's Fair who had to be able to state that the Statue of Liberty is 152 feet high and that the Empire State Building, including the television mast on top, soars to a height of 1,472 feet.

Thirteen million U.S. women between the ages of eighteen and twenty-eight have a theoretical right, if they are high school graduates, unmarried and white, to be crowned Miss America while the band plays "Pomp and Circumstance." And they can live out a nonalcoholic, cigarette-less Cinderella existence for a year riding in shiny, new Oldsmobiles and boosting Fralinger's Salt Water Taffy, wearing the gold-filled sorority pin of Mu Alpha Sigma, which is sorority Greek for Modesty, Ambition and Success. Today the idea of leggy promotions has been expanded to include a Miss Universe, Mrs. America, and Miss Teen-Ager—what a lift for the pubescent psyche. Among the princesses engaged in merchandising work are Miss Tall, Miss Can Opener and a Hot Rod Queen. Miss Hampshire travels under the aegis of the Hampshire Meat Hog Conference. The A.F.L.-C.I.O. has its own Union Maid. Yet not all the girls pursue the dream to the end. In 1963, to the astonishment of the three thousand persons present, the just-crowned Miss Louisiana went to the microphones with tears in her eyes to renounce the diadem, a thousand-dollar scholarship, a thousand-dollar wardrobe, a watch and a shot at the Miss America title, all for the love of a man. While the assistant beauties began to whimper, too, Miss Louisiana's mother, stunned, shook her head in shocked disbelief.

If a statuesque young lady undulates through the lobby of a large commercial hotel draped with a banner proclaiming her as "Miss Wellbilt," it is a safe bet that a convention is in progress. There are other indicia. Delegates wear badges of cellulose acetate lettered with their names and addresses. The delegates travel endlessly up and down in the crowded elevators, the man in the rear always shouting at the last possible minute, "Let me off at the Grand Ballroom" while a wit, raising his arms with difficulty in the tightly filled car, asks a colleague, "Shall we dance?" At breakfast the conventioneers all sit down on one side of the table, their wives on the other. They recollect their manners. Embarrassed, they laugh and move so as to sit alternately while a wife says, "He can sit there if he will be good."

Americans are undoubtedly convention-happy since some 20,-000 national, regional and state gatherings are held each year in the United States, with an attendance estimated at well over ten million. How much the delegates spend per diem, how long they stay, are the subject of anxious study by the convention bureaus of all major U.S. cities. Now they even go overseas to hold their meetings. Las Vegas, San Francisco and Miami are old stuff. Time-saving jets take the lucky appliance dealers to San Juan, Honolulu, or the Philippines, and Hong Kong is predicted as the next stop. Or, facing the other way, there are the attractions of Europe. General Electric, despite cultural differences, visa problems and language differences, has held a convention on the Aegean Sea. In Europe businessmen may meet royalty or the heads of state, talk to personalities far more interesting than the waitress in the Town Room of Detroit's Sheraton-Cadillac Hotel.

The American trade association breaks sharply with the European tradition of business secrets. Here the concept is to share knowledge, exchange ideas, see exhibits, get answers to specific problems. The delegates convene to talk it over. Macaroni manufacturers do it. Dahlia growers do it. So do the New York Cemetery Superintendents. The National Association of Former FBI Agents, with chapters in all fifty states, will gather in St. Louis in 1966, with much to chew over—memories of old stake-outs and details about the new developments in electronic snooping, such as the tiny microphone that can be concealed in the olive in a martini cocktail.

Chinchilla breeders hold national conferences. So do toymakers and the National Peanut Council. Anybody can be a delegate to something and need never be lonely in this great, yeasty, mobile country of ours. And there's an organization for every interest—the Association of Grandmothers' Clubs, the Dale Carnegie Alumni Association, circus fans, autograph collectors, canary lovers and cat lovers. The last two meet in separate locations to avoid conflict-of-interest difficulties. Planning in depth is required to pull off a successful convention. The Texas Funeral Directors & Embalmers Association, for instance, knew long ago that it would be meeting in Corpus Christi in June of 1965 and the Western Young Buddhists Association that they would head for Fresno. Right now, the American Association of Nurse Anaesthetists have their convention cities lined up for every year up to the big Chicago meeting in 1980.

Contrary to the popular impression, wives are welcomed at conventions. The old hands who manage these affairs know that the presence of wives enforces a modicum of good deportment, assures a respectable audience for the early morning panelists. Wives like to travel to New York City. This is an important influence in making it a leading convention city. In New York the mesdames can see a fashion show, tour Macy's store, take home a dress with a New York label, enjoy the boat trip around Manhattan Island. There is always a hospitality suite at convention headquarters offering coffee, doughnuts and contacts. The standard arrangements in-

clude at least one big luncheon with wives receiving orchid corsages and free tickets to television studios. If the budget is modest,
they can always put on sensible shoes and walk around Greenwich
Village and imagine it is Soho or feed the pigeons at St. Mark's-in-
the-Bouwerie.

Out-of-town visitors, known not unkindly in the patois of Times
Square as "popeyes" or the "white-shoe trade," may pick up valuable pointers from the hotel convention manager, who tactfully explains to the women how to be properly suited, heeled, pearled
and generally under-stated in a Chanel-type suit, basic black dress,
drip-dry blouse and lingerie. Much of this advice would be applic-
able to other cities and may be readily available from similar
sources. The Manger hotel chain, for one, has issued a little kit
which brings out these points tactfully and warns against slacks,
shorts or white shoes for women who will feel more secure in New
York if they don't look as though they were in town on a one-day
excursion ticket from Meriden. In justice to visitors who might get
a complex over being spotted as hicksters, it should be quickly said
that there really are no certain stigmata of the tourist in New York.

"You've got to remember," a shill for one of the sight-seeing
tours said recently, "that a lot of New Yorkers look like they've
never been to New York, too."

It's just as the man said, except that perhaps a camera is the complete give-away.

In every large American city elaborate luncheon meetings are
held every day and day after day to convey information via chalk
talks, slide projectors, demonstrations, banners and exhortations,
all being wheeled out for such diverse purposes as to inspire the
stewardess supervisors of an airline or introduce insurance agents
to a new health policy. A "Man of the Year" is handed a silver tray.
The Society of American Travel writers hear a panel discussion.
The problems of textbook publishers and of Jello are aired. And
then all too soon comes the public dinner with the chicken and
pleas, the long speeches and the popping of flash bulbs. A novel and
merciful idea for a new kind of dinner was unveiled in 1964 by a
New York State Senator, Jerome L. Wilson, a politician with a
light touch. Wilson raised funds for his campaign by mailing out
engraved invitations to a twenty-five-dollar-a-plate non-banquet
which would have no speakers, no waiters, no menu and no attendance. Mr. Wilson explained:

"There will be no undercooked chicken or off-green peas. The coffee won't turn cold before the introductions are finished. No endless parade of speakers . . . will drone into the night. . . ." Wilson assembled an impressive list of non-speakers, headed by New York's Mayor Robert F. Wagner. All accepted with pleasure the invitation not to speak.

The convention world supports a remarkable range of services and accessories—certificates of award, banquet favors, stenotype reporters, flags and bunting, security guards, art studios which provide sketch artists to limn prominent figures on the platform, headsets for multilingual conventions, orchestras, photographers and at least one philosopher, Martin C. Briggs, who can set out a forty-minute repast of wit, wisdom and hilarity. The four thousand men's-wear retailers who gathered in Los Angeles in 1964 could have inspected nearly three hundred exhibition rooms if they had wished to. They could listen to a steel band, receive free haircuts, shines and manicures. It is chic to like pro football and very "in" to know a player personally. So the clothiers carried home little white footballs autographed by Y. A. Tittle and Hugh McElhenny of the New York Giants football team. And to round off the opportunities for interesting contacts, they met Primo Carnera and Mitzi Gaynor and were photographed à la Polaroid with Playboy Club Bunnies in stagey poses. The wear and tear of life among the delegates was tacitly acknowledged when two hundred fashion editors gathered to see what the New York manufacturers had created for spring and summer apparel. Each visitor received an exquisite velvet, white-satin-lined jewel case. Inside, the weary ladies found fifty aspirin tablets.

19

―――――――――――――――

LAND OF THE SECOND CHANCE

Manners in the United States probably represent behavior at its lowest ebb since the early days of the barbarian invasions of ancient Rome, according to the social historian, Mr. Cleveland Amory. A more lenient judgment is presented by Mr. Arthur H. M. Hillis, a British civil servant who came over as a Commonwealth Fund Fellow and concluded: "I think that Americans at home are the politest people I know, with both the politeness of natural good manners and an engaging touch of formal courtesy that has something eighteenth-century and Virginian about it, like the origins of the Republic itself. . . ."

The British have, in fact, been treating us quite handsomely in recent years. When Alfred North Whitehead, the mathematician and philosopher, moved his household goods from Cambridge, England, to Cambridge, Massachusetts, he expressed the opinion that the people of the United States were the kindest ever produced by any civilization; and Sir Harold Nicholson, the scholar-diplomat, has praised "the mass manners of the United States" without, he says, in the least bit comprehending them. Yet there is a confusion of voices. *L'Osservatore della Domenica,* the Vatican's daily newspaper, has flung out against the women who visit Rome in skin-tight slacks, their minds "full of standardized ideas about Italy based on Neapolitan lyrics, macaroni and great lovers."

Miss Amy Vanderbilt avoids moralizing, accepts matter-of-factly the principle of change, assures her readers that the social laws, or guidelines, as she prefers to call them, will inevitably change with all sorts of innovations—in the mechanics of living, with political upheavals, legislation, the effects of technology, wars and economic developments. The same idea was current as far back as the ninth century, summarized in the line *Omnia mutantur nos et mutamur in illis;* the times change and we change with them. In her various writings Miss Vanderbilt deals briskly with the topics of our times —the problem drinker, bikinis and stretch pants, inter-faith weddings, divorce etiquette, elopements and civil marriages. She has not yet, so far as I know, tackled the social complexities of the pre-marital pregnancy or the situation which has arisen of elderly couples who are living together—should one say in sin?—without either civil or religious sanction. This surprising development is an unexpected consequence of the Social Security Act. When a woman outlives her husband, she gets part of his Social Security benefits only as long as she stays single. The payments cease upon her remarriage on the theory that her new spouse becomes responsible for her support. But if he is a retired man himself, living on eighty-five dollars a month, he cannot afford the theory.

A central question is how unbuttoned our manners can get and continue to perform the essential function of making contacts between human beings pleasurable or at least endurable. No one is suggesting out loud a return to finical artificialities, or what the social critic, Paul Goodman, has called "the icy grin of the upper middle class." But we have traveled a far piece since even the adjustable Emily Post interpreted the social law on such now-remote topics as whether a lady's maid could appear in bobbed hair (she could not) and how to live graciously with only one or two full-time, live-in servants.

Today's off-hand manners run from casual to sloppy. But appearances, to the extent that they suggest there aren't any standards at all, are deceptive. There always are standards. The fact that a young man does not call upon his fair lady bearing a nosegay or a

slender volume of sentimental verses does not support the infer-
ence that he is lacking in devotion. All that has changed is the
style. He does bring his offering. It is a fluffy, stuffed animal for her
collection or the latest hit record. For her part, the young woman
will not hesitate to go to the door barefoot, wearing blue jeans, her
hair done up in pin curls. She will say "Hi" with easy poise. Her
date, if temporarily short of funds, will say so and suggest they stay
home and play records.

Formality is on the run even among the highly favored. Nelson
("Rocky") Rockefeller also says "Hi" when out meeting the people, or sometimes it is "Hi, fella." He introduces his wife by her
nickname, "I want you to meet Happy." Mrs. William Scranton of
Pennsylvania followed the informal or Rotarian pattern when she
saluted the crowds during the 1964 Presidential campaign with a
forthright, "Hi, I'm Mary, Bill's wife."

The trend toward a casual mode of living has been accompanied
by, and to a substantial degree caused by, the disappearance of domestic servants. This social revolution has affected even the rich
rich. A good illustration is the adjustment which Miss Louise A.
Boyd of San Francisco, mining heiress and explorer, has made to
the new austerity. Miss Boyd, reputed once to have shot nineteen
polar bears in one day, although she believes it was only four or
five and insists they were needed for food, has sold her baronial
estate to the Elks. She now lives in an apartment with no other
help than a butler, cook, personal maid, chauffeur and cleaning
woman.

For most American women who run a home, push wire carts
through the lonely, cavernous supermarket, shuttle children to the
meetings of the Brownies and Cub Scouts and manage to cook and
serve pleasant little dinners for eight, there is no domestic service
at all. It has been eliminated because of the cost, because more
attractive job opportunities are available, because of U.S. immigration policy and most of all because of the aversion of the native-
born to the performance of domestic tasks. What American girl
with a high school diploma, for instance, images herself as a trim
little maid dressed in lilac print gown, muslin apron and little
white cap surmounted with a matching lilac bow, trotting to the
front door and bringing in the tea service?

There is a menial connotation about being told to use the service entrance of an apartment house which stirs up deep antago-

nisms. Sometimes the prickly reactions of the family jewel turn on semantics. Is a cook who has been on the job for thirty years a servant or a member of the family? Sometimes there are subtle distinctions of position. Building managers often permit nurses and governesses to enter the lobby and use the front elevators even when not accompanied by a tenant child or dog but bar other members of the domestic staffs.

Apartment dwellers like the epaulets, heavily padded shoulders, braid and trimmings once considered essential for the well-dressed doorman; or the English-butler style—wing collars and Ascot ties. Older residents of Manhattan may remember when London Terrace put its commissionaires in "Bobby" uniforms. Today the doorman wants to look like an executive, just as the janitor is happier when he performs his duties under the name of custodian or superintendent. Doormen prefer the same Ivy League business suit of charcoal gray that has become the uniform of the tenants. As one commented bitterly when asked to put on a costume trimmed in gold lamé to match the marquee:

"Do you want me to look like Liberace?"

Not everyone is grieving; the Martin Manulises, for instance, who live the Simple Life in fashionable Bel Air, a lush and expensive island of exclusiveness surrounded by the sprawl of Los Angeles. The Manulises prefer not to be fenced in by a dinner hour determined by cook's convenience. Mr. Manulis has explained: "We have a little woman named Katherine Manulis who comes in and does dinner every night."

This point of view is held quite generally in the "button-down bastions" of upper-upper life in southern California. There the social sets go in more for swimming pools, tennis courts and exotic gardens than the traditional full-scale service staff. Back in the eastern seaboard environment, former Assistant Secretary of State for Near Eastern and South African Affairs, Phillips Talbot, and Mrs. Talbot entertained regularly for the ambassadors of the eighteen countries which fell within Mr. Talbot's jurisdiction. They did it with no household help. Mrs. Talbot did the cooking in advance. When the guests arrived, Bruce, 12, answered the bell in a smart white cotton twill jacket, served the canapés and, with Nancy, 15, waited on the table, silently poured the wine. Both coped with the logistics expertly under a self-imposed rule against fraternizing with the guests.

For most families the hope of domestic graces lies in the expansion of outside services—window-washing, floor-scraping, power garden equipment, pushbutton shopping and cookery, pre-fried bacon and ultra-sonic dishwashers. A large commercial linen renter in New York will even rent mink stoles. Social callers are no longer expected at the front door except upon appointed occasions since there is no one to open it and say "The missus ain't here"; and it has become downright rude to drop in at any home that has a telephone. When the doorbell rings today it can only mean a canvasser offering something for sale, Girl Scout cookies, a set of plastic dishes or a Fabulous French Fry Potato Cutter.

Hostesses no longer expect Old World manners from their guests. But there is a minimum below which it is not safe to fall. The yawn should be covered. An open mouth in rhythmic motion is still not pleasant to view. Pointing and personal questions are just as much under the taboo as they were in the Victorian Age. It is still useful to know how to go down a receiving line, whether asparagus is a finger food and what to do with an artichoke. And, as X. J. Kennedy has said poetically, even in the Automat, a gentleman taking soup does not fan it with his hat. Zero Mostel, the antic thespian who calls his wife, Kate, "Snakemouth," once told his friend, Sam Jaffe, while dining in a restaurant, "You know . . . people will put up with anything . . ." And to prove it he leaned over and wiped his mouth on a stranger's tie. What happened? The man thanked him. But it is pertinent to add that Mostel is a very large man.

With all that has been thought and said about American conformity, regional folkways continue to thrive. A man driving a car across the United States doesn't need to wear a tie to be seated in any eating place in those parts of the West where the management offers a second cup of coffee free. But when a tie-less young nuclear engineer tried to enter the dining room of a beach club on Long Island he got a beating for his uncouth manners. A potential danger in having guests in for dinner was underlined a few years ago when a Mrs. Lawrence Onish of New York attempted to carve a turkey and sliced Mrs. Eugene Wallman's foot instead. Mrs. Wallman sued for $100,000. The judge, fortunately for the hostess, agrees with her contention that "it is well settled in New York that a social guest is a mere licensee who must take the premises as he finds them and to whom the host owes only the duty to avoid the maintenance of traps or dangerous defects. . . ."

The concept of what constitutes good smoking manners has

changed radically in some ways, remains rooted in tradition in others. When is it all right to pull out a pack of cigarettes? Almost any time. Cigarette smokers are not expected to ask permission to light up any more. But pipe smokers should be careful about pipe dottle and sucking noises. The considerate cigar smoker does not cultivate the long ash or talk with his cigar in his mouth. An ash tray, even if it is of silver and bears an aristocratic crest, even if it came from the Excelsior Hotel in Florence, makes many non-smokers ill if filled with used cigar butts. "One has no right to inflict a disgust upon another," was a rule of gentle behavior a century ago. It holds today. A gentleman removes the paper band from the cigar. The origin of this ritual is lost in the mists of the past. But the rule is iron-clad.

Women who smoke are expected to be equipped with their own cigarettes and matches and not just sit there, cigarette poised, trying to force some man to come and light it. But a man can, if he chooses, get a reputation for being really charming by carrying a lighter even if he doesn't smoke himself. That's what Michael Rennie does and you must know how the women feel about him.

The Surgeon-General's report on smoking and health made public early in 1964 modified at least for a time the profile of the nation's smoking habits. Women experimented with tiny, rhinestone-studded pipes and small, slender cigars to help them kick the cigarette habit. One store in New York puts up a special blend called Girl's Pipe Tobacco. The Cigar Institute of America has announced that there are two hundred thousand women cigar smokers now, including such leaders of important peer groups as actresses Anne Baxter and Hermione Gingold. Mrs. Wilma Soss, perennial gadfly of corporate management, turned up at an annual meeting of the Liggett and Myers Tobacco Company with a meerschaum pipe, a package of Chesterfield cigarettes and some advice for the company about developing a lighter smoking tobacco to "entice" the lady pipe smoker.

Chewing tobacco has disappeared from polite society. The spittoon vanished from trade catalogues around 1929. But in the Chamber of the House of Representatives where many prerogatives of a more uncouth age are jealously guarded, a gleaming row of stainless steel cuspidors is lined up behind the railing at the side of the Chamber leading to the cloak rooms. The Senate likewise provides a few of the receptacles necessary to the happiness of the old breed of southern senator. The reader should not conclude, from what has been said in these paragraphs, that the tobacco manufacturers are caught, in the Texas phrase, "between a rock and a hard place." Sales soared for cigars, pipe tobacco and snuff. Lose it on the apples, runs the old saying, make it up on the bananas.

The decencies of drinking wine and spirits were not considered to be a suitable topic for exegesis by most of the behavior writers during the century when all alcoholic beverages were lumped together as the Demon Rum. There have been encouraging signs of a greater finesse since the country recovered from the horrors of Prohibition. More people are drinking, but per capita they drink less. Intemperance is definitely not part of the approved social pattern. Chicago has calmed down noticeably in regard to sipping rather than gulping. It is rated as a one-and-a-half drink town now at lunch time. Los Angeles and San Francisco rate three, but there is a special weighting factor here: the data supporting the statement was gathered in advertising circles. The drinkingest city in North America is Montreal where it is impolite to take less than four cocktails at lunch.

"Man does not need alcohol," declares Dr. Harold Fallding, the sociologist, "but it does add something—rather like art, an adornment." And Dr. Giorgio Lolli, speaking at a symposium on "Alcohol and Civilization" at the University of California, saw no reason to abolish the cocktail. In his view alcohol is neither good nor bad. It is amoral. The key question is who drinks it, when, how much, why and in what form. But Dr. Lolli did suggest nibbling while taking an aperitif and spacing out the refills.

The etiquette of drinking situations needs to be codified. But a few pointers are merging out of experience. If you don't drink, decline quietly, without making a noisy virtue out of it. When asked what you will have, give a clear, decisive, specific answer. Be ready for the question and say distinctly, "I'll take bourbon on the rocks with a little water" or whatever your pleasure is. Don't practice alcoholic upmanship by asking for something that might stump a professional bartender and will quite possibly make your host either ridiculous or furious. It is all very well for Mrs. Paige Monteagle, of the opulent world of San Francisco blue bloods, to ask for a Suffering Bastard when she lunches in the Captain's Room at Trader Vic's, a drink which she has described as dry rum with a cucumber in it. Most hosts will not have a cucumber imme-

diately available or much variety in the rum classification. Therefore, the considerate guest settles for something less exotic.

One way to keep an even keel is to avoid half-soling; that is,
accepting refills when the glass is only partially empty. The
thoughtful host will not push the drinks, either, in a mistaken gesture of overanxious hospitality when the glasses are still in good
working order; unless, that is, he wishes to see some lady who just a
moment ago was crouching there demurely in her basic black and
pearls suddenly brim over, snatch off her wiglet and slap it over the
bald pate of the guest of honor in a gust of alcoholic whimsy.

If a "nice" woman of 1864 were to meet a woman of similar
reputation and position in the mid-1960's, the feelings of each
about the absurdity and indecency of the other would be deep-
seated and mutual. Each represents a response to the imperious
need to look "right" in accordance with current fashion which always employs the principle of exaggeration in order to renew the
impression. Hemlines at present reveal a greater expanse of leg
than has been on view since the 1920's. This has created an acute
leg problem, a dilemma of kneecap aesthetics which has been happily solved by André Courrèges, the Paris couturier, by introducing a boot whose height makes the exposed kneecap endurable.
Petti-pants—panties tapered to the knee—restore a modicum of de-
cency for the woman of 1965 who cannot sit in skirts that are both
too short and tight without risk of over-exposure.

Ideals of feminine allurement also change with geography, cultural background and different time periods. The Caribs of Suri-
nam admire large calves. The French women of the Directoire
wore a framework which made them look pregnant. The Ruku-
yenn of Guiana also esteem the large abdomen. It is not different
with us, except that our standards shift suddenly in response to
commercial manipulation. In the 1880's the bustle made the
derrière look like a shelf. In the nineties the soubrettes introduced
the bass-viol figure. In the 1920's of the John Held caricatures,
woman was tubular. Now well-rounded buttocks are held in such
affectionate regard that Nemo is manufacturing girdles which
stretch lace over molded foam-rubber padding to produce "Fanny
Falsies" that "add more wow to your wiggle." The Size B produces
sufficient exaggeration for the average figure or in extremis, there
is the C curve "for the miserably minus."

This rear-view expansion of the silhouette has been explained scientifically by Dr. Erwin O. Strassman, Professor of Clinical Obstetrics and Gynecology in the College of Medicine at Baylor University. In a flowering culture like that of the Renaissance, Dr. Strassman says, the admired types are the Titians and Rubens ladies. Men recognize them instinctively as women who will function well as females. Women react to the reaction, with bustles, pads and other aids to remedy any deficiency. Ours, then, must be a new Golden Age.

Dr. Strassman also made another off-the-cuff comment which stirred up a storm of comment. "The bigger the breasts," he remarked, "the lower the IQ." Mamie Van Doren replied through the press that she had had the biggest bust and the lowest IQ of anyone in her high school class, but added, "Who cares about IQ?" Not everyone, certainly. A group of Canadian fraternity men wrote to Dr. Strassman, "Three cheers for the girls with the big measurements and the low IQ's."

Fashion, that group compulsion which no individual in our culture can resist without incurring penalties, can make a costume modest or immodest. If a fad lasts long enough to become conventional it can even reshape the standard of propriety by which it is judged, and neither church nor state can do much beyond fume and exhort. But the fashion that moves too far, too fast, may be rejected. The topless bathing suit of 1964 got more mileage in the press than on the sands. Few women have followed the dictate for the naked look even as far as the transparent bodice, the "No-bra" bra or the fishnet bathing suit. The Baptists of Dallas picketed a specialty shop which displayed a topless bathing suit on a dummy and the Reverend Ed Watt, pastor of the Carroll Avenue Baptist Mission, said if the trend is not stopped the next thing will be the topless shorts. The Reverend Watt's distress is understandable but his conclusion is erroneous since it disregards the well-established anthropological principle that fashion is irrational.

Consider dark sunglasses as another exhibit in evidence. These glasses were first associated with the movies. They were worn by people whose work was presumably hard on the eyes. Then the glasses became a symbol, by association of ideas. Celebrities, the movie-rich, adopted them as a disguise. Everybody liked the idea, climbed aboard the vogue and wore it out. Now the glasses are back again, some with lenses as big as bagels. They combine the virtues of an attention-getter with a cozy sense of security, like the one-way window used in the spying dodge. It may be true for a brief while the dark sunglasses swaying above the eye-line will suggest to the passengers on the evening bus that someone of renown is standing on their toes. But the idea will not last. David Freedman, associate artistic director of the New York Shakespeare Festival, explains why: "If you're really 'in' you wouldn't be caught dead wearing them indoors or at night because you'd look like somebody who is 'out' but is trying to look 'in.' "

In our contemporary feminized society the male plumage is subdued except for the bold-patterned sports shirt, worn only for recreational hours. The fashion note is, otherwise, quiet elegance and no jewelry to speak of, except in Texas where a member can appear in the Fort Worth Club wearing his initials worked out in diamonds on his finger ring and matching belt buckle. With the tub and needle shower universally available, colognes and lotions are no longer a substitute for the bath but simply accessories whose clever trade names suggesting black panthers and mustaches attempt to make the toiletries a virility symbol.

But the bath is assumed. In fact it has been judicially determined that it is a union official's duty to bathe before attending a banquet. Clarence L. Greenwell, an alternate delegate to the Amalgamated Association of Street, Electric Railway and Motor Coach Employees of America, slipped in the bath tub while getting ready to attend an Amalgamated banquet. The injury which he sustained forced him to leave his job. The Union argued that Mr. Greenwell, a former driver for the transit company in the District of Columbia, was not entitled to workmen's compensation. But the courts upheld the plaintiff's argument that he was entitled to partial permanent disability since the risks of bathing were a job-connected hazard of attending official dinners.

As the long love affair between the American people and the automobile pushes the industry to turn out some nine million passenger cars a year, the machine continues to make significant contributions to American manners. Cultural indicators may be read in small acts such as the way couples sit in an automobile. Working-class wives sit with their husbands, one pair in front, the other in the back seat. Middle class men sit in front, the wives behind. In more sophisticated circles, each husband sits next to the other man's wife. An automobile can even be the outlet for ethnocentric feelings. Lady Sassoon, the former Evelyn Barnes of Kingsport,

Tennessee, known as "Barnsie" to her intimates, keeps the back-home touch by driving about London and the Home Counties in a cream-colored American station wagon with Texas license plates.

The driver to whom his automobile is a mustang to be subdued is the social pariah of the highways. But the automobile has also given us the all-weather gentleman who mans the gas pumps and speeds the parting motorist with a warm farewell, "You hurry right back, now." The car pool has developed its own code of civil behavior: be prompt, be responsible. Don't ask others to make a detour while you pick up an air conditioner. Keep the newspaper tucked away and make a fair contribution to the general conversation.

Good talk, oldest form of entertainment known to man, continues to be a stumbling block, as it was to our forebears. Perhaps alcoholic beverages are so firmly imbedded in our life today in part because they create a common ethos and loosen shy tongues. The difficulties of those who lack verbal acuity are reflected in the common reference to something being a "conversation piece." This principle is well-recognized by the sales people at the extraordinary Neiman-Marcus department store in Dallas, where they recommend a wide range of unusual merchandise on the ground that it is a "conversation starter." Typical selections are polar-bear rugs, Chinese opium beds for non-opium smokers, a fourteen-karat gold dog-bone and a fur-covered waste basket.

In most situations today the easy-does-it approach to chatting is the right one. In Texas, the greeting is "How y' doin?" Or, "You all right?" And from there it is no trick at all to move on to robust anecdote, sports, oil wells, bridge and personal plans. In Butte, Montana, there is an equally stylized exchange:

"How's she goin'?"

"Good. And you?"

"No use complaining. Nobody listens."

Also acceptable when friends meet at Main and Broadway in Butte are these hello manners. The opening remains the same, but the first speaker may come back with a modulation:

"Can't hardly kick. Who'd pay me any mind?"

At parting the formula runs:

"Well, I have to mosey. Tap 'er light, kid."

"Take care" is the antiphonal response to this as one friend moseys up Main, the other west on Broadway.

Compliments are now permissible provided they are at least sixty per cent true. The right word is the word of sense, not of sensibility. It's bitch, not lady dog; bathroom, not the Little Girls' Room; sweat, not perspire; old people, not Senior Citizens; God, not The Man Upstairs. Dangerous subjects now, as they always have been, are age, ailments, pregnancies. Tap other people's status symbols lightly. When you refer laughingly to "You know—maple people" or families who display bronzed baby shoes on the mantel, you are asking for what you will probably get. Don't interrogate lawyers on how the case is coming, pester doctors for free medical advice, belabor writers to help you market *your* book or pretend to be a hipster when talking to jazz musicians. "A musician," says Mrs. Mary Lou Munson, in her sensible *Practical Etiquette for the Modern Man,* "can spot you immediately as a phoney."

The older idea of how to shine conversationally has been touched upon in an earlier chapter. It revolved around acquiring and giving out miscellaneous bits of arcane information when the dinner is over but it is too early to go home, some such remark as "In eastern Uganda it is no longer compulsory to take part in the rain-making dances." This gambit was never any good, of course. A suggestion more attuned to reality has come recently from Dr. George W. Crane, who signs himself in his scientific writings as Ph.D., M.D., and member of a body known as the Pan American Psychological Association. Lucille H., aged nineteen, a stenographer with better than average looks, whose eyes have often made people think of Elizabeth Taylor, wrote to Dr. Crane that, with all her advantages, she simply could not line up a boy friend.

Dr. Crane's answer was, in essence, to break the ice with conversation. Like the life insurance salesman, Dr. Crane urged, Lucille should go where the prospects are and get them talking. The Doctor did not stop with vague generalities. Lucille could say it's a jolly party, isn't it? If the young man can only say uh-huh, she is instructed to follow with:

"My, but you have large, muscular hands. I'll bet you could hold a basketball in one hand, couldn't you?"

All this requires is a yes or no answer. But persistence is essential. Before giving up on the big hands, another try might be:

"I'll bet you'll make a great surgeon or artist with those long, strong fingers."

Play the averages, Dr. Crane counsels, and goes back again to his analogy of the successful insurance salesman. Remember, he sells only one out of fifteen prospects. Dr. Crane has a mnemonic device that helps immensely. It is DEAR HOME PALS. Each letter stands for a topic of conversation. "D" reminds Lucille to bring up something about the drama. If the boy's mind continues to be a blank, she hands him an easy either/or question from the cinema world:

"Do you like Rock Hudson better than Clint Walker?"

"E" represents entertainment in the Dr. Crane system, leading into fishing, chess, reading a book, or does he like best to go off on long hikes all by himself? "R" calls up the idea of family relations:

"Do they all have blue eyes like you?"

This is particularly good because it gets the conversation on a personal basis with intimate overtones. And so on to "L" which stands for literature. Again the lady should lay down a reasonable choice—no highbrow stuff—before the prospect:

"Which magazine do you read most, *Reader's Digest* or the *Saturday Evening Post?*"

The final "S" stands for "sex differences" and has great possibilities because it offers the boy, if he cares to grasp the nettle, an opening for expressing strong views on girls who wear mandarin fingernails and drink whiskey. "S" is, obviously, a reprise of the personal note. Dr. Crane says it takes only half an hour to memorize DEAR HOME PALS. But it is enough to bring a man to the altar and an exchange of eternal vows in a pretty candlelight ceremony.

There have always been modish ways of sitting, eating, drinking, dancing, standing and walking. A feminine affectation from the past was the Alexandra limp. The dandies of the 1880's carried their elbows raised and slightly projecting, to suggest that they were horsey fellows. There were, and are, similar shifting patterns of what is stylish involving the use of the right catchwords and inflections. Can a person of mature years learn a new way of speaking? Professor Alan S. C. Ross, well-known British philologist, maintains that one can't. Professor Ross coined the terms U, to designate the usages of the upper class; and non-U to describe the speech associated with a lower class origin. The principles, if not the details, apply also to the looser American social system, for here too it can be a professional advantage to a man, if he practices corporation law, to have a speaking voice that is unmistakably Old New York with a touch of Harvard and Wall Street.

But speech expert Maxeda von Hesse thinks American regionalisms can be smoothed out by the individual himself. Mrs. Edward J. MacMullan, the Philadelphia social secretary, concurs and has conducted classes in correct speech. But Dr. Harvey Halpern, instructor in speech pathology at Queens College, warns against the do-it-yourself approach. Go to a clinic, he advises, or a therapist. George Bernard Shaw's fascination with phonetics gave the world the delightful Eliza Doolittle who, you will remember, was saying in the first act of *Pygmalion*, "Bucknam Pellice" and "Cheer ap, Keptin; n' baw ya flahr orf a pore gel" and in Act IV had pulled off a stunning social triumph with hired diamonds and an acquired diction which, thanks to Professor Higgins, gave Eliza the classmarks of a duchess.

Because of the power of the mass media, we are almost drowned today in habit-forming words and phrases which are meretricious but hard to resist, like *glamorous, fabulous, finalize* and those creations with suffixes ending in -*wise*—housing-*wise*, client-*wise*; while Washington bureaucracy has contributed such neologisms as *overkill, fallout, manpowerization.* Jack Tinker, the New York advertising man, blames advertising for exhausting *white, power, mild, refreshing* and *relief.* Rudolph Flesch cites as currently dangerous words, *catalyst, charismatic* (this among the Phi Beta Kappa set), *rationale* and *viable.* And how about *bit*—"sick of the bouffant bit" —*bugged* and *do a flip?*

There are social advantages, to be sure, which accrue from a command of the vowel sounds and tropes which are current among fashionable people. "A footman may swear," Dean Swift reminds us, "but he cannot swear like a lord." For only those with access to select company can keep up with the new terms minted by the town wits, with a sure sense for when to take them up and when to discard the old for the new. Thus the use of a rapidly changing and specialized idiom serves as a quick means of determining whether new people are *we* or *they.* Nancy Hale, in *Dear Beast,* a novel about a Vermont girl who married a Virginian and moved on to New York to take in the cocktail parties as a sort of cram course, has her heroine speak with admiration of the vocabularies she encountered at the literary receptions. Everybody who was anybody in New York, she found, said "dichotomy." She looked the word up and was astonished to find that all it meant was division into parts; "but why say 'division' when you could say 'dichotomy'? It seemed beyond words worldly." In reviewing Miss Hale's book,

Charles Poore, daily book critic of *The New York Times,* predicted that the lady would soon catch up with "ambivalence" and talk portentously of books that could be read on two or three levels —"as if they had been written for the escalator trade."

People in the arts are enjoying an unprecedented boom as social ornaments, starting at the bottom with writers, who are complained of for a tendency to monopolize the conversation, and followed on a rising scale by those in the performing arts. That explains a remark made by Elia Kazan on an occasion when he was attending an important function in Washington. The noted Broadway producer observed somewhat testily the stir among the guests as James Reston of *The New York Times* walked in. Said Kazan: "What's with this society? They treat a news columnist like he was Marlon Brando?"

At the dazzling top stand the artists. They gather at the fall gallery openings to renew summer art colony friendships, accept the congratulations of well-wishers and meet dealers and collectors while uniformed maids struggle to move their trays of canapés and cocktails through a swirl of beards, turtle-neck sweaters, trench coats, slouch hats, mixed with full-length chinchilla coats and the latest Paris fashions. The openings sometimes provide orchestras for dancing, flowers floating in pools and guests floating, too, in pools of Scotch and Seagram's. At the top of these affairs is the elaborate black-tie reception where those in the New York-Philadelphia-Palm Beach orbit turn up regularly and an ambassador's wife in a Dior gown sips and chats with an artist so famous that he can appear in clam-digger slacks and a plaid shirt. Snatches of conversation, not necessarily about art, cut through the din:

"Did you hear that Iris' dachshund tore her mink coat to shreds?"

"Yugoslavia in the spring is absolutely marvelous!"

Unusual enough to be remarked upon in this context was the comment made by Mrs. Jason Robards, Jr., (Lauren Bacall) at a champagne party honoring the Spanish painter, Count Luis Quintanilla:

"I want to look at the pictures as it so happens."

The purchasers of today's easel art come from the affluent society, some with knowledge and taste and all of whom have at their disposal a seemingly endless supply of the latest abstractionists, French impressionists and genuine old masters, plus the houses or yachts for displaying them. A rich collector may even commission a new work of art. The Spanish surrealist, Salvador Dali, who rarely ventures into portraiture, is considering at this writing capturing the likeness of Mrs. Marjorie Merriweather Post, the Post Toasties heiress. And Mrs. Post, amused by the gifted Dali, is reported to be considering whether she wishes to sit for the artist whose works include "Debris of an Automobile Giving Birth to a Blind Horse Biting a Telephone." Also active and exercising a democratizing influence in the field of portraiture is Van Dyke Oil Portraits, Ltd., which maintains a stable of artists who paint "in rich oils" on canvas "from old or new photos." The Van Dyke people point out, "No longer need you envy those fortunate enough to own a family oil portrait."

It is undoubtedly true that some collectors are attracted to fine art because of its appeal as an exciting speculation. But many more take their treasures seriously for their aesthetic value, as the late Mrs. Katherine Witten demonstrated at a formal dinner she gave at her Connecticut Avenue apartment in Washington. During the dessert course a large oil painting toppled from the wall, fell over the head of a United Nations ambassador and came to rest around his ears, leaving him looking like a startled rabbit. While the guests gathered around to voice their concern and inquire about his possible injuries, the hostess' first words were: "Damn! That was one of my best paintings."

In between those who are in steel, cornflakes, oil or Greek shipping and those who buy the silk screen reproductions of Van Gogh's "Drawbridge at Arles" for $3.95, fall the moderately or Westchester-rich. There is a cultural explosion occurring among the split levels and the flowering dogwood. Walls are painted white or off-white to set off canvases framed in pickled woods, or mounted unframed. Art—not Utrillos or Dufys, of course, but original oils and water colors—now ranks with riding power mowers, power boats and fertilizer spreaders as an expression of the upper-suburban ethic.

American women continue to enjoy residuary benefits of being a scarce article, even though the supply today is ample. Tocqueville said, "I have nowhere seen woman occupying a loftier position," and Miss Gayle Brew of Chicago, an airline stewardess, says it is still true:

"My reaction is that the girls and women in this country never had it so good. I'm a student of history. I know that in no period of recorded history have women been placed on such a high pedestal by their men."

Yet since women have been explained by the Freudian revelation and now compete in the labor market, it is no longer necessary for a man to give up his seat to a woman when riding the bus at rush hour unless she is well advanced in pregnancy. In fact, a polite man today has been defined as "the one who offers a lady a seat when he gets off the bus." Women on the executive level carry credit cards and reach casually for the check when having a business luncheon with a man. But this is not every woman's dish of tea, with the culture-roles so overturned. Studies conducted by Young and Rubicam, a New York-based advertising firm with vast technical resources, have turned up the information that the typical American housewife is totally conventional. Betty Frieden, the feminologist, is in despair over the young women who, since World War II, have turned away from the hard-won gains for a new "privatism," following in their real lives the kittenish heroines met in women's magazine fiction who find their fulfillment in vacuuming the living room while wearing eye make-up, constructing endless piles of peanut-butter sandwiches and discovering a softer toilet paper. Thomas C. Mendenhall, President of Smith, largest of the women's colleges in the eastern Sisterhood, also believes that the process of emancipation is lagging, although it is a fact that there were, when recently counted, twenty-nine "Smithies" in the Peace Corps.

Although the gentlewoman, the true lady, is a lovely phenomenon which has not perished from the earth, such terms of reference are not widely used today and the ideal is not subscribed to by all women, certainly not by the girl who wrote to Dorothy Dix: "I read your articles on how to be a perfect lady and as a result am home every night." In the United States today about all that "Ladies" means is a public convenience or the women's apparel industry. We do hold firmly to First Lady. This term caused a painful misunderstanding for the Englishman, so the story goes, who heard that Lady Bird frequently traveled with President Johnson. The Britisher remarked that he could not understand why Lord Bird permitted it.

The word gentleman, as the mark of the man-as-he-should-be, is in a similar state of disarray. Again this is more a matter of terminology than of substance. A man is expected to measure up to the duties which go with position and responsibility. The medieval knight was accomplished in the appropriate sports. The Company president can shoot—birds or golf—follow the hounds and cut a good figure at the Hunt Ball. With his touch for handling people, his grace under pressure, his recreational skills, his deepening culture as educational standards rise, the professional manager, the civil servant of business, may turn out to be the new version of the gentleman. A. N. Whitehead thought this was quite likely to occur. It is the task of the American universities, he said, to civilize business, or better, as he put it, "to get business men to civilize themselves . . . for if America is to be civilized, it must be done . . . by the business class, who are in possession of the power and the economic processes."

In Richmond, Virginia, and similar self-contained social entities, "People just *know* who is in" if they are familiar with the terrain. More typically in the U.S. the lines are shifting, vague, representing delicate distinctions in life styles. New groups are rapidly joining the white-collar class—market research analysts, engineers, technicians, accountants, optical physicists, computer programmers, Ph.D.'s trained in analog circuitry, all of whom Louis Harris, the public opinion poll analyst, identifies as the New America. They are suburbanites who work in the new sophisticated industries, "a new group on the make"; who are going, so to speak, all the way with R.C.A. For them, as they regard their television antennas stippling the skyline, the eternal flame of the cookout grill flickering through the charcoal, these are the good *new* days.

A sensitivity about addresses often develops. The residents of the community of Briar Park, Long Island, went to federal court to get a classier post office address than Levittown. Rye Acres, which is in Port Chester, New York, insists upon having its mail delivered from the Rye post office. The Westchester Country Club, actually in Harrison, New York, has a Rye address. North Stamford home owners prefer to believe they live in New Canaan, but the Stamford post office deplores this autism and pays no attention to it. What's in a name? A great deal, apparently. Riverdale pretends it is not in the Bronx, pants pressers put "Sutton" in their firm names though they are located nowhere near exclusive Sutton Place; and Fourth Avenue, between Seventeeth Street and Thirty-second Street in New York, is now legally known as Park Avenue

South. But a man who went there and looked says "It still looks like Fourth Avenue." No one seems to feel that all this is absurd but rather that it is at the worst an amiable weakness, an understandable expression of the social push-up.

The desire to be somebody special became a realizable goal for millions of Americans when the median family income rose fifty per cent in the 1950's and continued to rise steeply in the following decade. The classic economic pyramid has bulged out in the middle, pulling in and flattening at the bottom so that now it is shaped like a diamond. This means a wider diffusion of the middle class way of life. Outhanging sports shirts are worn on the job. The dinner pail is disappearing. Clerks are now Administrative Assistants and a group of West Coast junk dealers have banded together as the Auto Dismantlers Association of Southern California. Symbolic minutiae continue to convey subtle overtones of social difference—a familiarity with wine cookery, for instance, the ability to refer to particular sidewalk cafés in Paris or "taking" *American Heritage* magazine.

Historically, Americans have always shown a special facility for living in a fluid society. Horace Greeley not only told the young man to go West, but also added, "and grow up with the country." "Wandering about," remarked the royal governor, the Earl of Dunmore, of the Americans, "seems engrafted in their Nature"; and in the twentieth century Archibald MacLeish sings, "America is west and the wind is blowing." Even our figures of speech reflect movement: *go-getter, going places, I'm on my way,* and the cheerful variant, *I don't know where I'm going but I'm on my way.* It is almost like a pilgrimage, this tidal wave of students, retired people moving their family goods to Florida, the southwest and California, gypsying trailer families, management men transferred by "the Company," refugees from state taxation, from a spouse or the police. All demonstrate that the United States is The Land of the Second Chance for all who participate in what a French source has called La Grande Parade Americaine.

This lateral movement provides a sort of counterpoint to the opposite principle of stability which is represented by Richmond, Philadelphia or Cotton Center, Texas, where the people in charge of the institutional life—the school board and the Baptist Church— are known as Old Timers because they arrived in western Hale County before 1924. Most Americans live outside such structured situations where the nice people know who is who. The newcomer anywhere finds the badges of belonging important—an assured manner, church affiliation, country-club membership, a son in the armed forces who is a commissioned officer rather than a soldier or seaman. Hope is endemic and frequently justified. Vacancies in the next higher circle serve usefully to keep the career open to the talents, softening caste antagonisms, assuring that the behavior of all will be more plastic. We have tried a number of aristocracies in America, based upon a religious sanction, upon landed proprietorships, on prior immigration, on the cultural flowering of New England. None has demonstrated real staying power.

When we look back at the Victorian period, with its affectations, its stiffness, its studied style, one sees that there has been a gain in directness and simplicity, in lightness and pace. There has been a marked improvement in the way people treat those to whom they do not have to behave gently. There is little calculated rudeness. Actually, the easier manners of today, it may be argued, call for a finer tact, a surer taste, than did the stiff conventions which once held sway in the citadels of privilege. A mannerly youth says "Can you go to the movies Saturday night?"; not, "What are you doing Saturday night?" And for the same old good reasons. There are fewer rules. Those that hold are followed more seriously. All the essentials of that universal consideration which has marked the person of breeding in all societies are evident in the outlook of the nine-year-old boy who declared:

"I have good manners. I say good night and good morning. I say hello and goodby, and when I see dead things lying around the house I bury them."

As Geoffrey Woodhead, a Commonwealth Fund scholar, said of our countrymen with carefully balanced antithesis: "Their Constitution is much less perfect, and they themselves are much more admirable, than they ever seem able to realize."

BIBLIOGRAPHY

Bibliographical information is annexed to the individual sketches in the standard work of collective American biography, *The Dictionary of American Biography*, Allen Johnson and Dumas Malone, eds., 22 v. New York: 1928-44; and *Supplements* edited by H. E. Starr, R. L. Schuyler and E. T. James, patterned after the English *Dictionary of National Biography*, Leslie Stephen and Sidney Lee, eds., 22 v. London: 1908-09, which was also frequently consulted in connection with the earlier chapters of the present volume. An indispensable bibliographical aid is the *Harvard Guide to American History*, compiled by Oscar Handlin, A. M. Schlesinger, S. E. Morison, Frederick Merk, A. M. Schlesinger, Jr., and P. H. Buck. Cambridge, Massachusetts: 1954. Also valuable: the annual volumes of indexed *Writings on American History* published since 1902 and issued since 1918 as part of the American Historical Association *Report*, edited currently by James R. Masterson. I found useful the lists of books, articles and documents prepared by Wood Gray for quarterly publication in *The American Historical Review*.

Other aids which I consulted include G. E. Noyes, *Bibliography of Courtesy and Conduct Books in Seventeenth-Century England*. New Haven: 1937; William Matthews, compiler, *American Diaries. An Annotated Bibliography of American Diaries Written Prior to the Year 1861*. Berkeley: 1945; K. G. Hornbeak, "The Complete Letter-Writer in English, 1568-1800," *Smith College Studies in Modern Languages*, XV, Nos. 3-4. Apr.-July, 1934; Ruth Kelso, "The Doctrine of the English Gentleman in the Sixteenth Century, with a

Bibliographical List of Treatises on the Gentleman and Related Subjects Published in Europe to 1625," *University of Illinois Studies in Language and Literature,* XIV, Nos. 1-2. Feb.-May, 1929; E. A. Leonard, S. H. Drinker, M. Y. Holden, *The American Woman in Colonial and Revolutionary Times, 1565-1800. A Syllabus with Bibliography.* Philadelphia: (c. 1962); M. R. Bobbitt, compiler, *A Bibliography of Etiquette Books Published in America Before 1900.* New York: 1947.

Allan Nevins, *America Through British Eyes,* New York: 1948, a collection of narratives of travel, contains much bibliographical information. A critical evaluation of such narratives, old but still useful, is *America and her Commentators.* New York: 1864, by H. T. Tuckerman. The field of American periodicals is covered in F. L. Mott, *A History of American Magazines.* 4 v. Cambridge, Mass.: 1957. Contemporary scholarly writings are equipped with footnotes, chapter notes or a formal bibliography which point the way to relevant sources and authorities. Examples, selected at random, are Merle Curti, *The Growth of American Thought.* New York: (c. 1951); C. K. Shipton, *New England Life in the 18th Century. Representative Biographies from Sibley's Harvard Graduates.* Cambridge, Mass.: 1963; or L. B. Wright, *The First Gentlemen of Virginia. Intellectual Qualities of the Early Colonial Ruling Class.* San Marino, Calif.: 1940.

The present writer, concerned with the general reader, has not wished to make of this book an ossuary of the whitened bones of academic research. But there is sufficient disclosure of the underpinning upon which the text rests. The author will be glad to furnish any serious inquirer with volume, number and page references connected with the development of any topic.

Short titles are used when the title is excessively long. Etiquette books cited refer to the edition used, not necessarily the first. Some references have been inserted into the main text for flavor and are not repeated in the bibliography.

PRIMARY SOURCES

Allen, Fred, *Much Ado About Me.* Boston: (c. 1956).
(Allestree, Richard), *The Whole Duty of Man, Laid Down in a Plain and Familiar Way, for the Use of all, but Especially the Meanest Reader.* . . . Edinburgh: 1741.
Arthur, E. B., *My Husband Keeps Telling Me to Go to Hell.* Garden City, N.Y.: (c. 1954).
Beecher, C. E., *Educational Reminiscences and Suggestions.* New York: 1874.
———— *Miss Beecher's Domestic Receipt Book.* . . . New York: 1846.
———— *A Treatise on Domestic Economy, for the Use of Young Ladies at Home, and at School.* New York: 1846.
———— and H. B. Stowe, *The American Woman's Home: or, Principles of Domestic Science: being a Guide to the Formation and Maintenance of Economical, Healthful, Beautiful, and Christian Homes.* New York: 1870.
Beecher, Lyman, *The Autobiography of Lyman Beecher.* Barbara M. Cross, ed., 2 v. Cambridge, Mass.: 1961.
Bent, George P., *A Pioneer's Historical Sketches.* Chicago: n.d.
Blair, Walter, *Native American Humor.* San Francisco: (c. 1960).
Bloom, Sol, *The Autobiography of Sol Bloom.* New York: 1948.

(Bloomfield-Moore, Clara Sophia Jessup), Mrs. H. O. Ward, (pseud.), *Sensible Etiquette of the Best Society.* . . . Philadelphia: 1878.

The Book of Complete Information About Pianos. Wing & Son. New York: (c. 1906).

(Braddy, Nella), *The Book of Business Etiquette.* Garden City, N.Y.: 1923.

Brown, Leonard, "Belshazzar's Feast," *Cabin Home Papers.* Des Moines: 1892.

Burnaby, Andrew, *Travels Through the Middle Settlements in North-America. In the Years 1759 and 1760.* . . . Ithaca, N.Y.: (1960).

Byrd, William, *The Great American Gentleman. William Byrd of Westover in Virginia. His Secret Diary for the Years 1709-1712.* L. B. Wright and Marion Tingling, eds. New York: (c. 1963).

—— *The London Diary (1717-1721) and Other Writings.* L. B. Wright and Marion Tingling, eds. New York: 1958.

—— *The Writings of Colonel William Byrd of Westover in Virginia Esqr.* J. S. Bassett, ed. New York: 1901.

Canby, H. S., *The Age of Confidence. Life in the Nineties.* New York: (c. 1934).

Caples, John, *Making Ads Pay.* New York: (c. 1957).

Carpenter, F. G., *Carp's Washington.* Frances Carpenter, ed. With an Introduction by Cleveland Amory. New York: (c. 1960).

Casa, Giovanni della, *Galateo of Manners & Behaviors.* With an Introduction by J. E. Spingarn. Boston: 1914.

Castiglione, Count Baldesar, *The Book of the Courtier.* L. E. Opdycke, tr. New York: 1929.

Catalogue and Buyers' Guide. No. 56. Fall and Winter. 1894-95. Montgomery, Ward & Co. (Chicago: n.d.).

Catalogue of Portraits in the Essex Institute, Salem, Massachusetts, Covering Three Centuries, with an Introduction by H. W. Foote. Salem, Mass.: 1936.

Chambers, William, *Things as They Are in America.* Philadelphia: 1854.

Chastellux, Marquis de, *Travels in North America in the Years 1780, 1781 and 1782 by the* . . . *A Revised Translation with Introduction and Notes by H. C. Rice, Jr.* 2 v. Chapel Hill: (c. 1963).

Chesterfield, P. D. S., 4th Earl of . . . , *Letters Written by the late Right Honorable Philip Dormer Stanhope, Earl of Chesterfield, to his Son, Philip Stanhope, Esq.* . . . 2 v. Boston: 1779. Vol. II published at Newburyport: 1779.

Child, L. M., *Letters from New York.* New York: 1847.

Clark, T. D., ed., *Bluegrass Cavalcade.* Lexington (Ky.): 1956.

Cleveland, R. E., and others, *Our Society, A Complete Treatise on the Usages that Govern the Most Refined Homes and Social Circles.* . . . Detroit, Mich.: 1891.

Cong. Rec. 63 Cong. 3 Sess. House Debate Dec. 22, 1914.

Cooley, E., M.D., *A Description of the Etiquette at Washington City.* Philadelphia: 1830.

The Crockett Almanacs, Nashville Series, 1835-1838. F. J. Meine, ed. Chicago: 1955.

Danckaerts, Jasper, *Journal of Jasper Danckaerts, 1679-1680.* B. B. James and J. F. Jameson, eds. New York: 1913.

Day, C. W., *The American Ladies and Gentleman's Manual of Elegance, Fashion, and True Politeness.* Auburn (N.Y.): 1854.

—— *Hints on Etiquette and the Usages of Society; with a Glance at Bad Habits.* New York: 1844.

Dow, G. F., *Every Day Life in the Massachusetts Bay Colony.* Boston: 1935.

Etiquette At Washington. By a Citizen of. . . . Baltimore: 1849.

Fay, Amy, *Music-Study in Germany. From the Home Correspondence of Amy Fay.* Chicago: 1888.

Franklin, Benjamin, *The Writings of.* . . . A. H. Smyth, ed. 10 v. New York: 1905-07.

Furness, C. J., *The Genteel Female. An Anthology.* New York: 1931.

Furnivall, F. J., *A Book of Precedence.* Early English Text Society. London: 1869.

The Barber and the Historian. The Correspondence of George A. Myers and James Ford Rhodes, 1910-1923. J. A. Garraty, ed. Columbus (Ohio): 1956.

Guazzo, Stefano, *The Civile Conversation of M. Steeven Guazzo . . . with an Introduction by Sir Edward Sullivan.* 2 v. London: 1925.

The Habits of Good Society: a Handbook for Ladies and Gentlemen. . . . New York: 1874.

Hall, F. H., *Social Customs.* Boston: 1887.

Hamilton, Dr. Alexander, *Gentleman's Progress. The Itinerarium of . . . 1744.* Carl Bridenbaugh, ed. Chapel Hill: 1948.

Harland, Marion (Terhune, Mrs. M. V. H.), and Virginia Van de Water, *Everyday Etiquette.* Indianapolis: (c. 1907).

────── *Marion Harland's Autobiography. The Story of a Long Life.* New York: 1910.

Harrison, Mrs. Burton, *Recollections Grave and Gay.* New York: 1911.

Hartley, C. B., *The Gentlemen's Book of Etiquette and Manual of Politeness.* Boston: (c. 1860).

Hartley, Florence, *The Ladies' Book of Etiquette and Manual of Politeness.* Boston: (c. 1860).

Harvard Portraits. A Catalogue of Portrait Paintings at Harvard University. . . . Allan Burroughs, ed. Cambridge, Mass.: 1936.

Hawthorne, Nathaniel, *The American Notebooks.* . . . Randall Stewart, ed. New Haven: 1932.

Hazard, T. R., *The Jonny-Cake Papers of "Shepherd Tom" Together with Reminiscences of Narragansett Schools of Former Days.* . . . Boston: 1915.

Hedrick, U. P., *The Land of the Crooked Tree.* New York: 1948.

Hewitt, E. W., *Those Were the Days.* . . . New York: (c. 1943).

Hill, T. E., *Hill's Manual of Social and Business Forms.* Chicago: 1879.

Hitchcock, Enos, *Memoirs of the Bloomsgrove Family.* . . . 2 v. Boston: 1790.

Houghton, W. R., and others, *American Etiquette and Rules of Politeness.* Chicago: 1882.

Hutchinson, Thomas, *The History of the Colony and Province of Massachusetts-Bay.* . . . L. S. Mayo, ed. 3 v. Cambridge, Mass.: 1936.

Jones, Hugh, *The Present State of Virginia from Whence is Inferred a Short View of Maryland and North Carolina.* R. L. Morton, ed. Chapel Hill: 1956.

Josselyn, John, *An Account of Two Voyages to New-England, Made During the Years 1638, 1663.* Boston: 1865.

Keim, D. R., *Hand-Book of Official and Social Etiquette and Public Ceremonials at Washington.* Washington: (c. 1889).

Kent, C. H., *How to Achieve Success. A Manual for Young People.* New York: (c. 1897).

Chicago Yesterdays. A Sheaf of Reminiscences. Caroline Kirkland, comp. Chicago: 1919.

The Ladies' Home Journal Treasury, J. M. Brown, ed. New York: (c. 1956).

The Ladies' Science of Etiquette. By an English Lady of Rank. . . . New York: 1844.

(Lavin, E. M.), *Good Manners.* New York: 1888.

Lewis, H. C., *Louisiana Swamp Doctor. The Writings of Henry Clay Lewis alias "Madison Tensas, M.D."* J. Q. Anderson, ed. Baton Rouge: (c. 1962).

(Longstreet, A. B.), *Social Etiquette of New York.* New York: 1885.

Lynde, Benjamin, *The Diaries of . . . and of Benjamin Lynde, Jr.* . . . F. E. Oliver, ed. Boston: 1880.

Journal of William Maclay, United States Senator from Pennsylvania, 1789-1791. E. S. Maclay, ed. New York: 1890.

Ibid., Introduction by C. A. Beard. New York: 1927.

Mann, T. C., and Janet Greene, *Over Their Dead Bodies.* Brattleboro Vt.: 1962; q. in "Over Their Dead Bodies," *Chicago Daily News Panorama,* Mar. 9, 1963.

Marryat, Captain Frederick, *Diary in America.* Jules Zanger, ed. Bloomington (Ind.): (c. 1960).

Martens, F. H., *The Book of Good Manners, a Guide to Polite Usage for all Social Functions.* New York: 1923.

McAllister, Ward, *Society as I Have Found It.* New York: (c. 1890).

Mencken, H. L., *Americana.* New York: 1925.

Miller, N. H., Edgar Lansdorf and R. W. Richmond, *Kansas in Newspapers.* Topeka, Kansas: 1963.

────── and J. W. Snell, *Why the West Was Wild. A Contemporary Look at the Antics of Some Highly Publicized Kansas Cowtown Personalities.* Topeka, Kansas: 1963.

Moore, J. H., *The Young Gentleman and Lady's Monitor.* . . . New York: 1806.

Morison, S. E., *One Boy's Boston. 1887-1901.* Cambridge: (c. 1962).

Mussey, Barrows, ed., *Yankee Life by Those Who Lived it.* New York: 1947.

Nevins, Allan, comp., *America Through British Eyes.* New York: 1948.

"Our Drummer." Butler Brothers Catalogue. Spring, 1904. Chicago: 1904.

Peacham, Henry, *The Compleat Gentleman.* . . . London: 1661.

Peale, R. S., ed., *The Home Library of Useful Knowledge . . . Self-Instruction in All Branches of Popular Education.* Chicago: 1887.

Piano Travelers' Association Book. National Piano Travelers' Association. n.p.: 1916.

Poore, B. P., *Perley's Reminiscences of Sixty Years in the National Metropolis.* . . . 2 v. Philadelphia: (c. 1886).

Pope, John, *A Tour Through the Southern and Western Territories.* Richmond: 1792.

Post, Emily, *Etiquette in Society, in Business, in Politics and at Home.* New York: 1924.

Prentis, N. L., *A Kansan Abroad.* Topeka, Kansas: 1878.

Price, Lucian, *Dialogues of Alfred North Whitehead.* Boston: (c. 1954).

Putt, S. G., ed., *Cousins and Strangers. Comments on America by Commonwealth Fund Fellows from Britain, 1946-1952.* Cambridge, Mass.: 1956.

Quinn, A. H., ed., *Representative American Plays.* New York: (c. 1917).

Randolph, Mrs. Mary, *The Virginia Housewife.* . . . Baltimore: 1838.

Richardson, Samuel, *Familiar Letters on Important Occasions*. Introduction by
B. W. Downs. London: (1928).

(Ruth, J. A.), *Decorum, a Practical Treatise on Etiquette and Dress of the
Best American Society*. . . . New York: 1879.

Schurz, Carl, *The Autobiography of Carl Schurz. An Abridgment in one Volume by Wayne Andrews. With an Introduction by Allan Nevins*. New
York: (c. 1961).

Slayden, Ellen Maury, *Washington Wife. Journal of Ellen Maury Slayden from
1897 to 1919*. New York: (c. 1963).

Smith, Mrs. S. H., *The First Forty Years of Washington Society*. Gaillard Hunt,
ed. New York: 1906.

Swift, Jonathan, *The Works of*. . . . 19 v. Boston: 1883.

Tasistro, L. F., *Etiquette of Washington*. Washington: 1866.

Thornwell, Emily, *Lady's Guide to Complete Etiquette*. . . . Chicago: 1888.

Tonk, William, *Memoirs of a Manufacturer*. New York: 1926.

Trollope, Anthony, *North America*. Donald Smalley and B. A. Booth, eds. New
York: 1951.

Trollope, Frances, *Domestic Manners of the Americans . . . With an Introduction by Michael Sadlier*. New York: 1927.

*True Politeness, A Hand-Book of Etiquette for Gentlemen, By an American
Gentleman*. New York: (c. 1846).

*A Mirror for Americans. Life and Manners in the United States 1790-1870 as
Recorded by American Travelers*. W. S. Tryon, ed. 3 v. Chicago: (c.
1952).

de Valcourt, Robert, *The Illustrated Book of Manners: a Manual of Good
Behavior and Polite Accomplishments*. Cincinnati: 1866.

Washington, George, . . . *Rules of Civility and Decent Behaviour in Company and Conversation*. Charles Moore, ed. Boston: 1926.

———— *The Writings of*. . . . W. C. Ford, ed. 14 v. New York: 1889-93.

Weems, Mason Locke, . . . *His Works and Ways*. E. E. F. Skeel, ed. 3 v. New
York: 1929.

Wells, R. A., *Manners, Culture and Dress of the Best American Society*. . . .
Springfield, Mass.: 1890.

White, W. B., *The Player-Piano Up-To-Date*. New York: (c. 1914).

Whittier, J. G., *The Complete Works of*. . . . Boston: 1904.

Winthrop, John, *The History of New England 1630-1649*. James Savage, ed. 2
v. Boston: 1853.

Young, J. H., *Our Deportment*. . . . Detroit: 1881.

SECONDARY WORKS

Abels, Jules, *The Rockefeller Billions*. . . . New York: (c. 1965).

Adams, B. P., *About Books and Children*. New York: (c. 1953).

Adams, Henry, *History of the United States*. 9 v. New York: 1889-91.

Allen, F. L., *Only Yesterday*. . . . New York: 1931.

*The American Heritage Cookbook and Illustrated History of American Eating
& Drinking*. n.p.: (c. 1964).

Amory, Cleveland, *The Proper Bostonians*. New York: 1947.

———— *Who Killed Society?* New York: (c. 1960).

Atherton, Lewis, *Main Street on the Middle Border*. Bloomington (Ind.): 1954.

Bainbridge, John, *The Super-Americans. A Picture of Life in the United*

States, as Brought into Focus . . . in . . . Texas. Garden City, N. Y.: 1961.

Baron, Stanley, *Brewed in America. A History of Beer and Ale in the United States.* Boston: (c. 1962).

Becker, Stephen, *Comic Art in America.* New York: 1959.

Beebe, Lucius, and Charles Clegg, *The American West. The Pictorial Epic of a Continent.* New York: 1955.

Benson, M. S., *Women in Eighteenth-Century America. A Study of Opinion and Social Usage.* New York: 1935.

Beveridge, A. J., *Abraham Lincoln, 1809-1858.* 2 v. Boston: 1928.

Blesh, Rudi, and Harriet Janis, *They All Played Ragtime.* New York: 1950.

Bleyer, W. G., *Main Currents in the History of American Journalism.* Boston: (c. 1927).

Bliven, Bruce, Jr., *The Wonderful Writing Machine.* New York: (c. 1954).

Boatright, Mody C., *Folk Laughter on the American Frontier.* New York: 1949.

Bolton, C. K., *Portraits of Persons Born Abroad Who Came to the Colonies in North America Before the Year 1701.* 3 v. Boston: 1919.

Bracken, Peg, *I Try to Behave Myself. . . .* New York: (c. 1964).

Bradley, Van Allen, *Music for the Millions. The Kimball Piano and Organ Story.* Chicago: 1957.

Branch, E. D., *The Sentimental Years. 1836-1860.* New York: 1934.

Bridenbaugh, Carl, *Myths and Realities. Societies of the Colonial South.* Baton Rouge: (c. 1952).

—— and Jessica, *Rebels and Gentlemen. Philadelphia in the Age of Franklin.* New York: (c. 1942).

Bruce, P. A., *Social Life of Virginia in the Seventeenth Century.* Lynchburg, Va.: 1927.

Buchanan, Aimee, *The Lady Means Business . . . the Career Woman's Own Machiavelli.* New York: (c. 1942).

Buck, S. J., and Elizabeth Hawthorn, *The Planting of Civilization in Western Pennsylvania.* (Pittsburgh): 1939.

Burt, Nathaniel, *The Perennial Philadelphians. The Anatomy of an American Aristocracy.* Boston: (c. 1963).

Butler, Frank, *Frank Butler's Book of the Boardwalk.* Atlantic City: 1952.

Campbell, Hannah, *Why Did They Name it . . . ?* New York: (c. 1964).

Carney, M. L., *Etiquette in Business.* New York: (c. 1948).

Carson, Gerald, *The Social History of Bourbon. An Unhurried Account of our Star-Spangled American Drink.* New York: (c. 1963).

—— *One for a Man, Two for a Horse, A Pictorial History . . . of Patent Medicines.* Garden City, N.Y.: (c. 1961).

Caughey, J. W., *Hubert Howe Bancroft, Historian of the West.* Berkeley: 1946.

Chase, Gilbert, *America's Music from the Pilgrims to the Present.* New York: (c. 1955).

Chidsey, D. B., *John the Great . . . John L. Sullivan.* Garden City, N.Y.: 1942.

Clark, F. E., *Our Business Boys.* Boston: (c. 1884).

Cobb, I. S., *Exit Laughing.* Indianapolis: 1941.

Cohn, D. L., *The Good Old Days.* New York: 1940.

(Collier, Price), *America and the Americans. . . .* New York: 1897.

Colman, E. M., *Seventy-five Years of White House Gossip from Washington to Lincoln.* Garden City, N.Y.: 1926.

Conventions: An American Institution. J. S. Turner, ed. (Cincinnati: n.d.).

Cooke, Charles, *Playing the Piano for Pleasure.* New York: (c. 1941).

Cox, W. R., *Luke Short and his Era*. Garden City, N.Y.: 1961.

Croly, Mrs. J. C. (Jennie June), *The History of the Woman's Club Movement in America*. New York: (c. 1898).

Cummings, R. O., *The American Ice Harvests. A Historical Study in Technology. 1800-1918*. Berkeley: 1949.

Curti, Merle, *The Growth of American Thought*. New York: (c. 1951).

Curtiss, F. H., and John Heard, *The Country Club 1882-1932*. Brookline, Mass.: 1932.

Dannett, S. G. L., and F. R. Rachel, *Down Memory Lane*. . . . New York: (c. 1954).

Dexter, E. A., *Colonial Women of Affairs*. Boston: 1924.

Dexter, F. B., *Biographical Sketches of the Graduates of Yale College with Annals of the College History*. 8 v. New York: 1885-1912.

Dibble, R. F., *John L. Sullivan*. Boston: 1925.

Dick, Everett, *The Dixie Frontier. A Social History of the Southern Frontier from the First Transmontane Beginnings to the Civil War*. New York: 1948.

Dolson, Hildegarde, *The Great Oildorado*. New York: 1959.

Dowdey, Clifford, *The Great Plantation*. . . . New York: (c. 1957).

Dulles, F. R., *The United States Since 1865*. Ann Arbor: (c. 1959).

Earle, A. M., *Colonial Dames and Good Wives*. Boston: 1895.

—————— *Two Centuries of Costume in America*. 2 v. New York: 1903.

Ellet, Mrs. E. F. L., *The Queens of American Society*. New York: 1867.

Emmet, Boris, and J. E. Jeuck, *Catalogues and Counters*. (Chicago: 1950).

Evans, Bergen, *A Natural History of Nonsense*. New York: 1946.

Ferguson, C. W., *Fifty Million Brothers. A Panorama of American Lodges and Clubs*. New York: (c. 1937).

Finley, R. E., *The Lady of Godey's, Sarah Josepha Hale*. Philadelphia: 1931.

Fish, C. R., *The Rise of the Common Man, 1830-1850*. A History of American Life, v. VI. New York: 1927.

Fitzpatrick, J. C., *George Washington Himself*. Indianapolis: 1933.

Fowler, Gene, *Skyline. A Reporter's Reminiscences of the 1920's*. New York: 1961.

Freeman, D. S., *George Washington. A Biography*. 7 v. New York: 1948-57.

Friedan, Betty, *The Feminine Mystique*. New York: (c. 1963).

Fuller, W. E., *RFD, the Changing Face of Rural America*. Bloomington: (c. 1964).

Furman, Bess, *White House Profile. A Social History of the White House*. Indianapolis: 1951.

Gannett, Lewis, *Cream Hill. Discoveries of a Weekend Countryman*. New York: 1949.

Goodsell, Willystine, *Pioneers of Women's Education in the United States*. . . . New York: 1931.

Gould, John, *Monstrous Depravity. A Jeremiad and a Lamentation*. New York: 1963.

Gould, M. E., *Early American Wooden Ware & Other Kitchen Utensils*. Springfield, Mass.: 1942.

Gray, J. T., *A Kentucky Chronicle*. New York: 1906.

Gray, R. K., *Eighteen Acres Under Glass*. Garden City, N.Y.: 1962.

Green, C. M., *Washington, Capital City 1879-1950*. 2 v. Princeton, N.J.: 1963.

Griswold, R. W., *The Republican Court*. . . . New York: 1855.

Harlow, A. F., *Weep No More, My Lady*. New York: 1942.

Harmer, R. M., *The High Cost of Dying*. New York: (c. 1963).

Hart, J. D., *The Popular Book. A History of America's Literary Taste*. New York: 1950.

Harveson, M. E., *Catherine Esther Beecher, Pioneer Educator*. Philadelphia: 1932.

Hecht, Ben, *Gaily, Gaily*. Garden City, N.Y.: 1963.

Herron, Paul, *The Story of Capitol Hill*. New York: (c. 1963).

Hibben, Paxton, *Henry Ward Beecher: An American Portrait*. New York: (c. 1942).

Holbrook, S. H., *The Golden Age of Quackery*. New York: 1959.

Holmes, F. L., *Side Roads*. . . . Madison: 1949.

Hoyt, Harlowe, *Town Hall Tonight*. New York: 1955.

Hunt, C. L., *The Life of Ellen H. Richards 1842-1911*. Washington: 1958.

Hunt Clubs and Country Clubs in America. Boston: 1928.

Jeffries, O. G., *In and Out of the White House . . . from Washington to the Eisenhowers*. New York: (c. 1960).

Johnson, Clifton, *Old-Time Schools and School-Books*. New York: 1963.

Kalaver, Lucy, *The Private World of High Society*. New York: (c. 1960).

Kane, H. T., *Gentlemen, Swords and Pistols*. New York: 1951.

Kennedy, E. R., *The Contest for California in 1861. How Colonel E. D. Baker Saved the Pacific States to the Union*. Boston: 1912.

Kittredge, G. L., *The Old Farmer and his Almanack*. Cambridge: 1924.

Klapp, O. E., *Heroes, Villains, and Fools. The Changing American Character*. Englewood Cliffs, N.J.: (c. 1962).

Krapp, G. P., *The English Language in America*. 2 v. New York: 1925.

Kronenberger, Louis, *Company Manners*. . . . Indianapolis: 1954.

LaPiere, Richard, *The Freudian Ethic*. New York. (c. 1959).

Lehmann-Haupt, Hellmut, L. G. Wroth and R. G. Silver, *The Book in America. A History of the Making and Selling of Books in the United States*. New York: 1952.

Lerner, Max, *America as a Civilization. Life and Thought in the United States Today*. New York: 1957.

Lewis, Paul, *Queen of the Plaza. A Biography of Adah Isaacs Menken*. New York: (c. 1964).

Leyburn, J. G., *The Scotch-Irish. A Social History*. Chapel Hill: (c. 1962).

Loesser, Arthur, *Men, Women and Pianos*. . . . New York: 1954.

Lutes, D. T., *The Country Kitchen*. Boston: 1946.

Malone, Dumas, *The Story of the Declaration of Independence*. New York: 1954.

(Manning, Mario), Fairfax, Beatrice, *Ladies Now and Then by*. . . . New York: 1944.

Mason, J. E., *Gentlefolk in the Making. Studies in the History of English Courtesy Literature . . . from 1531 to 1774*. Philadelphia: 1935.

Masterson, J. R., *Tall Tales of Arkansas*. Boston: (c. 1943).

May, H. F., *The End of American Innocence*. . . . Chicago: (c. 1964).

McMaster, J. B., *A History of the People of the United States from the Revolution to the Civil War*. 8 v. New York: 1883-1913.

Mencken, H. L., *The American Language*. . . . Fourth ed. and Two Supplements, abridged, with annotations and new material, by R. I. McDavid, Jr. and D. W. Maurer. New York: 1963.

Miller, N. E., and John Dollard, *Social Learning*. New Haven: 1941.

Miller, N. H., "Kansas Newspapers to 1900," *Kansas: the First Century*, J. D. Bright, ed. New York: 1956.

Mitchell, E. V., *Concerning Beards*. New York: 1930.

Mitford, Nancy, ed., *Noblesse Oblige*. . . . New York: (c. 1956).

Morison, S. E., *Builders of the Bay Colony*. Boston: 1930.

―――― *The Puritan Pronaos. Studies in the Intellectual Life of New England in the Seventeenth Century*. New York: 1936.

―――― *Three Centuries of Harvard 1636-1936*. Cambridge, Mass.: 1936.

Morris, Lloyd, *Not So Long Ago*. New York: (c. 1949).

―――― *Postscript to Yesterday*. . . . New York: (c. 1947).

Mott, F. L., *A History of American Magazines, 1741-1905*. 4 v. Cambridge, Mass.: 1957.

Munson, M. L., *Practical Etiquette for the Modern Man*. New York: (c. 1964).

National Associations of the United States. Jay Judkins, ed. Washington: 1949.

Nicholson, Harold, *Good Behaviour, being a Study of Certain Types of Civility*. Garden City, N.Y.: 1956.

Owsley, F. L., *Plain Folk of the Old South*. (Baton Rouge): 1949.

Papashvily, H. W., *All the Happy Endings. A Study of the Domestic Novel in America*. . . . New York: 1956.

Parkhill, Forbes, *The Wildest of the West*. (Denver: 1957).

Parrington, V. L., *Main Currents in American Thought*. . . . New York: (c. 1930).

Pearson, Edmund, *Queer Books*. Garden City, N.Y.: 1928.

Peck, G. W., *Peck's Bad Boy and his Pa*. (New York: c. 1958).

Plum, D. A., and G. B. Dowell, *The Great Experiment; a chronicle of Vassar*. Poughkeepsie, N.Y.: 1961.

Post, Edwin, *Truly Emily Post*. New York: (c. 1961).

Presbrey, Frank, *The History and Development of Advertising*. Garden City, N.Y.: 1929.

Quincy, Josiah, *Memoir of the Life of Josiah Quincy Jun. of Massachusetts: by his Son*. . . . Boston: 1825.

Randall, R. P., *Mary Lincoln*. . . . Boston: 1953.

Reynolds, Reginald, *Beards*. . . . Garden City, N.Y.: 1949.

Roberts, C. M., *Washington, Past and Present. A Pictorial History of the Nation's Capital*. Washington: (c. 1950).

Ross, Ishbel, *Crusades and Crinolines*. . . . New York: (c. 1963).

―――― *Ladies of the Press*. . . . New York: 1936.

Ross, Lillian, *Reporting*. New York: 1964.

Rourke, Constance, *American Humor*. . . . New York: (c. 1931).

Rowsome, Frank, Jr., *They Laughed When I Sat Down. An Informal History of Advertising*. . . . New York: (c. 1959).

Sachse, W. L., *The Colonial American in Britain*. Madison: 1956.

Sandburg, Carl, *Abraham Lincoln. The Prairie Years*. 2 v. New York: (c. 1926).

Schlesinger, A. M., *Learning How to Behave. A Historical Study of American Etiquette Books*. New York: 1946.

―――― *The Rise of the City. 1878-1898*. A History of American Life. v. X. New York: (1961).

Schlesinger, A. M., Jr., *The Age of Jackson*. Boston: 1949.

Seager, Robert, II, *And Tyler Too. A Biography of John & Julia Gardiner Tyler*. New York: (c. 1963).

Shaplen, Robert, *Free Love and Heavenly Sinners. The Story of the Great Henry Ward Beecher Scandal*. New York: (c. 1954).

Shipton, C. K., *New England Life in the 18th Century. Representative Biographies from Sibley's Harvard Graduates*. Cambridge, Mass.: 1963.

Singleton, Esther, *Social New York Under the Georges 1714-1776*. New York: 1902.

Smith, Merriman, *The Good New Days. A Not Entirely Reverent Study of Native Habits and Customs in Modern Washington.* Indianapolis: (c. 1962).

Solomon, B. M., *Ancestors and Immigrants. A Changing New England Tradition.* Cambridge: 1956.

Spaeth, Sigmund, *The Facts of Life in Popular Song.* New York: (c. 1934).

Spillane, Daniel, *History of the American Pianoforte.* New York: 1890.

Spruille, J. C., *Women's Life and Work in the Southern Colonies.* Chapel Hill: 1938.

Stanard, M. N., *Colonial Virginia, its People and Customs.* Philadelphia: 1917.

Stern, M. B., *We the Women. Career Firsts of Nineteenth-Century Women.* New York: 1963.

Stevens, W. B., *Grant in Saint Louis.* St. Louis: 1916.

Stewart, G. R., *American Ways of Life.* Garden City, N.Y.: 1954.

Stiles, H. R., *Bundling; its Origin, Progress and Decline in America.* Albany: 1871.

Stowe, H. B., *Household Papers and Stories.* In *The Writings of.* . . . 16 v. Boston: 1896.

Sullivan, Mark, *Our Times.* 6 v. New York: 1926-35.

Sumner, W. G., *Folkways.* Boston: 1940.

Sylvester, Robert, *No Cover Charge. A Backward Look at the Night Clubs.* New York: 1956.

Tandy, Jennette, *Crackerbox Philosophers in American Humor and Satire.* New York: 1925.

Thaman, Sister M. P., *Manners and Morals of the 1920's. A Survey of the Religious Press.* New York: (c. 1954).

Thomas, B. P., *Abraham Lincoln.* New York: 1953.

Townsend, W. H., *Lincoln and Liquor.* New York: 1934.

Tuckerman, H. T., *America and Her Commentators.* . . . New York: 1864.

Turberville, A. S., *English Men and Manners in the Eighteenth Century.* New York: 1957.

Tyler, A. F., *Freedom's Ferment. Phases of American Social History to 1860.* Minneapolis: 1944.

Vanderbilt, Amy, *Amy Vanderbilt's New Complete Book of Etiquette. The Guide to Gracious Living.* Garden City, N.Y.: (c. 1963).

Van Doren, Carl, *Benjamin Franklin.* New York: 1938.

Vidich, A. J., and Joseph Bensman, *Small Town in a Mass Society. Class, Power and Religion in a Rural Community.* Garden City, N.Y.: (c. 1948).

Wallis, C. L., *Stories on Stone. A Book of American Epitaphs.* New York: 1954.

Wecter, Dixon, *The Saga of American Society. A Record of Social Aspiration.* New York: 1937.

Weeden, W. B., *Economic and Social History of New England. 1620-1789.* 2 v. Boston: 1890.

Wertenbaker, T. J., *The First Americans 1607-1690.* A History of American Life. v.II. New York: 1927.

—— *Patrician and Plebeian in Virginia.* Charlottesville: 1910.

Wilcox, R. T., *Five Centuries of American Costume.* New York: (c. 1963).

—— *The Mode in Costume.* New York: 1944.

—— *The Mode in Hats and Headdress.* New York: 1952.

Winston, R. W., *Andrew Johnson, Plebeian and Patriot.* New York: (c. 1928).

Wood, M. I., *The History of the General Federation of Women's Clubs for the First Twenty-Two Years of its Organization.* New York: (c. 1912).

Woodham-Smith, Cecil, *The Reason Why.* New York: 1960.
Wright, L. B., *The First Gentlemen of Virginia. Intellectual Qualities of the Early Colonial Ruling Class.* San Marino, Calif.: 1940.
Wright, Richardson, *Grandfather Was Queer. Early American Wags and Eccentrics from Colonial Times to the Civil War.* Philadelphia: (c. 1939).
Wright, T. G., *Literary Culture in Early New England 1620-1730. Edited by his Wife.* New Haven: 1920.
Young, J. H., *The Toadstool Millionaires. . . .* Princeton, N.J.: 1961.

LOCAL HISTORY

Coffin, Joshua, *A Sketch of the History of Newbury, Newburyport, and West Newbury from 1635 to 1845.* Boston: 1845.
Dedmon, Emmett, *Fabulous Chicago.* New York: (c. 1953).
Durrett, R. T., *The Centenary of Louisville.* Filson Club Publications. No. 8. Louisville, Ky.: 1893.
Folsom, George, *Saco and Biddeford.* Saco: 1830.
Harlow, A. F., *The Serene Cincinnatians.* New York: 1950.
Hunt, Inez, and W. W. Draper, *To Colorado's Restless Ghosts.* (Denver: c. 1960).
Lewis, Oscar, *The Town that Died Laughing. The Story of Austin, Nevada, Rambunctious Early-Day Mining Camp, and its Renowned Newspaper, The Reese River Reveille.* Boston: (c. 1955).
Mayer, G. M., *Once Upon a City. New York from 1890 to 1910.* New York: 1958.
McWilliams, Carey, *Southern California Country.* New York: (c. 1946).
Miller, Max, *Holladay Street.* New York: 1962.
Morris, Lloyd, *Incredible New York. High Life and Low Life of the Last Hundred Years.* New York: (1951).
Rogers, W. G., and Mildred Weston, *Carnival Crossroads: the Story of Times Square.* New York: 1960.
Rose, W. G., *Cleveland, the Making of a City.* Cleveland: (c. 1950).
Ross, J. A., *Historical Sketch of Hampton, N.H.* Haverill, Mass.: 1901.
Smith, W. C., *Queen City Yesterdays. Sketches of Cincinnati in the Eighties.* Crawfordsville, Ind.: 1959.
Sprague, Marshall, *Newport in the Rockies. The Life and Good Times of Colorado Springs.* Denver: (c. 1961).
Stiles, H. R., *Ancient Windsor.* 2 v. Hartford, Conn.: 1891.
Thomas, Lately, *A Debonair Scoundrel. An Episode in the Moral History of San Francisco.* New York: (c. 1962).
Zeisloft, E. I., *The New Metropolis. . . .* New York: (c. 1899).

PAMPHLETS

The Bath and You. Cleanliness Bureau. New York: n.d.
Conmy, P. T., *The Origin and Purposes of the Native Sons and Daughters of the Golden West.* San Francisco: 1956.
Crane, Dr. George W., *How to Improve Your Personality Plus the Formula for being an Interesting Conversationalist.* N.p.; n.d.

Dahlgren, Mrs. M. V., *Etiquette of Social Life in Washington*. Washington: 1876.

Introducing SPEBSQSA. A Fact Book. . . . Kenosha, Wis.: (1964).

Kellogg, Mrs. E. E., *A Talk with Girls*. Battle Creek, Mich.: n.d.

A List of Items of Interest in the Library and Museum of the Society of California Pioneers. San Francisco: 1931.

Mott, F. L., *The Magazine Revolution and Popular Ideas in the Nineties*. Worcester, Mass.: 1954.

Ogle, Charles, *Speech of Mr. Ogle, of Pennsylvania, on the Regal Splendor of the President's Palace. Delivered in the House of Representatives, April 14, 1840*. N.p.; n.d.

"The Perfect Secretary." A Handbook of Office Behavior. . . . Pittsfield, Mass.: 1954.

Pinkham, L. E., *Guide to Health and Etiquette*. Lynn, Mass.: n.d.

(Shook, L. G.), *"Etiquette of the Motor" by Count Umberto Benito* (pseud.) (Los Angeles, Calif.: c. 1930).

A Short Tour Through the United States & Canada October 10th to December 31st, 1832. The Journal of Lieut. George Kirwin Carr. Deoch Fulton, ed. New York: 1937.

Singleton, J. C., *The Telephone Comes to St. Louis*. N.p.; n.d. Reprinted from *Bull. of the Missouri Hist. Soc.* v. 10. Oct., 1953.

Teiser, Ruth, *This Sudden Empire, California. The Story of the Society of California Pioneers 1850 to 1950*. San Francisco: 1950.

Vail, R. W. G., *Moody's School of Good Manners: A Study in American Colonial Etiquette*. N.p.; n.d. A separate repr. from *Studies in the History of Culture*. Feb., 1942.

Woodcock, Thomas S., *New York to Niagara, 1836*. The Journal of. . . . Deoch Fulton, ed. New York: 1938.

You and Your Telephone. New York Telephone Company. New York: (194?).

SERIAL PUBLICATIONS

Basler, R. P., "The Authorship of the 'Rebecca' Letters." *The Abraham Lincoln Quar.*, v. II, No. 2. June, 1942.

"The Centennial of the J. Walter Thompson Company, Commemorating 100 Years of American Advertising." *Advertising Age*, v. 35. No. 49. Dec. 7, 1964. Section 2.

Ibid., Tyler, W. D., "A Gallery of American Advertising . . . Reviewed."

Tharp, L. H., "The Song That Wrote Itself." *Amer. Heritage*, VIII, No. 1, Dec., 1956.

Rogers, Agnes, "The Undimmed Appeal of the Gibson Girl." *Amer. Heritage*, IX, No. 1. Dec., 1957.

Durant, John and Alice, "A Century of Cooperstown." *Amer. Heritage*, X, No. 1, Dec., 1958.

Levin, A. L., "Miss Knight Abroad." *Amer. Heritage*, XI, No. 3. Apr., 1960.

"The Bard Unblemished." *Amer. Heritage*, XI, No. 4. June, 1960.

Carson, Gerald, "They Knew What They Liked." *Amer. Heritage*, XII, No. 5. Aug., 1961.

Cowley, Robert, "Ask the Man Who. . . ." *Amer. Heritage*, XV, No. 5. Aug., 1964.

Forester, C. S., "Bloodshed at Dawn." *Amer. Heritage,* XV, No. 6. Oct. 1964.

Pierson, G. W., " 'A Restless Temper. . . .' " *Amer. Hist. Rev.,* LXIX, No. 4. July, 1964.

Levine, G. N., and L. A. Sussman, "Social Class and Sociability in Fraternity Pledging." *Am. Jour. of Sociology,* LXV, No. 4. Jan., 1960.

Palmore, E. B., "Ethnophaulisms and Ethnocentrism." *Am. Jour. of Sociology,* LXVII, No. 4, Jan., 1962.

Smart, G. K., "Private Libraries in Colonial Virginia," *Am. Lit.,* v. 10, No. 1. Mar., 1938.

Slater, Joseph, "Music at Col. Grangerford's: A Footnote to Huckleberry Finn." *Am. Lit.,* v. 21, No. 1. Mar., 1949.

"Comparison Between Certain French and American Customs." *Amer. Museum,* IV, No. 2. (1788).

Gleason, Philip, "The Melting Pot: Symbol or Confusion?" *Am. Quar.,* XVI, No. 1. Spring, 1964.

Bridges, W. E., "Family Patterns and Social Values in America, 1825-1875." *Am. Quar.,* XVII, No. 1. Spring, 1965.

Ibid., Conner, Paul, "Patriarchy: Old World and New."

Friedrich, Otto, "A Vivacious Blonde Was Fatally Shot Today, or How to Read a Tabloid." *Am. Scholar,* v. 32, No. 3. Autumn, 1959.

Kazin, Alfred, "The Scholar Cornered. . . ." *Am. Scholar,* v. 33, No. 2. Spring, 1964.

Keniston, Ellen, and Kenneth Keniston, "An American Anachronism, The Image of Women and Work." *Am. Scholar,* v. 33. No. 3. Summer, 1964.

Hatch, D. L., and M. A. Hatch, "Criteria of Social Status as Derived from Marriage Announcements in the *New York Times.*" *Am. Sociological Rev.,* v. 12, Aug., 1947.

Read, A. W., "Words Indicating Social Status in America in the Eighteenth Century." *Am. Speech,* Oct., 1934.

Cresswell, T. J., "What Did Peaches Browning Say?" *Am. Speech,* XXXVII, No. 1. Feb., 1962.

Ackerman, L. M., " 'Lady' as a Synonym for 'Woman.' " *Am. Speech,* XXXVII, No. 4. Dec., 1962.

Hancock, C. R., " 'Lady' and 'Woman.' " *Am. Speech,* XXXVIII. No. 3. Oct., 1963.

Lipski, P. W., "The Introduction of 'Automobile' into American English." *Am. Speech,* XXXIX, No. 3. Oct., 1964.

Newberry, Farrar, "The Concatenated Order of Hoo-Hoo." *Ark. Hist. Quar.,* XXII. No. 4. Winter, 1963.

(Parton, James), "The Piano in the United States." *Atlantic Monthly,* July, 1867.

"Mail Bag," *Barrytown* (N.Y.) *Explorer.* VII. No. 7. Dec., 1964.

Walker, Diedrich, "A Lament Over New Year Calls." *Bonfort's Wine and Spirit Circular,* Jan. 10, 1898.

"Ladies' Auxiliary." *Brotherhood of Maintenance of Way Employees Jour.,* v. 74. No. 2. Feb., 1965.

Weiss, H. B., "American Letter-Writers, 1698-1943." *Bull. N. Y. Public Library,* v. 48. No. 12. Dec., 1944.

———— "Part II—Conclusion," *Bull. N. Y. Pub. Lib.,* v. 49. No. 1. Jan., 1945.

Garnsey, C. J., "Ladies' Magazines to 1850." *Bull. N. Y. Pub. Lib.,* v. 58. No. 2. Feb., 1954.

Smith, L. S. "Sunday at the Glen House. A Letter of 1880 Describing the Simple Pleasures of Early Rochester Life." *Bull. of the Rochester Museum of Arts and Sciences,* v. 29. No. 1. Jan., 1956.

Hadley, Chalmers, "The Society for the Suppression of Music." *Bull. of the Hist. and Phil. Soc. of Ohio,* v. 11 (Oct.), 1953.

"Drinkers Seek the 'Light.' " *Business Wk.,* Feb. 23, 1963.

"Salesgirl—but Does She Sell?" *Bus. Wk.,* Sept. 14, 1963.

"Company Santas Sober Up." *Bus. Wk.,* Dec. 14, 1963.

"Employees at Play are Big Business." *Bus. Wk.,* Apr. 11, 1964.

"Pollsters Check—and Check Again." *Bus. Wk.,* Sept. 12, 1964.

"All the World's a Stage for Business Meetings." *Bus. Wk.,* Feb. 6, 1965.

"Etiquette in Washington," *Chi. Hist.,* III, No. 10. Winter, 1953-54.

Quinn, M. L., "I'll Teach You Piano in Quarter Usual Time." *Cosmopolitan,* Oct. 1920. An advertisement.

Wallace, S. A., " 'Letters of the Presidentess,' Julia Gardiner Tyler, 1844-1845." *Daughters of the Am. Rev. Mag.,* v. 87. No. 5. Whole No. 706. May, 1953.

"Etiquette Hints." *Designer,* Nov., 1902.

Recknagel, H. J., "Women in White Collar Jobs . . . (1910-1950)." *Dissertation Abstracts,* 14:253-4.

"To Market, To Market . . . Millions of Patents." *Du Pont Stockholder,* Summer, 1960.

"The Business of Beauty Contests." *The Economist,* CXCII, No. 6055. Sept. 12, 1959.

Cerruti, James, "The Cigar: Noblest Smoke." *Esquire,* July, 1955.

Shepard, R. F., "The Etiquette of the Executive Lunch." *Esquire,* Nov., 1963.

Pew, W. A., "Lady Arbella and Her Friends." *Essex Institute Hist. Coll.,* LXVI. July, 1930.

Walker, H. L., "Bundling and the Law. A Footnote to American Social History." *Florida Law Jour.,* v. 27.

"Old Colony Club Fires Annual Cannon, Then Eats its 'Souquetash.' " *Food Marketing in New England,* v. 24. No. 2. Autumn, 1963.

"Odd Clubs & Good-Humored Societies." *Food Marketing in N.E.,* v. 25. No. 1. Summer, 1964.

"Smart Dog Kittery." *Food Marketing in N.E.,* v. 25. No. 1. Summer, 1964.

"Backwash." *Food Marketing in N.E.,* v. 25. No. 2. Autumn, 1964.

"Queens of Foods." *Food Marketing in N.E., loc. cit.*

Champlin, J. D., Jr., "The Manufacture of Ancestors." *Forum,* X (1890-91); 565-72.

Roberts, Darrell, "Duel in the Georgia Capital." *Georgia Hist. Quar.,* XLVII. No. 4. Dec., 1963.

Huneker, James, "The Passing of the Piano." *Harper's Bazaar,* v. 33, May 12, 1900.

Whitney, C. W., "Evolution of the Country Club." *Harper's Mag.,* XC (1894); 16-33.

White, W. A., "The Country Newspaper." *Harper's Mag.,* v. 132, May, 1916.

Hearth and Home. Scattered material, advertisements, in issues of Jan.-Mar., 1915; and Oct.-Nov., 1916.

Meyer, K. E., "Clubs: Selective and Otherwise." *Holiday,* v. 31. No. 4. Apr., 1962.

"Servicing for the Seventies . . . More and Better Services. . . ." *Investor's Reader,* July 10, 1963.

"Regal Cola." *Investor's Reader,* Mar. 4, 1964.

Bertsch, W. F., "Native Sons and Daughters of Kansas." *Jayhawk Mag.*, v. 2. No. 2. Feb., 1929.

Dondero, G. A., "Why Lincoln Wore a Beard." *Jour. of the Ill. State Hist. Soc.*, XXIV. No. 2. July, 1931.

Rutledge, W. S., "Dueling in Antebellum Mississippi." *Jour. of Miss. Hist.*, XXVI. No. 3. Aug., 1964.

Howes, Cecil, "Pistol-Packin' Pencil Pushers." *Kans. Hist. Quar.*, XIII. No. 2. May, 1944.

"From the Sumner County Press (Wellington) . . . July 30, 1874." *Kans. Hist. Quar.*, XXI. No. 8. Winter, 1955.

"Bypaths of Kansas History . . . Keeping the Peace at Cherryvale." *Kans. Hist. Quar.*, XXVI. No. 1. Spring, 1960.

Socolofsky, H. E., "The Private Journals of Florence Crawford and Arthur Capper 1891-1892 —Concluded." *Kans. Hist. Quar.*, XXX, No. 2. Summer, 1964.

Hamblin, D. J., "Big Mouth + Massive Wit + Soul of a Daffodil = Zero." *Life*, v. 57. No. 23. Dec. 4, 1964.

"Beauty and the Devil." *Lit. Digest*, v. 81. May 31, 1924.

Tooker, John, "Hello Girls of Long Ago." *Long Island Forum*, v. 16 (June).

Knight, Patricia, and Polly Ross, "Washington Job Hunt." *Mademoiselle*, Nov., 1955.

"Letters of Molly and Hetty Tilghman. Eighteenth Century Gossip of Two Maryland Girls." J. H. Pleasants, ed. *Md. Hist. Mag.*, XXI.

Thaemert, E. A., "The Beard is Coming Back as a Masculine Adornment." *Master Barber & Beautician*, Apr., 1961.

Chevalier, L. R., "The High IQ and the Small Bosom, Do They Really Go Together?" *McCall's*, XCII. No. 6. Mar., 1965.

McCloskey, J. C., "Jacksonian Democracy in Mrs. Kirkland's *A New Home— Who'll Follow?*" *Mich. Hist.*, v. 45. No. 4. Dec., 1961.

Borough, R. W., "Saturday Afternoon Town." *Mich. Hist.*, v. 48. No. 2. June, 1964.

Ullman, Mrs. Joseph, "Pioneer Homemaker." *Minn. Hist.*, v. 34. No. 3. Autumn, 1954.

Shoemaker, F. C., "Presentation of 'Award of Merit' to the Native Sons of Kansas City." *Missouri Hist. Rev.*, v. 47. July, 1953.

Bidstrup, D. J., "The Background of Public Speaking in Missouri 1840-1860." *Missouri Hist. Rev.*, XXXVI. No. 1. Oct., 1941.

Arnett, F. S., "American Country Clubs." *Munsey's*, XXVII. No. 4. July, 1902.

Ashton, L. S., "The Last Lesson Before Vacation." *Musician*, v. 18, 1913; 303.

"Kay Arboit Night at Chicago." *National Shorthand Reporter*, XI. No. 2. Nov., 1949.

Carson, Gerald, "Rum and Reform in Old New England." *New-England Galaxy*, VI. No. 3. Winter, 1965.

Parkes, H. B., "New England in the Seventeen-Thirties." *New Eng. Quar.*, III. No. 3. July, 1930.

Carpenter, F. I., "Puritans Preferred Blondes. . . ." *New Eng. Quar.*, IX, 1936.

Walcott, R. R., "Husbandry in Colonial New England." *New Eng. Quar.*, loc. cit.

Whitehill, W. M., "The Vicissitudes of Bacchante in Boston." *New Eng. Quar.*, XXVII. No. 4. Dec., 1954.

Seigel, J. P., "Puritan Light Reading." *New Eng. Quar.*, No. 2. June, 1964.

"Prettiest Businessmen Ever . . . Turn Beauty into Booty." *Newsweek*, Sept. 18, 1961.

Dana, Nathalie, "Lenox Hill in the 1880s: A Girl's Memories . . . Part I.
. . ." *New-York Hist. Soc. Quar.*, XLVI. No. 2. Apr., 1962.
—— ". . . Part II. . . ." *New-York Hist. Soc. Quar.*, XLVI. No. 3. July,
1962.
Wilson, Edmund, "Books of Etiquette and Emily Post." *New Yorker,* v. 23.
Pt. 2. July 19, 1947.
Schlesinger, E. B., "The Nineteenth Century Woman's Dilemma and Jennie
June." *New York Hist.*, XLII. No. 4. Oct., 1961.
Boyd, Ernest, "Beards in America." *New Statesman and Nation,* Aug., 1931.
"In Lightest Washington." *New Statesman,* v. 63. May 11, 1962.
Meyer, K. E., "Sex in Washington." *New Statesman,* v. 64. Sept., 28, 1962.
Dow, G. F., "Men's Frocks of Other Days." *Old-Time New Eng.*, XII. No. 4.
Apr., 1922.
Crane, Dr. G. W., "Solve Your Dilemma." *Opportunity*, Dec., 1954.
Rice, Mrs. William, "Ryefield; Or, a Town in the Connecticut Valley. . . ."
Papers and Proceedings of the Connecticut Valley Hist. Soc. 1876-1881.
Q. in "From the Times," *New-Eng. Galaxy*, VI. No. 1. Summer, 1964.
Morison, S. E., "Precedence at Harvard College in the Seventeenth Century."
Proc. Amer. Antiq. Soc., v. 42. Pt. 2. N.S. Oct., 1932.
Adams, C. F., "Some Phases of Sexual Morality and Church Discipline in
Colonial New England." *Proc. Mass. Hist. Soc.*, Second Ser. VI. 1890-
1891.
Howe, M. A. D., "Biographer's Bait. A Reminder of Edmund Quincy." *Proc.
Mass. Hist. Soc.*, LXVIII. Oct. 1944-May, 1947.
Loring, A. P., Jr., "A Yankee Points the Way to His Posterity." *Proc. Mass.
Hist. Soc., loc. cit.*
Seaver, H. L., "Hair and Holiness." *Proc. Mass. Hist. Soc., loc. cit.*
Sachse, W. L., "Harvard Men in England, 1648-1714." *Pub. Colonial Society
Mass.*, XXXV. *Transactions* 1942-1946.
Greene, E. B., "The Code of Honor in Colonial and Revolutionary Times,
with Special Reference to New England." *Pub. Colonial Soc. Mass.*,
XXVI. *Transactions* 1924-1926.
"Obituary Notes . . . Emily Post." *Publishers' Weekly*, Oct. 3, 1960.
Thompson, Craig, "How's Your Telephone Etiquette?" *Sat. Eve. Post.*
Tompkins, R. S., "Confederate Daughters Stand Guard." *Scribner's*, XCII.
No. 1. July, 1932.
Woodbury, Margaret, "Public Opinion in Philadelphia, 1789-1801." *Smith
Coll. Studies in History*, V. Numbers 1, 2. Oct. 1919-Jan. 1920.
Mayer, K. B., "The Changing Shape of the American Class Structure." *Social
Research*, XXX. Winter, 1963.
Lee, C. P., "Decline and Death of the Southern Gentleman." *Southwest Rev.*,
XXXVI. No. 3. Summer, 1951.
Bailey, W. C., "The Status System of a Texas Panhandle Community." *Texas
Jour. Sci.*, v. 5. Sept., 1953.
"The Guider: Manners." *Time*, Mar. 1, 1963.
"Diplomacy, The Party Line." *Time*, Nov. 22, 1963.
Pyle, Howard, "Let's Dry Up the Office Christmas Party." *Today's Health,*
v. 40. Dec., 1962.
Town Topics, the Journal of Society, LIV. No. 2. July 13, 1905. Miscellaneous
editorial news items.
"Woman's Auxiliary News." *The Union Postal Clerk & Postal Transport Jour.*,
v. 61. No. 2. Feb., 1965.
Kelso, Ruth, "The Doctrine of the English Gentleman in the Sixteenth Cen-

tury, with a Bibliographical List of Treatises on the Gentleman and Related Subjects Published in Europe to 1625." *Univ. of Ill. Studies in Lang. and Lit.,* XIV. No. 1-2. Feb.-May, 1929.

Reed, Nita, "Country Dance Forty Years Ago." *Vt. Hist.,* XXIII. No. 2. Apr., 1955.

Scribner, R. L., "The Code Duello in Virginia." *Va. Cavalcade,* III. No. 2. Autumn, 1953.

Davis, C. C., "The Small Bang at Bangs." *Va. Cavalcade,* XI. No. 2. Autumn, 1961.

Troubetzkoy, Ulrich, "Enough to Keep a Byrd Alive." *Va. Cavalcade, loc. cit.*

"Virginia Gleanings in England." *Va. Mag. of Hist. and Biog.,* XX (1912).

Stebbins, Hal, "Advertising . . . A Capsule History." *West. Adv.,* LXXX. No. 17, Apr., 1964.

Garlington, Jack, "Culture in Our Town." *West. Humanities Rev.,* 9. (Summer), 1955.

Wilson, W. E., "Hyperbole: Hot or Cold." *West. Humanities Rev., loc. cit.*

"Williamsburg—the Old Colonial Capital . . . III Cradle of the Revolution." *Wm. and Mary College Quar.,* XVI. No. 1. July, 1907.

"Punishment for Duelling." *Wm. and Mary Coll. Quar.,* XVI, No. 2. Oct., 1907.

Dawes, N. H., "Titles as Symbols of Prestige in Seventeenth-Century New England." *Wm. and Mary Coll. Quar.,* 3 Ser., VI, 1949.

World Convention Dates, Mar., 1964. Scattered editorial material.

Pierson, G. W., "The Moving American." *Yale Rev.,* XLIV. No. 1. Sept., 1954.

Steeholm, Clara, "My Kind Physician—Dr. Gilbert Titus Pearsall." *Yearbk. of the Dutchess County Hist. Soc.,* v. 29, 1944.

NEWSPAPERS

Any issue of any newspaper published in the United States is a probable source of data delineating American manners. My obligations vary widely in this field from a slender hint, a phrase, an idea, a touch of satire or social comment, encountered in one issue of a newspaper, to the extensive use I have made, for example, of the *Chicago Tribune* or the social reporting of Charlotte Curtis in *The New York Times* during 1963-65. I have drawn in some degree on news reports or feature articles for the years cited from the following:

Amarillo Globe, Oct. 27-Nov. 3, 1930; *Battle Creek Daily Moon,* Oct., 1895; *Battle Creek Journal,* Feb. 26, 1875; *Boston Daily Globe,* Jan. 1, 1901; *Boston Evening Transcript,* Jan. 2, 1901; *Chi. Daily News Panorama,* various dates, 1964-65; *Chi. Sun-Times Midwest Mag.,* Jan. 26, 1964; *Chi. Tribune,* 1888, 1926, 1928, 1935, 1951-52, 1961, 1963-65; *Cincinnati Post,* Feb. 2, 1934; *Cleveland Plain Dealer,* 1923, 1957; *Cleveland Press,* Apr. 2, 1946; *Columbia* (Mo.) *Herald,* July 28, 1899, quoted, *Missouri Hist. Rev.* XLIX, No. 4., July, 1955; *Courier-Jour.,* Oct. 15, 1961; *Daily News* (N.Y.), 1959, 1961, 1965; *Detroit Free Press,* June 10, 1957; *Emporia Gaz.,* Jan. 1, 1962; *Battle Creek Enquirer and News,* 1948, 1958; *Helena* (Mont.) *Independent-Record,* Oct. 4, 1963; *Kansas City Labor Beacon,* Feb. 19, 1965; *Los Angeles Times,* Jan. 17, 1965; *Louisville Times,* Oct. 11, 1961; *Massachusetts Spy,* July 1, 1795; *Montana Standard-Post,* Nov., 1964; *National Observer,* Apr. 15, 1963; *N. Y. Herald Tribune,* 1954, 1959-61, 1964-65; *N. Y. Times,* 1932, 1946, 1955-57, 1959-65; *N. Y. World-Telegram and Sun,* Dec. 9, 1963 and Jan. 7, 1964; *Omaha World-Herald,* Oct. 17, 1964; *Patent Trader* (Mt. Kisco, N. Y.), Mar. 19, 1964; *Poughkeepsie Journal,* Jan. 22, 1964; *Roll Call,* 1964-65; *St. Louis Globe-Dem.,* June 28, 1964;

Sunday Herald Leader (Lexington, Ky.), June 7, 1964; *Sunday News* (N. Y.), 1946, 1961, 1965; *Sunday Star* (Wash., D. C.), June 23, 1957 and June 4, 1961; *Topeka Daily Capital*, 1904, 1924, 1961; *Wall St. Jour.*, Nov. 5, 1962 and Jan. 7, 1965; *Washington Post*, Jan. 31, 1965; *Washington World*, Feb. 10, 1964; *Wichita Eagle*, Oct. 27, 1930.

MANUSCRIPTS

Angle, Paul M., Letter, Oct. 30, 1965.

Cady, E. H., "The Concept of the Gentleman in Representative American Authors." 1943. (University of Wisconsin Library.)

"Concord Monthly Meeting Minutes 1684-1824." (Hist. Soc. of Pa.)

Dawes, Norman H., "Social Classes in Seventeenth-Century New England." 2 v. 1940-41. (Harvard Univ. Library.)

Dean, Grant Talbot, Letters, Mar. 28, 1963; Dec. 27, 1963; Sept. 22, 1964; Jan. 21, 1965; Jan. 25, 1965.

Ewbank, H. L., Jr., "The Art of Conversing. Rhetorical Theory in the Behavior Books of Nineteenth Century America." 1952. (Univ. of Wisconsin Library.)

Fennelly, Catherine, Letter, Mar. 31, 1964.

Flint, Herbert, "Journalism in Territorial Kansas." 1916. (Kansas State Historical Society Library.)

Heston, H. N., Letter, Mar. 9, 1965.

Houlette, W. D., "Plantation and Parish Libraries in the Old South." 2 v. (Univ. of Iowa Libraries.)

Hutchens, C. K., Letter, Oct. 27, 1964.

Krettek, Germaine, Letter, Oct. 12, 1964.

(Leland, C. G.), "Rules of Etiquette for Men About Town, or the Manual of Fashionable Impoliteness. Collected, Selected and Recollected by the Chevalier." (Hist. Soc. of Pa.)

Manwaring, Mrs. C. F., Letter, Oct. 14, 1964.

Moskowitz, Milton, Letter, Feb. 19, 1965.

Murphy, Mrs. M. M., Mar. 26, 1964.

Plum, D. A., Letter, Nov. 6, 1964.

Scriven, Margaret, Librarian, Chicago Hist. Soc. Memorandum. May 12, 1964.

Snell, J. W., "Calico Queens and Painted Ladies. Prostitution on the Cowtown Frontier." Speech before the Kansas City Posse of the Westerners. May 12, 1964.

Stevenson, Paul, Letter, Feb. 19, 1965.

Thompson, L. S., Letter, Apr. 1, 1964.

Watters, R. E., "The Vogue and Influence of Samuel Richardson in America. A Study of Cultural Conventions 1742-1825." 1941. (Univ. of Wisconsin Library.)

Williams, R. N., 2nd, Letter, Feb. 24, 1965.

BIOGRAPHICAL COLLECTIONS, CYCLOPEDIAS AND LITERARY HISTORIES

Biographical Directory of the American Congress 1774-1927. (Wash.): 1928.

The Cambridge History of English Literature, Sir. A. W. Ward and A. R. Waller, eds. 14 v. Cambridge: 1921-31.

Current Biography, Maxine Block and others, eds. New York: 1941, 1954.

Dictionary of American Biography.

Dictionary of American History, J. T. Adams, ed. 5 v. and index volume. New York: 1940.

Dictionary of National Biography.

Encyclopedia of American History, R. B. Morris, ed. New York: (c. 1953).

Encyclopaedia Britannica. 32 v. 11th Ed.

Encyclopaedia of Etiquette. Emily Holt, ed. Garden City, New York: 1923.

Encyclopaedia of the Social Sciences. E. A. R. Seligman, ed., 15 v. New York: 1930-34.

Literary History of the United States, R. E. Spiller, Willard Thorp, T. H. Johnson, H. S. Canby, eds. New York: 1953.

Oberholtzer, E. P., *The Literary History of Philadelphia.* Philadelphia: 1906.

The Oxford Companion to American Literature, J. B. Hart, ed. New York: 1956.

Shuck, O. T., ed. *Representative and Leading Men of the Pacific.* . . . San Francisco: 1870.

MISCELLANEOUS

"Beards." File Box of clippings, scrapbooks, ms. notes, cartoons, etc. (Rare Book Room, N. Y. Pub. Library.)

Guckenheimer Sour Kraut Band. Collection of news releases and comments upon the organization, supplied by Richard Gump.

"Hair-Cutting and Curling Room." Advertising circular. Boston: 1846-47. (Landauer Collection, N.-Y. Hist. Society.)

The Society for the Preservation and Encouragement of Barber Shop Quartet Singing in America, Inc. Booklets, photocopies, periodicals relating to the Society's activities. Kenosha, Wisconsin.

Index

★ ★ ★

Index prepared by Alice and Sidney Mason.

Trades (*See also* specific jobs, places): and clubs, 254-55
Travel, 23-24, 27, 93-94, 295. *See also* specific places
Travelers' Aid Society, 228
Treasury Department, 264
Tremont House (Boston), 85
Trenchers, 13
Trenton, N. J., 36
Trite phrases, 188-89
Trollope, Anthony, 85, 92, 104, 151
Trollope, Mrs. Frances, 76, 83, 85, 89, 147; on Congress, 98; on "genteel" era, 147, 148; on ministers' treatment of women, 91; on women's lack of politeness, 92
Trovatore, Il (Verdi), 163
True Confessions, 213
Truman, Harry S., 199, 250
Trumbull, Lyman, 123
Trumbull, Mrs. Lyman (Julia Jayne), 123
Tulsa, Okla., 258
Tuners, piano, 162
Turkey trot (dance), 231
Twain, Mark, 61, 152, 159; Huck Finn quoted, 157
Tweedsmuir, John Buchan, Lord, 241
Twentieth century, 224-96 (*See also* specific customs, manners); beards in, 138-141; business manners, customs, folkways, 261-76; clubs, organizations, societies, 240-60; society news in, 202-23; women compared to 19th century, 284-285
Tyburn, executions at, 23
Tyler, John, 139, 212
Tyler, Mrs. John (Julia Gardiner), 77, 102, 139, 212
Tyler, Royal, 40
Typewriter Trade Journal, 266
Typewriters, typists, 265, 266

"Uncle Sam," as beardless symbol, 131
Uncle Tom's Cabin (Stowe), 239
Underhill, Capt. John, 7, 54
Union Club (New York City), 218, 242, 243
Union League Club (New York City), 243
Union Maid, 273
Union publications, 4, 208
United Confederate Veterans, 251
United Daughters of the Confederacy, 140, 248, 251
United States Military Academy (West Point), 132, 192
U. S. School of Music, 164, 237

Universities. *See* Colleges and universities
Unloveliness of Love-Lockes, The (Prynne), 130
Upper classes, 3ff., 8-9ff., 12-13 (*See also* Gentlemen; specific customs, manners, periods, places, etc.); and chaperones, 228; language of, 194, 298 (*See also* Language); social scale, 186; Southern aristocracy, 41-53 *passim*
Urbino, 20, 21
Usher, Sarah, 55
Ustinov, Peter, 139

Valcourt, Robert de, 76, 87, 168, 180
Vallee, Hubert Prior (Rudy), 253
Van Buren, Martin, 75, 102, 106
Van Corlear, Mrs. 55
Vanderbilt, Mrs. Alfred, 214
Vanderbilt, Amy, 167, 214-15, 278; on business world etiquette, 262, 266
Vanderbilt, Gladys, 212
Van de Water, Virginia, 261
Van Doren, Mamie, 285
Van Dyck, Sir Anthony, 129-30
Van Dyke Oil Portraits, Ltd., 292
Van Vooren, Monique, 216
Vassar, Matthew, 145
Vassar College, 145, 192
Veblen, Thorstein, 210
Veering, John, 10
Veiled Prophet's Ball, 78, 218
Vermont, 260
Vespasian, 84
Vest, Mrs. George Graham, 105
Veterans. *See* Army
Vice-presidents, business, 79
Victoria, Queen, 75, 200, 225
Victorian era, 142-154, 169, 296. *See also* specific manners
Villa Venice (nightclub), 219
Villains, beards as marks of, 135
Vincent Club, 221
Vindication of the Rights of Women (Wollstonecraft), 56
Virginia, 34, 42-53 *passim*, 61, 76; Baptists jailed in, 91; and dueling, 116, 118, 127; hair styles in, 131; harpsichords in, 156; and titles, 73
Virginia City, Nev., 71
Virginia Gazette, 48
Virtue in Humble Life . . . , 62
Voice, use of the, 262-63, 266-67, 268-69, 289. *See also* Language
Vose pianos, 160
Votey, Edwin S., 164
Voting (*See also* Elections): religious re-

About the Author

GERALD CARSON was born in Carrollton, a county seat town in Illinois, graduated from the University of Illinois, where he also did graduate work, and has worked in the newspaper, editorial and advertising fields in New York City.

Turning from a business career to full-time research and writing in 1951, Mr. Carson has been a student of American attitudes, manners and folkways, including the ways Americans have lived their private lives and made their livings. His *The Old Country Store* won the John H. Dunning Prize of The American Historical Association and was listed in 1954 by The American Library Association as one of the Fifty Notable Books of the year.

Gerald Carson is a frequent contributor to *The New York Times Book Review, American Heritage* magazine and other periodicals. He is a member of the Advisory Board of *American Heritage* and of various historical societies and associations, including the Society of American Historians. Mr. Carson now lives and writes in a country setting near Millerton, New York.